Taxing Capital Income

Also of interest from the Urban Institute Press:

State Tax Policy: A Political Perspective, second edition,
by David Brunori
Encyclopedia of Taxation and Tax Policy, second edition, edited by
Robert D. Ebel, Joseph J. Cordes, and Jane G. Gravelle
Local Tax Policy: A Federalist Perspective, by David Brunori

Edited by

**Henry J. Aaron,
Leonard E. Burman,
and C. Eugene Steuerle**

Taxing Capital Income

THE URBAN INSTITUTE PRESS
Washington, D.C.

THE URBAN INSTITUTE PRESS
2100 M Street, N.W.
Washington, D.C. 20037

Library of Congress Cataloging-in-Publication Data

Taxing capital income / edited by Henry J. Aaron, Leonard E. Burman, and C. Eugene Steuerle.
   p. cm.
  Includes bibliographical references and index.
  ISBN 978-0-87766-737-7
  1. Capital levy—United States. 2. Taxation—United States. I. Aaron, Henry J. II. Burman, Leonard. III. Steuerle, C. Eugene, 1946-
  HJ4133.U5T39 2007
  336.24'2—dc22
                       2007007974

Printed in the United States of America

10 09 08 07   1 2 3 4 5

THE URBAN INSTITUTE is a nonprofit, nonpartisan policy research and educational organization established in Washington, D.C., in 1968. Its staff investigates the social, economic, and governance problems confronting the nation and evaluates the public and private means to alleviate them. The Institute disseminates its research findings through publications, its web site, the media, seminars, and forums.

Through work that ranges from broad conceptual studies to administrative and technical assistance, Institute researchers contribute to the stock of knowledge available to guide decisionmaking in the public interest.

Conclusions or opinions expressed in Institute publications are those of the authors and do not necessarily reflect the views of officers or trustees of the Institute, advisory groups, or any organizations that provide financial support to the Institute.

Contents

Introduction

Whether to tax wealth or income from wealth is a perennial issue. In 1942, President Roosevelt considered adding a large, new consumption tax exempting savings as a way to finance World War II, but ultimately settled on making the income tax much more robust. *Blueprints for Basic Tax Reform,* a 1976 Treasury Department study, examined both comprehensive income and consumption tax options, without picking a best option. Sweeping income tax reform followed ten years later in the Tax Reform Act of 1986. Rather than abandoning taxation of capital income, the 1986 legislation reinforced the taxation of income for all sources in a lower-rate, broader-based, structure. In 2005, the President's Advisory Panel on Federal Tax Reform offered a choice of income and consumption tax options, but the income tax option included new tax breaks on capital income, and the consumption tax option featured a supplemental tax on dividends and capital gains to maintain progressivity. If history is any guide, ambivalence on this issue is the norm even among disciples of tax reform.

There are a variety of consumption tax proposals; each aims to exempt most capital income and eliminate the inherent tax penalty on saving built into the income tax. Since wealthy people own most capital, these options would appear to redistribute tax burdens from the rich to everyone else. Many analysts believe that taxing only consumed income would promote economic efficiency, and some believe that the extent of redistribution could be limited. Are the claimed gains in economic efficiency from encouraging saving enough to justify the alleged loss in fairness from reducing tax burdens on those most able to pay?

This book aims to examine not just these abstract arguments but the practical issues that shifting from an income tax to a consumption tax would raise. Theoretical analysis typically compares the instantaneous replacement of comprehensive progressive income taxes with equally comprehensive, but usually less progressive, consumption taxes. The models often suggest that the largest efficiency gains would result primarily from imposing new taxes on retirees and other past savers, who are in no position to alter the investments they already made or their labor supply.

Such models are misleading in several ways. First, neither the United States nor any other nation has a truly comprehensive income tax. Capital income is taxed at widely varying rates, and some is not taxed at all. Some analysts and advocates question whether we actually do tax capital income under our income tax and, if so, by how much.[1] Joel Slemrod and several discussants examine that question in part I.

Whether or not we tax capital income, a more fundamental question is whether we should. To answer this question, one must consider taxes as they are or can be applied, not as imagined abstractions. If capital can only be taxed imperfectly under an income tax and if exempting capital income from tax opens new opportunities for tax avoidance under a consumption tax, is it clear which system is fairest, or simplest, or even most efficient? Eric Toder, Kim Rueben, and George Zodrow consider different perspectives on those questions in part II.

Two practical difficulties involve problems in taxing capital income when it can be moved freely across borders and when complex financial transactions can be used to conceal it. If capital income is exempt, how can government prevent taxpayers from masking earnings from labor as exempt capital income? Is it possible to exempt capital income without exempting a significant share of labor income as well? In part III, Julie Roin looks at the implications of global enterprises for the sustainability of the income tax, Edward Kleinbard develops an innovative new system that attempts to solve the principal problems in the current porous income tax, and Joseph Bankman and Michael Schler try to determine which tax regime is likely to be more successful or more shelter-proof in light of institutional constraints. That these authors cannot agree, even among themselves, underscores the challenge.

This volume will not settle the debate over whether to tax income or consumption, but will illuminate many practical issues that policy-makers and the public should consider in evaluating proposals that call for converting income to consumption taxes. Although the contributors have rendered difficult topics comprehensible, their analysis is grounded in reality, which makes it complex. Given the stakes, we believe that working through these analyses is a worthwhile investment.

What Is Capital Income?

Measuring or even defining the income from capital—essentially returns from assets or saving—may seem straightforward, but it is not. Some capital income is easy to recognize: interest on bonds, dividends paid on stock, profit from the sale of a house, royalties paid to the owner of a patent, and rent received for leasing an apartment. But measuring capital income is more difficult if one adjusts for inflation or depreciation. Measuring the returns from a business, which may have branches all over the world, is vastly more complex.

Capital income consists of three types of returns:

- The first element is compensation the owner receives for *deferring* use of the funds invested in an asset. The longer the deferral, the larger the total payment. For example, total interest paid over the life of a 10-year bond typically exceeds total interest paid over the life of a six-month note.
- The second component is compensation to the owner for bearing *risk*. Those undertaking risky projects have to be paid more on average to give up control of their funds than do those undertaking safe investments. The higher the risk, the higher must be the expected (or average) return.
- The third component is an *extra return* that can arise on unique assets, or from market power, or luck. That extra return is not necessary to compensate the owner for deferring use of the funds or for bearing risk. Extra returns may be called windfall profits, infra-marginal returns, super normal returns, or rents. Super normal returns may derive from many sources, including unexpected changes in demand for land or natural resources, monopoly power, or even legislative favor.

Why Taxation of Capital Income Is Important

Whether and how much to tax capital income is important for at least five reasons. First, for a given amount of income tax revenue, taxing capital less means taxing labor more. Capital income taxes therefore critically influence the distribution of tax burdens.

Whether this trade-off holds over the long run is a matter of considerable debate. Some believe that capital income taxation may indirectly make workers worse off over time by reducing their wages. According to this position, capital taxes lower saving, thereby raising the cost of capital and depressing investment, which slows the growth of worker productivity and wages. Chapters 2 and 3, by Toder and Rueben and by Zodrow, and the commentaries by Auerbach and Weisbach, illustrate these disagreements.

Second, taxation of capital income determines the relative treatment of savers and consumers. If all income is taxed, whether saved or consumed, the consumer pays tax once on income that finances the consumption, but the saver pays both the tax on this initial income and, later, an additional tax on the capital income earned on the savings. Taxing that return means that deferred consumption is taxed more heavily than immediate consumption.[2] This second round of tax may distort the timing of consumption and favors those who consume now over those who wait.

Third, the consumption tax debate is intimately intertwined with the debate over progressive taxation. By definition, capital income flows disproportionately to owners of capital—that is, those holding wealth. Capital income is much less evenly distributed than labor income. Capital income taxes, therefore, fall disproportionately on the wealthy. For given tax rates on labor income or consumption, how heavily capital is taxed partly determines the relative taxation of the rich and the poor. Some suggest that taxing heavy consumers (mostly richer people) at much higher rates than light consumers (mostly those with lower incomes) can achieve progressivity. To mimic the distribution of tax burdens under the income tax while exempting saving, however, could require extremely high consumption tax rates. A rate of over 100 percent of the value of the consumption could be required, since high-income families spend only a fraction of their incomes.

Fourth, measuring capital income is notoriously hard and getting harder as globalization and the complexity of capital transactions increase. In fact, much of the cost of complying with and administering the income tax goes into identifying and computing capital income. How the rules for taxing capital income are designed interacts with these developments to determine the cost of compliance and administration.

Many factors contribute to this complexity:

- By its very nature, capital income involves combinations of transactions that occur over two or more periods. Thus, investors must often keep detailed records.
- Increasingly, these transactions involve currencies of different nations, the relative values of which fluctuate.
- Capital income is computed net of the decline in value of capital goods from use and obsolescence, but this loss is generally estimated (for example, from depreciation schedules) and may deviate significantly from the actual loss of value for any given asset.
- Capital income and expense are not adjusted for inflation for tax purposes. When inflation is 4 percent, a bond-holder who receives a 6 percent interest rate must pay tax on the full 6 percent, but the real income is only 2 percent of the value of the bond—the 6 percent of interest income less the 4 percent drop in the real value of the bond. Similarly, bond issuers are entitled to deduct all of the interest but do not have to pay tax on the gain in wealth resulting from a drop in the real value of the debt they owe. This situation creates opportunities for tax avoidance (see section on "tax arbitrage"). (Indexing the measurement of capital income and expense for inflation, however, would create significant new complexities.)
- Capital assets increase or decrease in value constantly, but gains or losses are typically taxed, if they are taxed at all, only when an asset is sold.[3] That is, taxes are usually based on realizations rather than accruals of income. Calculating these gains and losses usually entails records spanning many years. The deferral of tax until an asset is sold is valuable to investors, both because it is effectively an interest-free loan from the government and also because it creates tax avoidance opportunities (especially when deductions may be taken before the corresponding income is taxed).
- Increasingly, capital transactions involve many parties to whom various interests in gains and losses are legally assigned. Some investors pay no U.S. tax on much of their income. This group

includes insurance companies (which pay no tax on income earned on some reserves held on behalf of policyholders), nonprofits (such as foundations, hospitals, and universities), and foreign investors. Through these so-called "tax indifferent parties," investment planners not only avoid taxes but turn the tax system into a subsidy machine by assigning deductions to investors with tax liabilities while assigning income to tax-exempt entities or to taxpayers who face low rates.

- Transactions may be designed to reduce tax liability by exploiting differences in tax rules applying to different assets and legal entities. If transactions are without "economic substance," they are illegal in principle, although the application of this common law doctrine varies from jurisdiction to jurisdiction and from case to case. Determining when there is enough economic substance to legitimate a transaction is an arcane exercise. Because the IRS audits only a fraction of such transactions, some taxpayers now engage in an "audit lottery," undertaking transactions that may be, or are known to be, illegal in the expectation that auditors will never catch them.

Finally, capital income is often hard for administrators to spot. This problem is particularly serious when taxpayers receive income from abroad. Some foreign nations—so-called "tax havens"—encourage investors to hide assets there by refusing to cooperate with U.S. tax collectors. Some taxpayers go to great effort to hide capital income, forcing administrators to spend time and money to try to find out where capital income goes.

Despite this complexity, it is not clear that exempting capital income from tax would simplify compliance or administration. Under current law, capital gains are taxed at lower rates than ordinary income, and a whole industry is devoted to contriving schemes to transform highly taxed labor income into lightly taxed capital gains. The introduction of low tax rates on dividends has created similar incentives to transform labor income into dividends. If capital income is entirely tax-free, the payoff from such tax shelters would grow, although the disallowance of deductions for interest expense would complicate such schemes. Joseph Bankman and Michael Schler (chapter 6) reach opposite conclusions on whether replacing the income tax with a consumption tax would simplify tax compliance and administration.

Current Taxation of Capital Income

The classical definition of income is the amount that can be spent without depleting net worth. In the case of labor earnings, the concept seems straightforward. Workers can consume wages and salaries without changing their net worth. Wages and salaries are clearly taxable under an income tax. Computing capital income is inherently more complex because it accrues over time. In practice, different rules apply to different forms of capital income and to different taxpayers.

A Panoply of Rules

Table I.1 illustrates the variety of tax rules governing asset transactions and asset income. The diversity of rules means that disputes are bound to arise over the classification of particular transactions. Should a payment to a lender by a borrower be treated as interest (taxable to the recipient and deductible to the payer) or repayment of principal (neither taxable nor deductible)? If people sell stock, are they doing so as investors, in which case long-term gains are taxed at lower than normal rates and losses are deductible only up to limits, or as stock traders, in which case gains are fully taxable and losses are fully deductible against ordinary income as they accrue (whether or not the asset is sold)?

Table I.1 does not begin to convey the complexity associated with taxation of capital income. Kleinbard, for instance, demonstrates how the tax treatment of complex financial instruments can result in what he calls a "tax pastry," with some income being recognized currently, some deferred, some favored, and some penalized, depending on the instrument's formal characteristics (chapter 4).

International Transactions

International transactions pose particular challenges that are growing in importance. Globalization facilitates both legal and illegal attribution of income to foreign rather than U.S. sources. As Julie Roin demonstrates (chapter 5), cross-border trade in finished and unfinished goods and financial instruments has increased sharply. It is not unusual, for example, for a company to produce, in several countries, components that are assembled into finished goods in another country for sale in still other countries. This company could have financed construction of each fac-

Table I.1. Current Law Tax Treatment of Capital Income and Expense for Selected Items

Item	Taxability (if receipt) or deductibility (if outlay)
Interest, rents, royalties (except interest on state and local government bonds, which is exempt)	Taxable
State and local bond interest	Exempt
Proceeds from borrowing (or repayments of principal)	Exempt
Purchase of any asset (other than to close a short sale)	Exempt
Accrued depreciation	Taxable
Accrued capital gains and losses	Deferred
Accrued capital gains and losses on puts, calls, and certain other financial derivatives	Taxable
Profits of single proprietors and partnerships	Taxable
Retained corporate earnings (to shareholders)	Deferred
Private pension income (financed by an individual with after-tax income)	Taxable
"Tax sheltered" savings, including 401(k)s, IRAs, and employer-financed defined benefit pensions	Exempt
Social Security	Partially taxed
Health savings accounts	Subsidized
Sales of assets	
Realized long-term capital gains	Partially taxed
Realized short-term capital gains	Taxable
Realized capital losses, long term or short term	Partially deductible
Special treatment for certain investors or assets	
Historic property, low-income housing, and certain energy investments, research, and experimentation	Subsidized
Insurance companies—investment yield on policyholder reserves	Exempt
Gains and losses on asset purchases and sales by companies whose business is trade in those assets	Taxable

tory with loans or stock sales in still other countries. The United States taxes all income, wherever earned, of corporations chartered in the United States. But it imposes taxes only when foreign subsidiaries of U.S. companies transfer income to their U.S. chartered parents. Before the funds are transferred to U.S. parent corporations, other nations have typically taxed the income earned by these foreign subsidiaries. To prevent multiple taxes on the same income and high cumulative tax rates, the United States allows U.S. chartered companies a credit for foreign taxes paid. The credit is intended not to exceed the tax liability that would have resulted had the income been earned in the United States.

Perhaps the major challenge in taxing international transactions is determining where the income was actually earned. This determination is important because tax rates vary widely from country to country and among types of assets. Taxpayers have an incentive to exploit these differences by allocating income to low-tax jurisdictions and deductions to high-tax jurisdictions. When members of a commonly owned corporate group trade among themselves, transactions are not at "arm's length" and the companies have considerable flexibility in setting the prices paid for trade in such items as intellectual property, professional services, and commodities. The resulting controversies over "transfer pricing" employ a small army of lawyers, accountants, and economists to help companies defend their decisions and to help tax authorities challenge them. These controversies and the associated costs have little redeeming social value and generate considerable cost. Roin believes that a perfect system of measuring capital income in an international context is infeasible when some tax havens have an incentive to help international scofflaws. However, increased enforcement, conforming rules and information-sharing agreements among countries, and improved measurement systems would help. Many of these issues associated with taxing companies based on geographical location of activity do not go away with consumption taxes.

Tax Arbitrage

Nonuniform taxation of different assets, liabilities, and taxpayers creates the opportunity for tax arbitrage. Tax arbitrage denotes the way in which taxpayers are able not simply to save taxes by investing in tax-preferred assets, but to leverage or multiply up tax breaks through various combinations that usually involve borrowing and lending (or analogous transactions) at the same time (Steuerle 1985). Sometimes the tax rate will end up being negative.

The costs of tax arbitrage transactions can offset a significant share of the tax savings they produce. Especially in the case of complex transactions, these costs take the form of fees to attorneys and brokers and other transactions costs.

Multiple Layers of Taxation

While tax arbitrage can reduce or eliminate tax burdens (or even turn them into subsidies), multiple layers of taxation can result in higher-than-intended tax rates. Ordinary corporate profits, for example, may be taxed in full at the corporate level and then taxed again at the individual level when dividends are paid or shares are sold. Although the low tax rate on dividends and capital gains can make certain investments attractive tax shelters when the underlying asset is not taxed at the business level, the additional individual-level tax can constitute double taxation if income is fully taxed at the business level. Layers can also be added through the multinational and multistate systems that Roin examines (chapter 5), as well as in the complex financial instruments of the Klein-bard analysis.

Proposals to Reduce or Eliminate Capital Income Tax

Given these difficulties, it is not surprising that proposals for reforming the taxation of capital income come in many forms, including complete replacement of the income tax with a consumption tax, removal of various taxes on capital income, and changes in how the income tax treats capital income.

Consumption taxes come in many flavors. Many states and localities have adopted general and specific sales taxes. All developed countries other than the United States have adopted value-added taxes (VAT). The VAT is assessed on each business approximately on the difference between its sales revenues and the cost of goods and services purchased from other companies. When investment outlays are fully deductible in the year the investment is made, value-added taxes are equivalent to consumption taxes. If only depreciation is deductible, value-added taxes fall on income. In most countries, sales taxes and consumption-type value-added taxes supplement income taxes. Some U.S. groups have suggested that a large retail sales tax should replace personal and corporation income taxes (and perhaps other taxes as well).

Because consumption is defined as income less change in net worth, consumption can be taxed by setting the tax base equal to income less net saving. This approach requires either some form of wealth accounting or measures of all transactions into and out of designated accounts (gross saving or deposits less gross "dissaving" or withdrawals) to approximate the change in net worth.

Value added is the sum of labor compensation and business cost flow. VATs tax both components at the business level. "Flat taxes" are VATs that tax labor compensation at the household level and cash flow at the business level. For instance, if a company buys inputs for $100, pays wages of $700, and sells output for $1,100, its total value added is $1,000 ($1,100 in sales minus $100 of inputs). Under the VAT, the $1,000 is taxed at the company level. Under a flat tax, the $1,000 is divided into two parts. The $700 labor component is taxed at the household level, and the remaining $300 is taxed at the company level. In almost all VATs and flat taxes, the company tax is deferred if earnings are retained and invested, as investments produce immediate deductions. In that case, profits effectively are not taxed until consumed.

One important difference distinguishes the two taxes. Under the flat tax, the household tax may be applied to earnings above an exemption. This zero rate for earnings below the exempt amount introduces an element of progressivity not present in the VAT. The so-called "X tax" not only includes an exemption, but also applies progressive rates to labor income above the exemption. Both the flat tax and the X tax represent coherent reforms that could replace the income tax system.

Some so-called consumption tax plans propose selective or piecemeal modifications to the current system. In many cases, the principal effect of such changes would be to open new tax avoidance opportunities. One such proposal would permit unlimited deposits in individual retirement accounts or other accounts receiving similar preferential tax treatment while continuing to allow deductions for interest payments. Under this scenario, people would be able to borrow, deduct interest costs, and deposit funds in tax-free accounts, saving nothing on balance but generating tax savings. Legislators could pass complex rules to try to limit such schemes, but the financial reward is so great from such arbitrage transactions that the rules would be unlikely to keep up with the tax avoidance schemes.

What Do We Know about Taxing Capital Income?

Although analysts disagree intensely about many aspects of capital income taxation, they concur substantially on some important conclusions. To begin with, taxes on capital, like all taxes, distort behavior. Most analysts agree that taxing capital income sometimes treats savers unfairly relative to consumers who have the same initial ability to pay tax but do not save. Accounting for capital, tax planning, and sheltering income undeniably contribute to tax complexity. Other agreed-upon sources of complexity, distortion, and unfairness include taxing capital income on a realization basis, improperly measuring capital income in the presence of inflation, and determining the location of income in companies with international transactions and operations in multiple jurisdictions.

Do We Tax Capital Income?

Analysts do not agree how much capital income is actually taxed. If effective capital income tax rates are as low as some suggest, the transition to some form of consumption tax might not be especially jarring (and might offer even larger efficiency gains than implied in simple theoretical models). Unfortunately, how much capital income is taxed is not clear. Is all capital income taxed, including the return to risk taking and windfall or monopoly profits, or just the return to waiting, which forms a small part of total capital income? Is the relevant rate in measuring the burden of capital income taxation the average tax rate or the marginal tax rate on new investments?

Joel Slemrod tries to answer these vexing questions in chapter 1. He presents three measures of the capital income tax burden—capital taxes as a share of capital income, the hypothetical tax rate on a new project, and an empirical measure of the marginal effect of taxation on returns to capital. The different measures suggest that the *effective* marginal tax rate on returns to saving is between 14 and 24 percent. Jane Gravelle questions some of Slemrod's assumptions in her comments on chapter 1. She estimates that the actual burden is somewhat higher than he does. She also stresses the importance of differences in tax rates on various sorts of capital.

Should We Tax Capital Income?

A key issue in assessing tax reform proposals is the size of current tax distortions to consumption, saving, and investment and the potential efficiency gains from switching to a consumption tax base. Economists agree that many potential gains in efficiency implied from conversion to a consumption tax arise from taxing "old capital"—that is, from taxing the consumption financed out of previously taxed income. Such taxation, however, raises issues of fairness and administrative feasibility. Apart from fairness, it is unclear that such a windfall tax on old capital could ever be imposed without distorting behavior. Taxpayers would have to believe that the confiscation of old wealth will not be repeated. Without such faith, they may shape economic decisions to shield themselves from the risk of anticipated tax increases, for example, by avoiding saving or deferring investment while awaiting the next set of rule changes.

Many opponents of consumption taxes are concerned more about an erosion of tax progressivity than about the merits of one tax base over another. Many consumption tax proposals, along with companion proposals to eliminate the estate tax, would reduce progressivity. Whether this outcome is necessary is also subject to disagreement. In chapter 2, Zodrow argues that progressivity could be maintained under a consumption tax. To do so would require curtailing almost all tax preferences that benefit the wealthy and minimizing transition relief for old capital. If these steps are not taken, Zodrow acknowledges that maintaining progressivity might require extremely high (and possibly unacceptable) maximum tax rates as well as possibly retaining an estate tax. Thus, the desirability of tax reform may hinge on the political feasibility and effectiveness of assessing such taxes on the wealthy.

Analysts disagree even on whether and how much the income tax penalizes savers relative to nonsavers. While a case can be made for not taxing normal or safe returns from capital, not taxing exceptional returns, such as those from monopoly, or even returns to risk taking, is harder to justify. In chapter 3, Toder and Rueben argue that only a small portion of total capital income reflects the normal or safe return.

Many consumption taxation advocates hold that whether one pays taxes now or later is not important provided that the *amount* of tax increases with the rate of return on the underlying asset. For example, if tax rates rise, Alan Auerbach explains that a consumption tax amounts to a tax on capital income because current consumption is treated more favorably than deferred consumption (see comment to chapter 2). But the timing of taxes may be important. If one regards taxes as the price of public services and such services provide the legal and social protections essential for the security of capital income, then recipients of such income may properly be held responsible for bearing some of the costs of those arrangements. Deferring the taxes required to pay for today's benefits well into the future, perhaps to future generations, results in a temporal mismatch between when benefits are received and when they are paid for. Because tax changes occur continuously, it is doubtful whether a fair distribution of payments for benefits received can be achieved with so much deferral.

Simplicity is a frequently claimed virtue of consumption taxes because they would eliminate the need to calculate depreciation and capital gains and to track complex arrangements, such as installment sales where payments and deliveries are made over time. However, businesses would still need to account for capital income to allocate their investments efficiently. Corporations long ago introduced modern capital income accounting to meet their needs to plan operations efficiently and to report to shareholders. If computation of taxable income exactly matched internal business requirements, no appreciable simplification would result from abandoning the income tax. But computation of taxable and business income are not identical. Thus, some accounting simplification might still result from a switch to a tax system that does not impose the requirements of the current income tax. The size of such savings is less clear.

Can We Tax Capital Income?

In many cases, implicit income taxes are likely to be retained even with a conversion to a consumption tax. Government policies require many people and some businesses to measure income for other purposes. For example, in many transfer programs, including cash assistance and subsidies for education, housing, or purchase of food, benefits are reduced as income increases. To reduce benefits without regard for capital income would hardly be sensible, and basing benefits on consumption is neither administratively feasible nor sensible.

Whether or not the income tax is reformed, income accounting will still be required for these other governmental systems. Further, most states and nations use income accounting. Thus, businesses and individuals subject to state or foreign taxation will still have to compute capital income, as Julie Roin notes in chapter 5.

Nor would a switch to consumption taxation eliminate opportunities for tax avoidance and evasion, as Joseph Bankman and Michael Schler explain in chapter 6. They and Julie Roin warn that companies still must allocate their sales and many of their intracompany or related transfers to the right jurisdictions at the right prices. Schler and Bankman point out that a consumption tax of the flat or X type would create new tax planning opportunities. They agree that controlling these opportunities would be difficult, but they disagree on whether complexity and tax cheating opportunities under a consumption tax would worsen or improve.

The fundamental reason why tax reform cannot eliminate complexity, tax avoidance, and evasion is that these problems emerge from politics and the complexity of modern economic activity. For example, whatever the tax system, accounting sophistication and politics are likely to cause legislators to favor small over large businesses. If differences in treatment exist, taxpayers will try to exploit them.

International trade and capital flows create the additional opportunity to hide assets abroad, and a switch to consumption taxation will increase these opportunities. If a filer hides assets abroad, the government loses tax on income from those assets under an income tax. With a flat or X tax, an asset hidden abroad can end up reducing the tax base by the entire value of the asset. For example, hiding $100 of an asset abroad in one year would reduce the income tax base by $5 if the rate of return is 5 percent. Hiding the same asset could reduce the consumption tax base by $100.

Further, a consumption tax would defer massive amounts of tax as filers take deductions for the full value of current investments. Schler worries that deferring so much more tax under a consumption tax than occurs under an income tax, where only depreciation is available upon purchase of assets, will create massive incentives for filers and their accounting and legal representatives to craft new tax shelters that neither legislators nor administrators can fully anticipate. Joseph Bankman views this risk as inadequate grounds for rejecting a consumption tax, given all the ways that capital income can be sheltered under an income tax.

In chapter 4, Ed Kleinbard acknowledges that financial instruments can be manipulated to avoid tax but believes that this problem can be fixed. He examines two reforms. Under one, most capital income would be taxed at the corporate level but still on a realization basis. Under an alternative that he designed, capital income would be taxed currently on an approximation or "imputed" basis in cases where there are no realizations of income. He also favors a simplified system of accounting for different types of capital costs (such as traditional depreciation). These accounting changes combined with the imputation system would minimize the possibility of tax planning and avoidance. Not everyone agrees, and Kleinbard himself calls for further analysis of his proposed changes.

Conclusion

The debate over taxing capital income is centuries old. Recent research has added theoretical insights and empirical knowledge. Certain tried and true principles of reform remain generally accepted. The best hope for reducing tax-based distortion and simplifying compliance and administration lies in curtailing special exceptions, exclusions, deductions, and credits. This formula applies as much to income as to consumption tax reform. The rate reduction made possible by broadening the tax base further reduces distortions and enhances fairness because the value of remaining tax deductions and exclusions declines when rates are lowered.

We believe that any broad expansion of consumption taxation would use a value-added tax base. All developed countries that have adopted VATs already have income taxes. VAT revenues could finance large personal exemptions under the income tax, freeing many filers from income tax burdens, as Michael Graetz (1997) suggests. Even without direct adoption of a VAT, most well developed proposals for conversion of the income tax base to a consumption tax base have built upon a VAT-like structure. Other attempts, such as personal consumption taxes (based on measuring changes in net worth) and very high retail sales taxes, have floundered over issues of administration and enforcement.

Under any tax system, the wealthy likely will pay a significant share of the tax and far more than they receive in cash or in-kind benefits. Thus, overall fiscal progressivity is almost inevitable, even if the degree and method of achieving progressivity are contentious. This debate is inescapable and desirable.

Estimates of the gains from a switch to a consumption tax all rest on highly abstract models of the economy. The estimates are extremely sensitive to assumptions. Moreover, economists cannot determine with certainty even such key matters as how heavily capital is currently taxed.

Under these circumstances, a wholesale switch in the tax system is a large and risky step. Whether the switch will, in the end, raise or lower welfare may depend on politically sensitive matters, such as how much transition relief is provided to owners of capital when the system is changed.

NOTES

1. President George W. Bush's Council of Economic Advisers has argued that the switch from an income tax to a consumption tax would be far less disruptive than many assume because so much capital income is already exempt from tax (Economic Report of the President 2005). The Office of Management and Budget made a similar argument in arguing that the baseline tax system for examining "tax expenditures"—that is, tax provisions that deviate from the norm—might just as well be a consumption tax as an income tax (OMB 2006).

2. For example, if the interest rate is 5 percent, then, before taxes, $1.00 today is the equivalent of $1.05 a year from now. If capital income is taxed at, say, a 20 percent rate, 1 cent (20 percent) of the 5 cent return to waiting would be paid in tax. Thus, the tax reduces the return to waiting by 20 percent. If the taxpayer was just indifferent between current consumption and future consumption at the 5 percent tax rate, he or she would not be willing to lend (i.e., would increase current consumption) when saving is subject to tax.

3. Although many gains and losses are recognized for tax purposes only when assets are sold, in the case of some financial market derivatives and some financial asset traders and brokers, accrued gains and losses are computed regularly, even when the underlying assets has not been sold, based on market prices.

REFERENCES

Council of Economic Advisers. 2005. *Economic Report of the President.* Washington, DC: U.S. Government Printing Office.

Graetz, Michael. 1997. *The Decline (And Fall?) of the Income Tax.* New York: Norton & Norton Co.

Office of Management and Budget. 2006. "Tax Expenditures." Section 19, Budget of the U.S. Government, Fiscal Year 2007. Analytical Perspectives. Washington, DC: Superintendent of Documents.

Steuerle, C. Eugene. 1985. "Taxes, Loans, and Inflation." Washington, DC: The Brookings Institution.

PART I
Do We Tax
Capital Income?

1

Does the United States Tax Capital Income?

Joel Slemrod

Examining how the United States taxes capital income is a crucial step for understanding whether to replace what we have with a system that exempts capital income from tax, as any consumption tax would.[1] How profound a change moving to a consumption tax would be has been called into question by recent claims that we now collect little or no tax on capital income, that the differences between income and consumption-based taxation of capital income are smaller than once believed, and that there is little capital income to be taxed.[2] These arguments also suggest that piecemeal tax changes that extend tax preferences to saving and investment might push the tax system "beyond" a consumption-based tax system to one that provides a net subsidy to saving and investment.

How—and how much—capital income is taxed has both equity and efficiency implications. Its importance for vertical equity stems from how starkly the wealth distribution is skewed. According to the 2001 Survey of Consumer Finances, the richest 1 percent owns nearly one-third of total net worth, and the next 9 percentiles own more than another third. In contrast, the 50 percent of families with the lowest net worth own less than 3 percent of net worth.[3] The wealth inequality produces a similar inequality in the receipt of capital income.

The battle is drawn because many economists argue that the efficiency costs of taxing capital income are large and avoidable under alternative tax systems, both because taxing capital income reduces the incentive to save and invest (and the relative price of current consumption) and because it distorts the allocation of current capital to productive uses and the allocation of risk among individuals. Thus, while many analysts argue that taxing capital income creates more damaging distortions than would result from collecting the same amount of revenue from taxes on consumption or labor income, many others (and sometimes the same people) are concerned that a failure to tax capital income could undermine progressivity.

The equity and efficiency issues are conceptually different, though related. For example, such inframarginal tax features as capped tax preferences may affect distribution by reducing the tax burden of those who take advantage of the preferences, but do not raise savings incentives for those subject to the caps. More directly, the choice of tax base and the progressivity of the tax system are not, in theory, linked—a country may levy a highly progressive consumption tax or a proportional or even regressive income tax, for example. Consumption taxes widely used internationally and by states (principally the value added tax and retail sales tax) often produce more regressive tax distributions than most graduated income taxes. However, progressive consumption tax plans do exist, such as the X tax (a version of the Hall-Rabushka flat tax developed and championed by David Bradford that has graduated rates on individual labor income rather than a flat rate) and the USA Tax (a graduated personal expenditure tax championed in the mid-1990s by Senator Pete Domenici [R-NM] and former Senator Sam Nunn [D-GA]). Indeed, the growth and investment tax proposed in 2005 by the President's Advisory Panel on Federal Tax Reform builds on the X-tax idea but is in fact a hybrid because it does not exempt capital income from personal tax, as a true flat tax or X tax would.

This article presents and critiques three approaches to quantitatively estimating the extent of U.S. capital income taxation in recent years and, finally, attempts to reconcile the answers the three methods provide. (An appendix lays out in rigorous mathematical language the arguments the chapter makes.) The focus here is on incentives to save and invest, rather than how the tax system affects the distribution of tax burden and welfare. Two theoretically appealing methods of calculating how much the U.S. taxes capital income that are conceptually similar but have distinct computational strengths and weaknesses suggest that the revenue collected is fairly small and the tax rate at the margin of new saving and investment is well below the corporate statutory rate or the top personal income tax rate. This implies that the effect of moving from the current tax system to a pure consumption tax—which would levy no marginal tax on capital income—on the incentive to save and invest would not be nearly as large as shifting from a pure income tax to a pure consumption tax.

Summarizing in one number the effect of taxation on the incentive to save and invest is not straightforward and requires a careful manipulation of data guided by a coherent conceptual framework. Starting with a conceptually correct measure, it becomes possible to use inevitably imperfect and incomplete data to estimate the real-world value of the conceptually correct measure.

The measure should focus on the *marginal* investment and saving decision. As an example, consider the case where the risk-free after-tax hurdle rate is 2 percent, and a business is considering two investments it believes will earn a certainty-equivalent of 8 and 3 percent pretax rate of return, respectively; call the former an "inframarginal" investment opportunity and the latter a "marginal" one. In the absence of any tax, the business should proceed with both investments. A 50 percent tax on the pretax rate of return will make the marginal project no longer attractive (it yields only 1.5 percent after tax, less than the hurdle rate), but the inframarginal investment is still worth doing (it yields 4 percent after tax, above the hurdle rate). Indeed, the extent to which a tax system reduces the rate of return on any inframarginal investment—and the revenue it collects—is irrelevant for understanding the impact on investment. A pure consumption tax does not affect the pretax rate of return on the marginal investment, and thus does not influence investment. It may, though, raise revenue by reducing the pretax rate of return on inframarginal investments; this revenue is sometimes referred to as coming from the tax on *pure profits.*

A similar issue arises when, as is generally the case, the return to investment is subject to risk. When the return to investment is uncertain, the investment will in equilibrium earn a higher expected return—a *risk premium*—to compensate the holders of the risk. A tax on risky returns will, on average, raise revenue, but it also reduces the required risk premium in the same proportion as it reduces the expected value, if the tax system treats profits and losses symmetrically. Even if the tax treatment is not exactly symmetrical, the tax revenue raised overstates the tax disincentive to invest because it misinterprets the revenue collected on the risk premium as a disincentive to invest rather than as a fair premium for the reduction in risk caused by the tax levy.

The conceptually correct measure must take into account the tax system currently in place and possible future changes in the tax system. Past tax systems are not directly relevant for this measure. Data generated by past tax systems can, though, be helpful if they shed light on important aspects in the current system, such as how much tax arbitrage erodes the marginal impact of differential tax rates on various means of holding assets or how much the current tax base includes revenue collected on pure profits and risk premiums. Tax collections data also reflect institutional details of the tax system, including special tax provisions and lax enforcement methods, for which measurement methods based on hypothetical investments and parameter assumptions have difficulty accounting. This information is especially valuable if there have been few recent changes in the tax system because, in this case, current data—which reflect both the current tax system and the traces of previous tax systems—provide a more accurate picture of the impact of the current system on saving and investment decisions.

A Tax-Collections-Based Measure

The most straightforward approach to measuring the tax burden on capital income is the ratio of capital income taxes paid to a measure of capital income.[4] This measure is calculated by categorizing each particular tax base as being capital or not (or, in practice, as a mixture of capital and noncapital). Once this is done, one simply sums the revenue from the taxes on capital, and then divides this sum by the total capital income associated with the capital income tax bases. In principle, the taxes on capital include both taxes assessed on income flows and those levied on capital stocks, such as property taxes, wealth taxes, and estate taxes.[5]

The measure is "backward looking" because the estimates it produces depend on the history of investment as well as on historical tax rules. The potential advantage is that tax collections data reflect the institutional details, including special tax provisions and lax enforcement; methods based on hypothetical investments and parameter assumptions have difficulty accounting for these factors.

The two main problems with such measures is that they rely on fairly arbitrary categorizations of what is a tax on capital income (and what is capital income) and, as detailed in the appendix, do not deal appropriately with risk and pure profits.

A careful tax collections–based measure for the recent U.S. tax system has been made using data from the Organisation for Economic Co-operation and Development (OECD) on national income and revenue statistics, which contain time series on revenue collected from various types of tax (Carey and Rabesona 2004). Table 1.1 presents figures that follow this procedure for the latest year U.S. data are available, 2002, and also for the year 2000 to neutralize the impact of 2002 being a recession year.[6] To make the figures more comparable with the alternative measurements discussed below, the calculations for federal tax only are also broken out for 2002.

This procedure produces a federal-tax-only capital income tax rate of 24.1 percent for 2002. These calculations provide a useful reality check to the less straightforward procedures discussed next, but as measures of the disincentive effects on savings and investment (as the authors admit), these estimates are suspect on many grounds. First, they accept all corporation taxes as taxes on capital income and therefore disregard the possibility that any of it represents pure profit, risk premiums, or the shifting of labor income into the tax base (Gordon and Slemrod 2000). Second, the calculation of household-level taxes on capital income is very crude, relying on an assumption that households face identical effective tax rates on capital and labor income, so that household capital income taxes are calculated by simply assigning total personal taxes to capital or labor based on the ratio of capital income to labor income. In making this division, all self-employed income is considered to be capital income. Further, the data do not account for such factors as special arrangements for the preferential taxation of capital gains, pensions and tax-preferred individual accounts, the deductibility of interest, or the arbitrage that occurs when individuals with high marginal taxes borrow from individuals with low marginal taxes or tax-exempt institutions.

In addition, this measure is backward looking, and so will inaccurately measure incentives for new saving and investment to the extent that the tax law has changed, the productivity of investment has changed, or the growth rate of real investment varies from the real interest rate. If these conditions are not satisfied, the tax collections–based measure will misestimate the true effective tax rate. For example, consider the implications of making this calculation for a recession year when current investment and profits are low relative to past years and, most important,

Table 1.1. Tax Collection–Based Measures, 2000 and 2002

	2000	2002	2002, federal only
Capital taxes			
Household taxes on individuals	523,150	434,652	359,006
= Taxes on individuals × share of capital income in household income	1,223,590 × .428	1,040,034 × .418	
Taxes on income, profits, and capital gains of corporations	254,984	185,893	159,755
Social Security taxes on self-employed or nonemployed	34,020	36,180	36,180
Taxes on property	295,105	329,184	27,242
Taxes on motor vehicles	6,684	6,807	0
Total capital taxes	1,113,943	992,716	578,941
Capital income			
Net operating surplus of the overall economy	2,305,500	2,399,100	2,399,100
Capital income tax ratio			
	48.3%	41.4%	24.1%

Sources: OECD National Accounts, OECD Revenue Statistics, and author's calculations.

Notes: All figures, except the capital income tax ratio, are in $millions.

Share of capital income in household income = [(unincorporated business net income) + (interest, dividends, and investment receipts)] / [(wages and salaries of dependent employment) + (unincorporated business net income) + (interest, dividends, and investment receipts)].

Net operating surplus equals business income net of taxes on productions and imports (less subsidies) and depreciation, but before subtracting financing costs.

In calculating the federal portion of capital taxes, it is assumed that the share of capital income in total household income is the same at the federal and state/local level, and federal taxes on property include only estate and gift taxes.

low relative to the current depreciation allowances associated with the high investment rates of the precedent years. In this case, the tax rate measure will underestimate the true effective tax rate; at peaks in the business cycle, the tax collections–based measure will be too high. With regular cycles, the problem could be attacked by taking averages over complete cycles. In practice, the calculations underlying table 1.1 produce a lower number in the recession year 2002 compared with 2000, 41.4 percent versus 48.3 percent for all levels of tax, but many other things certainly changed between 2000 and 2002—and many other issues remain unresolved—for these two figures to be considered the upper and lower bounds on the right answer for the early 2000s.

Hypothetical Project-Based Measures

The standard approach to summarizing the tax system's effect on saving and investment is based on calculating, for a hypothetical marginal investment project, the difference between the pretax return to capital and the after-tax return to savers.[7] A marginal project is one whose after-tax return equals the required after-tax return, no more and no less. Understanding the impact of the tax system on saving and investment means focusing on the marginal investment since changes in how this investment is taxed will affect investment decisions; in contrast, if a tax feature reduces the after-tax return of inframarginal investments (i.e., those that are worth doing in any event), it might have distributional effects but would not change how much investment is carried out.

If taxable income measured true income, then (putting aside personal-level taxes on corporate income and future tax changes), the effective tax rate on a marginal investment would be equal to the statutory rate. But, for many reasons, taxable income does not equal true income. One important reason is that the tax law allows assets to be depreciated based on fixed schedules for a small number of asset categories. To the extent that true economic depreciation differs from tax depreciation allowances, taxable income will differ from true income over the useful life of the asset. Because of the time value of the money, a firm saves more in present value from a tax depreciation schedule that is accelerated relative to true economic depreciation because this lowers its taxes paid earlier and increases them later.

The effective tax rate provides a single constant tax rate applied to economic income that evens out the overstated and understated tax burdens in particular years. Considering only taxes at the business level, it is that tax rate that makes the following equation hold:

$$(1-t)\rho = r.$$

In this equation, ρ denotes the real pretax rate of return on the marginal investment and r is the required after-tax real return that investors require. Solving that equation shows that

$$t = (\rho - r)/\rho.$$

When taxes are also paid at the personal level,[8] the effective tax rate is defined as that tax rate that makes the following equation hold:

$$(1-t)\rho = s,$$

where s is the real after-tax rate of return savers receive. Thus, the total effective tax rate is equal to $(\rho - s)/\rho$.

Calculating an effective tax rate requires making a number of assumptions. These include, but are not limited to, the true pattern of economic depreciation for each type of capital asset, the effective tax depreciation schedule, the required (hurdle) rate of return, the statutory tax rates that apply, and firms' sufficient taxable income against which to deduct depreciation allowances. In addition, one needs to know the required rate of return on investment, how capital is financed, and in what form individuals hold, directly or indirectly, these assets. Errors in measuring any of these values will produce inaccurate measurements of the effective tax rate. Finally, the procedure generally assumes that the current tax system will stay in place forever. The following explains how the Congressional Budget Office (CBO) (2005) and Jane Gravelle (1994, 2004, 2005) calculated the effective tax rate.

The CBO methodology calculates a single aggregate statistic for all capital and for broad categories of capital (i.e., corporate, noncorporate) by first calculating before-tax rates of return (ρ) for each of 49 asset types and then averaging these values within a category using as weights the share of the current capital stock in the category. All businesses are assumed to be profitable. Marginal investments are assumed to be financed in proportion to the existing patterns of finance and that the tax rate on dividends matters in proportion to the fraction of after-tax profits paid out as dividends. The effective tax rates are computed under the assumption that any provisions of the 2001 and 2003 tax acts not already expired by 2008 will be made permanent.

Two of CBO's methodological choices are worth special attention. The first is the CBO's treatment of risk. Although the conceptual model on which this method rests requires a careful differentiation between expected values of uncertain returns and risk-free returns, the discussion of the CBO's underlying model does not provide this other than to say the expected earnings on an investment must be sufficient to recover the hurdle rate. When the CBO implements the conceptual model, it measures the hurdle rate (r) as a weighted average of the Baa corporate bond rate and the real equity return after corporate tax, neither of which is a risk-free measure. The report admits that "the methodology for computing effective tax rates does not adequately treat the taxation of risky returns, so some analysts recommend [using as the hurdle rate] a rate with less risk, such as the yield on Treasury bonds" (CBO 2005). The report says that using the Treasury bond rate would not change their qualitative findings.[9]

Second, although the CBO methodology generally assigns marginal saving to categories that reflect tax status (i.e., nontaxable with binding limits, nontaxable with no binding limits, temporarily deferred, or fully taxable), it adjusts for the fact that, because of statutory limits on contributions to IRAs and 401(k) plans, marginal saving must be directed elsewhere. The CBO estimates that 46 percent of marginal saving was done by families constrained by a limit; these limits reduce marginal saving in fully taxable form from 55 to 64 percent.

The CBO report concludes that the effective tax rate on capital income is 13.8 percent, composed of a 26.3 percent rate on corporate capital income, a 20.6 percent rate on noncorporate capital income, and a −5.1 percent rate on owner-occupied housing (table 1.2).[10]

Gravelle follows a similar methodology. She starts by calculating effective tax rates for 22 types of equipment and 6 types of structure (intangible assets are ignored) using estimates of asset lives and assumptions about the interest rate, the inflation rate, the assumed rate of debt finance, and the applicable tax rates. As in CBO (2005), the hurdle rate

Table 1.2. Hypothetical Project-Based Measure of the Effective Tax Rate on Capital Income (%)

	CBO	Gravelle
Corporate, firm-level only	n.a.	27
Corporate, total	26.3	32
Noncorporate	20.6	18
Owner-occupied housing	−5.1	2
Overall	13.8	23

Sources: CBO (2005, 12) and Gravelle (2004, 3)

is not a risk-free rate. The calculations account for a bonus depreciation at 30 percent for 2002 and 50 percent in 2003, and a reduction in the tax rate for capital gains and dividends from 20 to 15 percent in 2003.[11]

Table 1.2 presents the calculated values from Gravelle (2004) of the forward-looking, hypothetical project–based measure of the tax on capital income for 2003. The overall rate is 23 percent, compared with the 13.8 percent CBO calculated. One reason for the discrepancy is that Gravelle's baseline calculations purposely do not take into account the tax benefits to saving that come from pensions and individual retirement accounts, even though half of interest, dividends, and capital gains are received through these tax-exempt vehicles. Gravelle (2004, 4) argues that ignoring their effect is appropriate because many investments in these forms are made up to the maximum contribution limit and "even where investments are not at the limit all marginal investments may still not flow through the tax-favored account." This is an extreme version of the CBO procedure for dealing with this issue outlined above. Gravelle notes, though, that there is probably some marginal effect, and correcting for this can have a big effect on the estimated tax rates. If the individual income tax rate on these forms of income is set to half the statutory value, to reflect the share of nontaxed investment returns, the estimated total effective tax rate falls 6 percentage points, assuming the lower individual rates on capital income put in place in 2003 (8 points lower, with the permanent individual rates); the rate on the corporate sector falls 10 points (8 points assuming the permanent tax rates), and the noncorporate rate falls 5 points. This adjustment makes Gravelle's overall estimate equal to 17 percent, closer to the CBO estimate of 13.8 percent.

The GKS Approach

A series of papers have proposed and implemented a different method—referred to as the GKS method after its authors, Gordon, Kalambokidis, and Slemrod—of assessing whether, and how much, the United States taxes capital income.[12] As discussed in detail in the appendix, the underlying conceptual basis of the measure is exactly the same measure that underlies the hypothetical-project method; indeed, under certain conditions, the two methods produce exactly the same measure for a given tax system. The difference is the empirical approach to *measuring* the effective tax rate on saving and investment. The new empirical approach is based on computing the difference between actual tax revenues and the hypothetical revenues collected under a particular type of consumption tax system (an R-base tax) with the same rate structure. The base of the tax, dubbed an "R tax" by the Meade Committee (1978), excludes financial income, disallows interest deductions, and replaces depreciation, amortization, and depletion deductions with expensing for new investment. The tax base is essentially the same as the Hall-Rabushka flat tax and, in its graduated form, is closely related to the X tax proposed and studied extensively by David Bradford. To calculate the revenue that would be collected under an R-base tax, the R-base corporate taxable income and tax liability are computed using aggregate data on depreciation allowances, interest deductions, and investment expenditures; the first two are added back into the tax base and the third is subtracted. Next, the individual taxable income under the R base (accounting for the individual tax base implications of changes in corporate tax payments) is estimated using microdata from public-use individual tax returns; a tax calculator computes the tax revenue that would be collected if the current individual tax rate structure were applied to the individual R base. Given the limitations of the aggregate corporate tax data and the individual tax return data, performing this hypothetical calculation requires detailed assumptions (Gordon and Slemrod 1988; Gordon, Kalambokidis, and Slemrod 2004a, b; Gordon, Kalambokidis, Rohaly, and Slemrod 2004).

Because the R-base tax is a form of consumption tax, it does not distort investment incentives. The GKS measure is based on the notion that the difference between the taxes actually collected and the taxes collected under a nondistortionary alternative tax system is informative about how much distortion the tax system creates. Measuring an effective tax rate on capital in this way has two main advantages. Because an R-base tax would collect (expected) tax revenue that does not reflect any distorting taxation of capital income, only the excess of current tax collections reflects distortion to decisions; thus, the GKS measure automatically and simply corrects a tax collections–based measure for the problem of confounding capital income with either pure profits or a risk premium. Second, it does not require calculating a host of parameters, such as the asset-specific rates of economic depreciation, the effective tax rate on components of corporate and personal taxable income, debt-to-capital ratios, and dividend payout ratios.[13] To the extent that these features of the tax system matter, the GKS method picks them up via their impact on tax collections. For example, the rate of economic depreciation, which must be estimated under the hypothetical-project method, plays no role in the calculation of the GKS measure (although the observed pattern of depreciation deductions for tax purposes does.)

The principal disadvantage of the GKS approach is that it is not forward looking. Thus, recent changes in the tax system can contaminate the measure, though adjustment can be made to approximately reflect recently changed tax law and business-cycle effects. Its accuracy also depends on whether the economy's recent growth rate is approximately the risk-free rate of interest because, to the extent it is not, the ratio of investment to depreciation allowances at any one time will not reflect the forward-looking present-value difference to a business between immediate expensing and depreciation.

The authors (including Jeff Rohaly) estimated the GKS measure in 2004 and examined how far recent tax reforms had moved the tax system toward (or beyond) a consumption tax system.[14] Using data from 2000 (adjusted to reflect the U.S. economy in the year 2004) on corporate taxes and simulations provided by the Urban–Brookings Tax Policy Center Microsimulation Model for the individual income tax liabilities, the authors find that the United States would lose about $64 billion of tax revenue if it switched the system to an R-base consumption system ($30.1 billion at the corporate level and $33.7 billion at the individual level). Table 1.3 presents some details of these calculations. What table 1.3 does not show is that the authors estimate that moving to an R base would exempt from tax $626.1 billion of interest receipts and other capital income but disallow $357.8 billion of interest deductions, for a net drop of $268.2 billion in taxable income. The net reduction in taxable income is $293.3 billion, resulting in a decline of $33.7 billion in tax liability; this is starkly lower than the estimated household tax on capital income by

Table 1.3. The GKS Measure of the Effective Tax Burden on Capital Income, 2004

	Corporate	Household	Total
Tax collections with 2002–2003 capital income tax provisions	201.5	832.8	1,034.3
Tax collections under an R-base tax	171.4	799.1	970.5
Difference	30.1	33.7	63.8

Source: Gordon, Kalambokidis, Rohaly, and Slemrod (2004)
Note: All numbers in $billion.

the tax collections–based procedure discussed earlier. The ratio of the estimated change in tax liability to the estimated change in taxable income is just 0.115, reflecting the fact that the disallowed interest deductions are concentrated among those in the top brackets, whereas the exempted capital income receipts tend to be received relatively more by those in lower tax brackets.

Converting the $63.8 billion estimate for the difference in tax collections between the current system and an R-base tax with the same rate structure into a tax rate requires dividing the former by an estimate of the capital stock times the after-business-tax real interest rate (plus another term discussed in the appendix). According to the Bureau of Economic Analysis, the current-cost net stock of corporate and residential fixed assets was $22.3 trillion in 2004. Using 2 percent for this adjusted, risk-free rate of return for the denominator produces an estimate of the effective tax rate of 14.3 percent ($63.8 billion divided by $446 billion).

These estimates presume that the changes in capital income taxation enacted in 2002 and 2003, most importantly bonus depreciation and the lower tax on dividend receipts, are in place. Not considering bonus depreciation, as might be appropriate given the fact that it was not extended into 2005, would add about $25 billion to the GKRS estimate of capital income tax collections, pushing the 14.3 percent estimate toward 20 percent.[15]

Finally, GKRS (2004) estimates the effect of significantly expanding tax-free savings accounts (to $50,000 per married couple, $25,000 for single filers), similar to what the Bush administration proposed in 2003 and likely to be reconsidered in the future. Depending on the method of modeling this policy change, GKRS finds that the expanded accounts could push the U.S. tax system *beyond* a consumption tax in the sense that revenue would be lost from the attempt to tax capital income. Two alternative methods suggest that the aggregate tax revenue from (the attempt to) tax capital income would be either just $20 billion or minus $44 billion.[16]

The Right Answer

Three approaches to measuring the effective marginal federal tax rate on capital income produce similar estimates, ranging from 24 percent in the tax collections–based measure, 14 to 23 percent for the hypothetical project–based measure, to 14 to 20 percent under the GKS method assuming that the real interest rate is 2 percent.[17] Because the latter two have a rigorous conceptual underpinning, more weight should be given to those results.[18] To be sure, the conclusions of both of these methods are subject to the accuracy of a host of assumptions and data analysis choices.

Conclusions

Two theoretically appealing methods of calculating how much the United States taxes capital income—conceptually similar but with distinct measurement strengths and weaknesses—suggest that the amount of revenue collected is fairly small and the tax rate at the margin of new saving and investment is well below the corporate statutory rate or the top personal income tax rate. This suggests that moving to a pure consumption tax, which would levy no marginal tax on capital income, would not affect the incentive to save and invest as much as shifting from a pure income tax to a pure consumption tax. Because the current system generates differential tax rates depending on the physical asset, the business financing method, and the tax status of the business and saver, a pure consumption tax would also improve the efficiency of the allocation of capital and risk for any given amount of saving, investment, and capital. However, further expanding tax-preferred savings accounts (and/or accelerating depreciation) while retaining interest deductibility would arguably push the tax system *beyond* a consumption tax in the sense that it would subsidize saving and investment compared to a world with no taxes.

T his appendix provides a more rigorous explanation of the conceptual underpinnings of the methods this chapter discusses.[19]

Hypothetical Project–Based Measure

The conceptual framework revolves around the presumption that any profit-maximizing firm will acquire the productive services of a new capital good as long as the present discounted value of the stream of returns it generates exceeds the cost of acquiring the asset; thus, for the marginal project, the present discounted value of the returns equals the acquisition cost. Normalizing the pretax price of the capital good to be one, we can write the single-period-equivalent maximization problem as

(A-1) $$\text{Max } f(K) - (r + \delta)K,$$

where $f(K)$ is the output produced with the capital stock K, r is the discount rate (equal to the real opportunity cost of funds), and δ is the per-unit rate (assumed to be exponential) of economic depreciation of the capital good. The solution to this problem is characterized by the following condition for the marginal investment:

(A-2) $$f'(K) - \delta = r.$$

Here $f' - \delta$ is the annual net-of-depreciation return to one unit of capital. In equilibrium, it equals the alternative rate of return to savings for the firm's shareholders, r.

Now introduce a business-level tax on the revenue the investment generates, at the rate of u, and allow the purchaser of the capital asset to deduct a prespecified stream of depreciation allowances.[20] Think of the present discounted value of the tax savings generated by the depreciation allowances as a reduction in the acquisition cost of the asset. Let z be the present value of depreciation deductions per dollar of acquisition cost, so that uz is the present value of the tax savings resulting from the deductions allowed on one dollar of new investment. As a result, only $(1 - uz)$ dollars need to be raised from investors to finance a dollar of new investment. Similarly, only $\delta(1 - uz)$ dollars need to be raised in each future period to cover replacement expenditures. With these adjustments, equation (A-2) becomes

$$(A\text{-}3) \qquad f'(K) = \frac{(r + \delta)(1 - uz)}{(1 - u)},$$

which can be rewritten as

$$(A\text{-}4) \qquad f' - \delta = r + \frac{u(r + \delta)(1 - z)}{1 - u},$$

where the K term has been dropped for notational convenience.

The second term of the right-hand side of expression (A-4) captures the extent of any tax distortion, measuring the difference between the net-of-depreciation return to capital and the investors' return to savings. It will be convenient for future purposes to denote the numerator of this term by $\Delta \equiv u(r + \delta)(1 - z)$. One can think of Δ as measuring the extra taxes due as a result of using depreciation rather than expensing (in which case $z = 1$ and $\Delta = 0$), measured as a constant figure in each year. To pay these extra taxes while still yielding a return of r to investors, the firm needs to earn an extra $\Delta/(1 - u)$ before taxes. For future reference, note that Δ rises with r: for given tax parameters, the higher the opportunity cost of capital, the higher the disincentive is to invest.

Now define the "effective tax rate," m, as that tax rate on net-of-depreciation income, $f' - \delta$, that leads to the same equilibrium value of $f' - \delta$, given r, that arises under the actual tax law. By definition, then, m satisfies the following equation:

(A-5) $$(f' - \delta)(1 - m) = r,$$

where the equilibrium f' is characterized by equation (A-4). We then find, using equations (A-4) and (A-5), that

(A-6) $$m = \frac{\Delta}{(1 - u)r + \Delta}.$$

Note that the correct calculation of m relies on accurately measuring (in addition to u and z) δ, the rate of economic depreciation, which is notoriously difficult to do. Two special cases are worth pondering. The first is expensing, under which all investment expenditures are deductible from taxable income when incurred. In this case, $z = 1$, so that $m = 0$ *regardless of the value of u or δ*. The other case of interest is the pure income tax, under which depreciation allowances exactly mirror economic depreciation. Then $z = \delta/(r + \delta)$. If $\delta/(r + \delta)$ is substituted for z in expression (A-4), then $m = u$, implying that the tax system is a true income tax that at the margin taxes away exactly the fraction u of the net-of-depreciation return.

Tax Collections–Based Measure

How does the effective tax rate calculated in this way relate to the amount of taxes *collected* on capital income and the ratio of taxes collected to capital income? To answer this question, note that the taxes paid in some year t equal

(A-7) $$TC_t = u\left[f_t(K_t) - \int_{s=0}^{\infty} d_{s,t-s} I_{t-s}\, ds \right],$$

where $d_{s,t-s}$ equals the depreciation deductions allowed for s-year-old capital originally purchased in year $t-s$, based on the tax law in force in year $t-s$. Capital purchased in year $t-s$ is denoted by I_{t-s}. Now consider the following measure of the average tax rate on capital income:

$$(A\text{-}8) \qquad\qquad m_{TC} = \frac{TC_t}{\left(f_t(K_t) - \delta K_t\right)},$$

which is tax collected divided by capital income net of true depreciation. This measure of the average tax rate exactly equals the marginal effective tax rate on investment, m, if four conditions hold. The first two are that the tax law remains fixed over time and that there are no business cycle effects, so that f_t does not vary over time. The third is that real investment has been growing at rate r. Only when this assumption holds will the pattern of current depreciation allowances due to past capital investments mimic the pattern of depreciation allowances a current investment will generate in the future. The fourth critical assumption is that production is characterized by constant returns to scale. Under this assumption, $f' = f(K)/K$; that is, the marginal product of capital equals the average product of capital. This assumption rules out pure profits, ensuring that the return to inframarginal investment is the same as for the marginal investment.

GKS Measure

The GKS measure is based on the difference between the amount of tax collected under current law and what tax collections would be under an R-base tax, a tax first developed (and named) in the Meade Committee report (1978). The R base excludes financial income, disallows interest deductions, and replaces depreciation, amortization, and depletion deductions with expensing for new investment. The base is essentially the same as the Hall-Rabushka flat tax, and in its graduated form is closely related to the X tax proposed and studied extensively by David Bradford. The difference between how much the actual tax system raises and the amount of revenue a hypothetical R-base tax (with the same tax rate structure) raises can be converted into an effective tax rate comparable to the two measures already derived.

To see this, let TR be the the tax that would be collected under an R-base tax, holding both the return to capital and the capital stock at current levels, rather than at the values they would have in the equilibrium with an R-base tax. Because the R base allows immediate expensing of investment, this is equal to

(A-9)
$$TR_t = u(f_t(K_t) - I_t).$$

The difference between taxes collected under the current law relative to an R-base tax that does not distort capital investments, $TC - TR$, equals the net taxes collected on income/deductions from financial assets (dividends, interest, and capital gains) plus the effects on tax revenue from use of depreciation and amortization rather than expensing for new investment. This expression equals:

(A-10)
$$TC_t - TR_t = u\left(I_t - \int_{s=0}^{\infty} d_{s,t-s} I_{t-s} ds\right).$$

Assuming an unchanging tax law and real investment growing at rate r, this expression simplifies to $u(r + \delta)(1 - z)K = \Delta K$, where Δ is defined as earlier.[21]

To measure an effective tax rate associate with this method, Gordon, Kalambokidis, and Slemrod (2004b) proposed the following definition:

(A-11)　$$m_{GKS} \equiv \frac{(TC_t - TR_t)/K}{(1-u)r + (TC_t - TR_t)/K} = \Delta/((1-u)r + \Delta)$$

Note a few things about m_{GKS}. First, if the current tax system were equivalent to an R-base tax (and continuing to assume an unchanging tax law and real investment growing at rate r), so that z is equal to one, TC would equal TR, so that $m_{GKS} = 0$, regardless of the value of u or r. Second, if TC was a pure income tax, so that $z = \delta/(r + \delta)$, then $m = m_{GKS} = u$.

Therefore, under a long list of strong assumptions, all three methods of measuring the effective tax rate on capital income produce the same answer, correctly measuring the disincentive to invest due to taxes.

Keeping in mind the conceptual relationship and similarities among these three measures is helpful when one tries to estimate them for a world and a tax system that are incredibly more complex than the simple model I've just presented. Given the space constraints of this article, it is infeasible to work through how these simple models might be expanded to address these complexities. Volumes have been devoted to just this task.[22] Because this chapter focuses on quantitative estimates for the U.S. economy, in place of an exhaustive (or even adequate) treatment of all the issues that arise, the following sections explain a few key issues that come up in evaluating the quantitative measurements.[23]

Debt versus Equity Finance and Personal Tax

The taxation of capital income depends on whether the capital is provided to the business in the form of debt or equity finance. Payments to the providers of debt finance (lenders) are deductible when calculating taxable business income, but payments to the providers of equity finance (shareholders) are not. The return to the suppliers of capital to corporations is also taxed differently at the personal level, with interest receipts generally fully taxed (unless received via a tax-favored savings vehicle) and the returns to share ownership taxed differently, depending on whether the return comes in the form of dividends, share appreciation, or some alternative means of distributing profits from the corporation to the shareholders.

How this pattern of taxation affects the marginal tax on saving and investment is quite controversial, in part because the equilibrium pattern of finance and risk ownership is unclear in a world of graduated personal tax rates and also because of the "new view versus old view" controversy that concerns whether the personal tax on dividends reduces the return to investment for established corporations on investments financed with retained earnings. Nevertheless, with some assumptions, the earlier expressions can be modified to deal with these issues. For example, following King and Fullerton (1984), one can assume that a marginal dollar of investment is financed by b dollars of debt and $(1 - b)$ dollars of equity, and that businesses are constrained to use no more than an exogenously given debt-capital ratio. Similar assumptions must be made about equilibrium corporate payout policy and, importantly, to what extent tax-preferred savings plans apply to marginal saving.[24]

Risk

Risk is inherent to the saving and investment process because it involves the uncertain future. How does risk change the measurement of effective tax rates on capital income? If the marginal return to investment is random, then in equilibrium, the investment will earn a higher expected return—a risk premium—to compensate the risk holders. Under certain conditions, expression (A-4) continues to hold where f' is now interpreted as the certainty-equivalent value of the marginal product (expected value minus the risk premium). The critical assumption is that the tax system reduces the required risk premium in the same proportion as it reduces the expected value, which will occur if the tax system treats profits and losses symmetrically.

In this case, both the hypothetical-project and GKS measure of the effective tax rate remain correct. However, the tax collections–based measure is no longer correct because it includes the tax revenue collected on the risk premium as part of the numerator and the risk premium itself as part of the return to capital in the denominator; for this reason, it is biased toward the statutory rate, u, with the bias being larger, the larger the risk premium is relative to the certainty-equivalent rate of return.[25] Intuitively, this measure misinterprets the tax revenue collected on the risk premium as a disincentive to invest rather than as a fair premium for the reduction in risk caused by the tax levy.[26]

(Pure) Profits

The maintained assumption that constant returns to scale (CRS) characterize the production function implies that if, as competitive markets ensure, factors are paid their marginal products, payments to the factors will exactly exhaust business revenues, leaving no pure, or economic, profits. What if production functions exhibited decreasing returns to scale, so that paying factors their marginal product implied positive pure profits? This would not bias either the hypothetical-project or GKS measure of the tax rate, which are focused on the incentive to save and invest in the marginal project. In the GKS case, because the revenue collected on pure profits under the current system would also be collected under an R-base tax with the same rate structure, the presence of pure profits has no effect on the calculation of $TC - TR$, the critical input into m_{GKS}. The presence of pure profits does, though, affect the calculation of the tax collections–based method, which depends on the CRS assumption that $f' = f/K$, or $f = f'K$. If, instead, $f = f'K + \pi$, then the expression (A-8) incorrectly includes $u\pi$ in the numerator and π in the denominator. As in the case of risk, this measure is biased toward the statutory tax rate u, and the bias increases with the extent of pure profits; the measure misinterprets the revenue collected from pure profits as evidence of a disincentive to marginal investments. Unlike the case of risk, though, a tax on inframarginal profits may reduce the after-tax return to saving even as it does not reduce the incentive to save or invest.[27]

Summary

Some economists have argued that switching to a consumption tax would not be a monumental shift because much capital income is untaxed. This chapter described three methods for calculating how much the United States taxes capital income and concludes that the revenue collected is fairly small and the tax rate at the margin of new saving and investment is well below the corporate statutory rate or the top personal income tax rate. Thus, moving from our current system to a pure consumption tax would not increase incentives to save and invest nearly as much as moving from a pure income tax to a pure consumption tax.

All three methods for measuring capital income taxation have advantages and disadvantages.

First approach. A straightforward ratio of capital income taxes paid to a measure of capital income produces an effective federal capital income tax rate of 24.1 percent for 2002. This measure is backward looking in that it relies on historical investments and tax rules that change, but it reflects institutional details that hypothetical methods cannot.

Second approach. The difference between the pretax return to capital investments and the after-tax return to savers is calculated for a hypothetical marginal investment project. Focusing on the marginal investment is key to understanding the impact of the tax system on saving and investment since changes in how this investment is taxed affect investment decisions. It requires estimates of economic depreciation, which are highly uncertain. Using this approach, the Congressional Budget Office concluded that the effective tax rate on capital income is 13.8 percent; Jane Gravelle found that it is 17 or 23 percent.

Third approach. This empirical approach is based on computing the difference between actual tax revenues and an estimate of the revenues that would be collected if the normal rate of return on capital were tax exempt. Using data from 2000 on corporate taxes and simulations provided by the Urban–Brookings Tax Policy Center, the method found that in 2004 the United States would lose about $64 billion of tax revenue if it switched to an R-base (similar to a flat tax or X tax) consumption tax system, and the effective tax rate on capital is about 14 percent.

NOTES

I am grateful for the outstanding research assistance provided by Johannes Becker, and for innumerable conversations on this topic over the past two decades with Laura Kalambokidis and, especially, Roger Gordon. Henry Aaron, Len Burman, Jane Gravelle, Reed Shuldiner, and George Zodrow provided helpful comments on an earlier draft. For the record, though, any mistakes in this chapter are entirely my own responsibility.

1. As noted below, to be precise, a consumption tax exempts from tax the risk-free return to capital.

2. A century ago, most economists thought that capital and labor income should indeed be taxed differently, and capital income should be taxed at a *higher* rate than labor income. Back then, the terms used were earned income (derived from personal exertion) and unearned income (derived without personal exertion) or as Gladstone termed the distinction, "industrious" and "lazy" incomes. The dean of American public finance at the time, Edwin Seligman of Columbia University, argued that the distinction is based on the equality of sacrifice related to the creation of income: "The sacrifice involved in earning a given amount of income is a very different thing from the sacrifice involved in receiving an equivalent of unearned income" (1914, 24). When preferential treatment of earned income was adopted in the 1907 British income tax, Seligman gushed over its introduction, saying that, since the close of the 18th century, it had been "demanded by numberless critics and reformers" (1914, 206). In the budget statement of May 7, 1908, Prime Minister Asquith said that differentiation of earned and unearned incomes had removed "the most crying grievances and inequalities which have marred the equity and clogged the efficiency of the income tax" (quoted in Seligman 1914, 207).

The United States also considered the possibility of a higher rate on unearned income, both in the 1894 federal income tax that was eventually ruled to be unconstitutional as well as in the debate leading to the original modern income tax passed in 1913. In fact, in 1913, Senator Coe Crawford proposed a lower tax on earned income that was explicitly modeled after the U.K. provision. The proposal was ultimately rejected and then referred to committee for further study without ever emerging (see 50 Cong. Rec. 3815 [1913]). In 1924, an earned income tax provision was passed but was repealed a year later, perhaps because of the difficulty defining earned income. See Kornhauser (1994).

More recently, the Tax Reform Act of 1969 introduced a maximum tax on "earned" income, which the Economic Recovery Tax Act of 1981 repealed.

3. To be sure, some wealth inequality would arise due to life-cycle variations in wealth holdings even if all families had identical lifetime patterns of wealth accumulation. But this explains only a small fraction of wealth inequality. See Kennickell (2003).

4. It is the analogue to expression (A-8) of the appendix.

5. A number of studies have used observed revenue collections to obtain an approximation of the effective marginal tax rate on capital. For example, Martin Feldstein and Lawrence Summers (1979) calculate an average effective tax rate on corporate-source income equal to corporate taxes paid plus personal taxes due on corporate dividend and interest payments, as a proportion of capital income, measured using accounting data.

6. The methodology is based on one proposed by Enrique G. Mendoza, Assaf Razin, and Linda L. Tesar (1994). Carey and Rabesona (2004) suggest some corrections, mainly concerning the choice of the numerator variables, and test the impact of relaxing some of the Mendoza assumptions (e.g., splitting self-employed income between labor and capital and accounting for the preferential taxation of pension funds). After all adjustments, the measure discussed in the text would have to be increased by between 0.3 and 4.4 percentage points.

7. It is based on expression (A-6) of the appendix. While expression (A-6) pertains to firm-level taxes only and a single hypothetical investment, estimating the effective marginal tax rate on capital for the aggregate U.S. economy is much more complicated, requiring several additional assumptions, often about the effect of the personal taxation of capital investment returns.

8. For an investment in a pass-through business entity, only the personal tax applies.

9. This statement is accurate. However, distinguishing between the risk-free rate and a risky rate is essential for understanding the implications of the average amount of revenue collected for a marginal effective tax rate on capital, and in correctly measuring the GKS measure of that concept discussed below.

10. The CBO calculates an 18.2 percent effective tax rate on tenant-occupied housing.

11. Other key assumptions are that the nominal interest rate is 7.5 percent, the inflation rate is 2 percent, the real return to equity is 7 percent, with 4 percent (or 57 percent of real profits) paid as dividends, and that half of financial assets are held in exempt forms, such as pensions and IRAs.

12. Joel Slemrod, Roger Gordon, and, beginning in 2004, Laura Kalambokidis. GKRS (2004) includes Jeff Rohaly as a coauthor.

13. It does, though, require other assumptions.

14. In the first application of this method, Gordon and Slemrod (1988) found that, under a simulated R-base tax in 1983, the tax liability of nonfinancial corporations would increase by $22.6 billion and individual tax liability would fall by $15.2 billion. On net, therefore, Gordon and Slemrod (1988) estimated that the 1983 income tax system collected $7.4 billion *less* in tax revenue than an R-base would have, even though an R-base tax imposes no distortion to savings or investment decisions; this implies that the tax on capital income was on balance *negative*. Even allowing for the inaccuracies of this method, since this figure is a small fraction of total tax revenue, the implication of this result is that, in 1983, the U.S. tax system imposed little or no burden on the return to capital.

Gordon, Kalambokidis, and Slemrod (2004a) repeated this exercise using data from 1995 and found a somewhat different result. In 1995, switching to an R-base tax would have reduced corporate tax liability by $18.0 billion and individual tax liability by $90.1 billion, for a net revenue loss of $108.1 billion. Between 1983 and 1995, apparently the environment had changed so that significant revenues from taxing capital income were collected, in part because of the drop in nominal interest rates from 1983 to 1995 that reduced the tax savings from arbitrage through the use of debt.

15. The GKS approach implicitly assumes that the effect of capped tax-preferred savings vehicles on the marginal after-tax rate of return to saving is equal to the average effect; this probably underestimates the true effect at the margin of the current system.

16. The method that yields the higher number allows half of the stated limit, as a way to approximate the long-term consequences of the statutory annual limits, figuring 10 years of contributions and a 5 percent rate of return. The alternative method imposes no individual tax on interest income, dividends, or capital gains.

17. The comparison is not perfect in part because the analyses refer to different years. My update of the Carey and Rabesona (2004) analysis is for 2002, the Gravelle (2004) numbers I cite refer to 2003 assuming tax rates continue at their 2003 levels, CBO (2005) applies to 2005 law assuming the indefinite extension of provisions in place in 2008, and GKS refers to 2004. Neither the tax collections–based method nor the GKS method is forward looking, so they do not make explicit assumptions about future tax provisions.

18. One unsettling, and unsettled issue, is the role the real interest rate plays in assessing whether and how much the United States taxes capital income. Some, such as Hubbard (2005), have argued that the essential difference between an income tax and a consumption tax is how the risk-free real return to capital (i.e., the two taxes treat the return to risk and pure profits essentially the same) is treated; because this rate is very low, the difference between the two taxes is minimal. This issue is critical to the exercise of this chapter if only because it suggests that the tax *rate* stressed here is not as important as the tax *wedge* between the pretax and after-tax return. To see this, look at expression (A-4) and assume that the tax depreciation allowances are exactly equal to economic depreciation $(z = \delta/(r + \delta))$, so that expression (A-4) becomes

$$f' - \delta = r/(1 - u).$$

In this case, the tax rate measure, m, equals the statutory rate u. But the wedge between the pretax and after-tax rate of return is equal to $ru/(1 - u)$. The smaller is r, the smaller is the wedge created by any effective tax rate m. For example, assume that $u = 0.333$. If $r = 0.02$, then expression (A-12) says that the tax system increases the equilibrium marginal rate of return on capital from 0.02 in the absence of taxes to 0.03. If, alternatively, $r = 0.06$, then taxes increase the equilibrium marginal product from 0.06 to 0.09, or by three times as much as when $r = 0.02$. Whether this corresponds to a much larger reduction in the demand for capital depends on the nature of the production function, in particular whether the marginal product of capital declines at the same rate around different values of f'. If the marginal product is a linear function of K, then the higher is r, the larger is the implied reduction in K caused by any given value of m. If, on the other hand, the marginal product is a constant-elasticity function of K, then the level of r is irrelevant.

19. The discussion in this section draws on the exposition in Gordon, Kalambokidis, and Slemrod (2004b).

20. To simplify the exposition, I ignore inflation and investment tax credits.

21. This calculation makes use of the fact that if real investment and capital stock are growing at rate r, then at any time $I_t = (r + \delta)K_t$.

22. I have in mind King and Fullerton (1984), OECD (1991), and Sorensen (2004).

23. Among the issues not addressed are how taxes affect the choice of business organizational form, churning of capital assets, and international considerations (e.g., do the tax measures calculated here measure taxation on capital located in the United States or on capital owned by U.S. citizens?). The first two are addressed in Gordon, Kalambokidis, and Slemrod (2004b).

24. More discussion about how to reconcile the details of personal taxation with the hypothetical project–based and GKS methods is in Gravelle (1994, 2004, 2005) and Gordon, Kalambokidis, and Slemrod (2004b), respectively.

25. The measure is biased toward u because it adds uRK to the numerator and RK to the denominator; where R is the risk premium; the bigger R is, the more this will move the ratio toward u.

26. Put this way, this argument is clearly related to the argument first made by Domar and Musgrave (1944) that taxes reduce the after-tax riskiness of risky investment.

27. Taxation of some pure profits might provide disincentives for some other decisions, however.

REFERENCES

Carey, David, and Josette Rabesona. 2004. "Tax Ratios on Labor and Capital Income and on Consumption." In *Measuring the Tax Burden on Capital and Labor,* edited by Peter Birch Sorensen (213–62). Cambridge, MA: MIT Press.

Congressional Budget Office. 2005. "Taxing Capital Income: Effective Rates and Approaches to Reform." Washington, DC: Congressional Budget Office.

Domar, Evsey D., and Richard A. Musgrave. 1944. "Proportional Income Taxation and Risk-Taking." *Quarterly Journal of Economics* 38(3): 388–422.

Feldstein, Martin, and Lawrence Summers. 1979. "Inflation and the Taxation of Capital Income in the Corporate Sector." *National Tax Journal* 32(December): 445–71.

Gordon, Roger H., and Joel Slemrod. 1988. "Do We Collect Any Revenue from Taxing Capital Income?" In *Tax Policy and the Economy,* vol. 2, edited by Lawrence H. Summers (89–130). Cambridge, MA: MIT Press.

———. 2000. "Are Real Responses to Taxes Simply Income Shifting between Corporate and Personal Tax Bases?" In *Does Atlas Shrug? The Economic Consequences of Taxing the Rich,* edited by Joel B. Slemrod (240–80). Cambridge, MA: Harvard University Press.

Gordon, Roger H., Laura Kalambokidis, and Joel Slemrod. 2004a. "Do We Now Collect Any Revenue from Taxing Capital Income?" *Journal of Public Economics* 88(5): 981–1009.

———. 2004b. "If Capital Income Taxes Are So High, Why Do We Collect So Little Revenue? A New Summary Measure of the Effective Tax Rate on Investment." In *Measuring the Tax Burden on Capital and Labor,* edited by Peter Birch Sorensen (99–128). Cambridge, MA: MIT Press.

Gordon, Roger H., Laura Kalambokidis, Jeffrey Rohaly, and Joel Slemrod. 2004. "Toward a Consumption Tax, and Beyond." *American Economic Review, Papers and Proceedings* 94(2): 161–65.

Gravelle, Jane G. 1994. *The Economic Effects of Taxing Capital Income.* Cambridge, MA: The MIT Press.

———. 2004. *Historical Effective Marginal Tax Rates on Capital Income.* Washington, DC: Congressional Research Service.

———. 2005. *Capital Income Tax Provisions and Effective Tax Rates.* Washington, DC: Congressional Research Service.

Hubbard, R. Glenn. 2005. "Would a Consumption Tax Favor the Rich?" In *Toward Fundamental Tax Reform,* edited by Alan J. Auerbach and Kevin A. Hassett (81–94). Washington, DC: AEI Press.

Kennickell, Arthur. 2003. "A Rolling Tide: Changes in the Distribution of Wealth in the U.S., 1989–2001." Working Paper No. 2003-24. Washington, DC: Federal Reserve Board.

King, Mervyn A., and Don Fullerton. 1984. *The Taxation of Income from Capital.* Chicago: University of Chicago Press.

Kornhauser, Marjorie E. 1994. "The Morality of Money: American Attitudes toward Wealth and the Income Tax." *Indiana Law Journal* 70(Winter): 119–70.

Meade Committee. 1978. *The Structure and Reform of Direct Taxation.* Boston: Allen and Unwin.

Mendoza, Enrique G., Assaf Razin, and Linda L. Tesar. 1994. "Effective Tax Rates in Macroeconomics: Cross-Country Estimates of Tax Rates on Factor Incomes and Consumption." *Journal of Monetary Economics* 34(3): 297–323.

OECD. 1991. *Taxing Profits in a Global Economy: Domestic and International Issues.* Paris: OECD.

Organisation for Economic Co-operation and Development. See OECD.

Seligman, Edwin R. A. 1914. *The Income Tax: A Study of the History, Theory, and Practice of Income Taxation at Home and Abroad.* New York: The MacMillan Company.

Sorensen, Peter Birch, ed. 2004. *Measuring the Tax Burden on Capital and Labor.* Cambridge, MA: MIT Press.

Reed Shuldiner

The taxation of capital is clearly a core question in the debate over a shift to a consumption tax or reform of the income tax. Less clear is how much the current U.S. income tax actually taxes capital and hence the significance of a shift in the tax base away from capital. Joel Slemrod's chapter makes a valuable contribution to this debate by examining three measures of the tax on capital and providing estimates of the effective tax rate on capital based on those measures. One issue he raises that is discussed here is the importance of differentiating between different returns to capital. In particular, the view that consumption taxes do not tax returns to capital, and income taxes do, is seriously incomplete. A fuller understanding of this issue is important to the debate over the choice of taxes.

The Importance of Separating Different Returns from Capital

The return to capital consists of three components: the normal risk-free return to savings, the return to risk bearing, and above-market returns or pure profits. The risk-free return is simply the market price for deferring consumption. It means that all else equal, the consumer values future consumption less than current consumption. With respect to the risk-free return, the conventional wisdom is correct: a pure income tax taxes the risk-free return and a pure consumption tax does not. The source of the exemption of the risk-free return under a consumption tax is that by allowing a deduction for investment, rather than making the taxpayer wait to recover basis, the government essentially funds its share of the investment. When the investment is used in the future, the apparent tax is in essence not a tax but a return to the government's investment.

As a consequence of taxing the risk-free return, an income tax distorts the choice between current and future consumption. This distortion is a principal reason that many people prefer a consumption tax. It should be noted too that, by increasing the price of future consumption, the tax on the risk-free return also imposes an indirect tax on labor (Bankman and Weisbach 2006). Yet, as Slemrod notes, from an equity point of view, the tax on the risk-free return is important because the distribution of capital, and hence the risk-free return, is highly skewed. In theory, more steeply graduated rates on labor income could make up this loss of progressivity. Whether the progressivity of the tax on labor income would increase as part of a switch to a consumption tax is, of course, subject to doubt. Finally, it is worth noting that a pure wage tax, like a consumption tax, imposes no burden on the risk-free rate of return. The importance of the taxation of the risk-free return depends critically on the size of the risk-free return.

In practice, the income tax does not always tax the risk-free return. Under the U.S. income tax, such forms of savings as retirement savings and municipal bonds are tax-free and others may be subsidized. Some savings may bear an implicit tax (e.g., municipal bonds); others are unlikely to bear an implicit tax (e.g., retirement savings). Similarly, we do not know how much a U.S. federal consumption tax would exempt the risk-free return. For example, if the rates of taxation changed over time, the tax could impose a substantial burden on (or subsidy of) capital.

The second type of return is the return to risk bearing. When investors make risky investments, they expect a higher rate of return to compensate for the risk. This is referred to as the risk premium. At first, the risk premium appears fully taxed under an income tax. That, however, is not correct. The key observation is that while the income tax does take a share of the risk premium, it also takes a share of the underlying risk. More to the point, the risk sharing by the government exactly compensates for the risk premium the government receives. (Another way to state the same thing is that the government's share has zero market value [Domar and Musgrave 1944; Gordon 1985; Gentry and Hubbard 1997].) Of course, taxpayers may still object to this mandatory sharing arrangement because they prefer to bear more risk and to receive a greater premium. If that is the case, however, taxpayers can simply increase their amount of pretax risk.

Similarly, in the case of a consumption tax, the government shares the risk premium and the risk, and, therefore, there is no effective tax on the risk premium. By contrast, under a wage tax, there is no risk sharing (of capital income) by the government.

Because both the pure income and pure consumption tax do not tax risk, but merely share risk, there is no efficiency cost with respect to bearing risk with either tax. Researchers have argued, however, that the failure to tax the risk premium raises equity concerns. Two independent arguments have been made. The first is that individuals with greater risk tolerance and greater wealth are able to earn greater risk premiums and, therefore, have higher levels of consumption (Zelenak 2004). While this is true, devising a tax to capture the risk premium seems unlikely to be practical. The second argument made in response to the failure to tax the risk premium is based on a misunderstanding. Some have argued that winners and losers are different and that tax burdens should reflect this difference. This second argument, however, fails to account for the fact that both income and consumption taxes differentiate between winners and losers. Under an income and a consumption tax, gains and losses are shared with the government. Hence winners pay more tax and losers pay less tax. By contrast, a wage tax, sometimes seen as a prepaid consumption tax, does not differentiate between investment winners and losers and does not collect a share of the risk premium.

However much income and consumption taxes do not share in gains and losses is because of imperfections in the taxes. For example, under the income tax, some gains can be held until death and then forgiven, while some losses can be taken currently. In other circumstances, gains are taxed currently and losses are deferred, potentially indefinitely. Graduated rates may also have the effect of taxing gains more heavily than losses.

The third type of returns from capital are what Slemrod refers to as pure profits or inframarginal returns. Pure profits are unlike both risk-free returns and returns to risk bearing in that they reflect opportunities not generally available in the market. Pure profits are also different in that they are taxed by both pure consumption taxes and pure income taxes. Importantly, pure profits can generally be taxed without adverse efficiency consequences.[1] Thus, the taxation of pure profits is an attractive feature of both types of taxes. By contrast, a wage tax, despite being described as a prepaid consumption tax, does not tax pure profits and is therefore generally inferior to both consumption and income taxation.

Once again, however, qualifying the claims made is necessary. In practice, whether an income or consumption tax captures pure profits depends on how the tax is implemented. For example, under the current income tax, pure profits held in the form of capital appreciation are often forgiven at death and may or may not be captured by the estate tax. Similarly, it is often argued that a consumption tax can be implemented on a prepaid basis. For example, under current law, taxpayers are permitted to invest assets in either a conventional individual retirement account (IRA) or a Roth IRA and both are considered to provide treatment like a consumption tax. If, however, a taxpayer has an opportunity to invest IRA assets in a form that will generate pure profits, those returns will be captured by a conventional IRA and lost by the Roth IRA. Thus, when it comes to pure profits, questions of implementation are more important than whether the tax is a consumption or income tax. The foregoing points are summarized in table C.1.

One implication that flows from this analysis is that, in measuring the tax on capital for comparing income and consumption taxes, picking a metric that distinguishes between these types of returns is important. Thus, Slemrod rightly rejects what he refers to as the tax collection–based measure because it includes the government's share of the risk premium and taxes on pure profits, thus overstating the difference between consumption and income taxation. The tax collection–based measure also suffers from other serious flaws. For example, it treats all income of unincorporated businesses as income from capital despite the fact that large portions of such income are from labor, not capital. It also

Table C.1. Comparison of Tax Bases

Type of return	Income	Consumption	Wages
Normal risk-free	Taxes	No	No
Risk premium	Shares	Shares	No
Monopoly returns	Taxes	Taxes	No

assumes that a prorata share of taxes on individuals is on capital, despite the fact that rates on capital income are often lower than rates on labor. Even if corrections were made for such problems, correcting for the inclusion of the risk premium and pure profits would be extremely difficult.

As the other two measures Slemrod considers, the GKS measure and the forward-looking measure both correctly account for risk and pure profits. Both are, therefore, inherently superior to the collections measure. The forward-looking measure has two principal advantages. First, it focuses on the forward-looking investment decision. Second, it provides separate estimates for different sectors. Given the wide range in effective tax rates in different sectors of the economy, an aggregate measure can be misleading. For example, for 2003, Gravelle estimates rates from a high of 32 percent for corporate capital to a low of 2 percent for owner-occupied housing. Blending these rates into an average rate of 23 percent hides substantial tax-induced inefficiencies.

The principal disadvantage of the forward-looking measure is its difficulty accounting for the details of law and practice that influence tax burdens. For example, it cannot account for the effect of tax shelter activity or noncompliance. This problem is solved by the GKS measure, which is founded on collection data and accounts for such details. In summary, while neither measure is perfect, they complement each other and together give some confidence in the range of estimates provided.

What Is the Risk-Free Rate of Return?

A second implication of table C1.1 is the importance of the level of the risk-free rate.[2] The usual approach is to look at the rate for the U.S. Treasury 30-day bill (T-Bill), adjusted for inflation, as the best measure of the risk-free rate. That rate historically has been quite low. For example, Bankman and Griffith (1992) and Bradford (1996) suggest that the rate has been in the range of 0.5 to 1.0 percent. Based on this low rate, some have suggested that the difference between an income tax and a consumption tax is small and relatively inconsequential (Weisbach 2004). By contrast, my calculations suggest that the risk-free rate is significantly greater and that, therefore, the difference between the income tax and the consumption tax is significant.

My conclusions are based on several factors. First, the best estimate of future T-Bill rates substantially exceeds 0.5 to 1.0 percent. Second, the T-Bill rate is an inappropriate benchmark; a longer-term rate should be used. Finally, for whatever rate is chosen, a one-year investment horizon is too short. I consider each of these factors in turn.

Bankman and Griffith (1992) base their estimate of the T-Bill rate on data published by Ibbotson Associates showing that the average real T-Bill rate over the period 1926 to 1989 was 0.5 percent. As a prediction for the future, however, that historical figure is too low. The primary problem has to do with the choice of time period. The period 1926 to 1989 includes the postwar period when there was substantial unanticipated inflation. As a result, risk-free rates computed on an ex post basis were artificially low. For example, from 1945 to 1972, the real return on T-Bills averaged negative 0.5 percent (Jagannathan, McGrattan, and Scherbina 2001). If a different period is chosen, the rate changes dramatically. For example, from 1802 to 1997, the rate averaged 2.9 percent. More recently, from 1972 to 1999, the rate averaged 1.5 percent. Putting aside considerations of term, a risk-free rate of 1.5 percent in future years seems more likely than a rate of 0.5 percent.

A separate question is whether the T-Bill is the correct benchmark. For any given investment horizon, the appropriate risk-free investment would be a bond of the same maturity. Any shorter-term obligation would expose the investor to reinvestment risk. If, for example, investors have a 20-year horizon, the appropriate benchmark rate would be the 20-year Treasury Bond, which has generally had much higher yields than the one-month T-Bill. For example, from 1802 to 1997, the 20-year bond averaged 3.5 percent. From 1972 to 1999, it averaged 3.3 percent. Thus, an expected risk-free rate on the order of 3.0 to 3.5 percent seems like a more reasonable prediction.

The counter argument to using a long-term bond rate as the risk-free rate is that long-term bonds have inflation risk. If inflation risk is a concern, the solution is to look to Treasury Inflation-Protected Securities (TIPS) for a benchmark rate. TIPS were first issued in 1997, so there is not a substantial historical record. Since inception, the real coupon rate on TIPS has varied from a low of 1.625 percent to a high of 4.25 percent. The unweighted average real coupon has been about 3 percent, again suggesting that a rate of around 3 percent for the risk-free rate is appropriate.

Regardless of whether the best estimate of the future risk-free rate is as low as 0.5 percent or as high as 3 percent, ultimately the question is whether an income tax that taxes the risk-free rate is significantly different from a consumption tax that does not. For this purpose, the question of investment horizon is again relevant. In particular, there is no reason to think that one year is the correct frame of reference. In the extreme, if an individual has an infinite horizon, regardless of the risk-free rate of return, a tax that collects 23 percent of the income from capital is equivalent to the government taking 23 percent of the taxpayer's wealth.

For a less extreme example, consider a 40-year-old considering deferring current consumption until age 70. Given a 1 percent risk-free rate of return, a tax that collects 23 percent of annual income increases the price of future consumption by about 10 percent. If the risk-free rate is 3 percent, the tax increases the price of future consumption by over 30 percent. Thus, even at modest rates of return, over long periods of time the tax burden of the income tax is substantial.

As is clear from these conference papers, the significance and the merits of a move from the current income tax to a consumption tax remains open to vigorous debate. As we engage in that debate, understanding how much various taxes do and do not tax capital is important. Professor Slemrod's chapter is a valuable contribution toward that debate.

NOTES

1. To the extent that pure profits represent returns to labor income, taxing pure profits does distort labor supply. Of course, such pure profits would also be taxed under a perfect wage tax. Taxing pure profits can also distort location decisions (Slemrod, chapter 1).

2. The risk-free rate of return is important because it is the base on which the capital portion of the income tax is imposed. It is also important in the context of chapter 1 because it directly enters the computation of effective tax rates under both the GKS and forward-looking measures.

REFERENCES

Bankman, Joseph, and Thomas Griffith. 1992. "Is the Debate between an Income Tax and a Consumption Tax a Debate about Risk? Does It Matter?" *Tax Law Review* 47:377–406.

Bankman, Joseph, and David Weisbach. 2006. "The Superiority of an Ideal Consumption Tax over an Ideal Income Tax." *Stanford Law Review* 58(1413).

Bradford, David F. 1996. "Some Fundamental Transition Issues." In *Frontiers of Tax Reform,* edited by Michael J. Boskin. Stanford, CA: Hoover Institution Press.

Jane G. Gravelle

Does the United States tax capital income? I believe the answer to this question is yes. But the equally important question is, how much? Joel Slemrod settles on about 14 percent. My own view is that the tax rate on capital income is probably higher, but that includes low or negative tax rates on owner-occupied housing and tax rates of as much as 40 percent on corporations. Some important assumptions in calculating how much capital income is taxed include whether the current tax cuts will be made permanent and how much investment in tax-preferred savings accounts is marginal.

To answer these questions, one needs a measure of capital income taxes. Chapter 1 proposes three measures. The first is the hypothetical investment approach that estimates the stream of returns from investments using an after-tax discount rate and then estimates the pretax return. This measure is conceptually straightforward, and its main drawback is that it depends on measuring some important values that are difficult to determine, one of the most important being economic depreciation. A tax rate calculation takes the difference between the pretax rate of return and the after-tax discount rate and divides it by the pretax rate of return. This type of tax rate is often referred to as a marginal effective tax rate, or METR.

The second measure is straightforward in concept as well: it involves dividing collected taxes by an estimate of the pretax return. This is known as average effective tax rate, or ATR. This lessens some measurement demands, but involves allocating shares of proprietors' income and partners' income between capital and labor and estimating individual taxes on capital income.

A conceptual problem with ATR is that it can be strongly influenced by timing and cannot reflect, except in certain circumstances, a measure of the tax rate similar to that using a hypothetical investment. Only in two circumstances—when the growth rate equals the discount rate, or when tax depreciation equals economic depreciation—does this measure correspond to the hypothetical investment measure. In addition, this measure, unlike the measure generated from a prospective investment, cannot be used to estimate the differential tax rates across different types of investments.

The third type of tax rate uses a measure of tax receipts, developed in a series of papers, which measured the difference between the revenues collected and the revenues that would be collected under an "R-base" consumption tax—a consumption tax based on only real assets. This measure is referred to as the GKS measure after its authors, Roger Gordon, Laura Kalambokidis, and Joel Slemrod.

In general, the GKS approach can measure a component of the tax burden, namely a component of the firm level tax. But it cannot accommodate such other tax effects as debt finance, personal-level taxes, and owner-occupied housing. It also requires estimates of the capital stock. Further, discrepancies between the growth rate and discount rate are even more troubling for this measure than for the ATR measure. Consequently, this discussion will rely on the investment-based measure (METR) and the collections measure (ATR).

The most appropriate measure, conceptually, of the marginal effective tax rate, is the one derived from the investment approach, assuming that one is interested in how capital income taxes affect savings and investment. Can the collections-based measure (ATR) be used to check on the marginal effective tax rate measure?

As noted above, an important reservation about the collections-based measure is how it compares when the growth rate is not equal to the discount rate, a more realistic assumption, and how different tax regimes affect it. To explore this issue, it is necessary to examine specific measures of the economic depreciation rate, or δ. In these conceptual investigations, the METR or hypothetical investment yields the correct answer, and the purpose is to determine how close the collections measure comes to yielding the correct answer.

Table C.1. Effective Tax Rates for Equipment, Firm Level, and Equity Investment (Steady State)

	Expensing	Fast depreciation	Economic depreciation	Slow depreciation	No depreciation
METR	0	24	35	46	68
ATR	19	29	35	41	68

Sources: Author's calculations.

Note: METR = marginal effective tax rate; ATR = average effective tax rate

In tables C.1 and C.2, the METR refers to the marginal tax rate derived from the hypothetical investment approach and the ATR to the average tax rate based on collections. Table C.1 estimates rates for a typical equipment investment, with the geometric depreciation rate (δ) equal to 15 percent. Table C.2 estimates rates for a typical building, with δ equal to 2.5 percent. The after-tax return, r, is 5.5 percent and the statutory tax rate is 35 percent. Fast depreciation sets the tax depreciation rate to twice the economic rate, and slow depreciation sets it to one-half the economic rate.

These calculations indicate that, for many cases, the average tax rate (or collections measure) provides a good approximation. If current depreciation values are close to economic depreciation, as the METR estimates suggest, the collections base is also a good approximation.

Chapter 1 also discusses risk, excess profits, and inframarginal investment. It is possible to explore risk by a simple assumption that the depreciation deductions, which are certain, are discounted at a riskless rate (assumed to be 2 percent) and the risky cash flows are discounted at a risky

Table C.2. Effective Tax Rates for Real Estate, Firm Level, and Equity Investment (Steady State)

	Expensing	Fast depreciation	Economic depreciation	Slow depreciation	No depreciation
METR	0	29	35	40	44
ATR	19	31	35	38	44

Sources: Author's calculations.

Note: METR = marginal effective tax rate; ATR = average effective tax rate

Table C.3. Effective Tax Rates for Equipment, Firm Level, and Equity Investment (Steady State) with Risk

	Expensing	Fast depreciation	Economic depreciation	Slow depreciation	No depreciation
METR	0	22	35	49	82
ATR	19	28	35	43	67

Sources: Author's calculations.

Note: METR = marginal effective tax rate; ATR = average effective tax rate

rate (5.5 percent). This assumption can be used to generate the marginal product of capital and calculate the tax measures. In the case of the METR, the tax rate is calculated as a certainty equivalent and all flows are discounted at the certain rate, but the other measures use the differential discounting scheme to yield an observed marginal product of capital. The risky results are shown in tables C.3 and C.4, also for equipment and structures.

The ATR (collections measure) is a poorer approximation than without risk but is still a relatively good approximation if depreciation is close to economic depreciation.

These illustrations, even when including risk, have abstracted from many other issues. The tax rate measure should also capture the deductibility of interest; tax rates on unincorporated business investments, interest, dividends, and capital gains; and the treatment of owner-occupied housing. Another important issue, and one difficult to assess, is whether and how to adjust for assets held in such tax-exempt forms as IRAs and pension plans. Many of these issues are difficult to solve. In the latter case, one could

Table C.4. Effective Tax Rates for Real Estate, Firm Level, and Equity Investment (Steady State) with Risk

	Expensing	Fast depreciation	Economic depreciation	Slow depreciation	No depreciation
METR	0	26	35	43	55
ATR	19	31	35	39	45

Sources: Author's calculations.

Note: METR = marginal effective tax rate; ATR = average effective tax rate average taxes across tax-exempt assets and taxable ones based on the shares of each. Or one could argue that these investments, or most of these investments, should not be treated as marginal. For some assets, such as defined-benefit pension plans, the investor has no direct control over investment. Contributions to elective plans are often at the maximums and even where they are not, the tax benefits come with liquidity constraints that reduce their subjective value.

To follow up on the question of how much capital income is taxed, compare the two measures for current law without the special dividend and capital gains provisions enacted in 2003 and without any of the bonus depreciation. My calculations of the METR indicate a tax rate of 30 percent if the assets in IRAs and 401(k)s are not accounted for.

A collections measure should be reasonably close to the METR measure since depreciation is relatively close to economic depreciation and since these rules have been in effect for equipment (which accounts for most gross investment) since 1986 and for structures since 1986 or 1993, which is close to a steady state. Using the data in table 1.3, the collections-based (ATR) measure is calculated on the same overall basis (i.e., ignoring the untaxed IRA and 401[k] assets), and, after subtracting employment and property tax and adding bonus depreciation, yields a rate of about 23 percent. However, to make this rate on the same footing as the METR, other taxes should be subtracted from the base, yielding a rate of about 27 percent.

The year 2002 might not be a good year for estimating the permanent (pre-2001) tax rate because during a recession, corporate profits and profit taxes tend to fall, as table 1.3 shows. If we apply the 2002 federal share (after correcting for bonus depreciation) for the corporate income tax and household taxes on individuals to the 2000 data, the resulting tax rate is 36 percent. Thus, measured on the same basis, the collections base seems to confirm a tax rate of around 30 percent, with one year yielding a 27 percent tax rate and the other a 36 percent tax rate.

The tax rate depends, however, on the tax regime and how pensions and IRAs are treated. If tax-favored investment through IRAs and pensions is weighted with taxable returns (treated as marginal), the METR falls to 22 percent. If the dividend and capital gain relief enacted in 2003 is made permanent, the tax rates are 26 percent, treating the tax-favored accounts as inframarginal, and 20 percent, treating the accounts as marginal. Hence, these measures suggest the tax rate is 20 percent or more. But corporate-sector taxes may be close to 40 percent, while owner-occupied housing is subject to negligible and possibly negative taxes (with unincorporated businesses in between).

The Congressional Budget Office (CBO 2005) has recently completed its own METR study. These tax rates are several percentage points lower than my calculations. For permanent tax law with pensions and IRAs not treated as marginal, the CBO's estimate is 23 percent; my estimate is 30 percent. These differences are almost entirely due to the weighting of business assets and owner-occupied housing in the capital stock. Both estimates show similar tax rates for the three sectors: corporate is about 40 percent, noncorporate business is 22 percent (my estimate) to 26 percent (CBO estimate), and owner-occupied housing is 2 percent (my estimate) to negative 2 percent (CBO estimate). The CBO study has much larger weights for owner-occupied housing (based on 2002 levels). Some small part of this difference is because my estimates do not include land, which is reproducible and more important for owner-occupied housing (excluding land from the CBO study increases overall rates by about a percentage point), but most of the difference reflects recent significant growth in housing as a share of the capital stock. Whether this increased share is a permanent change or simply reflects a combination of the housing bubble that drove up the price index for housing and expanded investment, and business cycle effects that slowed investment in the corporate sector (inventories were also smaller in 2002 than in 2000), remains to be seen. This comparison illustrates, however, the sensitivity of an overall marginal tax rate estimate to capital stock measures.

For the temporary lower rates, CBO estimates a rate of 18 percent compared to my rate of 26 percent. As with the permanent rates, these differences largely reflect the share of housing, particularly owner-occupied housing.

The CBO study's base case constructs tax rates in which IRAs and pensions play a marginal role but do not have fixed weighting based on asset shares. The weighting is based on the fraction of these assets that have an effect at the margin, that is, on the last dollar of investment. For example, a taxpayer contributing at the IRA limit would not have the IRA benefit for the next dollar of investment, while a taxpayer contributing below the limit would. Based on that allocation, the tax rates are 17 percent under permanent law and 14 percent with dividend and capital gains relief, placing the overall, economy-wide average at less than 20 percent. As noted earlier, a major reservation about treating these investments as marginal is that individuals do not have direct control over the amounts in traditional pension plans and that all of these tax-favored accounts come with strings attached that impose an implicit tax.

Note also that none of these measures include the estate and gift tax, which appears to increase the tax about 1 percentage point based on a 2002 collections-based measure and would, of course, depend on which tax regime is considered.

The evidence suggests that there is a significant tax on capital income; the magnitude of this tax before recent tax changes may have been closer to 20 or 30 percent, depending on the treatment of pensions and IRAs, and the weights for business assets and housing. The 2001 to 2003 tax cuts reduced those rates by 3 to 5 percentage points. Perhaps more importantly for tax policy, however, are significant differences in the tax treatment of different assets, differences that are smaller under temporary tax law but that persist. That, perhaps, is an issue as important as the overall magnitude of the tax.

REFERENCE

Congressional Budget Office. 2005. "Taxing Capital Income: Effective Rates and Approaches to Reform." Washington, DC: Congressional Budget Office.

PART II
Should We Tax Capital Income?

2

Should Capital Income Be Subject to Consumption-Based Taxation?

George R. Zodrow

In 2005, the report of the President's Advisory Panel on Federal Tax Reform proposed two alternative approaches to tax reform. If implemented, both plans would move the tax system farther away from the full taxation of capital income that is the hallmark of a true income tax. However, the panel did not recommend enacting a true consumption tax—instead, both proposals were hybrid income-consumption taxes. The report thus highlights the uncertainty regarding the appropriate tax treatment of capital income, the focus of this book. This chapter examines the central issue the panel faced—whether to implement full-scale consumption-based taxation of capital income.

Introduction

Not surprisingly, separating the topic of this part, "should we tax capital income," from the other topics in this book ("do we" and "can we" tax capital income) is difficult. After all, a key argument proponents of consumption-based taxation make is that accurately measuring and taxing capital income is difficult, especially in the face of increasing international capital mobility and tax-sheltering activity, and that, in practice, much capital income escapes taxation under the income tax. This chapter, however, ignores these issues and assumes that accurately taxing capital income at a reasonable cost is possible. It considers several preliminary issues and then turns to an analysis of the desirability of consumption-based taxation of capital income.

Is a "Pure" Consumption Tax More Likely Than a "Pure" Income Tax?

Experience has shown taxing all income as accrued is difficult. Practical requirements for a tax based on realizations—loosely speaking, actual sales—rather than on accrued values, plus the difficulties in measuring economic depreciation and adjusting for inflation, make accurate income measurement exceedingly difficult.[1] By comparison, similar conceptual issues do not beset a consumption-based tax.[2] Of course, "real world" consumption taxes would be more complex than their idealized versions, especially if the United States' trading partners continued to rely on income taxes. Moreover, many of the implementation problems that plague the income tax also arise under a consumption tax.[3] Nevertheless, consumption is inherently easier to measure than income.

Beyond measurement issues, both the corporate and individual income taxes are riddled with special deductions, exemptions, and other forms of preferential tax treatment, most of which would be eliminated under current consumption-tax reform proposals (and could also be eliminated under an income tax reform). Could any consumption tax reform that survived the political process maintain "purity?" Several factors suggest some room for cautious optimism. Under the corporate tax, a uniform marginal effective tax rate of zero on all forms of investment could serve as a natural floor to preferential tax treatment, at least if there were greater political resistance to outright subsidies than to mere reductions in tax liabilities, especially given current budget exigencies.[4] Of course, recent reforms—including (temporary) accelerated depreciation, extensions of small business expensing, and reductions in tax rates on capital gains and dividends—were not accompanied by limits on the deductibility of interest expenses, as is required to avoid negative effective tax rates. Nevertheless, in the 1980s, public outcries at the tax sheltering and tax loss trading associated with negative effective tax rates at the business level provide some support for the notion of a "zero rate floor" as they prompted passage of the Tax Reform Act of 1986 and the elimination of the safe-harbor leasing provisions of the Economic Recovery Tax Act of 1981.

There is less cause for optimism on the individual side. Pressure to maintain popular deductions would be intense under any fundamental tax reform, although the lure of lower tax rates and the prospect of significant simplification would hopefully offset some of this pressure. Some limits on current deductions might be palatable, especially if the limits target higher-income taxpayers who benefit most from rate reductions. For example, the "upside-down subsidy" nature of the current deduction for home mortgage interest implies benefits highly concentrated among the wealthy (Carasso, Steuerle, and Bell 2005). Proposals to convert the deduction to a credit, subject it to a cap and eliminate it for second homes—as the president's tax reform panel recommends—might be feasible as a means of reducing top rates.

Introducing super-majority requirements for raising rates or adding preferences and reenacting "pay-as-you-go" budget rules would also help limit tax preferences. Legislators might be more likely to enact these budget rules under a large-scale reform of the tax structure than under a more modest income tax reform (Auerbach and Hassett 2005b; Bradford 2005). Finally, in addition to eliminating current deductions, legislators could introduce new (perhaps capped) deductions for investments in human capital that are not only politically popular, but have the advantage of being consistent with the principles of consumption-based taxation (Judd 2001). To sum up, there are several reasons why a new consumption tax, enacted in the context of fundamental tax reform, might attain a greater degree of "purity" than would be possible under an incremental reform of the current income tax. Of course, whether such arguments prove compelling in the end, and whether such reforms would be sustainable, is highly speculative.[5]

Would a consumption tax be less susceptible to the tax sheltering activity that has plagued the income tax?[6] Some tax experts argue that many tax sheltering schemes, most of which involve manipulations of provisions related to the taxation of capital income, would not be possible under a consumption tax (Bankman 2004). But the validity of this argument in the "real world" would depend a great deal on the specific details of the plan enacted.[7] For example, some argue that the flat tax and the X tax are more easily evaded than other consumption tax options, primarily because they are "open" tax systems that allow business deductions even when there are no offsetting inclusions (e.g., purchases from individuals, tax-exempt institutions, or foreigners).[8] Similarly, Schler and Bankman in chapter 6 identify sheltering opportunities under the flat tax and the X tax.

Thus, the relative importance of sheltering opportunities under the income tax and the various consumption tax options is unclear, partly because there is so little international experience with direct consumption taxes.[9] It is important to note, however, that the economic models of income and consumption taxation described in this chapter assume effective enforcement and thus do not take into account differences in susceptibility to tax sheltering.

Consumption-Based and Income-Based Taxation of Capital Income

The essential difference between consumption and income-based taxes is in how they treat capital income. Although consumption taxes are often described as exempting the capital income included in the base of an income tax, the differences in tax treatment under the two approaches are subtler than this simple characterization suggests. The purchases of investment goods, for instance, are not included in a consumption tax, either due to immediate deductions (expensing), exemptions, or credits. Such treatment is more generous than the treatment provided under an income tax, which allows only deductions for economic depreciation. More specifically, allowing expensing is sufficiently generous to exempt only the normal return to investment.[10] However, as recent literature has stressed, capital income consists of four conceptually separate components.[11] The risk-free return that compensates individuals for deferring consumption, often described as the "return to waiting," is tax exempt under a consumption tax but is fully taxed under a comprehensive accrual income tax. In contrast, the tax treatments of the other three components of capital income—above-normal returns and the returns to risk taking, which include the expected risk premium and returns that reflect good or bad luck—are similar under income and consumption taxes. Thus, the difference between the tax treatment of capital income under income and consumption taxes is limited to taxation of the risk-free return, which is fully taxed under income taxes and exempt under consumption taxes.

The implications of this point are quite interesting and have not been fully investigated. Risk-free real returns to capital have historically been quite low, especially in periods of high inflation, with average rates ranging from roughly 0.5 to 3 percent (Avi-Yonah 2004). This suggests that the literature may have overstated differences between income and consumption taxes.[12] In particular, most computer simulation models assume perfect competition and ignore uncertainty; they thus may overstate how much capital income is taxed under the income tax, as well as the efficiency gains obtained by moving to a consumption tax. On the other hand, since these models usually ignore inflation, they also understate how much normal returns to capital are taxed under an unindexed income tax. Sorting out these effects is a useful avenue for future research.

International Issues

Increasing globalization also plays a critical role in the debate on the appropriate taxation of capital income (see chapter 5). Many administrative problems would arise if the United States implemented a consumption-based direct tax system while its trading partners continued to tax income. In particular, avoidance schemes based on the differential treatment of capital income would be problematic under certain forms of consumption taxation, and the transfer pricing problems that plague the income tax would also arise in certain cases (Avi-Yonah 2004; Bradford 2003; McLure and Zodrow 1996; Weisbach 2000). Yet adoption of a consumption tax would also allow substantial simplification of international tax rules (Ballard 2002; Weisbach 2000).

From a theoretical perspective, globalization reinforces the case for consumption-based tax treatment of capital income. In particular, the optimal tax rate on capital income is zero for countries that are small open economies and thus face a fixed after-tax return to internationally mobile capital (Gordon 1986; Razin and Sadka 1991).[13] A fixed international rate of return implies that taxes cause capital outflows that lower the productivity of immobile factors in the taxing country—especially land and relatively immobile labor—and thus lower wages and land rents by the full amount of the tax plus its efficiency cost (excess burden). The clear implication is that, solely from the viewpoint of the residents of the taxing country, it is preferable simply to tax local residents directly.[14] This strong result has been qualified in various ways in the literature (see Zodrow 2006). Nevertheless, on balance, international capital mobility strengthens the case for consumption-based tax reform (see Ballard 2002).

An Overview of the Literature

The debate on the relative merits of income and consumption taxation has generated a voluminous literature.[15] This section focuses on three important sets of results in the literature on optimal capital income taxa-tion, as well as various qualifications to those results, and then considers some additional issues.

Results from Infinite Horizon Models
Analyzing Efficiency Issues

The most striking result in this literature involves optimal capital and wage income taxation in models with individuals assumed to have infinite life-times. Such models can be loosely justified as representing a parent whose welfare depends on her children's welfare, on her grandchildren's welfare, etc. Within this context, several researchers have shown that, in the long run, the optimal capital income tax rate is zero (Chamley 1986; Judd 1985).[16] The intuition behind this result is straightforward. By reducing the after-tax interest rate, a capital income tax raises the price of future consumption. Although this distortion may be modest over the short term, it grows exponentially with time, so that even a small capital income tax rate will eventually be highly distortionary. Since the indi-viduals in these models have perfect foresight over an infinite lifetime, such a tax highly distorts their consumption patterns, with significant declines in saving and capital accumulation.

Indeed, one infinite horizon model that includes both representative workers and capitalists shows that the negative effects of a capital income tax on labor productivity and wages are so great that the optimal capital income tax rate is zero even if the government is concerned only about the welfare of workers (Judd 1985). A second message of the infinite horizon models is that, even though capital income taxation should be avoided entirely in the long run, existing capital should be taxed to the maximum extent feasible, since such taxation represents a "lump sum" or nondistortionary source of revenue.[17]

The large saving responses that characterize infinite horizon models imply that consumption tax reforms would yield large growth effects (Engen, Gravelle, and Smetters 1997).[18] Yet the policy implications of these results are open to debate. In particular, some researchers argue that returns to human capital investments should also be exempt from tax (Jones, Manuelli, and Rossi 1993; Milesi-Ferretti and Roubini 1998). To the extent the costs of obtaining human capital are forgone earnings, this is not an issue since such costs are effectively "deductible." However, if the direct costs of making an investment in human capital (e.g., tuition, books, and fees) are not deductible, the logic underlying the zero capital income tax result also implies that the associated wage income should not be taxed. That is, tax exemption of the income to physical capital under a consumption tax should be accompanied by deductibility of the direct costs of investing in human capital, at least to the extent such investments do not reflect consumption expenditures (Judd 2001).

More importantly, many observers hesitate to draw policy implications from models that assume infinitely lived individuals. Beyond questions on the validity of using this representation of altruism across generations, such models cannot address the critical issues related to the intergenerational redistribution and transitional problems consumption tax reforms raise. Accordingly, most policy analyses of consumption tax reforms have focused on life-cycle models with an overlapping generations structure.[19]

Results from Life-Cycle Models Analyzing Efficiency Issues

The basic structure described above also characterizes the simplest version of the traditional life-cycle model, except that the representative individual has a two-period life cycle: supplying labor (demanding leisure), purchasing goods, and saving during the earnings period, and drawing down savings during the retirement period. A tax on wage income in this context is equivalent to a uniform consumption tax in the two periods, while a tax on capital income effectively acts as a tax on future consumption. The optimal capital income tax problem is thus analogous to the issue of whether uniform or differential taxation of consumption commodities is desirable. As is well known, uniform commodity taxation is efficient only under certain circumstances. Specifically, the optimal capital income tax rate is zero (implying uniform taxation of consumption in both periods, as would occur under a consumption or wage tax) only if first and second period consumption are equally complementary with leisure.[20]

The conditions for the optimality of uniform commodity taxation require that decisions on choices among consumption commodities must be separable, or independent of the decision on how much labor to supply (leisure to demand). Also, individual tastes must be homothetic with respect to the consumption goods, which implies that increases in wealth are distributed proportionately across consumption in all periods (Auerbach 1979). There is, of course, no guarantee that individual tastes will satisfy these two conditions, although such an assumption is plausible at least to a first approximation.[21] In sum, the simple two-period model arguably suggests a presumption that an optimal tax system exempts capital income from taxes.

The applicability of the simple two-period model, however, is limited. A more complete analysis requires that a more detailed model of individual life-cycle optimization be combined with production and incorporated into an overlapping-generations, general equilibrium structure of the economy. These concerns are addressed in an overlapping generations model, constructed in 1981 by Lawrence H. Summers, composed of life-cycle savers who have a 50 year adult life (the last 10 of which are spent in retirement), supply labor inelastically, and experience exponential wage growth (Summers 1981). The Summers model emphasizes that increasing the tax rate on capital income reduces the after-tax discount rate individuals use in estimating their human wealth—the present value of all future labor earnings—when making consumption and savings decisions. The resulting increase in human wealth prompts greater consumption early in life and thus, less saving. Simulations suggest that this human wealth effect is highly significant, implying that consumption tax reform would result in large steady state welfare gains. For example, in one central case, the enactment of a cash flow consumption tax results in a steady state welfare gain equal to 11.2 percent of lifetime income.[22] A wage tax reform in the Summers model would also increase steady state welfare but to a significantly smaller extent (7 percent of lifetime income), since existing capital is not subject to tax.[23]

The Summers model sparked a great deal of interest and additional research, most prominently the overlapping-generations, general equilibrium model constructed in 1987 by Auerbach and Kotlikoff.[24] This model allows labor-leisure choices in each period, assumes a "humpbacked" wage profile over the life cycle taken from the labor economics literature, and uses more conservative parameter values than those Summers utilizes.

As a result of these and other differences from the Summers model, the welfare gains obtained from a consumption tax reform in the Auerbach-Kotlikoff model are more moderate. For example, in a base case analysis, a cash flow consumption tax increases steady state welfare by 2.3 percent of the present value of "lifetime resources," which includes the value of leisure and is therefore a broader measure of welfare than that used by Summers.[25] A more recent version of the model estimates that implementing a retail sales tax or a value-added tax would increase long-run steady state welfare by 1.9 percent of lifetime resources; this corresponds to an efficiency gain for all future generations, holding constant the utility levels of all individuals alive at the time of enactment, equal to 6.4 percent of lifetime resources. By comparison, the Hall-Rabushka flat tax, due to its standard deduction and personal exemptions, results in smaller welfare and efficiency gains, as steady state welfare increases by 1.6 percent and the efficiency gain is more than halved to 2.8 percent. Reform-induced efficiency gains thus vary significantly across consumption tax reforms; in addition, these analyses show that adding progressivity and transition rules significantly reduces efficiency gains.[26]

Results from Models Analyzing Efficiency and Equity Issues

Equity concerns are also central to the debate on the desirability of taxing capital income. The literature has addressed issues of both horizontal equity (equal treatment of equals) and vertical equity (progressivity).

Equal Treatment of Equals

Before equity issues can be addressed, the period over which the ability to pay tax is to be measured must be determined. If this period is a single year, then potential rather than actual annual consumption is a plausible measure of ability to pay, and a comprehensive measure of income that includes all accrued capital income, often referred to as Haig-Simons income, is typically viewed as the appropriate tax base. In this case, horizontal equity implies that individuals with the same comprehensive income in a given year should pay the same tax.

However, consumption tax proponents have questioned the rationale underlying the Haig-Simons ideal. In particular, the basic life-cycle model implies that individual welfare is a function of consumption over the lifetime rather than annual income (Bradford 1980). In this case, the appropriate measure of ability to pay is an individual's "endowment"—the present value of lifetime wage earnings—and capital income merely represents compensation for deferred consumption.[27] On this view, a tax on consumption and a tax on wages satisfy horizontal equity, as the lifetime tax burdens under each approach equal the product of the tax rate and the present value of the endowment, independent of individual consumption and saving decisions. By comparison, an income tax taxes the return to saving, penalizing savers. Many researchers argue that a consumption tax is therefore the preferable option on horizontal equity grounds.

A more contentious issue is whether this argument should be extended to multiple generations, implying that economic resources should not be taxed until consumed.[28] Some tax experts argue the "dynastic" view— that bequests should be tax exempt as they represent a transfer of potential consumption to heirs. According to this view, under a prepaid tax like the flat tax or the X tax, inheritances should not be included in the tax base of the recipient (since the tax has already been paid); similarly, under a postpaid expenditure tax, "withdrawals" used to fund bequests should not be taxed, and inheritances should be taxed only when consumed. The sales tax or value-added tax approaches are inherently consistent with the dynastic view of equity, as tax is not assessed until consumption actually occurs.

By comparison, the "lifetime endowment" view of equity underlying the life-cycle model described above argues that people should be taxed on all resources available during their lives, including inheritances, whether used for consumption or bequests. Therefore, the correct base for measuring ability to pay tax is lifetime income, including inheritances (Aaron and Galper 1985). Under a prepaid tax like the flat tax or the X tax, both the recipient and the donor will pay tax on intergenerational transfers. Under a postpaid expenditure tax, "withdrawals" used to fund bequests should be taxed and should also be in the recipient's tax base. Proponents of the dynastic equity view argue that such treatment creates a tax bias against saving and transfers in the form of bequests relative to other forms. In contrast, proponents of the lifetime endowment equity view argue that such treatment is essential to ensure all individuals with the same lifetime resources are treated equally (and to limit transfers of huge fortunes across generations). The choice between the two approaches obviously involves personal value judgments. However, it is important to note that the choice between the dynastic and lifetime endowment views of equity has similar implications for the designs of both income and consumption taxes, and is relevant primarily to the extent that capital income taxation is perceived to supplement poorly administered estate taxes (or to substitute for nonexistent estate taxes).[29]

Progressivity

Progressivity is also a contentious issue in the income versus consumption tax debate. Although a complete exploration of the optimal progressivity of the tax system is beyond the scope of this chapter, the following discussion examines whether capital income taxation is necessary to achieve an appropriate level of progressivity.

In a seminal paper published in 1976, Atkinson and Stiglitz construct a model of optimal commodity and wage taxation. The Atkinson and Stiglitz model focuses on whether differential commodity taxation is desirable to achieve a society's equity goals if wages are taxed optimally and individuals differ only in their skill and wage levels. Within this context, differential commodity taxation is unnecessary if the conditions for uniform commodity taxation (described above) are satisfied. The intuition behind this striking result is that an appropriately progressive wage tax can achieve all distributional goals since individuals differ only in their skill levels and at any given skill level, all individuals have the same earnings and consumption pattern.

A number of recent papers provide qualifications to the Atkinson and Stiglitz result. For example, if demands for leisure and consumption goods vary within a given skill class, differential commodity taxes may further the redistribution that occurs under the progressive wage tax. In a dynamic context, the implication is that, with more saving and higher levels of welfare, taxes on saving are desirable (Saez 2002). The practical relevance of this result, however, is open to question. With low national savings rates being a perennial concern, the desirability and political feasibility of a policy designed explicitly to penalize savers seems highly questionable (Weisbach and Bankman 2005; Naito 1999; Saez 2004; Stiglitz 1982).

Consumption-based taxation would thus appear preferable to income taxation in terms of providing equal treatment of equals, and progressivity goals in principle could be achieved with a suitably progressive consumption-based tax, such as the X tax or a progressive expenditure tax.[30] Indeed, a tax system that at least roughly replicates the progressivity of the current tax system across income classes seems a prerequisite for reform in most (although by no means all) circles, and such a constraint was imposed on the deliberations of the president's tax reform panel.[31] Such a result also cannot be obtained with a flat tax or a national retail sales tax (or VAT) plus rebate plan, as numerous studies have demonstrated that these plans involve a shift in tax burden from the very wealthy to a broadly defined middle class (Feenberg, Mitrusi, and Poterba 1997; Mieszkowski and Palumbo 2002).[32] Such a redistribution of tax burdens is undesirable, especially in light of the dramatic increase in income inequality over the past 30 years. Indeed, this concern is sufficiently important that Robert Hall, one of the creators of the original flat tax plan, now argues that a "tax design to fit the times might have two or even three different tax rates at the personal level" (Hall 2005, 75).

A natural question is whether the current distribution of the tax burden could in practice be replicated under a progressive consumption-based tax. Recent increases in income inequality are due primarily to an explosion in the compensation of the wealthy, while capital income has become increasingly less concentrated over time (Piketty and Saez 2003). As long as a consumption tax system subjects executives' compensation to the same level of tax as current law—for example, by including executive pay in the form of stock options in the individual-level tax—maintaining progressivity under a consumption tax should be feasible.[33] Still, replicating current tax burdens would require a progressive consumption tax rate with potentially high maximum tax rates. For example, one static revenue estimate of the effects of implementing an X tax with no transition relief while maintaining current tax preferences concludes that a revenue- and distributionally neutral reform would require a corporate tax rate and a top individual rate of 44 percent (see chapter 3). Such static estimates, however, are subject to the criticisms that they miss the primary advantages of a consumption tax reform, including its efficiency-enhancing behavioral responses, and overstate the regressivity of consumption taxes by focusing on annual rather than lifetime incidence measures.

These issues are addressed in a 2001 analysis that extends the Auerbach and Kotlikoff (1987) model to include 12 lifetime income groups (10 deciles, with the top [bottom] decile split into the top [bottom] 2 percent and the remaining 8 percent) (Altig et al. 2001). Simulations with this model indicate that using an X tax with a top marginal rate of 30 percent results in a long-run increase in output of 6.4 percent, coupled with long-run welfare increases for each of the 12 lifetime income classes of between 1 and 2 percent of full lifetime resources (including leisure). However, the transitional losses for the elderly that accompany these gains at the time of reform range between 1 and 2 percent of remaining lifetime utility; moreover, other simulations suggest that adding transition relief would significantly reduce, and perhaps even reverse, these long-run, steady-state welfare gains.

In addition, estimates of the regressivity of implementing a consumption tax are reduced by taking into account that high-income households often receive capital income as returns to risk-taking and economic rents, which are taxed similarly under income and consumption taxes. One estimate suggests this factor reduces the decline in the tax share paid by the top 5 percent of the net worth distribution by more than a third, relative to an analysis that assumes a consumption tax exempts all capital income (Gentry and Hubbard 1997).

Several researchers have investigated how much capital income is actually taxed under the current income tax (see chapter 1). One study found that an X tax implemented in 1983 would have raised no additional personal and corporate income tax revenues, and that the income tax burden on lower-income investors who tend to hold taxable bonds was greater than on higher-income investors who tend to borrow heavily to invest in assets that generate more lightly taxed capital gains (Gordon and Slemrod 1988).[34] A subsequent analysis of the 1995 tax system showed a similar distributive pattern for capital income taxes in the lower- and middle-income classes, but also showed that very high income taxpayers bore a significant portion of the capital income tax burden that year (Gordon, Kalambokidis, and Slemrod 2004). Indeed, in 2004, replacing the income tax with an X tax regime would have cost only $63.8 billion (less than 7 percent of combined personal and corporate annual income tax revenues) (Gordon et al. forthcoming).[35]

Finally, most dynamic models of consumption tax reform allow for only a single production good and do not capture the economic efficiency gains that arise from taxing investment more uniformly under a consumption tax, especially investment in owner-occupied housing, relative to other forms of investment.[36]

Although any conclusion from these analyses is tentative, they suggest that a progressive consumption tax reform could be designed without causing huge redistributions of income across income classes, at least if the growth effects such models predict in fact materialize and transition relief is limited. The reform would also have to be well-designed to improve economic efficiency. Yet, since considerable uncertainty remains about the accuracy of these models' predictions, implementing a slightly more progressive system than such models predict may be advisable to avoid unanticipated income redistributions (Auerbach and Hassett 2005a).

Additional Issues

The literature on income and consumption taxation has considered a host of additional issues relevant to the debate.

The Size of Behavioral Responses

One issue is whether the behavioral responses that the simulation models predict, especially labor supply and saving responses, are unreasonably large. Empirical estimates of labor supply responses to changes in taxation are typically low (Ballard 2002; Bernheim 2002; Engen et al. 1997; Gravelle 2002). Some simulated effects of consumption tax reforms are significantly larger than the current econometric literature implies. For example, one infinite-horizon study estimates that enacting a pure flat rate national retail sales tax with no exemptions or rebates would, in the short run, increase investment nearly 80 percent and labor supply 30 percent, and, in the long run, boost investment roughly 16.5 percent and labor supply 15 percent (Jorgenson and Wilcoxen 2002). Large, although typically more moderate, responses also characterize some life-cycle models, especially in the short run.[37]

Two factors, however, mitigate the validity of this criticism. First, as noted above, much recent literature has adopted more conservative assumptions in both model structure—for example, life-cycle rather than infinite-horizon models, perfect foresight rather than myopic expectations, and more careful modeling of the consumption tax–type features of the current income tax—and in parameter choices, resulting in more moderate behavioral responses, especially in the long run.[38] Second, the current econometric literature may not adequately capture the behavioral responses that would occur under fundamental tax reform. Econometric estimates of the response of saving to changes in the after-tax rate of return may inadequately capture the human wealth effect (Summers 1988). Recent research that examines differences in labor supply in the United States and Europe suggests that long-run labor supply responses to tax changes are considerably greater than those found in the microbased empirical literature, which typically studies data over a much shorter time period (Prescott 2005).

Alternative Models of Saving

Most analyses discussed in this chapter are based on the individual life-cycle model. Since this approach represents the "workhorse" model of individual behavior in neoclassical economics, this emphasis is not surprising. However, several researchers have suggested such models may present an incomplete picture of individual saving behavior.[39]

One argument is that saving reflects a precautionary motive, as individuals attempt to protect themselves against fluctuations in earnings and an uncertain lifetime (Engen and Gale 1996). When precautionary saving is added to a standard life-cycle model, the savings responses induced by a consumption tax reform fall dramatically, since precautionary saving is relatively unresponsive to changes in after-tax rates of return. As a result, the efficiency gains from switching to a consumption tax are significantly smaller than in alternative analyses that do not consider precautionary saving. The efficiency case for consumption tax reform is correspondingly weakened.

In addition, some individual saving may be undertaken to meet a goal that is fixed in dollar terms.[40] In this case, a consumption tax reform may reduce saving, as a higher after-tax rate of return helps achieve the savings target. One estimate attributes approximately a third of aggregate wealth to such precautionary saving motives, which again implies that life-cycle models overstate the savings responses that would occur with a consumption tax reform (Carroll and Samwick 1998). However, a more recent study places this figure at a much lower 10 percent (Hurst et al. 2005).

Another issue is that individuals may not be as free to borrow at any point in their life-cycle, especially early in life, as most analyses assume. Reform-induced efficiency gains might be muted if a large number of credit-constrained individuals, who consume all their after-tax earnings, are negatively affected by higher wage or consumption taxes under a consumption tax reform. However, a progressive consumption tax could address such liquidity problems by reducing tax rates on lower-income, credit-constrained individuals, an approach preferable to a progressive income tax that distorts individuals' saving decisions. Further, problems with liquidity constraints can be addressed more directly with transfer programs such as the earned income tax credit and presumably have been alleviated in recent years by easier access to credit card debt and tax-favored home equity loans (Hubbard and Judd 1986).

Uncertainties about future income levels could also make some capital income taxation desirable for credit-constrained individuals if it reduces the saving of individuals who save too much due to concern about future income declines (Aiyagari 1994; Chamley 2001). However, the desirability and political feasibility of a tax policy designed explicitly to penalize savers in the current low-saving environment is open to serious question.

Another potentially serious concern is that individual saving behavior is far more erratic than economic simulation models predict. Specifically, the relatively new field of behavioral economics has suggested new models that have implications for modeling individual saving behavior (Bernheim 1997, 2002). To cite one example, individual decisions may reflect a balancing of the desire for immediate gratification against the desire to engage in more prudent behavior by saving for the future. In this case, tax preferences for savings under the income tax imply government encouragement of saving that may successfully sway behavior away from immediate consumption, which such features as restrictions and penalties on withdrawals from tax-preferred savings plans and systematic payroll deductions for savings may reinforce. If such features are eliminated under a consumption tax reform, saving might decline. In particular, since employer-provided pensions would lose their relative tax advantage under a consumption tax reform, employers might reduce the extent of pension coverage (Bernheim 1997). As a result, savings might fall because some people would no longer be constrained to save more than they desired or be penalized for withdrawals from savings to finance current consumption. However, such effects might be partially, or even fully, offset if a consumption tax reform were perceived as government encouragement of all forms of saving.

Transitional Issues

Transitional issues present a formidable obstacle to enacting consumption tax reform. Most analyses have focused on two issues.[41] First, in the absence of transition rules, a consumption tax might result in a one-time fall in equity prices. Under a value-added tax or national retail sales tax, inflation in the form of a one-time, tax-induced increase in consumer prices would reduce the purchasing power of existing real assets. Under the direct consumption tax options, such as the flat tax, X tax, or expenditure tax, the relative value of existing capital would decline because remaining depreciation deductions would be denied while competing investments in new capital would be expensed; an equilibrium with equal after-tax returns on both new and old assets could occur only if the prices of old assets fell.[42] Second, a consumption tax might also push down the price of existing owner-occupied housing, which would lose its current tax advantages. Some observers have suggested that the asset prices could plunge 20 to 30 percent (Capozza, Green, and Hendershott 1996; Gravelle 1995).

However, these analyses neglect certain offsetting factors (Bruce and Holtz-Eakin 1999; Lyon and Merrill 2001; Zodrow 2002). Equity price declines, for instance, would be mitigated by the costs of adjusting the capital stock in response to reform, which imply that existing capital would earn above-normal returns during the transition to a new equilibrium. Simulation results suggest that adjustment costs alone play a significant role in reducing and, in some cases, eliminating reform-induced declines in equity values (Altig et al. 2001; Auerbach 1996).

Numerous factors, such as declines in interest rates and reductions in the supply of owner-occupied housing, would mitigate any tendency for house prices to fall (Diamond and Zodrow forthcoming; Gravelle 1996). One simulation suggests that the declines in the price of owner-occupied housing could be on the order of 3 to 5 percent, far smaller than those suggested above, and would dissipate relatively quickly over time (Diamond and Zodrow forthcoming).

Thus, transition problems may not be a "show stopper" for fundamental tax reform; indeed, transition relief should be minimized since transition rules significantly reduce the efficiency gains obtained from such a reform (Zodrow 2002). The relatively harsh transition rules that accompanied the enactment of the Tax Reform Act of 1986 suggest that transition relief could be limited under a consumption tax reform. However, political realities suggest that some transition rules are inevitable and will eliminate the need to create complex rules that limit attempts to avoid a one-time, reform-induced transition "hit" on existing capital (Pearlman 1996; Shaviro 2000; Weisbach 2003). If so, the costs of such transition rules should be kept to a minimum by using targeted grandfather rules (Zodrow 1992). For example, transition relief could be limited to allowing continued depreciation allowances only on long-lived assets, especially since recent equipment purchases have benefited from bonus depreciation. In addition, transition rules could be coupled with compensating provisions. For example, under the flat tax or X tax, phased-out deductions for home mortgage interest could be accompanied by similarly phased-out taxation of the associated interest income, and expensing of new investment might be limited to a fraction of the purchase price for firms with significant continuing deductions for depreciation on existing investment (Hall and Rabushka 1995).

Conclusion

The debate on whether capital income should be subject to consumption-based taxation has raged for many years. It is likely to intensify as the

United States examines various options for fundamental tax reform, including those the president's tax reform panel proposed in 2005. What lessons can be drawn from the voluminous literature on this subject?

The theoretical literature generally supports consumption-based taxation of capital income. Infinite horizon models provide the most clearcut result—a long-run optimal capital income tax rate of zero—due to ever-increasing distortions of future consumption and saving decisions. A similar result can be obtained in the context of life-cycle models, although it is more tenuous as it depends on unproven but plausible assumptions on individual tastes. In terms of tax fairness, consumption-based taxation provides for more equal treatment of equals, and a central theoretical result indicates that under the same assumptions on individual tastes, progressivity goals can be achieved with progressive direct taxes on consumption. Further, the low level of revenues capital income taxation collects under the current income tax suggests that approximating the current distribution of the tax burden is less difficult than might appear under a consumption tax. These results on the taxation of labor income are especially important to the current debate, as recent increases in income inequality are largely attributable to an explosion in executive compensation. Consumption taxes are also inherently simpler than taxes based on income, although some of this advantage would be muted as "pure" proposals for reform are modified to accommodate a variety of real-world complications and political pressures. Indeed, one critical factor in advancing the debate is the ongoing development of more fully specified reform proposals, with the work of David Bradford on his celebrated X tax—which formed the basis of one of the two reform proposals made in 2005 by the president's panel on tax reform—setting the standard for such endeavors.

The results of large-scale computer simulation models have played an important role in buttressing the case for consumption tax reform. Many of these models indicate that such a reform would generate impressive improvements in economic performance and gains in economic welfare, especially in the long run. Yet, these gains are significantly muted, and in a few cases, even reversed, once reform is accompanied by transition rules to protect old capital and as the progressivity of the tax system increases. This suggests that transition relief should be kept to a minimum in implementing a consumption tax reform. In addition, keeping rates relatively low by eliminating tax preferences at the business level and severely limiting them at the individual level, especially at the high end of the income distribution where the gains from reform are concentrated, is critical to attaining efficiency gains and achieving rough distributional neutrality. It is equally important to note that current models do not capture all of the potential efficiency gains from fundamental tax reform and so may understate the potential for such gains. Items often not considered (depending on the model) include the gains attributable to an improved allocation of capital across sectors, especially across housing and nonhousing production and across the corporate and noncorporate sectors, the benefits of increased inflows of foreign capital, the gains from eliminating financing distortions, the potential gains from a well-designed and simpler tax system that would require less resources for compliance and administration and be less susceptible to avoidance and evasion, and any positive additional benefits (e.g., on the growth rate of technological innovation) from tax-induced increases in investment (Stokely and Rebelo 1995).

This chapter suggests two directions for future research to clarify the main issues in the ongoing debate on fundamental tax reform.[43] The first is continued evolution of computer simulation models to capture more fully reform-induced efficiency gains and distributional effects on both current and future generations, and as many of the "real world" complications of reform as possible. The second is continued development of the structural details of consumption tax reform proposals to understand more clearly their economic effects and how effectively they would cope with various real-world complications, and to help in choosing among the prototypes for reform. Finally, it is important to note that piecemeal changes in the general direction of consumption tax reform run the risk of losing revenues and creating arbitrage opportunities while falling short of attaining all the potential gains that a well-designed reform package might achieve—gains that must be achieved for a consumption tax to be a desirable approach to reform.

Summary

Decades of economic research, including both theoretical arguments and computer simulation results, make a strong case for consumption tax reform on efficiency grounds and suggest that it should be possible to design a comprehensive consumption tax that would be sufficiently progressive to meet equity concerns. However, a "real world" reform would have to deal appropriately with transitional issues and be designed to limit opportunities for tax avoidance and evasion. The findings of this chapter indicate that

Theoretical models suggest that the optimal tax rate on capital income is zero, or at least approximates zero. Capital income taxation is unambiguously undesirable in the long run in analyses where individuals are assumed to have infinite lives (or care about future generations), as taxing capital income results in highly undesirable, ever-increasing distortions of consumption decisions that significantly reduce saving. Similar—although more tenuous—results are obtained in life-cycle models, where individual welfare depends on consumption and labor supply over a finite lifetime spent working and in retirement.

Consumption taxes are simpler than taxes based on income. Consumption is inherently easier to measure than income since it is difficult to tax all income as accrued, primarily due to problems in accurately measuring depreciation and adjusting for inflation. A consumption tax could also eliminate the special deductions, exemptions, and other forms of preferential tax treatment that complicate current law, although these could also, in principle, be eliminated under an income tax reform. A viable consumption tax would have to be designed to minimize new opportunities for tax avoidance and evasion, especially if our international trading partners continue to use income-based taxation.

A consumption-based tax could be designed to meet equity goals. Since the taxation of capital income under an income tax penalizes savers, most observers believe that a consumption tax is inherently preferable to an income tax in terms of providing "equal treatment of equals." Maintaining progressivity under a consumption tax should be feasible under a progressive tax that taxes compensation comprehensively, especially since capital income is taxed relatively lightly under current law. However, replicating current tax burdens without unacceptably high maximum tax rates would require significantly curtailing tax preferences that benefit the wealthy and minimizing transition relief.

Transitional issues present obstacles to consumption tax reform, but critics exaggerate the problems. Implementation of a consumption tax may reduce equity prices and housing prices in the short-term. However, a wide variety of other reform-induced factors mitigate this effect. Transition rules can protect asset owners, but they require higher tax rates and this can eliminate many of the gains from tax reform. Accordingly, transition rules should used sparingly and carefully.

NOTES

I would like to thank Alan Auerbach, Len Burman, John Diamond, and Joel Slemrod for helpful comments; Kevin Grahmann for outstanding research assistance at the beginning stages of this project; and Athiphat Muthitacharoen for his invaluable help in bringing this chapter to completion.

1. For example, see chapters 4 and 5 for discussions of the difficulties of taxing capital income; Shakow (1986) and Auerbach and Bradford (2004) discuss how a comprehensive income tax might be implemented.

2. See Bradford (1986) for a classic exposition of this argument. More recently, McCaffery (2005, 809) argues that a "great deal and possibly all of the mind-numbing complexity of America's largest and least popular tax follows from the decision to have a progressive personal income tax." Shaviro (2004, 92) stresses that "a consumption tax could offer enormous simplification advantages."

3. Schler and Bankman (chapter 6) address these issues in the context of a version of the X tax. In addition, Weisbach (2000), McLure and Zodrow (1996), and Feld (1995) discuss problems that would arise in implementing the flat tax, while Bradford (1996b) discusses problems raised by the taxation of financial institutions under prepaid consumption tax plans. Ginsburg (1995) analyzes issues raised by the USA tax proposal (which combined a business level value added tax with an individual level cash flow tax), and Murray (1997) addresses problems in implementing a national retail sales tax. Slemrod (2005) discusses the desirability of, and problems raised by, removing popular tax preferences, and Hubbard (2005a) discusses the administrative problems of integrating the corporate and individual income tax systems.

4. Note that if favorable treatment of some narrow classes of investment were deemed desirable (e.g., in research and development in order to capture significant positive externalities), carefully targeted expenditure programs could be utilized rather than general tax preferences.

5. International experience with the VAT may also be instructive in this regard. Although VATs are never completely uniform, preferences take the form of applying zero rates to certain commodities (typically on distributional grounds) or exempting certain activities (typically on distributional or administrative grounds), rather than business subsidies that give rise to negative marginal effective tax rates.

6. This is clearly related to the more general issue of whether a consumption tax would be simpler than an income tax, discussed by Slemrod (1996) and Gale and Holtzblatt (2002).

7. For example, McLure and Zodrow (1996) argue for a modified version of the X tax that would tax both real and financial transactions at the business level partly on the grounds that it would be less susceptible to evasion and avoidance, especially on international transactions.

8. By comparison, under the credit-method VAT utilized in Europe and elsewhere, firms get credits on their purchases only to the extent that they have invoices showing that their suppliers have paid the tax (McLure 1987).

9. A related question is why this international experience is so limited (beyond the extensive international experience with indirect consumption taxation in the form of the VAT), with the primary examples being the ACE (allowance for corporate equity) taxes

implemented in Croatia, Brazil, Italy, and Austria (Genser forthcoming). One factor played a critical role in halting several consumption tax reforms: the reasonable concern that the U.S. Internal Revenue Service would not deem a consumption-based business cash flow tax (e.g., under a flat tax, an X tax, or an expenditure tax) to be creditable against the domestic tax liability of U.S. multinationals (McLure and Zodrow 1998).

10. See Zodrow and McLure (1991) for a demonstration of this point.

11. See Weisbach (2004) and Hubbard (2005b) for comprehensive recent discussions, including demonstrations of all the basic points asserted in the text; see also Bradford (1986), Bankman and Griffith (1992), and Hubbard (2002).

12. Weisbach and Bankman (2005) and McCaffery (2005) stress this point. Note, however, that this argument in no way implies that the taxation of normal returns to capital is a trivial issue; see Aaron's comments in the concluding section.

13. This applies only for production-based taxes on capital income. By comparison, taxes on the capital income of all of a nation's residents, regardless of where it is earned, is in principle desirable but in practice exceedingly difficult to implement.

14. This result is closely related to the international tax competition literature; see Zodrow (2003) for a recent discussion.

15. For recent surveys, see Zodrow and McLure (1991), Gravelle (1994), Gordon (2000), Judd (2001), McCaffery (2005), and Weisbach and Bankman (2005).

16. For recent extensions, see Lucas (1990); Chari, Christiano, and Kehoe (1994); and Judd (1997, 1999).

17. Although the practical relevance of this result is generally limited, it is interesting to note that implementing a consumption tax may, depending on transition rules, achieve this result; this point is investigated further in the discussion of transition issues below. Note also that such a policy suffers from a "time inconsistency problem" in that although it may, in principle, be desirable to impose a huge tax on existing capital as part of an agreement to exempt future returns to capital, investors will understandably be suspicious that future governments will renege on the agreement and tax future accumulations of capital, in which case, the predicted positive effects on saving and capital accumulation will not fully materialize.

18. Indeed, Lucas (1990, 314), argues that consumption tax reform would trigger "the largest genuinely free lunch I have seen in 25 years in this business."

19. Note, however, that the insight that capital income taxes are highly distortionary for individuals with long time horizons is still relevant, if to a lesser degree, in lifecycle models. Indeed, because lifecycle models often assume away intergenerational altruism entirely, they may be understating the gains from consumption tax reform.

20. For example, see Feldstein (1978), Bradford (1980), King (1980) and, in an explicitly dynamic context, Atkinson and Sandmo (1980). Goods that are complements tend to be consumed together. More formally, leisure and a consumption good are complements if an increase in the price of the consumption good reduces the demand for leisure (and thus increases labor supply).
    The intuition underlying this result reflects a balancing of two considerations. Uniform taxation of consumption tends to be efficient, as it avoids tax distortions of intertemporal consumption allocation decisions. However, the inability to tax leisure directly implies that taxation of consumption goods will inefficiently reduce labor supply, so that differential taxation of consumption goods will be desirable if it can be used to offset the

tax-induced increase in leisure demand and the associated reduction in labor supply. If consumption in each of the two periods is equally complementary to leisure and thus affects labor supply in the same way, any rationale for differential taxation disappears, and uniform commodity taxation (a capital income tax rate of zero) is optimal.

21. For example, Atkinson and Stiglitz (1980, 437) conclude that separability is "an assumption that has been made in nearly all studies of demand and labor supply functions."

22. One reason for the large welfare gains obtained with a consumption tax reform is that the size of the existing capital stock under the income tax is suboptimal in the Summers model; such an assumption seems plausible and is consistent with the often-expressed concern that the United States saves and invests too little. Note, however, that many nontax government policies also affect the level of saving and the size of the capital stock, making it difficult to ascertain whether the capital stock is too large or too small.

23. This highlights the point, noted above, that a significant fraction of the efficiency gains obtained from a consumption tax reform is attributable to a one-time "hit" on old capital, reminiscent of the tax on existing capital that characterizes the infinite horizon models. In addition, Summers assumes that the government's budget must be balanced each year. As a result, any policy that defers taxes, such as a cash flow consumption tax or an income tax, will stimulate additional savings as individuals must save to finance the payment of future taxes; this additional savings would not occur under a wage tax reform, which reduces savings effects and thus the long-run welfare gains associated with its enactment.

24. The model is described in Auerbach and Kotlikoff (1987). See Auerbach (1996) for a recent analysis of fundamental tax reform using the Auerbach and Kotlikoff model and Kotlikoff (1998) for a discussion of its evolution.

25. By comparison, for the same reasons as in the case of the Summers model, the enactment of a wage tax (again without a complementary business tax) reduces welfare by 0.9 percent of the present value of lifetime resources.

26. Indeed, Auerbach also estimates that the efficiency gains associated with implementing the USA tax (Weidenbaum 1996), which provides for transition rules and multiple individual tax rates that range up to 40 percent as well as a variety of other features, are only 0.1 percent of lifetime resources.

A separate issue is whether the optimal capital income tax is zero in such overlapping generations models. Erosa and Gervais (2002) and Garriga (2003) show that this is not necessarily the case because individual utility functions are not necessarily characterized by separability in leisure and consumption. However, their "optimal" capital income tax rates are relatively small.

27. As explained below, when the basic life-cycle model is extended to include bequests and inheritances, the value of the individual endowment should include inheritances, and bequests should (arguably) be treated as consumption.

28. See Zodrow and McLure (1991) for further discussion.

29. Cremer, Pestieau, and Rochet (2003) show that capital income taxation may be desirable in a version of the Atkinson and Stiglitz (1976) model, modified to include bequests that are by assumption tax exempt, if the equity gains from indirectly taxing inherited wealth offset the efficiency costs of reducing saving and investment. Note also that capital income taxation can be justified as a proxy for a wealth tax that is assessed on the grounds that wealth confers utility beyond its consumption value in the form of

prestige, security, and power, including political power (Carroll 2000). However, consistent with the dynastic view of equity, Shaviro (2004) argues that such benefits reflect only the value of future consumption, which would be taxed fully under a consumption tax (although there would be no reduction in wealth accumulation under a consumption tax, in contrast to the case under an effective capital income tax).

30. Note that in addition to the vertical equity rationale, progressive taxation effectively provides social insurance against income fluctuations (Varian 1980).

31. Note, however, that even a "distributionally neutral" consumption tax reform will cause redistributions within income classes. Moreover, since low-income individuals pay little or no income tax and middle-income individuals already largely receive consumption tax treatment since most of their saving is in housing or retirement plans (see chapter 3), these redistributions will be concentrated in the upper-income classes, especially at the very top. One could argue that as long as reform is roughly distributionally neutral in the bottom four quintiles, redistributions among the top quintile may be of relatively little social concern.

32. As Fullerton and Rogers (1993) discuss, lifetime incidence analyses are preferable to studies based on annual income because they limit mismeasurement due to income fluctuations attributable to cyclical and lifecycle factors. For a dissenting view, see Barthold (1993).

33. Note that one potential advantage of the postpaid expenditure tax approach is that it may be relatively less susceptible to evasion in the form of converting labor income to exempt capital income (Weisbach 2000), although many such strategies are limited under the prepaid flat tax and X taxes by setting the top individual tax rate equal to the flat business tax rate.

34. Indeed, McCaffery (2005) argues that wealthy individuals can largely avoid taxation over their lifetimes by following a strategy of investing in, and then holding until death, assets that generate capital gains while financing current consumption with debt. See Gravelle's comments to part 1 for a critique of this approach that concludes that it understates how much capital income is taxed under the current income tax.

35. These authors also find that expanding prepaid savings accounts, as was proposed in 2004 and is currently being discussed, could result in a situation where the taxation of capital income loses revenue. This dramatically illustrates the point that piecemeal reforms that cobble together various elements of a consumption tax reform but do not include all of its features, including especially the elimination of interest deductibility, can be highly undesirable. In particular, the "five easy pieces" approach (Christian and Robbins 2002)—which would reduce rates (and eliminate the estate tax), allow expensing, and exempt capital income from taxation at the individual level without providing for consumption-based tax treatment of interest expense—loses revenue and creates arbitrage opportunities without gaining the advantages of consumption-based taxation in providing uniform tax treatment of all saving and investment decisions and a simplified tax system.

36. Note that such gains would not be obtained under an income tax reform—although more uniform treatment of business investment could be achieved (if economic depreciation were measured accurately and the appropriate adjustments for inflation were made), a move to more comprehensive taxation of business income would exacerbate the already large tax bias favoring owner-occupied housing over other forms of investment. The net result would likely be a relatively small efficiency gain or an efficiency loss. Note also that additional efficiency gains could be obtained with reforms that would

reduce the consumption distortions of the existing income tax, especially those attributable to tax preferences for fringe benefits; these potential efficiency gains, however, could be achieved with either income or consumption tax reforms, and would face the same political obstacles in either case.

37. See Gravelle (2002) for an extended discussion of this and other issues raised by the use of computable general equilibrium model to analyze the effects of consumption tax reforms.

38. The assumption of myopic expectations tends to overstate the short-run responses to the enactment of the consumption tax reform because individuals and firms do not take into account in their behavioral responses the decline in the interest rate over time that occurs with capital accumulation. More careful modeling of the many consumption tax–type features of the current hybrid income tax implies that enacting a consumption tax would change the current system less than if it were a true income tax (Engen and Gale 1996).

39. Indeed, Altig et al. (2001) note that in their simulations, they use a relatively low value of the intertemporal elasticity of substitution, a key parameter in determining saving responsiveness, to compensate for the lack of non-life-cycle saving motives in their model.

40. Samwick (1998) examines such "target saving."

41. For example, see Sarkar and Zodrow (1993), Bradford (1996a), Pearlman (1996), Shaviro (2000), and Zodrow (1997, 2002).

42. Note that existing assets could be put on an equal footing with new assets only if the remaining basis were expensed at the time of enacting a consumption tax reform.

43. See also Zodrow and Mieszkowski (2002).

REFERENCES

Aaron, Henry J., and Harvey Galper. 1985. *Assessing Tax Reform*. Washington, DC: Brookings Institution Press.

Aiyagari, S. Rao. 1994. "Uninsured Idiosyncratic Risk and Aggregate Saving." *Quarterly Journal of Economics* 109:659–84.

Altig, David, Alan J. Auerbach, Laurence J. Kotlikoff, Kent A. Smetters, and Jan Walliser. 2001. "Simulating Fundamental Tax Reform in the United States." *American Economic Review* 91:574–95.

Atkinson, Anthony B., and Agnar Sandmo. 1980. "Welfare Implications of the Taxation of Savings." *Economic Journal* 90:529–49.

Atkinson, Anthony B., and Joseph E. Stiglitz. 1976. "The Design of Tax Structure: Direct versus Indirect Taxation." *Journal of Public Economics* 6:55–75.

———. 1980. *Lectures on Public Economics*. New York: McGraw-Hill.

Auerbach, Alan J. 1979. "A Brief Note on a Nonexistent Theorem about the Optimality of Uniform Taxation." *Economic Letters* 3:49–52.

———. 1996. "Tax Reform, Capital Allocation, Efficiency, and Growth." In *Economic Effects of Fundamental Tax Reform*, edited by Henry J. Aaron and William G. Gale (29–73). Washington, DC: Brookings Institution Press.

Auerbach, Alan J., and David F. Bradford. 2004. "Generalized Cash-Flow Taxation." *Journal of Public Economics* 88:957–80.

Auerbach, Alan J., and Kevin A. Hassett. 2005a. "Conclusion." In *Toward Fundamental Tax Reform*, edited by Alan J. Auerbach and Kevin A. Hassett (149–58). Washington, DC: AEI Press.

———. 2005b. *Toward Fundamental Tax Reform*. Washington, DC: AEI Press.

Auerbach, Alan J., and James R. Hines. 2002. "Taxation and Economic Efficiency." In *Handbook of Public Economics*, vol. 4, edited by Alan J. Auerbach and Martin Feldstein (1347–1421). Amsterdam: Elsevier.

Auerbach, Alan J., and Laurence J. Kotlikoff. 1987. *Dynamic Fiscal Policy*. Cambridge, UK: Cambridge University Press.

Avi-Yonah, Reuven S. 2004. "Risk, Rents, and Regressivity: Why the United States Needs Both an Income Tax and a VAT." *Tax Notes International* 37(December 20): 177–95.

Balcer, Yves, Irwin Garfinkel, Kathy J. Krynski, and Efraim Sadka. 1983. "Income Redistribution and the Structure of Indirect Taxation." In *Social Policy Evaluation: An Economic Perspective*, edited by Elhanan Helpman, Assaf Razin, and Efraim Sadka (279–97). New York: Academic Press.

Ballard, Charles L. 1990. "On the Specification of Simulation Models for Evaluating Income and Consumption Taxes." In *Heidelberg Congress on Taxing Consumption*, edited by Manfred Rose (147–88). Berlin: Springer-Verlag.

———. 2002. "International Aspects of Fundamental Tax Reform." In *United States Tax Reform in the 21st Century*, edited by George R. Zodrow and Peter Mieszkowski (109–39). Cambridge, UK: Cambridge University Press.

Bankman, Joseph. 2004. "The Tax Shelter Problem." *National Tax Journal* 57:925–36.

Bankman, Joseph, and Thomas Griffith. 1992. "Is the Debate between an Income Tax and a Consumption Tax a Debate about Risk? Does It Matter?" *Tax Law Review* 47:377–406.

Barthold, Thomas A. 1993. "How Should We Measure Distribution?" *National Tax Journal* 46:291–99.

Bernheim, B. Douglas. 1997. "Taxation and Saving: A Behavioral Perspective." In *Proceedings of the Eighty-Ninth Annual Conference on Taxation*. Washington, DC: National Tax Association.

———. 2002. "Taxation and Saving." In *Handbook of Public Economics*, vol. 3, edited by Alan J. Auerbach and Martin Feldstein (1176–1207). Amsterdam: Elsevier.

Blumenthal, Marsha, and Joel Slemrod. 1995. "The Compliance Cost of Taxing Foreign-Source Income: Its Magnitude, Determinants, and Policy Implications." *International Tax and Public Finance* 2:37–54.

Bond, Stephen R., Michael P. Devereux, and Malcolm J. Gammie. 1996. "Tax Reform to Promote Investment." *Oxford Review of Economic Policy* 12:109–17.

Boskin, Michael J., ed. 1996. *Frontiers of Tax Reform*. Stanford: Hoover Institution Press.

Bradford, David F. 1980. "The Case for a Personal Consumption Tax." In *What Should Be Taxed: Income or Expenditure?* edited by Joseph Pechman (77–113). Washington, DC: Brookings Institution Press.

———. 1986. *Untangling the Income Tax*. Cambridge, MA: Harvard University Press.

————. 1987. "On the Incidence of Consumption Taxes." In *The Consumption Tax: A Better Alternative,* edited by Charles E. Walker and Mark A. Bloomfield (243–61). Cambridge, MA: Ballinger.

————. 1996a. "Consumption Taxes: Some Fundamental Transition Issues." In *Frontiers of Tax Reform,* edited by Michael J. Boskin (123–50). Stanford: Hoover Institution Press.

————. 1996b. "Treatment of Financial Services under Income and Consumption Taxes." In *Economic Effects of Fundamental Tax Reform,* edited by Henry J. Aaron and William G. Gale (437–60). Washington, DC: Brookings Institution Press.

————. 2003. "Addressing the Transfer-Pricing Problem in an Origin-Basis X Tax." *International Tax and Public Finance* 10:591–610.

————. 2005. "A Tax System for the Twenty-First Century." In *Toward Fundamental Tax Reform,* edited by Alan J. Auerbach and Kevin A. Hassett (81–94). Washington, DC: AEI Press.

Bruce, Donald, and Douglas Holtz-Eakin. 1999. "Fundamental Tax Reform and Residential Housing." *Journal of Housing Economics* 8:249–71.

Burton, David, and Dan Mastromarco. 1997. "Emancipating America from the Income Tax: How a National Sales Tax Would Work." Policy Analysis no. 272. Washington, DC: Cato Institute.

Capozza, Dennis R., Richard K. Green, and Patric H. Hendershott. 1996. "Taxes, Mortgage Borrowing, and Residential Land Prices." In *Economic Effects of Fundamental Tax Reform,* edited by Henry J. Aaron and William G. Gale (171–98). Washington, DC: Brookings Institution Press.

Carasso, Adam, C. Eugene Steuerle, and Elizabeth Bell. 2005. "Making Tax Incentives for Homeownership More Equitable and Efficient." Discussion Paper No. 21. Washington, DC: Urban–Brookings Tax Policy Center.

Carroll, Christopher D. 2000. "Why Do the Rich Save So Much?" In *Does Atlas Shrug: The Economic Consequences of Taxing the Rich,* edited by Joel Slemrod (465–84). Cambridge, MA: Harvard University Press.

Carroll, Christopher D., and Andrew A. Samwick. 1998. "How Important Is Precautionary Saving?" *Review of Economics and Statistics* 80:410–19.

Chamley, Christophe. 1986. "Optimal Taxation of Capital Income in General Equilibrium with Infinite Lives." *Econometrica* 54:607–22.

————. 2001. "Capital Income Taxation, Wealth Distribution, and Borrowing Constraints." *Journal of Public Economics* 79:55–69.

Chari, V. V., Lawrence J. Christiano, and Patrick J. Kehoe. 1994. "Optimal Fiscal Policy in a Business Cycle Model." *Journal of Political Economy* 102:617–52.

Christian, Ernest, and Gary Robbins. 2002. "Stealth Approach to Tax Reform." *Washington Times,* November 1.

Cnossen, Sijbren. 2000. "Taxing Capital Income in the Nordic Countries: A Model for the European Union?" In *Taxing Capital in the European Union,* edited by Sijbren Cnossen (180–213). Oxford: Oxford University Press.

Coakley, Jerry, Farida Kulasi, and Ron Smith. 1998. "The Feldstein-Horioka Puzzle and Capital Mobility: A Review." *International Journal of Finance and Economics* 3:169–88.

Cremer, Helmuth, Pierre Pestieau, and Jean-Charles Rochet. 2003. "Capital Income Taxation when Inherited Wealth Is Not Observable." *Journal of Public Economics* 87:2475–90.

Diamond, John, Craig Johnson, and George R. Zodrow. 1997. "Bequests, Saving, and Taxation." In *Proceedings of the Eighty-Ninth Annual Conference on Taxation.* Washington, DC: National Tax Association.

Diamond, John W., and George R. Zodrow. Forthcoming. "Consumption Tax Reform: Changes in Business Equity and Housing Prices." In *Fundamental Tax Reform: Issues, Choices, and Implications,* edited by John W. Diamond and George R. Zodrow. Cambridge, MA: MIT Press.

Engen, Eric M., and William G. Gale. 1996. "The Effects of Fundamental Tax Reform on Saving." In *Economic Effects of Fundamental Tax Reform,* edited by Henry J. Aaron and William G. Gale (83–112). Washington, DC: Brookings Institution Press.

Engen, Eric M., Jane Gravelle, and Kent Smetters. 1997. "Dynamic Tax Models: Why They Do the Things They Do." *National Tax Journal* 50:657–82.

Erosa, Andres, and Martin Gervais. 2002. "Optimal Taxation in Life-Cycle Economies." *Journal of Economic Theory* 105:338–69.

Evans, Owen J. 1983. "Tax Policy, the Interest Elasticity of Saving, and Capital Accumulation: Numerical Analysis of Theoretical Models." *American Economic Review* 73:398–410.

Feenberg, Daniel R., Andrew W. Mitrusi, and James M. Poterba. 1997. "Distributional Effects of Adopting a National Retail Sales Tax." In *Tax Policy and the Economy,* vol. 11, edited by James M. Poterba (49–89). Cambridge, MA: MIT Press.

Feld, Alan L. 1995. "Living with the Flat Tax." *National Tax Journal* 48(4): 603–17.

Feldstein, Martin. 1978. "The Welfare Cost of Capital Income Taxation." *Journal of Political Economy* 86:29–51.

Feldstein, Martin, and Phillipe Bacchetta. 1991. "National Saving and International Investment." In *National Saving and Economic Performance,* edited by B. Douglas Bernheim and John B. Shoven (201–20). Chicago: University of Chicago Press.

Feldstein, Martin, and Charles Horioka. 1980. "Domestic Savings and International Capital Flows." *Economic Journal* 90:314–29.

Fullerton, Don, and Diane Lim Rogers. 1993. *Who Bears the Lifetime Tax Burden?* Washington, DC: Brookings Institution Press.

———. 1996. "Lifetime Effects of Fundamental Tax Reform." In *Economic Effects of Fundamental Tax Reform,* edited by Henry J. Aaron and William G. Gale (321–47). Washington, DC: Brookings Institution Press.

Gale, William G. 2005. "Tax Reform Options in the Real World." In *Toward Fundamental Tax Reform,* edited by Alan J. Auerbach and Kevin A. Hassett (34–47). Washington, DC: AEI Press.

Gale, William G., and Janet Holtzblatt. 2002. "The Role of Administrative Issues in Tax Reform: Simplicity, Compliance, and Administration." In *United States Tax Reform in the 21st Century,* edited by George R. Zodrow and Peter Mieszkowski (179–214). Cambridge, UK: Cambridge University Press.

Gale, William G., and Joel Slemrod. 2001. *Rethinking Estate and Gift Taxation.* Washington, DC: Brookings Institution Press.

Garriga, Carlos. 2003. "Optimal Fiscal Policy in Overlapping Generations Models." Unpublished manuscript, Florida State University.

Genser, Bernd. Forthcoming. "The Dual Income Tax: Implementation and Experience in European Countries." *Finanzarchiv.*

Gentry, William M., and R. Glenn Hubbard. 1997. "Distributional Implications of Introducing a Broad-Based Consumption Tax." In *Tax Policy and the Economy,* vol. 11, edited by James M. Poterba (1–47). Cambridge, MA: MIT Press.

Gillis, Malcolm, Peter Mieszkowski, and George R. Zodrow. 1996. "Indirect Consumption Taxes: Common Issues and Differences among the Alternative Approaches." *Tax Law Review* 51(Summer): 725–74.

Ginsburg, Martin D. 1995. "Life under a Personal Consumption Tax: Some Thoughts on Working, Saving, and Consuming in Nunn-Domenici's Tax World." *National Tax Journal* 68:585–602.

Gordon, Roger H. 1986. "Taxation of Investment and Savings in the World Economy." *American Economic Review* 76:1086–1102.

———. 1992. "Can Capital Income Taxes Survive in Open Economies?" *Journal of Finance* 47:1159–80.

———. 2000. "Taxation of Capital Income vs. Labour Income: An Overview." In *Taxing Capital in the European Union,* edited by Sijbren Cnossen (15–45). Oxford: Oxford University Press.

Gordon, Roger H., and James R. Hines Jr. 2002. "International Taxation." In *Handbook of Public Economics,* vol. 4, edited by Alan J. Auerbach and Martin Feldstein (1935–96). Amsterdam: Elsevier.

Gordon, Roger H., and Joel Slemrod. 1988. "Do We Collect Any Revenue from Taxing Capital Income?" In *Tax Policy and the Economy,* vol. 2, edited by Lawrence H. Summers (89–130). Cambridge: National Bureau of Economic Research.

Gordon, Roger H., Laura Kalambokidis, and Joel Slemrod. 2004. "Do We Now Collect Any Revenue from Taxing Capital Income?" *Journal of Public Economics* 88:981–1009.

Gordon, Roger H., Laura Kalambokidis, Jeffrey Rohaly, and Joel Slemrod. Forthcoming. "Toward a Consumption Tax and Beyond." *American Economic Review, Papers and Proceedings.*

Goulder, Lawrence H., John B. Shoven, and John Whalley. 1983. "Domestic Tax Policy and the Foreign Sector: The Importance of Alternative Foreign Sector Formulations to Results from a General Equilibrium Tax Analysis Model." In *Behavioral Simulation Methods in Tax Policy Analysis,* edited by Martin Feldstein (333–68). Chicago: University of Chicago Press.

Graetz, Michael J. 2005. "A Fair and Balanced Tax System for the Twenty-First Century." In *Toward Fundamental Tax Reform,* edited by Alan J. Auerbach and Kevin A. Hassett (48–69). Washington, DC: AEI Press.

Gravelle, Jane G. 1994. *The Economic Effects of Taxing Capital Income.* Cambridge, MA: MIT Press.

———. 1995. "The Flat Tax and Other Proposals: Who Will Bear the Tax Burden?" Congressional Research Service Report for Congress, no. 95-1141E. Washington, DC: U.S. Library of Congress.

———. 1996. "The Flat Tax and Other Proposals: Effects on Housing." Congressional Research Service Report for Congress, no. 96-379E. Washington, DC: U.S. Library of Congress.

———. 2002. "Behavioral Responses to a Consumption Tax." In *United States Tax Reform in the 21st Century*, edited by George R. Zodrow and Peter Mieszkowski (25–54). Cambridge, UK: Cambridge University Press.

Grubert, Harry, and John Mutti. 1985. "The Taxation of Capital Income in an Open Economy: The Importance of Resident-Nonresident Tax Treatment." *Journal of Public Economics* 27:291–309.

Hall, Robert E. 2005. "Guidelines for Tax Reform: The Simple, Progressive Value-Added Consumption Tax." In *Toward Fundamental Tax Reform,* edited by Alan J. Auerbach and Kevin A. Hassett (70–80). Washington, DC: AEI Press.

Hall, Robert E., and Alvin Rabushka. 1983. *Low Tax, Simple Tax, Flat Tax.* New York: McGraw-Hill.

———. 1995. *The Flat Tax.* Stanford: Hoover Institution Press.

Harberger, Arnold C. 1995. "The ABCs of Corporate Tax Incidence: Insights into the Open-Economy Case." In *Tax Policy and Economic Growth,* edited by American Council for Capital Formation (51–73). Washington, DC: ACCF Center for Policy Research.

Hubbard, R. Glenn. 2002. "Capital Income Taxation in Tax Reform: Implications for Analysis of Distribution and Efficiency." In *United States Tax Reform in the 21st Century,* edited by George R. Zodrow and Peter Mieszkowski (89–108). Cambridge, UK: Cambridge University Press.

———. 2005a. "Economic Effects of the 2003 Partial Integration Proposal in the United States." *International Tax and Public Finance* 12:97–108.

———. 2005b. "Would a Consumption Tax Favor the Rich?" In *Toward Fundamental Tax Reform,* edited by Alan J. Auerbach and Kevin A. Hassett (81–94). Washington, DC: AEI Press.

Hubbard, R. Glenn, and Kenneth L. Judd. 1986. "Liquidity Constraints, Fiscal Policy, and Consumption." *Brookings Papers on Economic Activity* 2001(1): 1–50.

Hurst, Erik, Annamaria Lusardi, Arthur Kennickell, and Francisco Torralba. 2005. "Precautionary Savings and the Importance of Business Owners." NBER Working Paper no. 11731. Cambridge, MA: National Bureau of Economic Research.

Institute for Fiscal Studies (Meade Commission). 1978. *The Structure and Reform of Direct Taxation.* London: George Allen & Unwin.

Jones, Larry E., Rodolfo E. Manuelli, and Peter E. Rossi. 1993. "Optimal Taxation in Models of Endogenous Growth." *Journal of Political Economy* 101:485–517.

Jorgenson, Dale W., and Peter J. Wilcoxen. 2002. "The Economic Impact of Fundamental Tax Reform." In *United States Tax Reform in the 21st Century,* edited by George R. Zodrow and Peter Mieszkowski (55–88). Cambridge, UK: Cambridge University Press.

Judd, Kenneth L. 1985. "Redistributive Income in a Simple Perfect Foresight Model." *Journal of Public Economics* 28:59–83.

———. 1997. "The Optimal Tax Rate for Capital Income is Negative." NBER Working Paper no. 6004. Cambridge, MA: National Bureau of Economic Research.

———. 1999. "Optimal Taxation and Spending in General Competitive Growth Models." *Journal of Public Economics* 71:1–26.

———. 2001. "The Impact of Tax Reform in Modern Dynamic Economies." In *Transition Costs of Fundamental Tax Reform,* edited by Kevin A. Hassett and R. Glenn Hubbard (5–53). Washington, DC: AEI Press.

Kaplow, Louis. 2004. "On the Undesirability of Commodity Taxation Even When Income Taxation Is Not Optimal." Discussion Paper No. 470. Cambridge, MA: John M. Olin Center for Law and Economics.

King, Mervyn A. 1980. "Savings and Taxation." In *Public Policy and the Tax System,* edited by G. A. Hughes and G. M. Heal (1–35). London: Allen and Unwin.

Kotlikoff, Laurence J. 1996. "Saving and Consumption Taxation: The Federal Retail Sales Tax Example." In *Frontiers of Tax Reform,* edited by Michael J. Boskin (160–80). Stanford: Hoover Institution Press.

———. 1998. "The A-K Model—Its Past, Present, and Future." NBER Working Paper no. 6684. Cambridge, MA: National Bureau of Economic Research.

Lawrence, Emily C. 1991. "Poverty and the Rate of Time Preference: Evidence from Panel Data." *Journal of Political Economy* 99(1): 54–77.

Lucas, Robert E. Jr. 1990. "Supply-Side Economics: An Analytical Review." *Oxford Economic Papers* 42:293–316.

Lyon, Andrew B., and Peter R. Merrill. 2001. "Asset Price Effects of Fundamental Tax Reform." In *Transition Costs of Fundamental Tax Reform,* edited by Kevin A. Hassett and R. Glenn Hubbard (58–91). Washington, DC: AEI Press.

McCaffery, Edward J. 2005. "A New Understanding of Tax." *Michigan Law Review* 103:807–938.

McLure, Charles E. Jr. 1987. *The Value-Added Tax: Key to Deficit Reduction?* Washington, DC: AEI Press.

McLure, Charles E. Jr., and George R. Zodrow. 1996. "A Hybrid Approach to the Direct Taxation of Consumption." In *Frontiers of Tax Reform,* edited by Michael J. Boskin (70–90). Stanford: Hoover Institution Press.

———. 1998. "The Economic Case for Foreign Tax Credits for Cash Flow Taxes." *National Tax Journal* 51(1):1–22.

McLure, Charles E. Jr., Jack Mutti, Victor Thuronyi, and George R. Zodrow. 1990. *The Taxation of Income from Business and Capital in Colombia.* Durham, NC: Duke University Press.

Mieszkowski, Peter, and Michael G. Palumbo. 2002. "Distributive Analysis of Fundamental Tax Reform." In *United States Tax Reform in the 21st Century,* edited by George R. Zodrow and Peter Mieszkowski (140–78). Cambridge, UK: Cambridge University Press.

Milesi-Ferretti, Gian M., and Nouriel Roubini. 1998. "On the Taxation of Human and Physical Capital in Models of Endogenous Growth." *Journal of Public Economics* 70:237–54.

Murray, Matthew N. 1997. "Would Tax Evasion and Tax Avoidance Undermine a National Retail Sales Tax?" *National Tax Journal* 50:167–82.

Naito, Hisahiro. 1999. "Re-Examination of Uniform Commodity Taxes under a Non-linear Income Tax System and Its Implication for Production Efficiency." *Journal of Public Economics* 71:165–88.

Nielsen, Soren Bo, and Peter Birch Sorensen. 1994. "On the Optimality of the Nordic System of Dual Income Taxation." *Journal of Public Economics* 63:311–29.

Pearlman, Ronald A. 1996. "Transition Issues in Moving to a Consumption Tax: A Tax Lawyer's Perspective." In *Economic Effects of Fundamental Tax Reform,* edited by Henry J. Aaron and William G. Gale (393–427). Washington, DC: Brookings Institution Press.

Piketty, Thomas, and Emmanuel Saez. 2003. "Income Inequality in the United States, 1913–1998." *Quarterly Journal of Economics* 118:1–39.

Prescott, Edward C. 2005. "The Elasticity of Labor Supply and the Consequences for Tax Policy." In *Toward Fundamental Tax Reform,* edited by Alan J. Auerbach and Kevin A. Hassett (123–34). Washington, DC: AEI Press.

Razin, Assaf, and Efraim Sadka. 1991. "International Tax Competition and Gains from Tax Harmonization." *Economics Letters* 37:69–76.

Roubini, Nouriel, and Gian Milesi-Ferretti. 1998. "On the Taxation of Human and Physical Capital in Models of Endogenous Growth." *Journal of Public Economics* 70:237–54.

Saez, Emmanuel. 2002. "The Desirability of Commodity Taxation under Nonlinear Income Taxation and Heterogeneous Tastes." *Journal of Public Economics* 83:217–30.

———. 2004. "Direct or Indirect Tax Instruments for Redistribution: Short-Run versus Long-Run." *Journal of Public Economics* 88:503–18.

Samwick, Andrew A. 1998. "Tax Reform and Target Saving." *National Tax Journal* 51:621–35.

Sarkar, Shounak, and George R. Zodrow. 1993. "Transitional Issues in Moving to a Direct Consumption Tax." *National Tax Journal* 46:359–76.

Seidman, Laurence S. 1983. "Taxes in a Life Cycle Growth Model with Bequests and Inheritances." *American Economic Review* 73:437–41.

Shakow, David J. 1986. "Taxation without Realization: A Proposal for Accrual Taxation." *University of Pennsylvania Law Review* 134:1111–1205.

Shaviro, Daniel. 2000. *When Rules Change: An Economic and Political Analysis of Transition Relief and Retroactivity.* Chicago: University of Chicago Press.

———. 2004. "Replacing the Income Tax with a Progressive Consumption Tax." *Tax Notes* 102 (April 5): 91–162.

Slemrod, Joel. 1996. "Which Is the Simplest Tax System of Them All?" In *Economic Effects of Fundamental Tax Reform,* edited by Henry J. Aaron and William G. Gale (355–84). Washington, DC: Brookings Institution Press.

———. 2005. "My Beautiful Tax Reform." In *Toward Fundamental Tax Reform,* edited by Alan J. Auerbach and Kevin A. Hassett (135–48). Washington, DC: AEI Press.

Sorensen, Peter Birch. 1994. "From a Global Income Tax to the Dual Income Tax: Recent Reforms in the Nordic Countries." *International Tax and Public Finance* 1:57–79.

Starrett, David A. 1988. "Effects of Taxes on Saving." In *Uneasy Compromise: Problems of a Hybrid Income-Consumption Tax,* edited by Henry J. Aaron, Harvey Galper, and Joseph Pechman (237–68). Washington, DC: Brookings Institution Press.

Steuerle, Eugene C. 2004. *Contemporary U.S. Tax Policy.* Washington, DC: Urban Institute Press.

Stiglitz, Joseph E. 1982. "Self-Selection and Pareto Efficient Taxation." *Journal of Public Economics* 17:213–40.

Stokey, Nancy L., and Sergio Rebelo. 1995. "Growth Effects of Flat-Rate Taxes." *Journal of Political Economy* 103:519–50.

Summers, Lawrence H. 1981. "Capital Taxation and Accumulation in a Life Cycle Growth Model." *American Economic Review* 74:533–44.

———. 1988. "Comment." In *Uneasy Compromise: Problems of a Hybrid Income-Consumption Tax,* edited by Henry J. Aaron, Harvey Galper, and Joseph A. Pechman (259–65). Washington, DC: Brookings Institution Press.

U.S. Department of the Treasury. 1977. *Blueprints for Basic Tax Reform.* Washington, DC: U.S. Government Printing Office.

———. 1992. *Integration of the Individual and Corporate Tax Systems: Taxing Business Income Once.* Washington, DC: U.S. Government Printing Office.

Varian, Hal. 1980. "Redistributive Taxation as Social Insurance." *Journal of Public Economics* 14:49–68.

Weidenbaum, Murray. 1996. "The Nunn-Domenici USA Tax: Analysis and Comparisons." In *Frontiers of Tax Reform,* edited by Michael J. Boskin (54–69). Stanford: Hoover Institution Press.

Weisbach, David A. 2000. "Ironing Out the Flat Tax." *Stanford Law Review* 52:599–664.

———. 2003. "Fundamental Tax Reform: Does the X-tax Mark the Spot?" *SMU Law Review* 56:201–38.

———. 2004. "The Non-Taxation of Risk." *New York University Tax Review* 58:1–57.

Weisbach, David A., and Joseph Bankman. 2005. "The Superiority of a Consumption Tax over an Income Tax." Unpublished manuscript, University of Chicago Law School and Stanford Law School.

Zodrow, George R. 1992. "Grandfather Rules and the Theory of Optimal Tax Reform." *Journal of Public Economics* 49:163–90.

———. 1997. "On the Transition to Indirect or Direct Consumption-Based Taxation." In *Tax Conversations: A Guide to the Key Issues in the Tax Reform Debate,* edited by Richard Krever (27–59). London: Kluwer Law International.

———. 2002. "Transitional Issues in the Implementation of a Flat Tax or a National Retail Sales Tax." In *United States Tax Reform in the 21st Century,* edited by George R. Zodrow and Peter Mieszkowski (245–83). Cambridge, UK: Cambridge University Press.

———. 2003. "Tax Competition and Tax Coordination in the European Union." *International Tax and Public Finance* 10:651–71.

———. 2006. "Capital Mobility and Source-Based Taxation of Capital Income in Small Open Economies." *International Tax and Public Finance* 13: 269–94.

Zodrow, George R., and Charles E. McLure Jr. 1991. "Implementing Direct Consumption Taxes in Developing Countries." *Tax Law Review* 46(Summer): 407–87.

Zodrow George R., and Peter Mieszkowski. 2002. "The Fundamental Question in Fundamental Tax Reform." In *United States Tax Reform in the 21st Century,* edited by George R. Zodrow and Peter Mieszkowski (1–24). Cambridge, UK: Cambridge University Press.

Alan J. Auerbach

George Zodrow has deftly presented the issues relating to the choice between income and consumption taxation and reviewed the pertinent evidence. In the end, he is somewhat agnostic about whether the United States should attempt the switch from income to consumption taxation. Although theory and evidence suggest that consumption taxation can provide a more efficient and simpler tax system, transition problems and concerns over how "pure" the resulting consumption tax might be undercut the attractiveness of the move.

I am very much in accord with Zodrow's conclusions. The nearly religious fervor that often surrounds the debate seems misplaced, given that consumption taxes and income taxes are not necessarily that different; the chapter's title foreshadows the point that some capital income is in the tax base even under a consumption tax. But the details matter; for example, eliminating capital income taxes does not equate to taxing consumption, despite frequent claims to the contrary. While we may draw general lessons based on theory and evidence, arguing strongly for or against a consumption-tax reform without knowing all the details makes little sense. How progressive will the consumption tax be? How will existing assets be treated in transition? How many exclusions from the tax base will be carried over from the current system? The evidence suggests that some consumption-tax reforms would be beneficial and others would be damaging, and that knowing in which category a reform falls may be impossible until well after the dust settles and the reform is implemented.

Zodrow's chapter has two main sections, the first laying out the relevant issues and the second discussing evidence from theory and simulation models. The first issue addressed is whether a consumption tax is likely to be more "pure" than an income tax, in the sense of being broad-based and uniform. The bar is set pretty low here, given how "impure" the income tax has become. Zodrow first argues that a consumption tax might be more successful in the purity dimension because it is intrinsically simpler; that is, some of the complexity of the income tax is not gratuitous, but results from the inherent difficulty of measuring capital income. As a consumption tax does not tax capital income explicitly, the need for such measurement is obviated. I agree with this point, but would also point out an alternative that would preserve the income tax and yet not require the explicit measurement of capital income. This alternative—generalized cash-flow taxation (Auerbach and Bradford 2004)—would tax cash flows as under a consumption tax but at time-varying rates that would replicate the incentives and burdens of an income tax.

As to Zodrow's other arguments on why a consumption tax might be purer, I am less convinced. I have little confidence that a tax rate of zero on all assets would represent a compelling equilibrium, or that the search for progressivity would force the elimination of tax expenditures that benefit the well-to-do. But some forms of consumption tax—those imposed as indirect taxes—might be less susceptible to erosion, at least by existing tax expenditures. How the exclusion of employer-provided fringe benefits could be preserved under a retail sales tax, for example, is hard to see. Thus, while some types of consumption tax might lead to a simpler tax system, those that look more like the current tax system— particularly the flat tax and its generalization, the X tax, seem to convey little advantage in this dimension.

The next issue Zodrow tackles is the degree to which capital income is taxed under a consumption tax. As many authors have observed, it is useful to distinguish three components of the returns to capital: the safe rate of return, the excess return to risk-taking, and a residual component, rent, that includes returns to factors not easily replicated (unique skills, a particular location, etc.) as well as profits resulting from noncompetitive behavior. A broad-based income tax that provides for a full recovery of losses hits all three components, whereas a consumption tax hits all but the first, even though it is not imposed explicitly on capital income. Given that the safe rate of return, as represented perhaps by the return on Treasury bills, is very low, this comparison suggests that the income and consumption bases do not differ much, which is both good news and bad news for consumption tax advocates. It reassures opponents who worry about giving capital income a free pass, but it also leads one to wonder what all the excitement is about. How can such a small reduction in the burden on capital income lead to the large economic gains some have predicted? My response is that the differences between income and consumption taxes are larger than this discussion suggests. First, the capital income tax burden under the current income tax, expressed as a fraction of the safe return, is probably very high once one takes into account the lack of full loss offset as well as other provisions Zodrow mentions. Second, from a distributional viewpoint, we should leave out the tax on risk-taking in computing the share of capital income a consumption tax frees from taxation, as this component does not represent a true burden on the taxpayer. Thus, a much larger share of the relevant return to capital is dropped from the tax base when we move to a consumption tax. Finally, the economic gains typically estimated to flow from moving to a consumption tax come from three main sources: reductions in tax progressivity, reductions in the tax on the return to saving, and a levy on assets in existence at the time of transition. Only the second source is at issue when one considers how much the burden on the return to capital has been reduced.

Zodrow next considers the issues that arise when thinking about the United States in the broader international economy. He points out that the case against capital income taxation grows with international capital flows under a source-based tax, but also that this case may be tempered for a large country like the United States, and that conclusions are different under a residence-based tax system. Even under a residence-based system, though, encouraging saving may have larger economic benefits because a world capital market can absorb the additional saving without any noticeable erosion in the available rate of return. Indeed, I found this in a comparison of closed-economy and open-economy simulations of a move to consumption taxation (Auerbach 1996). Another point to mention here is that the taxation of rents under both income and consumption tax systems may become less attractive under source-based taxation because international mobility is not limited to tangible capital.

Moving on to consider theory and evidence, Zodrow starts with the result that, when households make consumption decisions over an infinite time horizon, capital income taxes are not desirable in the long run. The logic is simple. Capital income taxes discourage future consumption relative to current consumption. Because capital income taxes are imposed annually, the tax wedge facing consumption in the distant future is enormous. A key lesson of optimal tax theory is that the economic loss from a tax distortion grows with the square of the size of the distortion itself, so a lot of small tax wedges are better than a few large ones. But to avoid a tax wedge on future consumption that gets larger as the date of that consumption extends further into the future, we must get rid of capital income taxes at some point in the future. Indeed, the same argument applies to labor income, to the extent that such income results from nondeductible human capital investment, such as education and training.

While the logic of this result is compelling, its implications for tax policy are unclear. First, it does not apply unless households save as if they will live forever. Second, it does not rule out potentially high capital income taxes over an indefinite transition period—this is how the government is supposed to get a lot of its revenue to compensate for the eventual elimination of capital and even labor income taxes. An announced plan to eliminate capital income taxes as of some future date will, in theory, encourage saving for the long term, but only if it is seen as credible; and why should it be? This problem, it should be noted, applies to a plan to eliminate capital income taxes, not to a switch from income taxes to consumption taxes. There is a similar potential credibility problem in the latter case, though, in that the consumption tax without transition relief effectively imposes a levy on existing assets. A fear that additional future levies might occur could discourage saving, even if the one-time levy does not. But I see the credibility problem as being less important here than in the case of a plan to lower capital income taxes because the capital levy is part of a larger tax reform—the levy occurs as we move from an income tax to a consumption tax, and that transition cannot occur again unless we raise consumption taxes still further and tax income at negative rates. Ironically, for the same reason—that the capital levy is simply part of a larger tax policy change—some researchers have argued that transition relief should be provided (e.g., Kaplow 1986).

Moving on to the results of simulation models based on the more realistic assumption of finite household planning horizons and more realistic characterizations of the tax system, Zodrow points to what (not surprisingly) I consider the main lessons of these studies. First, there are large potential economic gains from a move to consumption taxation. Second, much or even all of these gains evaporate when progressivity is maintained and transition relief is provided to owners of existing assets. Third, a consumption tax with sufficient marginal rate flexibility can maintain progressivity throughout most of the income distribution. As Altig et al. (2001) illustrate, the long-run gains are relatively uniform for individuals ranging all the way from the bottom 2 percent to the top 2 percent of the income distribution in simulations where the X tax replaces the income tax. What this does *not* say, though, is that progressivity is maintained even within the top 2 percent of the income distribution; it is almost certain that those at the *very* top benefit. How much this matters depends on one's conception of vertical equity, but we should keep in mind that those in the top 1 percent or even the top 0.1 percent of the population account for a much larger share of the economy's income and an even larger share of tax payments under the income tax.

To evaluate the plausibility of the simulation models' predictions, one has to consider how realistic the models' key assumptions are. In particular, how accurate is the assumption of a life-cycle savings process in which the household, rational and informed, determines a plan for spreading its lifetime resources over consumption at different dates, from the present to the distant future? Much recent research suggests that the determinants of saving are more complex. Most households save for retirement, but a significant minority does not. Participation in tax-sheltered saving vehicles, such as 401(k) plans, appears to be influenced by employer-provided education and other plan attributes. These examples suggest that households may not know their own preferences or may not have stable preferences over time and, as Zodrow suggests, should make us wary of adopting a tax reform the attractiveness of which depends so heavily on households responding individually to an increased tax incentive to save. If adoption of a consumption tax eliminates the tax advantage of employer-sponsored savings plans and leads to their disappearance, might households save less rather than more? I agree with Zodrow's call for caution, but a deeper problem arises in this context. If households do not know their preferences or have preferences that change over time, what should the government's objective be? It is no longer sufficient to view the government's objective as maximizing the well-being of individuals when this well-being does not have a clear measure.

Because the treatment of assets in transition is an important determinant of whether a consumption tax can deliver long-run economic benefits, Zodrow considers specifically whether it will be politically possible to limit transition relief. He points out that the additional saving a consumption tax induces should spur asset demand that, in pushing asset prices generally upward, should partially offset the capital levy. Indeed, the simulation studies he cites typically show relatively low net declines in asset values, taking both factors into account. Thus, Zodrow argues, little transition relief may be justified. I agree with this conclusion, of course, but am skeptical that this argument will lessen the pressure for transition relief because the loss of tax benefits is quite direct, whereas the offsetting increase in asset values is a result that will be more difficult to trace to the tax reform. Thus, as in the case of trying to keep tax expenditures out of the new tax base, one may find more attractive a version of the consumption tax that precludes the provision of transition relief, or at least makes such provision more unwieldy.

Where does all this analysis leave us? Zodrow suggests that a key objective, if we move toward consumption taxation, is to limit the scope of transition relief. I agree, but I also am skeptical that this can be accomplished unless the consumption tax is implemented as an indirect tax like a retail sales tax or a VAT, in which case, progressivity must be sacrificed. Zodrow also points out that consumption taxes can convey benefits beyond those identified through simulation models by eliminating the differential taxation of capital and making the tax system simpler. But a simpler and more rational tax system is also potentially available through reform of the income tax, so we are back to the question of whether the switch to a consumption tax promotes these objectives. Again, I am skeptical if the consumption tax we consider is one in which individual assets and taxpayers can be treated differently. Thus, I remain a consumption tax agnostic, recognizing its potential benefits but wondering whether such benefits really exist.

REFERENCES

Altig, David, Alan J. Auerbach, Laurence J. Kotlikoff, Kent A. Smetters, and Jan Walliser. 2001. "Simulating Fundamental Tax Reform in the United States." *American Economic Review* 91(3): 574–95.

Auerbach, Alan J. 1996. "Tax Reform, Capital Allocation, Efficiency and Growth." In *Economic Effects of Fundamental Tax Reform,* edited by Henry Aaron and William Gale (29–81). Washington, DC: Brookings Institution Press.

Auerbach, Alan J., and David Bradford. 2004. "Generalized Cash-Flow Taxation." *Journal of Public Economics* 88(5): 957–80.

Kaplow, Louis. 1986. "An Economic Analysis of Legal Transitions." *Harvard Law Review* 99(3): 509–617.

3

Should We Eliminate Taxation of Capital Income?

Eric Toder and Kim Rueben

Current law taxes capital income only partially and unevenly across economic sectors and taxpayer groups (see chapter 2). Competing tax reform models have sought either to broaden the tax base and comprehensively tax capital income or to eliminate all such taxes by replacing an income tax with a consumption tax that exempts income from capital. The introduction to this volume traces the increasing popularity of such recent tax reform models as the flat tax or the X tax—both of which would exempt capital income from taxation (Bradford 1986; Hall and Rabushka 1995).

The Tax Reform Act of 1986 broadened the base of capital income taxation while lowering tax rates but fell far short of a fully comprehensive income tax. Major sections of the original U.S. Treasury Department proposal (1984) that would have moved toward a system that taxed all capital income once were discarded or modified before final enactment, while other provisions designed to curtail tax sheltering were added.[1] Most tax experts believe that a truly comprehensive income tax is either impractical or politically unacceptable because it would require assessing tax annually on changes in the value of all assets, with an adjustment for inflation that includes changes in the values of shares in nontraded companies and in the value of outstanding debt.[2] It could be equally unlikely, however, to convert the tax system to a comprehensive consumption tax that is easy to comply with and administer, is not subject to manipulation, and maintains the current distribution of the tax burden. Partial steps toward a consumption base through expanding or adding new preferences for capital income taxation, while maintaining the deductibility of interest, could significantly erode the tax base while failing to accomplish any of the goals that a comprehensive consumption base could achieve.

Much of the debate over the attractiveness of moving to a consumption-based tax or increasing the preferences for capital income involves subjective tradeoffs among different goals of tax policy. Ideally, taxes would be collected in a way that would minimally distort economic activity. This would best be accomplished by having the broadest base of goods and services taxed at the lowest rates needed to raise the funds required to carry out the business of government. Practically, the tax code is often used for goals other than simply financing government services, including encouraging certain behavior (home ownership, retirement saving) and redistributing resources (through progressive tax rates and earned income tax credits). Discussions of changing tax policy must weigh the different values placed on simplifying the tax law and the achievement of these other policy goals. Different people place different weights on these goals. It is important to keep these normative judgments in mind when evaluating both the current system and any system that is likely to be implemented. In our view, total removal of taxation of capital income is unlikely to lead to a large enough improvement in efficiency gain or simplification to offset the decline in the progressivity of the tax system. This judgment reflects both a technical assessment of the terms of the tradeoff and a view that further erosion of a progressive tax system is undesirable in today's context of increasing pretax income inequality and the need for raising more revenue to meet the needs of an aging population.

Discussions of tax policy generally, and capital income taxation in particular, abound in semantic confusion. If we define capital income in the strict economic sense as the reward for postponed consumption, then the base of an income tax that excludes capital income is economically equivalent to the base of a consumption tax.[3] But what we actually classify on tax returns as returns to capital—interest, dividends, and profits of corporations and unincorporated businesses—includes much more than this reward for waiting. Eliminating taxation on these returns will not necessarily lead to a consumption tax. Further, developing a comprehensive consumption tax that exempts only the "normal" return to capital income may turn out to be as difficult as developing a comprehensive income tax has been. We use the term "normal returns" to represent the income earned from capital in its classical sense—the reward for deferring consumption.

While other chapters in this volume examine in more detail the question of how much we do or can tax capital income in the aggregate, it is important to highlight the fundamental differences in how the current U.S. income tax treats low-, middle-, and high-income taxpayers. Low-income taxpayers, especially those with children, are for the most part exempt from income taxation. In fact, many receive income tax rebates from the Treasury. A married couple with two children under the age of 17 did not owe income tax in 2005 until income exceeded $37,000 per year. In 2005, low-income families received $47.3 billion per year in earned income and child tax credits in excess of income taxes they paid (Office of Management and Budget 2005). Although taxpayers must have earned income to receive these refundable tax credits, eligibility for the credits phases out based on a measure that includes income from capital. Eligibility criteria for assistance under many spending programs also are based either on a measure that includes capital income or on a separate measure of assets (Steuerle 2005).

For the most part, middle-income families pay *negative* taxes on capital income—that is, the tax system raises net returns above their pretax levels. The reason for this is that most of their savings is in the form of qualified retirement accounts, and other tax-deferred accounts, on which their investment income is exempt, and owner-occupied housing, on which they need not report imputed rent, but may deduct mortgage interest. To the extent they pay any capital income tax, it is largely due to the impact of the corporate income tax on their returns from saving in tax-deferred accounts. Most taxable capital income flows to the very highest-income families, who pay the bulk of capital income taxes. In 2005, taxpayers with income over $200,000 (3.2 percent of all tax units) received about 25 percent of all income, but received 68 percent of income from capital gains, dividends, and interest and 71 percent of business income (table 3.1). Taxpayers with income over $1 million received 45 percent of all dividends, interest, and capital gains. So the debate about eliminating capital income taxation is largely a debate about whether capital income taxes should be eliminated for the highest-income families and, to a lesser extent, for corporations. Who would benefit from elimination of corporation income taxes depends, of course, on

Table 3.1. Distribution of Capital Income by Cash Income Class, 2005

Cash income class (thousands of 2005 $)[a]	Tax Units[b]		Adjusted Gross Income		Interest Income, Capital Gains, and Dividends		Business Income	
	Number (thousands)	% of total	Amount ($ millions)	% of total	Amount ($ millions)	% of total	Amount ($ millions)	% of total
Less than 10	19,560	13.5	55,716	0.9	3,887	0.6	5,266	0.8
10–20	25,611	17.7	228,534	3.5	12,495	1.8	16,587	2.5
20–30	19,953	13.8	351,595	5.5	13,871	2.0	14,878	2.3
30–40	15,289	10.6	403,764	6.3	12,575	1.8	12,239	1.9
40–50	11,738	8.1	413,926	6.4	15,646	2.2	13,106	2.0
50–75	20,700	14.3	1,033,153	16.0	40,575	5.8	32,950	5.0
75–100	11,936	8.3	853,738	13.3	32,702	4.7	36,799	5.6
100–200	14,432	10.0	1,555,116	24.1	86,310	12.4	102,216	15.6
200–500	3,797	2.6	793,922	12.3	100,424	14.4	151,428	23.1
500–1,000	642	0.4	284,304	4.4	59,456	8.5	94,025	14.4
More than 1,000	335	0.2	522,227	8.1	314,282	45.0	220,378	33.7
All	144,573	100.0	6,441,556	100.0	698,847	100.0	654,415	100.0

Source: Urban–Brookings Tax Policy Center Microsimulation Model (version 0305-3A).

Note: Data are for calendar year 2005.

a. Tax units with negative cash income are excluded from the lowest income class but are included in the totals. For a description of cash income, see http://www.taxpolicycenter.org/TaxModel/income.cfm.

b. Includes both filing and nonfiling units. Tax units that are dependents of other taxpayers are excluded from the analysis.

the incidence of the corporate income tax—an issue on which the economics profession still lacks consensus.

Consumption Taxes and Yield-Exempt Income Taxes

In economic terms, capital income is the return to postponing consumption. By deferring consumption today and instead investing in productive assets, society can increase output and potential consumption tomorrow.[4]

Equivalence between a Consumption Tax and a Yield-Exempt Income Tax

A consumption tax is simply an income tax that exempts net saving from the tax base, or a yield-exempt income tax. All income accrued must be either spent or saved. If a person receives $200,000 in wages, interest, dividends, capital gains, and business profits (net of costs), then the entire $200,000 would be included in a comprehensive income base. If that person saved $40,000 of that income—through bank deposits, financial assets, or investment in a business—then his or her consumption tax base would be $160,000. If, instead of saving, the person withdrew $40,000 of assets for consumption (for example, by selling shares or withdrawing money from a bank account), he or she would pay tax on $240,000 of consumption.

Income ultimately is the source of all consumption. The key difference between the two tax bases is that under an income base all income is taxed in the year it accrues, while under a consumption base, tax is deferred until the income is consumed. In practice, this means that the $40,000 that is saved would be taxed under an income tax system because it is treated as simply a transfer of wealth from one form (cash) to another (a financial or real asset). Future returns from the wealth are also taxed, but withdrawals of the (previously taxed) principal are tax-free. Under a consumption tax, the entire asset purchase is deductible, but future net withdrawals from both income on the asset and returns of principal are subject to tax, the latter because the principal had not been taxed previously.

Under all consumption taxes, the purchase of an asset or saving is immediately deductible. Consumption taxes, however, can be implemented in a variety of ways (see figure 3.1).

Figure 3.1. Ways of Implementing a Consumption Tax

All consumption taxes exempt net saving, but consumption taxes can be collected in different ways.

- A retail sales tax is imposed on sales of goods and services by businesses to final consumers. Sales of capital goods to business should be excluded from the tax base.
- A subtraction-method value-added tax (VAT) is imposed on gross receipts of all businesses, less deductions for the cost of purchases of intermediate goods, including capital assets, from other businesses. Thus, a VAT is simply a retail sales tax collected at each stage of production instead of solely on final sales to consumers. An alternative form of VAT, widely used in Europe and elsewhere, is a credit-invoice VAT. Under a credit-invoice VAT, businesses pay tax on their gross sales, but claim a credit for taxes paid by businesses that sell goods and services (including capital goods) to them. The retail sales tax and the VAT share the property that all tax liability is imposed on businesses (although for this purpose, self-employed individuals would be treated as a business).
- The Hall-Rabushka (HR) tax is a special form of subtraction-method value-added tax that allows businesses to deduct both wages and intermediate purchases (again including capital goods) in computing taxable net receipts. The tax on the portion of value added that represents labor services is imposed on individual wage earners instead of businesses. Imposing a portion of the tax on wage earners makes it possible to make the tax system progressive either by exempting a portion of wages (as in the Hall-Rabushka flat tax proposal) or taxing wages on a graduated rate schedule (as in the X tax).
- Finally, it is possible to collect a consumption tax wholly from individuals by modifying the current income tax to allow an unlimited deduction for all saving and to tax all net borrowing, net asset sales, and net withdrawals from savings accounts. The Unlimited Savings Account (USA) tax plan introduced by Senators Nunn and Domenici in 1995 was a tax of this form.

The choice of how to collect a consumption tax has huge implications for costs of administration and compliance, evasion possibilities, and the ability to implement a progressive tax. Two points are worth noting. First, making a consumption tax progressive and enabling it to take account of family circumstances requires imposing some or all of the tax on individuals, as in the HR tax or the USA tax. Second, consumption taxes can either include or exclude purely financial transactions. A tax base that excludes "financial transactions," such as a VAT or HR tax, is referred to as an R base; "real returns" to businesses are in the base and taxed at the enterprise level, but financial returns resulting from businesses activities, including interest received and paid, dividends, and capital gains from sales of financial assets, are outside the tax base. In contrast, an individual-based consumption tax, such as the USA tax, is referred to as an R plus F base because it includes all asset transactions, whether from real or financial assets.[a]

---

a. The exclusion of financial transactions under an R-base tax can create anomalies and opportunities for evasion because the distinction between real and financial transactions is often murky (see chapter 4; Weisbach 2000).

If income from capital is *by definition* the reward for postponed consumption, a flat rate tax on consumption (income less net saving) can be shown to be equivalent to a flat rate tax on wages, provided that we ignore any potential tax on capital that exists at the time the taxes are introduced. Suppose an individual earns $100 in annual wages, which is used to purchase a bond with an annual interest rate of 10 percent. After a year, the amount in the account is $110. If the $110 is withdrawn for consumption in the second year and the tax rate is 20 percent, the net after tax available for consumption will be $88—80 percent of $110. Under a wage tax with the same rate, tax will be due in the year the wages are earned. Only $80 dollars will be available to invest. With no tax on interest income, the amount available for consumption after one year will be $88, exactly the same as under the consumption tax. In contrast, if income from capital is also subject to a 20 percent tax rate, the after-tax interest rate is reduced to 8 percent and the amount available for consumption in the second year is only $86.40—the original $80 invested plus $6.40 in after-tax interest.

Consumption Taxes and Above-Normal Returns

In this simple example, with capital income representing the reward for deferring consumption, a consumption tax is exactly the same as an income tax that exempts the return to saving. But individuals who invest in productive assets or financial claims to assets receive more than just the time value of money as a return (what we are calling the normal rate of return). Business profits, or dividends and capital gains received by individuals, include rewards for risk-bearing and entrepreneurial efforts. They also include economic rents and returns from inherited wealth.

The treatment of entrepreneurial income is especially relevant. The classic example is someone whose skill, enterprise, or brilliant new idea gives birth to a highly profitable enterprise. Successful entrepreneurs create wealth valued at many multiples of their financial investments. Their increase in wealth is really, in large part, income from labor services, but because it is capitalized into the value of the business, it is not taxable under current law unless the shares are sold during the owner's lifetime. Even if tax on the gain is ultimately paid, the real value of the tax is reduced by deferral and the income is assessed at preferential capital gains rates. The entrepreneur's annual profit from the business largely represents a deferred recognition of income from labor services that previously went untaxed.[5]

The question of how a consumption tax treats entrepreneurial returns and other excess returns can be analyzed in different ways (Toder 1997). Under a flat rate consumption tax implemented as a wage tax, the pre-tax return to investment is the same as the after-tax return. So if investors get a 25 percent rate of return pretax on saving, they will also get 25 percent under a consumption tax.[6] But the present value of tax payments, discounted at a risk-free rate, will be positive whenever the discount rate is lower than the return on the investment.

The key point is that, under a consumption tax, the government becomes a partner in the investment. It puts up a share of the capital but captures a share of the returns. Under an income tax, in contrast, the government captures a share of the returns, net of depreciation, but does not contribute to the investment.[7] If higher than normal returns are associated with scarce investment opportunities, monopoly rents, or a good idea that cannot be replicated, then government under a consumption tax can be an *unwanted* partner in the business. For every dollar of equity investors want to put in the high-return activity, they can only invest a fraction equal to $1 - t$ dollars and must settle for normal returns on the other t dollars they were previously going to invest.[8] To the extent that observed investment returns represent economic rents or returns to entrepreneurial activities (see figure 3.2), a consumption tax differs substantially from a yield-exempt income tax.

What Does Reported Capital Income Represent?

Income tax returns do not reveal what share of reported capital income represents normal returns to capital, but bits and pieces of evidence come

Figure 3.2. Example: Taxing Entrepreneurial Income

An entrepreneur (E) gets an idea on marketing a product of a large manufacturer to previously untapped groups. E starts a company and approaches the product's manufacturer (M) with an offer—"guarantee me exclusive marketing rights to these new market segments and give me a fixed percentage of all sales if I can develop the markets." M agrees, because E bears all the risk and M knows that if the new markets materialize, the deal will be profitable after paying E's fee.

E's marketing idea proves wildly successful. The fee generates revenue far in excess of marketing costs. E spends $1 million in upfront costs, including forgone earnings, payments to his employees, and investment in office equipment, to develop the new markets. As CEO, E takes a salary, but the remainder of the revenue, net of labor and other operating costs, comes to $50 million per year, which E spends on lavish homes, expensive cars and boats, and foreign travel. At a 5 percent discount rate, this stream of profits is worth $1 billion. At the end of 20 years, E decides to retire and sells the business for $1 billion.

Under a pure accrual income tax, E would pay tax on $999 million of accrued capital gain in the year the business starts generating revenue and establish a basis of $1 billion ($999 million of gain plus $1 million of capitalized outlays). E would then pay tax annually on the $50 million of net profit and would pay no tax on the final sale, which would yield a profit of zero. Under a pure consumption tax, E would deduct the $1 million upfront costs and would pay tax on the portion of annual receipt—the $50 million of annual profits and the $1 billion sales proceeds at the end—that is consumed instead of reinvested.

The difference between the income and consumption tax models is in the timing of the tax on the $999 million net gain from setting up the business. An income tax would include in the base $999 million of net gain in the first year, while a consumption tax would allow a deduction of $1 million of costs in the first year and then assess tax on whatever part of the $50 million in annual profits is consumed and on the $1 billion of sales proceeds 20 years later, providing those proceeds are not reinvested.

Under the current income tax, E would be able to deduct the portion of the $1 million start-up costs that represents payments to employees, but would have to capitalize the portion that represents buildings and equipment and recover those costs over time through depreciation. The $999 million of accrued capital gains would initially be exempt and the $50 million of annual profits would be taxable, just as under the consumption tax.[a] The $999 million of capital gain might be taxed at a reduced rate when E leaves the business, unless E could figure out a way to defer a taxable realization event until death, at which point E's heirs would inherit a basis of $1 billion in the business and no tax would be paid ever on the initial capital gain.

In contrast, under a tax on wages that exempts investment returns, E would pay tax only on salary from the business. The $999 million of gain would escape tax entirely, as would the $50 million of profit. In this example, current-law taxation of entrepreneurial income is much closer to a consumption tax base than to a comprehensive income tax because of the deferral of tax on the initial gain; it may also be more favorable than a consumption base if the entrepreneur can escape tax on the gain because of the step-up in basis at death. A yield-exempt income tax, in contrast, would impose much less tax on E than either a consumption tax or the current income tax. (Note that in this example, we are omitting discussion of estate and gift taxes because an estate tax could supplement either an income tax or a consumption tax.)

a. The profits would generate two levels of tax if the business were organized as a C corporation and E paid himself dividends, but would only be taxed once if organized as an LLC, a partnership, a sole proprietorship, or an S corporation.

from other sources. "Entrepreneurial households"—defined as households that own one or more active businesses with a total market value of at least $5,000—own a substantial share of household wealth and income, especially among those with high wealth (Hubbard and Gentry 2000). Entrepreneurial households also hold highly undiversified portfolios— that is, they are heavily invested in their own enterprises. While this cross-section evidence does not explain how the wealth was acquired (someone who saved to accumulate wealth or inherited money may have started a business later in life), it does suggest that a significant share of wealth may reflect past entrepreneurial profits rather than normal returns to saving.

Combining successive years of the Federal Reserve Board's Survey of Consumer Finances (SCF) with estimates of savings rate by age from the Consumer Expenditure Survey, Ed Wolff (1999) calculates that capital gains account for 75 percent of the growth in wealth for different age cohorts in both the 1962 and 1983 SCF surveys and 76 percent for cohorts in both the 1983 and 1992 surveys (Wolff 1999). While normal returns could come in the form of capital gains (to the extent they reflect retained corporate profits), this finding also suggests that unusually successful investments may largely generate the current wealth distribution.[9]

As an alternative way of addressing this question, we calculate the effects of switching from current law taxation of corporate income to taxation of corporate income under an R-base tax system by slightly modifying the calculations by Gordon, Kalambokidis, and colleagues (2004).[10] We find the percentage reduction in the tax base from the switch from depreciation and inventory capitalization to expensing by itself and interpret the change in capital recovery rules as eliminating tax on the share of all business returns (from both debt and equity) attributable to normal returns to capital. For the corporate sector, the new tax base would be equal to 68 percent of current taxable income arising in the corporate sector (including interest received by lenders to the corporate sector). So if moving to expensing can be interpreted as eliminating the tax on normal returns to capital, this implies that normal returns are roughly 32 percent of all corporate returns.

These data are suggestive of the income sources that generate wealth, but not the shares of wealth that people accumulate on their own instead of receiving as inheritances or gifts. A number of studies have estimated the share of wealth attributable to inheritances or gifts with widely divergent results, but some recent studies estimate that half to two-thirds of wealth comes from these sources.[11]

This research suggests that normal returns to saving may account for a relatively small fraction of what we measure as capital income. What comes out as measured capital income includes both a deferred recognition of disguised labor compensation plus some combination of rewards to risky investments and returns to inheritance. A tax based on wages alone, arrived at by exempting individual capital income under the current income tax and allowing the corporate tax base to erode, would fail to capture these returns.

Comparing Ideal Income and Consumption Taxes

Eliminating existing taxes on returns to assets would not necessarily lead to a consumption tax. But if either an ideal income tax or an ideal consumption tax could be implemented, which would be preferable? In other words, should normal returns to saving be excluded from the tax base? Whether consumption or income is the better tax base is one of the oldest issues in public finance.

Equal Treatment of Equals

One threshold question of fairness is whether the tax law treats people in the same circumstances equally. Whether both capital income and wages should be taxed may seem clear to those who believe that the tax system should treat people in equal circumstances even-handedly. Unfortunately, two different views exist.

One view holds that capital income should be taxed because otherwise the tax system would favor wealth holders over wage earners. Consider two taxpayers, K and L. K receives $50,000 per year of interest based on U.S. government bonds inherited from a relative. L is a schoolteacher and earns $50,000 per year. Taxing K's return from capital less than L's earnings from labor would seem to be unfair.

A different view is that capital income should not be taxed because doing so penalizes K's forebears, who at some point in the past earned and saved to accumulate the wealth on which K's capital income is based and paid tax on those earnings. Alternatively, K's wealth may have accrued from K's own past saving. Suppose, for example, that K and L are both schoolteachers earning $50,000 per year for 10 years and paying a 20 percent tax on their earnings, leaving them with $40,000 after tax. L spent

$40,000 each year on consumption, while K lived on just $30,000 and saved the remainder in U.S. government bonds at a 5 percent interest rate. Without any tax, K could have accumulated savings of $125,779 after 10 years. But if interest income is taxed at 20 percent per year, K's wealth would be reduced to $120,061.

This year, the tax on L's salary will be $10,000. But K will pay not only a $10,000 tax on current salary but another $1,200 on interest income. Further, K's interest income would have been $286 higher but for interest income tax paid in earlier years. So K's total tax burden is really $11,486. Why should K pay more tax than L when both had the same opportunities?

These examples illustrate two perspectives on the fairness of taxing capital income. The first is a question of whether the wealth was accrued out of previously taxed or untaxed income. This is primarily a question of whether a consumption tax is implemented by taxing current consumption or by taxing wages, while exempting returns to capital; if the latter, as indicated in the previous chapter, the tax might exempt returns from assets acquired with income that was never taxed. If the tax was imposed annually on current consumption, both K's interest and L's wages would be taxable, but only to the extent they were spent.

The second difference in perspective relates to determining the appropriate time frame to use in measuring the ability to pay tax. If annual accruals are the right measure of ability to pay, capital income should be in the base. But, using a longer time perspective, the second example shows how a tax on capital income can discriminate against the person who chooses to save for consumption later in life. More generally, if people leave no bequests, then the value of their lifetime resources (including inheritances, windfalls, and the present value of labor earnings) must equal the present value of their lifetime consumption (Bradford and U.S. Treasury Tax Policy Staff 1984; U.S. Department of the Treasury 1977). A flat rate consumption tax would impose the same tax on everyone with the same lifetime endowment, without regard to the timing of consumption or labor earnings. In contrast, for two people with the same endowment, an income tax that includes normal returns to capital in the base would impose a higher tax on the person who consumes later in life (saves more) and on the person whose earnings come earlier in life (and who therefore must save more than someone with a more back-loaded pattern of earnings to finance the same pattern of consumption).

The lifetime equity argument provides powerful reasons for supporting consumption taxes but also has its limitations. In the absence of perfect capital markets, people cannot always borrow and lend money at a risk-free rate so that current income as well as the present value of lifetime earnings can affect ability to pay. Congress cannot commit future Congresses to a stable tax policy. In cases where taxes must be raised temporarily (as in World War II), some argue that current income recipients (who may spend either today or in the future) should bear the burden instead of current spenders only (Graetz 1997). A model of "equal treatment of equals" based on a stable tax policy and the assumption that tax units are stable over a lifetime may not translate well to a world in which tax rates vary over time and tax units change as individuals marry, divorce, and die.

Most people do not share the lifetime perspective of economists and, as a result, the fairness of a tax system that exempts capital income may not be apparent to them. It is hard to justify, for example, imposing high tax rates as a share of income on young people who are borrowing to make ends meet simply because they can expect to earn higher income in the future. It is difficult to rationalize high tax rates on the income of those with temporarily low incomes from unemployment or business reverses, who must borrow to maintain living standards.

Progressivity

A corollary to the principle that people with equal ability should pay the same tax is that people who have more ability to pay should pay more tax. General tax principles do not say *how much* additional tax should be imposed on people with more ability to pay. We share the widespread view that the tax system should be progressive. In the current environment of increasing income inequality, tax reforms should not make the system markedly less progressive.[12] Not everyone will agree.

With the same rate structure, an income tax is more progressive than a consumption tax because the ratio of consumption to income declines with income. A consumption tax could be made as progressive as an income tax by changing the rate structure, but maintaining the current distribution of taxes by income or consumption class would require much higher marginal rates at the top consumption levels than the top marginal rates now applied to income. Further, implementing a progressive consumption tax would require collecting at least part of the tax from individuals. The feasibility of implementing a progressive consumption tax and the rate structure necessary to sustain current progressivity is examined below.

Consumption Taxes, Income Taxes, and Economic Efficiency

Taxes in general reduce economic efficiency because they impose a wedge between the price that buyers pay for goods and services (including services of labor and capital in production) and the price that sellers receive. This wedge prevents some transactions that would have been mutually advantageous to buyers and sellers in the absence of tax. Assuming that people act in their own best interests and that prices of goods sold in the marketplace reflect their additional value to society, taxes that distort economic choices may result in fewer products or cause a less valuable set of products to be made.

Imposing an equal tax on everyone (a head tax) will not distort economic choices because tax liability would not be affected by economic behavior. But head taxes impose a high burden on those with little ability to pay. Taxing all economic activities at the same rate would also not distort behavior, but it is only feasible to tax observed market transactions. In practice, the returns to time spent in leisure and home production cannot be taxed.

A wage or consumption tax is equivalent to a uniform tax on all goods purchased in the marketplace, with nonmarket production (leisure and home production) not subject to tax (see figure 3.3). Under certain assumptions, tax rates on all goods should be equal to minimize the economic cost of changes in behavior (Atkinson and Stiglitz 1976). Future consumption is one good that consumers purchase by forgoing consumption today. Therefore, uniform commodity taxation requires taxing consumption today at the same rate as consumption in future periods or, equivalently, not taxing capital income. If there is no initial endowment of wealth (no inheritances), capital markets are perfect, all income from capital represents the return from deferring consumption, the decision on what goods to purchase is separate from the decision of how much to work, and people have identical preferences, a consumption or wage tax will improve efficiency relative to an income tax or, in other words, the optimal tax rate on capital income is zero.

If decisions on labor supply and choices among consumption goods are not independent, a zero tax rate on capital income—that is, a consumption tax—is not always better than a tax that imposes a positive tax rate on capital income. In general, taxing at higher rates goods that are complements to the untaxed good (nonmarket production) can reduce the distortion against nonmarket production in the tax system.[13] If the

Figure 3.3. Distortions from Income and Consumption Taxes

Assume people choose among three activities: current consumption, future consumption, and current leisure. They need to work (sacrifice leisure) to earn the income to purchase current and future consumption goods and, in addition, may spend less than their income from working to purchase future consumption goods.

A consumption tax is neutral between current and future consumption because both goods are taxed at the same rate. But a consumption tax distorts the choices between leisure and current consumption and between leisure and future consumption because leisure is untaxed. An income tax distorts the choice between leisure and current and future consumption and also distorts the choice between current and future consumption by reducing the rate of return to saving. For example, suppose people save $100 this year and the pretax interest rate is 10 percent. By sacrificing $100 of consumption today, they can buy $110 worth of consumption goods next year. But if a tax at 25 percent is imposed on capital income, their rate of return is reduced to 7.5 percent and the same amount of saving only buys $107.50 worth of future consumption goods. An income tax makes future consumption relatively more expensive in terms of current consumption and thereby distorts the incentive to save.

An income tax can raise the same revenue at a lower rate than a consumption tax because the base of the tax is broader. So an income tax imposes a smaller distortion between leisure and current consumption. But it imposes a larger distortion between leisure and future consumption because of the inclusion of capital income in the tax base. In general, therefore, it cannot be said that an income tax distorts the incentives to work (sacrifice leisure) by less than a consumption tax.

Assuming that people's decision on how much to work is independent of their decision of how much of their income to save for future consumption (technically, the utility function is separable in leisure and consumption), then it can be shown that a consumption tax is unambiguously less distorting than an income tax. But an income tax might be less distorting than a consumption tax if leisure and future consumption are complements (working less raises the value of an additional dollar of future consumption), so that taxing future consumption is an indirect way of taxing the untaxed activity, leisure. Alternatively, if leisure and current consumption are complements, the optimal tax rate on capital income could be negative. So we cannot assert with certainty that a consumption tax is less distorting than an income tax, but in the absence of clear evidence on how capital income taxes might affect the labor leisure choice, many economists would take as a starting point that the tax rate on normal returns to capital should be zero.

reverse is true, however, or other circumstances apply, the optimal tax rate on capital income could be negative.[14]

Positive tax rates on capital income may be better than a zero rate for other reasons as well. A desire to redistribute income is one such reason. If individuals differ in their initial wealth and there is interest in reducing income inequality, social welfare can sometimes be improved by adopting a positive tax on capital income (Cremer, Pestieau, and Rochet 2001). If high-income earners have a higher taste for saving, a positive tax on capital income may be desirable under an income tax (Saez 2002).

Do high-income or high-ability individuals have higher tastes for saving? Is the value of wealth exactly equal to the future consumption it finances or does it have value in itself? Standard economic models do not do a good job of explaining the saving behavior of the very wealthy (Carroll 2000). It is not the case that high-income households save in their high-earning years just to consume in retirement or leave a bequest. Consumption by the wealthy does not increase enough in later periods to decrease wealth stocks, and the spending and saving patterns of these individuals also are not consistent with such other motivations for saving as maintaining precautionary balances or leaving a bequest. For the very wealthy, asset accumulation seems to have some benefit or utility beyond the consumption stream purchased by these goods—that is, from the accumulation of wealth in itself. If this hypothesis is true, then a tax on either wealth or capital income of high-income people can be a relatively efficient way to redistribute resources.

In summary, there is a general presumption that capital income should not be taxed if it all comes from deferred consumption—that is, there are no inheritances—and if wealth in itself provides no utility apart from financing future consumption. However, these conditions do not hold in the real world. The efficiency argument for not taxing capital income is therefore not necessarily conclusive. We must look more closely at how a tax system that exempts all income from capital would be implemented and how it would affect saving when compared with our current tax system, which is also not a pure income tax.

Implementing a Progressive Consumption Tax

Two prototypes of progressive consumption taxes have been proposed—a cash flow consumption tax collected only from individuals, and the X tax, which is collected from individuals on wages and from businesses on gross receipts less wages and purchases from other businesses.

Cash Flow Individual Consumption Taxes

One approach for developing a progressive consumption tax is to transform the current income tax system into a cash flow tax on individuals' consumption by allowing an unlimited deduction for all net deposits to qualified savings accounts and by requiring all loan proceeds to be included in the tax base. Graduated rates could be applied to individuals' cash flow consumption. Corporate profits could be taxed either under an R-base system or a cash flow R-plus-F base with or without expensing (see figure 3.1 for an explanation of these systems and of the differences between an R-base and an R-plus–F-base system) or not at all, if not paid out. No country has a tax system of this type. The U.S. Treasury proposed a graduated expenditure tax in 1942 as a war finance measure, but Congress rejected it summarily (Graetz 1997).

More recently, there have been two models advanced of a cash flow consumption tax. In January 1977, the Treasury Department described a model cash flow consumption tax for individuals, combined with elimination of the corporate income tax.[15] Senators Sam Nunn and Pete Domenici proposed the USA (for Unlimited Savings Account) tax in 1994. No administration ever advanced the Treasury Department model as a legislative proposal. The Nunn-Domenici proposal attracted little support in Congress.

A cash flow tax would most closely approximate a tax on annual consumption, but would add complexity by requiring taxpayers to keep track of all net saving and spending of savings on current expenses.[16] In particular, measuring whether deposits to savings accounts represented net saving or a transfer of old wealth would require a comprehensive wealth accounting when the system is introduced. In addition, politically necessary compromises, such as maintaining preferences for mortgage interest and municipal securities, and provisions to relieve individuals of double taxation on consumption from previously taxed wealth could open the system to significant tax avoidance.[17]

The Hall-Rabushka Flat Tax or X Tax

An alternative to the cash flow tax is an R-base business tax with wages taxed at the individual level, modeled on the Hall-Rabushka (1995) flat tax proposal (HR tax). This system combines a subtraction-method value-added tax with a deduction for wages and a personal tax on wages. Capital is expensed at the business level, so the tax base is consumption, not income.[18] Businesses may not deduct interest expense; individuals do not pay tax on interest, dividends, and capital gains. The HR tax applies a single rate to the business and individual tax bases but allows generous taxpayer and dependent exemptions to introduce a degree of progressivity in the wage tax on individuals.[19] The X tax is a variant of the HR tax with graduated rates for individuals (Bradford 1986).

While the HR tax proposes a broad tax base by disallowing individual deductions (including deductions for mortgage interest, charitable deductions, and state and local income taxes) and taxing employer-provided health insurance and other fringe benefits (by denying deductibility for fringe benefits from the business tax), most of these preferences could be retained within the HR framework. Retaining the mortgage interest deduction is possible but problematical because it allows individuals to engage in pure arbitrage by deducting interest on loans used to purchase tax-free interest-bearing assets. An earned income tax credit and other credits, either refundable or not, could also be retained within the HR framework.

The HR tax is much less complex than a personal cash flow consumption tax and also simpler than the current income tax. But part of this simplicity comes from the elimination of tax preferences that are unrelated to the switch from income to consumption taxation and that Congress may wish to retain. The HR tax would eliminate a number of administrative problems in the income tax associated with taxing capital income (Weisbach 2000), including all rules that relate to timing of income recognition and measurement of changes in net worth. But there are also significant administrative issues not present in the current tax that an HR-type tax would need to resolve. Among the serious problems are those that arise from inconsistencies between the treatment of real and financial transactions, ability to manipulate results through arrangements with taxpayers outside the system, and inconsistencies the new business tax would introduce between the U.S. and other countries' corporate tax rules.[20]

An interesting question is whether the HR tax is a yield-exempt tax base or a consumption tax that includes above-normal returns in the base. On the surface, the individual tax base appears as a yield-exempt system because it does not tax capital gains, dividends, or interest income, while allowing no deductions for asset purchases. In a closed economy (with no international capital flows), however, the effect of expensing and full inclusion of business income would be to reduce the purchase price of business assets to households, including the price of corporate shares, and to reduce after-tax income of households from business profits. In theory, the net effect would be the same as for a cash flow consumption tax that allowed deductibility of saving and taxed all returns from real and financial assets. The exception is for debt, which would be taxed in effect by a yield-exempt method. Because the tax rate on capital income is zero, interest rates and bond prices would be unaffected by the tax, relative to a no-tax world, so that interest would be taxed on a yield-exempt basis.

But a closer look suggests that an HR tax may in fact also operate to some degree as a yield-exempt tax for some equity investments. First, returns from foreign assets held directly by U.S. individuals would be wholly exempt from any U.S. tax under the HR plan. Second, because the proposed HR business-level tax, unlike European value-added taxes, is an origin-based tax with no tax on foreign source income, incentives to avoid tax by manipulating transfer prices would be substantial (Bradford 2005; Weisbach 2000). Corporations, for example, would have an incentive to shift income to overseas subsidiaries by understating the sales prices of intangible assets to them. The yield-exemption method of individual taxation places a substantial burden on enforcement of a business-level tax base that is subject to many opportunities for manipulation, if there is to be any taxation of investment returns at all, because there is no tax on distributions or capital gains from asset sales.

This foregoing description also assumes no transition rules: existing business assets would have a tax basis of zero and no further depreciation would be allowed. Retaining basis and capital recovery for old assets would make the HR tax base a yield-exempt tax for owners of claims to income from those assets. Further, even without transition rules, an origin-based tax of this variety exempts old wealth held by U.S. residents in the form of foreign assets (Grubert and Newlon 1995). As we discuss later, in practice, implementing these changes with no transition relief is probably politically infeasible. With the introduction of transition rules, costs of changing systems increase and much of the expected efficiency gain is lost.

If the United States were to implement a progressive tax on a base that excludes capital income, the most likely method would be a variant of this HR tax approach. The mechanics of how such a tax base would work, especially with regard to transition rules and with how changes in the corporate tax would be coordinated with other countries' tax rules, needs much further development. Following are some illustrative simulations of the distributional effects of moving to this tax base for capital income, both with and without changes in the rate structure that would be needed to maintain revenue neutrality. We then consider rates that would be necessary to maintain approximately the same current distribution of the tax burden as under current law.

Distributional Effects of Adopting an HR Tax Base

We simulate the effects of eliminating capital income taxation by replacing the current individual and corporate income taxes with an HR base tax, while maintaining all preferences in current law other than interest deductions. The simulations assume that there is no transition relief under the business tax, that the tax can be enforced as well as the current income tax, and that individuals cannot escape capital income taxation by shifting funds overseas any more than under the current system (however, see Bankman and Schler, chapter 6, as to the potential for increased opportunity for escaping taxation). The simulations also assume that the burdens of both the current and revised corporate income tax are borne by all recipients of income from capital, including recipients of income from tax-free retirement saving plans. The purpose is to illustrate the effects of replacing the current tax base with one that exempts income from capital.

The simulations, based on the Urban–Brookings Tax Policy Center (TPC) microsimulation model of the federal individual tax system, assume the elimination of all taxes on interest, dividend, and capital gains income and of deductions for mortgage interest, investment interest, and student loan interest. Current provisions remain for contributions to tax-deferred savings accounts on the grounds that deductible IRA provisions provide the same present value of tax benefits as eliminating taxation of capital gains, interest, and dividends from IRA investments, assuming the individual remains in the same tax bracket. We also maintain the current income tax bracket structure and all tax preferences not related to capital income taxation (such as the deductibility of state and local taxes and charitable contributions). The simulations also examine models in which the mortgage interest deduction is retained.

For corporations, the corporate tax base would be replaced with an R base, with no transition rules for old assets.[21] Note that the distributions presented are from a static model and assume no behavioral response. That is, individuals are assumed not to change their investment and savings decisions once these returns are no longer taxed.

The benefits of eliminating taxation of capital income accrue overwhelmingly to the highest-income taxpayers. As shown in table 3.2, taxpayers with income over $1 million receive 82.5 percent of the benefits and see their average federal tax burden drop by 20 percent. Taxes would increase for taxpayers with income between $75,000 and $200,000, largely because the loss of the mortgage interest deduction would outweigh benefits to them from lower taxes on interest, dividends, and capital gains and from the reduced burden of the corporate-level tax. Ranking taxpayers by income reveals that taxpayers in the top 1 percent of the distribution receive over 100 percent of the tax cut (table 3.3). The changes in tax burden are very small in the bottom four-fifths of the income distribution: slightly negative in the bottom three-fifths and slightly positive in the fourth quintile. The highest-income taxpayers receive the largest increase in after-tax income; for taxpayers in the top 0.1 percent of the distribution, after-tax income goes up by 11 percent.

Implementing these changes would reduce annual federal revenue by about $75 billion per year at 2005 levels. The cost of exempting capital income from taxation would be partly offset by the elimination of the mortgage interest deduction. If the mortgage interest deduction were retained (and household behavior did not change), the overall cost of the change would nearly double to $145 billion (see table 3.4, top panel).[22] With the mortgage interest deduction retained, taxes would decline on average for households with incomes between $75,000 and $200,000. The share of benefits going to taxpayers at the very top of the income distribution would fall, but the top 1 percent of households would still receive over half of the tax cut (see table 3.4, bottom panel). The majority of tax units in the bottom three-fifths would experience no change in their taxes.

If mortgage interest deductions were retained and savings and investment income were not taxed, individuals could reduce their tax liability without any change in saving or housing consumption by increasing their housing-backed debt and investing the additional funds in tax-exempt securities. To estimate the revenue loss from this arbitrage opportunity, we assume individuals raise their housing debt to 80 percent of

BASELINE DISTRIBUTION OF INCOME AND FEDERAL TAXES BY CASH INCOME CLASS, 2005

Cash income class (thousands of 2005 $)[a]	Tax Units[b]		Average income ($)	Average federal tax burden ($)	Average after-tax income ($)[c]	Average federal tax rate (%)[d]	Share of pretax income (%)	Share of posttax income (%)	Share of federal taxes (%)
	Number (thousands)	% of total							
Less than 10	19,560	13.5	5,618	200	5,418	3.6	1.3	1.5	0.2
10–20	25,611	17.7	14,885	706	14,178	4.8	4.4	5.2	1.0
20–30	19,953	13.8	24,715	2,488	22,227	10.1	5.6	6.4	2.7
30–40	15,289	10.6	34,863	5,023	29,840	14.4	6.1	6.6	4.2
40–50	11,738	8.1	44,824	7,501	37,323	16.7	6.0	6.3	4.9
50–75	20,700	14.3	61,482	11,337	50,145	18.4	14.5	15.0	12.9
75–100	11,936	8.3	86,246	17,261	68,985	20.0	11.8	11.9	11.4
100–200	14,432	10.0	133,489	29,744	103,744	22.3	22.0	21.6	23.7
200–500	3,797	2.6	287,471	72,859	214,612	25.3	12.5	11.7	15.3
500–1,000	642	0.4	678,426	184,509	493,916	27.2	5.0	4.6	6.5
More than 1,000	335	0.2	2,943,745	919,538	2,024,206	31.2	11.3	9.8	17.0
All	144,573	100.0	60,566	12,544	48,022	20.7	100.0	100.0	100.0

Source: Urban–Brookings Tax Policy Center Microsimulation Model (version 0305-3A).

Notes: Data are for calendar year 2005. Baseline is current law. Under the proposal, corporate tax revenue is assumed to be 76 percent of its current-law value.

a. Tax units with negative cash income are excluded from the lowest income class but are included in the totals. For a description of cash income, see http://www.taxpolicycenter.org/TaxModel/income.cfm.

b. Includes both filing and nonfiling units. Tax units that are dependents of other taxpayers are excluded from the analysis.

c. After-tax income is cash income less individual income tax net of refundable credits, corporate income tax, payroll taxes (Social Security and Medicare), and estate tax.

d. Average federal tax (includes individual and corporate income tax, payroll taxes for Social Security and Medicare, and the estate tax) as a percentage of average cash income.

Table 3.3. Exempt Capital Income from Taxation with Adjustment to Corporate Tax Revenue

DISTRIBUTION OF FEDERAL TAX CHANGE BY CASH INCOME PERCENTILE, 2005

Cash income percentile[a]	Percent of Tax Units[b]		Change in after-tax income (%)[c]	Share of total federal tax change	Average Federal Tax Change		Share of Federal Taxes		Average Federal Tax Rate[d]	
	With tax cut	With tax increase			$	%	Change (% points)	Under the proposal	Change (% points)	Under the proposal
Lowest quintile	19.6	0.9	0.3	0.7	−19	−7.9	0.0	0.4	−0.3	3.0
Second quintile	32.1	5.2	0.3	1.9	−49	−3.6	0.0	2.2	−0.3	6.9
Middle quintile	37.8	18.0	0.1	1.1	−28	−0.6	0.3	8.1	−0.1	14.1
Fourth quintile	42.1	38.8	0.0	−0.2	4	0.0	0.8	18.2	0.0	18.4
Top quintile	35.4	61.3	1.8	95.9	−2,493	−5.5	−1.0	70.9	−1.4	23.3
All	33.5	24.8	1.1	100.0	−520	−4.1	0.0	100.0	−0.9	19.9
Addendum										
Top 10%	36.2	62.5	2.7	102.5	−5,327	−7.5	−2.0	54.5	−2.0	24.1
Top 5%	41.2	58.3	3.8	108.5	−11,282	−10.1	−2.8	41.7	−2.8	24.5
Top 1%	54.8	45.1	6.7	101.7	−52,884	−15.9	−3.3	23.3	−4.7	24.9
Top 0.5%	60.2	39.8	7.8	92.9	−96,550	−17.9	−3.1	18.4	−5.4	25.0
Top 0.1%	72.0	28.0	10.6	71.4	−370,923	−22.7	−2.5	10.5	−7.2	24.6

Baseline Distribution of Income and Federal Taxes by Cash Income Percentile, 2005

| Cash income percentile[a] | Tax Units[b] | | Average income ($) | Average federal tax burden ($) | Average after-tax income ($)[c] | Average federal tax rate[d] | Share of pretax income (%) | Share of posttax income (%) | Share of federal taxes (%) |
	Number (thousands)	% of total							
Lowest quintile	28,340	19.6	7,487	242	7,245	3.2	2.4	3.0	0.4
Second quintile	28,910	20.0	19,134	1,377	17,757	7.2	6.3	7.4	2.2
Middle quintile	28,916	20.0	34,409	4,880	29,528	14.2	11.4	12.3	7.8
Fourth quintile	28,916	20.0	59,726	10,965	48,761	18.4	19.7	20.3	17.5
Top quintile	28,914	20.0	183,278	45,140	138,138	24.6	60.5	57.5	72.0
All	144,573	100.0	60,566	12,544	48,022	20.7	100.0	100.0	100.0
Addendum									
Top 10%	14,457	10.0	271,934	70,892	201,042	26.1	44.9	41.9	56.5
Top 5%	7,228	5.0	408,681	111,532	297,149	27.3	33.7	30.9	44.5
Top 1%	1,446	1.0	1,126,790	333,361	793,429	29.6	18.6	16.5	26.6
Top 0.5%	723	0.5	1,774,411	539,278	1,235,133	30.4	14.7	12.9	21.5
Top 0.1%	145	0.1	5,136,564	1,636,532	3,500,032	31.9	8.5	7.3	13.1

Source: Urban–Brookings Tax Policy Center Microsimulation Model (version 0305-3A).

Notes: Data are for calendar year 2005. Baseline is current law. Under the proposal, corporate tax revenue is assumed to be 76 percent of its current-law value.

a. Tax units with negative cash income are excluded from the lowest quintile but are included in the totals. For a description of cash income, see http://www.taxpolicycenter.org/TaxModel/income.cfm.

b. Includes both filing and nonfiling units. Tax units that are other taxpayers' dependents are excluded from the analysis.

c. After-tax income is cash income less individual income tax net of refundable credits, corporate income tax, payroll taxes (Social Security and Medicare), and estate tax.

d. Average federal tax (includes individual and corporate income tax, payroll taxes for Social Security and Medicare, and the estate tax) as a percentage of average cash income.

Table 3.4. Exempt Capital Income from Taxation, Retain Home Mortgage Interest Deduction with Adjustment to Corporate Tax Revenue

DISTRIBUTION OF FEDERAL TAX CHANGE BY CASH INCOME CLASS, 2005

Cash income class (thousands of 2005 $)[a]	Percent of Tax Units[b]		Change in after-tax income (%)[c]	Share of total federal tax change (%)[c]	Average Federal Tax Change		Share of Federal Taxes		Average Federal Tax Rate[d]	
	With tax cut	With tax increase			$	%	Change (% points)	Under the proposal	Change (% points)	Under the proposal
Less than 10	17.3	0.3	0.3	0.2	−15	−7.4	0.0	0.2	−0.3	3.3
10–20	28.5	1.9	0.3	0.8	−42	−6.0	0.0	1.0	−0.3	4.5
20–30	37.9	4.4	0.3	1.0	−74	−3.0	0.2	2.9	−0.3	9.8
30–40	44.1	8.0	0.3	1.0	−96	−1.9	0.3	4.5	−0.3	14.1
40–50	52.7	11.0	0.5	1.6	−200	−2.7	0.3	5.1	−0.5	16.3
50–75	63.3	12.7	0.8	5.7	−395	−3.5	0.6	13.6	−0.6	17.8
75–100	69.9	16.5	0.8	4.7	−567	−3.3	0.6	11.9	−0.7	19.4
100–200	74.7	20.2	1.3	13.4	−1,341	−4.5	0.9	24.6	−1.0	21.3
200–500	76.7	22.4	3.1	17.3	−6,595	−9.0	−0.2	15.1	−2.3	23.1
500–1,000	75.2	24.6	4.4	9.7	−21,893	−11.9	−0.3	6.3	−3.2	24.0
More than 1,000	77.4	22.5	9.5	44.4	−191,505	−20.8	−2.4	14.6	−6.5	24.7
All	46.6	8.7	2.1	100.0	−1,001	−8.0	0.0	100.0	−1.7	19.1

Change in federal revenue ($ billions)   −144.718

DISTRIBUTION OF FEDERAL TAX CHANGE BY CASH INCOME PERCENTILE, 2005

Cash income percentile[a]	Percent of Tax Units[b]		Change in after-tax income (%)[c]	Share of total federal tax change (%)	Average Federal Tax Change		Share of Federal Taxes		Average Federal Tax Rate[d]	
	With tax cut	With tax increase			$	%	Change (% points)	Under the proposal	Change (% points)	Under the proposal
Lowest quintile	19.7	0.6	0.3	0.4	−20	−8.2	0.0	0.4	−0.3	3.0
Second quintile	33.4	3.0	0.3	1.2	−60	−4.3	0.1	2.3	−0.3	6.9
Middle quintile	44.0	7.7	0.4	2.2	−107	−2.2	0.5	8.3	−0.3	13.9
Fourth quintile	61.8	12.5	0.7	7.2	−362	−3.3	0.9	18.4	−0.6	17.8
Top quintile	73.4	19.6	3.2	88.8	−4,441	−9.8	−1.5	70.5	−2.4	22.2
All	46.6	8.7	2.1	100.0	−1,001	−8.0	0.0	100.0	−1.7	19.1
Addendum										
Top 10%	76.5	20.7	4.1	82.2	−8,226	−11.6	−2.2	54.3	−3.0	23.1
Top 5%	77.4	21.6	5.1	75.6	−15,132	−13.6	−2.7	41.8	−3.7	23.6
Top 1%	76.1	23.8	7.4	58.4	−58,436	−17.5	−2.8	23.8	−5.2	24.4
Top 0.5%	76.3	23.6	8.3	51.3	−102,627	−19.0	−2.6	18.9	−5.8	24.6
Top 0.1%	79.9	20.1	10.8	37.8	−378,114	−23.1	−2.1	10.9	−7.4	24.5

Source: Urban–Brookings Tax Policy Center Microsimulation Model (version 0305-3A).

Notes: Data are for calendar year 2005. Baseline is current law. Under the proposal, corporate tax revenue is assumed to be 76 percent of its current-law value. Baseline distribution tables are given as the bottom panels of tables 3.2 and 3.3.

a. Tax units with negative cash income are excluded from the lowest income class but are included in the totals. For a description of cash income, see http://www.taxpolicycenter.org/TaxModel/income.cfm.

b. Includes both filing and nonfiling units. Tax units that are other taxpayers' dependents are excluded from the analysis.

c. After-tax income is cash income less individual income tax net of refundable credits, corporate income tax, payroll taxes (Social Security and Medicare), and estate tax.

d. Average federal tax (includes individual and corporate income tax, payroll taxes for Social Security and Medicare, and the estate tax) as a percentage of average cash income.

housing value (up to a maximum of $1 million) and calculate the result-
ing increase in mortgage interest deductions, assuming an interest rate
of 5 percent.[23] Under these assumptions, the cost of exempting capital
income and retaining the mortgage interest deduction would increase by
about $30 billion annually, to $176 billion. This assumption of arbitrage
reduces the share of benefits received by the very highest income taxpayers, in part because the $1 million cap in current law on deductible
mortgage interest debt limits their additional borrowing.

If these changes are offset by proportionate increases in individual and
corporate tax rates, to a top marginal rate of 37.4 percent on individuals
and corporations and a top individual alternative minimum tax (AMT)
rate of 29.9 percent, taxes would decline for the very highest income taxpayers, decline slightly for the very lowest income taxpayers, and increase
for all groups in between.[24] Average federal tax burdens would drop by
15 percent for taxpayers with income over $1 million and by 3.6 percent
for taxpayers with income between $500,000 and $1 million, but would
increase on average for all groups of taxpayers with income between
$20,000 and $500,000 (table 3.5, top panel). For these groups, the increase
in tax rates and the loss of the mortgage interest deduction would outweigh any benefits from lower taxes on interest, dividends, and capital
gains. Ranking taxpayers by income percentile (table 3.5, bottom panel)
shows similar results.

To simulate a consumption tax base that roughly maintains the current distribution of tax burdens, we increase individual and corporate rates
(but not AMT rates) to keep taxes, including the estimated corporate tax
burden, approximately constant in each tax bracket. This requires large
increases in the top two marginal rates; the top individual and corporate
rates rise from 35 to 44 percent.[25] At this corporate rate, assuming no
change in behavior, corporate revenue would be about 95 percent of revenue under current law.

This rate structure roughly maintains the current tax burden in each
of the bottom four fifths of the income distribution, but there would continue to be some big changes within the top fifth. Taxpayers with income
over $1 million would receive an average tax cut of almost $25,000, or
slightly over 1 percent of income, but taxpayers in income groups
between $100,000 and $1 million on average would all pay higher taxes
(table 3.6, top panel). Even within the very top income group, most individuals would pay higher taxes. Only the very small minority of taxpayers
with a very large share of their income coming from capital would benefit

Table 3.5. Exempt Capital Income from Taxation with Adjustment to Corporate Tax Revenue

REVENUE-NEUTRAL, PROPORTIONAL CHANGES TO INDIVIDUAL AND CORPORATE TAX RATES TO OFFSET INDIVIDUAL AND CORPORATE INCOME TAX CHANGE, DISTRIBUTION OF FEDERAL TAX CHANGE BY CASH INCOME CLASS, 2005

Cash income class (thousands of 2005 $)[a]	Percent of Tax Units[b]		Change in after-tax income (%)[c]	Average Federal Tax Change		Share of Federal Taxes		Average Federal Tax Rate[d]	
	With tax cut	With tax increase		$	%	Change (% points)	Under the proposal	Change (% points)	Under the proposal
Less than 10	16.4	2.9	0.2	−11	−5.4	0.0	0.2	−0.2	3.4
10–20	23.1	26.9	0.1	−18	−2.6	0.0	1.0	−0.1	4.6
20–30	24.3	54.8	−0.1	19	0.8	0.0	2.8	0.1	10.2
30–40	20.3	72.2	−0.4	115	2.3	0.1	4.3	0.3	14.8
40–50	19.5	78.2	−0.5	201	2.7	0.1	5.0	0.5	17.2
50–75	18.8	80.5	−0.7	357	3.2	0.4	13.3	0.6	19.0
75–100	16.5	83.3	−1.2	830	4.8	0.5	11.9	1.0	21.0
100–200	18.2	81.8	−1.7	1,755	5.9	1.4	25.1	1.3	23.6
200–500	28.8	71.1	−0.6	1,187	1.6	0.3	15.5	0.4	25.8
500–1,000	35.2	64.8	1.3	−6,568	−3.6	−0.2	6.3	−1.0	26.3
More than 1,000	46.3	53.7	6.8	−138,099	−15.0	−2.6	14.4	−4.7	26.6
All	20.4	55.6	0.0	1	0.0	0.0	100.0	0.0	20.7

(continued)

Table 3.5. (Continued)

DISTRIBUTION OF FEDERAL TAX CHANGE BY CASH INCOME PERCENTILE, 2005

Cash income percentile[a]	Percent of Tax Units[b]		Change in after-tax income (%)[c]	Average Federal Tax Change		Share of Federal Taxes		Average Federal Tax Rate[d]	
	With tax cut	With tax increase		$	%	Change (% points)	Under the proposal	Change (% points)	Under the proposal
Lowest quintile	18.0	7.8	0.2	−13	−5.5	0.0	0.4	−0.2	3.1
Second quintile	24.6	38.9	0.1	−12	−0.9	0.0	2.2	−0.1	7.1
Middle quintile	20.9	70.5	−0.4	105	2.2	0.2	8.0	0.3	14.5
Fourth quintile	18.5	80.6	−0.7	359	3.3	0.6	18.1	0.6	19.0
Top quintile	19.7	80.2	0.3	−425	−0.9	−0.7	71.3	−0.2	24.4
All	20.4	55.6	0.0	1	0.0	0.0	100.0	0.0	20.7

Addendum

Top 10%	22.9	77.0	0.9	−1,893	−2.7	−1.5	55.0	−0.7	25.4
Top 5%	27.9	72.1	1.9	−5,656	−5.1	−2.3	42.2	−1.4	25.9
Top 1%	37.5	62.5	4.5	−35,629	−10.7	−2.8	23.7	−3.2	26.4
Top 0.5%	41.4	58.6	5.6	−68,811	−12.8	−2.7	18.7	−3.9	26.5
Top 0.1%	51.8	48.2	8.3	−289,779	−17.7	−2.3	10.7	−5.6	26.2

Source: Urban–Brookings Tax Policy Center Microsimulation Model (version 0305-3A).

Notes: Data are for calendar year 2005. Baseline is current law. Under the proposal, the corporate tax rate is increased by 6.8 percent, from 35 to 37.4 percent resulting in corporate tax revenue that is 81 percent of its current-law value. Individual income tax rates would also rise by 6.8 percent, from 10, 15, 25, 28, 33, and 35 percent to 10.7, 16.0, 26.7, 29.9, 35.2, and 37.4 percent; the individual alternative minimum tax rates would rise from 26 and 28 percent to 27.8 and 29.9. Baseline distribution tables are given as the bottom panels of tables 3.2 and 3.3.

a. Tax units with negative cash income are excluded from the lowest income class but are included in the totals. For a description of cash income, see http://www.taxpolicycenter.org/TaxModel/income.cfm.

b. Includes both filing and nonfiling units. Tax units that are dependents of other taxpayers are excluded from the analysis.

c. After-tax income is cash income less individual income tax net of refundable credits, corporate income tax, payroll taxes (Social Security and Medicare), and estate tax.

d. Average federal tax (includes individual and corporate income tax, payroll taxes for Social Security and Medicare, and the estate tax) as a percentage of average cash income.

Table 3.6. Exempt Capital Income from Taxation with Adjustment to Corporate Tax Revenue

DISTRIBUTIONALLY NEUTRAL CHANGES TO INDIVIDUAL AND CORPORATE TAX RATES TO OFFSET INDIVIDUAL AND CORPORATE INCOME TAX CHANGE, DISTRIBUTION OF FEDERAL TAX CHANGE BY CASH INCOME CLASS, 2005

Cash income class (thousands of 2005 $)[a]	Percent of Tax Units[b]		Change in after-tax income (%)[c]	Average Federal Tax Change		Share of Federal Taxes		Average Federal Tax Rate[d]	
	With tax cut	With tax increase		$	%	Change (% points)	Under the proposal	Change (% points)	Under the proposal
Less than 10	15.7	0.5	0.0	-2	-0.9	0.0	0.2	0.0	3.5
10–20	44.1	3.0	0.1	-15	-2.1	0.0	1.0	-0.1	4.7
20–30	69.5	7.9	0.2	-42	-1.7	-0.1	2.7	-0.2	9.9
30–40	76.2	15.0	0.2	-56	-1.1	-0.1	4.2	-0.2	14.3
40–50	73.6	23.7	0.2	-83	-1.1	-0.1	4.8	-0.2	16.6
50–75	67.7	31.4	0.3	-141	-1.2	-0.2	12.8	-0.2	18.2
75–100	53.4	46.2	0.0	1	0.0	0.0	11.4	0.0	20.1
100–200	39.9	59.8	-0.4	407	1.4	0.3	24.0	0.3	22.6
200–500	32.8	67.1	-0.7	1,397	1.9	0.3	15.6	0.5	25.9
500–1,000	32.1	67.8	-1.7	8,475	4.6	0.3	6.8	1.3	28.5
More than 1,000	36.5	63.5	1.2	-24,506	-2.7	-0.5	16.5	-0.8	30.4
All	52.9	21.7	0.0	17	0.1	0.0	100.0	0.0	20.8

DISTRIBUTION OF FEDERAL TAX CHANGE BY CASH INCOME PERCENTILE, 2005

Cash income percentile[a]	Percent of Tax Units[b]		Change in after-tax income (%)[c]	Average Federal Tax Change		Share of Federal Taxes		Average Federal Tax Rate[d]	
	With tax cut	With tax increase		$	%	Change (% points)	Under the proposal	Change (% points)	Under the proposal
Lowest quintile	21.8	1.0	0.0	−3	−1.3	0.0	0.4	0.0	3.2
Second quintile	56.2	4.7	0.2	−29	−2.1	−0.1	2.2	−0.2	7.1
Middle quintile	75.3	14.9	0.2	−59	−1.2	−0.1	7.7	−0.2	14.0
Fourth quintile	68.1	30.8	0.3	−121	−1.1	−0.2	17.3	−0.2	18.2
Top quintile	42.7	57.0	−0.2	295	0.7	0.4	72.4	0.2	24.8
All	52.9	21.7	0.0	17	0.1	0.0	100.0	0.0	20.8
Addendum									
Top 10%	36.4	63.4	−0.2	490	0.7	0.3	56.8	0.2	26.3
Top 5%	33.5	66.3	−0.2	579	0.5	0.2	44.6	0.1	27.5
Top 1%	34.0	65.9	0.2	−1,336	−0.4	−0.1	26.4	−0.1	29.5
Top 0.5%	34.1	65.9	0.5	−5,951	−1.1	−0.3	21.2	−0.3	30.1
Top 0.1%	40.1	59.9	2.4	−83,340	−5.1	−0.7	12.4	−1.6	30.2

Source: Urban–Brookings Tax Policy Center Microsimulation Model (version 0305-3A).

Notes: Data are for calendar year 2005. Baseline is current law. Individual income tax rates would change from 10, 15, 25, 28, 33, and 35 percent to 9.5, 14.2, 23.5, 32.3, 37.4, and 43.9 percent (alternative minimum tax rates are unchanged from current law). The corporate rate would be equal to the top individual income tax rate of 43.9 percent resulting in corporate revenue that is 95.3 percent of its value under current law. Under the proposal, the aggregate sum of the individual and corporate tax burden remains approximately the same as under current law for individuals in each statutory individual income tax bracket. Baseline distribution tables are given as the bottom panels of tables 3.2 and 3.3.

a. Tax units with negative cash income are excluded from the lowest quintile but are included in the totals. For a description of cash income, see http://www.taxpolicycenter.org/TaxModel/income.cfm.

b. Includes both filing and nonfiling units. Tax units that are dependents of other taxpayers are excluded from the analysis.

c. After-tax income is cash income less: individual income tax net of refundable credits; corporate income tax; payroll taxes (Social Security and Medicare); and estate tax.

d. Average federal tax (includes individual and corporate income tax, payroll taxes for Social Security and Medicare, and the estate tax) as a percentage of average cash income.

from the change. For all income groups, the number of individuals facing tax increases is higher than those receiving tax cuts. For example, of those with cash income over $1 million, 63.5 percent of individuals would be subject to a tax increase, while only 36.5 percent would receive a tax cut.

So moving to a system that exempts savings from taxation would decrease the progressivity of the income tax system. It would also increase the size of the expected budget deficit unless offset by tax rate increases or reduction in other, noncapital income-related preferences. Roughly maintaining the progressivity of the tax system would require much higher top marginal tax rates. Maintaining the same tax burden at the very top of the income distribution would require adding another, even higher, tax bracket.

Departures from a Consumption Base

The simulations above assume a comprehensive consumption tax base could be implemented. But, as Bankman and Schler (chapter 6) and others have shown, there could be substantial departures from the flat tax base, and even with perfect enforcement, not all consumption arising from business profits would be taxed. Two other sources of departure from a consumption tax that would erode the tax base for high-income people would be transition rules and omissions of those provisions necessary to implement a consumption base that would *increase,* instead of reduce, tax liabilities for some individuals and companies. These transition rules, in large part, will decrease the expected efficiency gains and will introduce additional complications to the new system and further arbitrage opportunities for taxpayers.

Transition Rules and Taxation of Returns to Old Capital

A consumption base would exempt the normal return to new savings, but there would still be the issue of how to tax consumption financed with capital accumulated out of after-tax income under the current income tax. We follow others in referring to this as the *transition* problem. Eventually, all normal returns to capital will be exempt from tax. In the short run, however, a fairly large percentage of wealth that was accumulated with after-tax dollars could be taxed again when the funds are used for consumption.

The total wealth of U.S. households is estimated at about $45 trillion. Much of this wealth is in the form of assets such as pensions and unrealized capital gains, which have not yet been taxed. Excluding housing, the basis of private assets in the United States could be as much as $15 trillion.[26] Transition rules governing the treatment of consumption financed by existing wealth will determine to what extent these previously taxed savings will be subject to the consumption tax.

Transition rules might be considered necessary to relieve the tax burden on savers who have accrued savings from after-tax income and would be taxed again when those savings are spent under a consumed income tax. For example, without a transition rule for past savings, a retiree who accumulated $100,000 in a savings account with after-tax income before the imposition of a consumption tax would be taxed on withdrawals used for consumption. A transition rule could allow savings accumulated under the income tax to be separated from "new" saving and deducted from income. Such a rule could treat the $100,000 as tax-paid savings and would enable the retiree to make tax-free withdrawals from the savings account. It is difficult, however, to design a system that would differentiate between individuals who reduce their accumulated savings to consume, and individuals who only rearrange assets among accounts. Allowing tax-free withdrawals from past savings, for example, would enable any individual with accumulated wealth to gain a tax deduction simply by transferring old assets into "new" savings accounts. It would enable millionaires living off interest, for example, to receive the equivalent of tax-free interest income—a substantial benefit compared to current law.

If the consumption tax were in the form of a standard value-added tax (VAT) or flat tax that fell on consumption from old wealth from businesses, then transition rules could not distinguish among people based on whether they were saving or consuming out of old wealth. People would bear the transition burden either through higher prices or through lower asset values of their equity shares in business. Transition relief would be focused on businesses that had purchased assets capitalized under the prior income tax. They would see the basis of those assets reduced to zero in the absence of transition relief. Relief could take the form of allowing businesses to retain basis or some fraction of basis in old assets and allowing them to continue to recover basis in old assets through depreciation, or could allow for the immediate expensing of the remaining basis.

It is hard to imagine that a consumption tax could be enacted without some form of relief for businesses that had purchased assets before enactment of the tax. But such relief would be costly and would effectively move the system in the direction of a tax on wages instead of consumption, by exempting income from old capital from tax. It would also provide windfall gains to owners of existing assets who are planning to maintain their capital instead of spending it down (see figure 3.4).

Dessert without the Broccoli

Moving from current law to a consumption-base treatment of savings reduces the tax base to some degree and benefits many wealth holders. It also will raise taxes, however, on some individuals and businesses. As noted above, eliminating deductibility of interest will raise taxes on many middle- and upper middle–income individuals with large home mortgages and little taxable capital income. Eliminating interest deductibility

Figure 3.4. Winners and Losers From Transition to a Consumption Tax

Suppose an individual, A, had accumulated $100,000 of wealth under the current income tax from earnings and interest from taxable bonds. Suppose also that the marginal tax rate the individual faces is 28 percent and that on January 1, 2006, the income tax is repealed and a 28 percent consumption tax is imposed. Under an income tax, no further tax would be due if A immediately consumed the $100,000, but additional tax would be due on any interest income earned on the portion of the wealth that was not consumed. If the full $100,000 was retained and generated interest at 10 percent, the before-tax return would be $10,000 and the after-tax return, $7,200.

Under a consumption tax without transition rules, A would pay a 28 percent tax on spending from the wealth. That would permit $72,000 of immediate consumption or $7,200 a year, which has a present value of $72,000 at a 10 percent discount rate. By saving a portion of capital income, A could accumulate more wealth faster under the consumption tax than under the income tax. Thus, without transition rules, replacing the income tax with a consumption tax would hurt people who are dis-saving, help savers, and leave those who consume all their capital income (but none of their principal) in the same position. Those consuming their principal are likely to be older people who have saved for retirement in their working years. People who have saved in traditional tax-favored retirement accounts, however, would pay tax on their return of investment under both the current income tax and the proposed new consumption tax.

If transition rules allowed people to retain basis in their old assets, people spending from old wealth will be held harmless by the transition. But all other wealth holders will benefit; they will avoid the one-time "lump sum" transition tax on their wealth, while receiving a higher rate of return. In that sense, transition rules would confer a windfall gain on all wealth holders who are planning either to preserve or further enhance their capital.

will also raise taxes on highly leveraged businesses, especially those currently holding tax-favored assets or engaging in tax-sheltering transactions that lower taxes on their profits. Incremental movement toward eliminating taxes on capital income without taking the complementary steps of limiting interest deductions creates opportunities for taxpayers to reduce their tax liability without undertaking any additional saving. Instead they could engage in tax arbitrage, offsetting deductible interest payments against tax-free interest receipts.

The "five easy pieces" proposal (see figure 3.5) is one example of an incremental approach to eliminating taxation of capital income that

Figure 3.5. Five Easy Pieces

The "five easy pieces" proposal (Christian and Robbins 2002) would

- reduce marginal tax rates,
- eliminate taxes on capital gains and dividends,
- move toward expensing of business investments,
- eliminate the estate tax, and
- allow individuals to establish tax-free personal savings accounts, on top of retirement saving incentives already in the tax law.

The proposal is represented as an indirect approach to replacing the income tax with a consumption tax through incremental changes in the current system. The current administration and Congress have already enacted or partially enacted several of these items, including lower marginal tax rates, a temporary 15 percent rate on capital gains and dividends (recently extended through the end of 2010), partial expensing of business investments (now expired), and elimination of the estate tax for one year in 2010. The administration has proposed large tax-free personal savings accounts in previous budgets, but Congress has not enacted these proposals. Elimination of individual taxes on capital gains and dividends and expensing of business investments would also be part of the HR-type consumption tax option that we simulate in this section.

But these proposals do not represent a move toward a consumption tax because they retain deductibility of mortgage interest and interest deductions by corporate and noncorporate businesses. They effectively would allow a substantial erosion of the tax base by high-income taxpayers and businesses that could offset tax-free or tax-favored income from investments with fully deductible borrowing. In addition, there are no provisions to offset revenue losses; although the proposal would reduce the tax base, it would also reduce rates instead of raising rates or closing other tax preferences to finance the proposed tax cuts.

would substantially erode the tax base, while maintaining current-law incentives to borrow money by keeping interest deductibility. Major portions of the five easy pieces proposal have already been enacted. Further advancing this agenda would not be a move toward consumption taxation or economic neutrality, but instead a move to erode the tax base by enabling investors to engage in tax arbitrage transactions to reduce their tax liability. This proposal illustrates the dangers of incremental moves toward a consumption tax that start with the "easy" part, while ignoring the heavy lifting.

Saving, Growth, and Economic Efficiency

Elimination of capital income taxation could increase economic growth and efficiency by increasing private saving or by improving the efficiency of capital use.

Capital Income Taxes and Private Saving

Eliminating capital income taxation raises the after-tax return from new saving. Being able to spend more dollars in the future from sacrificing a dollar of current consumption gives people an incentive to save more (the substitution effect). But with a higher rate of return, people do not need to save as much to achieve a given future consumption target and so may choose to save less (the income effect).

The magnitude of the income effect varies across individuals and is highly sensitive to how the capital income tax cut is financed. If the tax change is revenue neutral (by, for example, financing it by higher taxes on labor income) and everyone has the same propensity to save, there would be no income effect overall. But changes in income distribution could influence private saving, depending on whether taxes are reduced for people with low or high propensities to save.

If elimination of capital income taxes is implemented as part of a reform that substitutes a consumption tax for the current hybrid income tax system, with no transition relief for consumption from old wealth, then the income effect could reinforce the substitution effect and also promote more saving. It would do this by redistributing tax burdens from those with high-saving propensities to those with low-saving propensities. In particular, some tax change burden would fall on retirees mostly consuming out of previously accrued wealth, while young people saving to finance their future retirement could see their taxes fall.[27]

If, instead, capital income taxes are reduced within the income tax system, while consumption from the proceeds of old wealth remains tax-free, existing wealth holders will receive a net tax cut and be able to consume more today, while maintaining planned future consumption. Under this scenario, taxes would be reduced for retirees and for those with large multigenerational fortunes and would be increased for younger people with income mostly from wages.

Empirical research on the relationship between private saving and the after-tax rate of return gives mixed results. One estimate shows a 10 percent rise in returns would increase saving by 4 percent, but subsequent studies found that these results were not robust with respect to changes in specification (Boskin 1978; Bosworth 1984; Howrey and Hymans 1980). Other studies have found more mixed effects of interest rates on saving (Blinder and Deaton 1985; Carlino 1982; Friend and Hasbrouck 1983; Skinner and Feenberg 1991).[28]

Simulation models estimating tax reform effects must make some assumption about the degree to which households substitute present for future consumption in response to a change in the after-tax return on saving. These assumptions can have a large effect on the simulated benefits of tax reform.[29]

Assuming that the choice between current and future consumption responds to the rate of return, simulation models show that replacing the current income tax with a consumption-based tax will raise economic efficiency and output in the long run, though the size of these gains varies with the assumptions made within the model.[30] Much of the efficiency gain from introducing a consumption tax comes from the implicit lump-sum tax on existing capital (figure 3.4). Transition rules would reduce these gains. For example, one study reported that replacing the current tax system with a proportional consumption tax would lead to a 9 percent increase in output with no transition rules, but less than 2 percent if graduated rates are retained and transition relief is provided by maintaining current depreciation allowances for existing capital (Altig et al. 2001).[31]

Saving Incentives under the Income Tax

Since the late 1970s, tax policy has sought to encourage private saving by broadening opportunities for workers to save a portion of their wages in

IRAs, 401(k) plans, and other qualified accounts. These accounts receive consumption tax treatment. Either the contribution is deductible, capital income from the assets is tax-free, and the proceeds of withdrawals are included in income; or deposits are from after-tax income, but earnings and withdrawals are tax free.

If the economic theory on saving behavior is correct, tax-preference accounts should not increase saving for those who would otherwise save more than the account limits. These accounts do not increase the return to an additional dollar of net saving, but instead just increase the returns to inframarginal saving that would have occurred without the tax preference. The accounts could increase net saving, however, by people who would not otherwise save as much as the contribution limit and cannot finance their contributions with tax-deductible borrowing at a rate close to the return they would be earning in the account. Penalties for early withdrawals render IRAs and 401(k) plans less liquid than other savings accounts. Consequently, households may consider them imperfect substitutes for other saving and may choose to finance a portion of their deposits by reducing current consumption.

Despite mixed research results in general, there is stronger evidence that IRAs and 401(k) plans increase saving of low- and middle-income taxpayers more than for others. Researchers cannot easily determine what households would have saved absent the incentives without further assumptions. We cannot simply assume that a positive correlation between contributions to tax-preferred accounts and total saving means that the accounts boosted saving.

Based on somewhat different identification strategies, research findings differ on whether contributions to tax-preference accounts increase overall saving or substitute for other saving (Engen and Gale 2000; Engen, Gale, and Scholz 1996; Poterba, Venti, and Wise 1996). Recent work, however, has shown that saving plans have raised wealth for relatively low-income households, but not for relatively high-income households and that increasing participation among low- and middle-income households is more likely to represent new saving (instead of asset shifting) than additional contributions by high-income households is (Engen, Gale, and Uccello 1999; Gale, Iwry, and Orszag 2005; Neuberger, Greenstein, and Sweeney 2005).

More recent research suggests that increased saving depends at least as much on how incentives are conveyed as on the actual financial benefit from the incentive. For example, evidence suggests that more people invest in 401(k) plans when employers automatically deposit money in the plan (with an option for an employee to opt out) than when the employee is simply offered an opportunity to contribute (Choi et al. forthcoming). These studies suggest that targeted savings plans designed to encourage broader participation could be much more effective in stimulating saving than increases in after-tax returns by themselves.

Because antidiscrimination rules require broad participation for qualification of 401(k) plans, many employers must offer generous incentives for low-income employees to participate, so that the plans will be available for the high-income savers who benefit the most. Over 80 percent of 401(k) plans include an employer match.[32] Removing taxes on income from capital would remove the incentive for employers to provide 401(k) plans for their workers. Paradoxically, the effect could be to reduce saving by employees who would no longer be receiving the matched contributions that characterize many 401(k) plans.

In conclusion, while in theory private saving should be higher under a consumption tax than under an income tax, eliminating capital income taxation could either increase or decrease private saving, *compared with current law*, if the responsiveness of saving to after-tax returns is low and if a consumption tax causes employers to stop subsidizing employee contributions to retirement saving plans. Absent more compelling evidence that eliminating capital income taxation in our current system would raise saving, arguments that cutting capital income taxes would increase saving, and thereby raise economic growth, are not persuasive.

Would Eliminating Capital Income Taxation Reduce Differentials in Tax Rates across Economic Sectors?

Even if aggregate saving does not increase, eliminating capital income taxation could raise output if it improves the efficiency of investment. In general, investors seek investments that yield the highest after-tax returns. If all tax policy is *neutral* among investments—by taxing all returns to capital at the same rate—then investments with the highest after-tax returns will also have the highest pretax returns, plus the highest economic productivity.

Both a comprehensive income tax and zero taxes on capital income are neutral among investments, but the current income tax is not. In practice, it is impossible to achieve perfect neutrality under an income tax because not all changes in net worth are measurable. In contrast, eliminating tax on capital income, at least in theory, accomplishes this goal by making all effective tax rates on capital income equal at a rate of zero. Economic models that assess the economic efficiency effects of tax reform find that equalizing tax rates across capital assets increases efficiency, especially by reducing the differentials between federal tax treatment of business capital and untaxed owner-occupied housing, and between corporate and noncorporate capital.

In practice, differences in effective tax rates across activities will not disappear under any consumption tax likely to be enacted. Differential taxation may be retained for such forms of tax-preferred noncapital income as employer contributions for health insurance and other fringe benefits, and for certain deductible consumption items. On the capital income side, for political reasons, Congress may choose to retain a mortgage-interest deduction or enact an alternative preference for owner-occupied housing. President George W. Bush's tax reform commission, for example, recommended retaining incentives for home ownership and charitable contributions.

While a consumption tax eliminates the problem of measuring changes in net worth for business assets, it creates new issues for measuring the tax base for investments in household capital and human capital—two very large sources of capital investment in the economy. To be consistent with the treatment of business assets, a consumption tax should allow a deduction for the purchase of household assets and then impose a tax on their imputed rental value. More likely, if they are taxed at all, household assets would be taxed under the prepayment method with the initial purchase taxed and returns exempt. The use of the prepayment method is equivalent in present value to consumption taxation for assets with normal returns, but would exempt large and unanticipated gains on housing. In principle, investments in human capital should be deductible under a consumption tax, but rules would be needed to determine what portion of educational and training outlays is investment in producing future taxable income, and what portion is current consumption or generates future untaxed benefits. Without any deduction for investments in human capital, a consumption tax would introduce a bias in favor of physical assets and against human capital. (The current income tax system allows partial expensing of human capital. The portion of costs that reflect forgone earnings are effectively deductible and a portion of outlays for tuition for postsecondary education benefit from either deductions or credits, but some of the expenses cannot be recovered either through expensing or deductions over time.)[33]

Conclusions

Unlike most other market-economy countries that have both income and consumption taxes, the United States does not impose a broad-based national consumption tax. The current federal income tax, however, is in reality a hybrid between consumption and income taxation. The debate about whether consumption or income is the appropriate base for taxation has been ongoing for generations. Under certain assumptions, consumption taxes can be shown to produce fewer distortions of economic decisionmaking than income taxes because consumption taxes are neutral in the choice between spending now or later and provide more even-handed treatment of people with an equal ability to pay tax over their lifetimes. If capital income is defined as the reward for waiting, then a consumption base tax can be shown to be equivalent to a tax base that exempts capital income. These two propositions form the core of the case to eliminate taxation of capital income. Some proponents of eliminating capital income taxation also assert that a tax base that excludes the return to saving would increase private saving and economic growth.

The neutrality arguments probably favor consumption taxes in the abstract, given economists' standard framework, but the conclusions could be different if ability and future consumption are complements. Income taxation also has a role if, unlike in the standard analytical framework, people seek wealth for multiple reasons. The case that consumption taxes are fairer than income taxes in a lifetime context is also less compelling when tax policies and the composition of tax units are changing over time than in the stable policy and demographic framework that some people assume.

The assumed equivalence between consumption taxes and income taxes that exempt the return to saving is especially problematic. Income that appears as returns to capital includes much more than compensation for sacrificing current consumption; it also includes economic rent, entrepreneurial profits, and returns from inheritances. A tax on annual consumption would capture these returns, but a yield-exempt tax would not. Evidence on the sources of capital income is fragmentary but indicates that normal returns account for a minority of individual wealth accumulation and corporate profits. A tax that excluded excess returns and returns from old wealth would be equivalent to a tax on wages alone. It would not have the efficiency properties of a consumption tax and would not equally impose the same burden on all people with an equal lifetime ability to pay.

Maintaining a progressive tax system requires imposing liability on individual taxpayers based on some measure of their well-being. A comprehensive consumption tax that included all income receipts in the tax base but allowed people and businesses to deduct all saving, while taxing all borrowing and all withdrawals from saving, could achieve that objective and arguably might be superior to an income tax. But no such tax is being seriously proposed, in part because imposing a comprehensive consumption tax on individual taxpayers is seen to be unacceptably complex. Instead, consumption tax advocates are promoting modified versions of the Hall-Rabushka tax plan. These plans would impose a graduated wage tax at the individual level, while moving the business tax base toward a consumption base by allowing expensing of new investments. In theory, this could result in a consumption base if, in addition to expensing and exemption of capital income, interest deductions are also eliminated, as the HR tax plan provides. But in practice, the result may be closer to a yield-exempt tax (with super-normal returns exempt) on wages alone.

Even if a consumption base could be implemented with an HR-type tax, the top tax rates would have to be raised substantially to maintain the current distribution of the tax burden—since taxable capital income is very highly concentrated among very high income taxpayers. Maximum tax rates of 44 percent on individual and corporate income would roughly maintain the current tax burden throughout most of the distribution but still result in sizeable tax cuts at the very top. So exempting taxes on capital income would lead to more distortions in behavior due to much higher marginal tax rates if implemented in a revenue-neutral way. Simply changing the tax base without offsetting changes in rates would reduce annual federal revenue by about $75 billion per year, at 2005 levels. This estimate assumes complete elimination of the mortgage interest deduction. If the mortgage interest deduction was retained (and household behavior did not change) the overall cost of the change would nearly double, and if arbitrage opportunities are exploited, the cost would increase even further.

Eliminating taxation of capital income could increase private saving and economic growth by raising after-tax returns to saving and could raise the productivity of the capital stock by eliminating tax differentials across assets, especially the favorable treatment of owner-occupied housing compared with business assets. But evidence of how saving responds to after-tax returns is weak, and there could be an offsetting drop in saving if eliminating capital income taxation causes employers to drop retirement plans. Efficiency of capital allocation would probably improve if capital income taxes were eliminated, but this requires that preferential treatment of housing be eliminated and may require special rules to address human capital investments.

An alternative to eliminating capital income taxes is to rethink the current tax treatment of returns to saving. Under current law, most capital income of middle-income taxpayers is already exempt from tax. One approach to reform would simplify the current complex set of retirement and other saving incentives and introduce new provisions to limit the ability to offset tax-free returns with interest deductions. This would move the system closer to one that exempts capital income for most taxpayers, while maintaining a residual capital income tax on high-income individuals and corporations. Another possibility would be introducing a value-added tax and using the revenue to remove most people from the individual income tax, while maintaining an income tax, at lower rates, on high-income individuals and corporations (Graetz 1997).

In conclusion, the case for eliminating all taxes on capital income of high-income people is problematic. Without substantially higher marginal tax rates, it would make the tax system less progressive, without any clear indication that it would raise saving, improve economic performance, result in a simpler tax system, and, on balance, reduce opportunities for tax-sheltering behavior. While an ideal consumption tax is potentially attractive, departures from the ideal, particularly through retention of interest deductions and transition rules that enable people to receive tax-free returns from old capital, could more than offset any potential economic benefits and allow many high-income people to avoid tax on large parts of their income that do not represent a return to new saving. These changes, in addition to eroding potential efficiency gains, would also further reduce the progressivity of our current tax system. Instead, more attention should be focused on alternatives to improve and simplify our current system.

Summary

Eliminating taxes on capital income would not promote progressivity or tax simplification. The principal gainers from eliminating capital taxes would be high-income households. Only a sharp increase in top marginal rates could maintain progressivity, and it is not clear any potential growth gains would be achieved, especially when transition relief is taken into account. Further, eliminating taxes on capital income in our system, without maintaining progressivity, would sacrifice equity for uncertain efficiency gains.

This chapter's findings include the following:

Replacing the current income tax with a consumption tax would have different effects on low-, middle-, and high-income taxpayers. Most low-income taxpayers are already exempt from income taxation; middle-income families generally make most of their investments in employer pensions, 401(k)s, IRAs, and housing—all of which are largely exempt from tax. So the debate is largely about whether capital income taxes should be eliminated for the highest-income families and, to a lesser extent, for corporations.

The very highest-income families pay the bulk of capital income taxes. In 2005, taxpayers with income over $200,000 received 68 percent of income from capital gains, dividends, and interest; those with income over $1 million received 45 percent.

Normal returns to saving may account for a relatively small fraction of capital income. Measured capital income includes recognition of deferred consumption and some combination of rewards to entrepreneurship, risky investments, and returns to inheritance.

Highest-income taxpayers benefit most from eliminating capital income taxation. If all taxes on interest, dividend, capital gains income, and interest deductions were eliminated, taxpayers with income over $1 million would get a 20 percent tax cut on average, based on a Tax Policy Center simulation (see table 3.2). Taxes would increase for taxpayers with income between $75,000 and $200,000, largely due to the loss of mortgage interest deduction. Retaining mortgage interest deductions while eliminating taxes on capital gains and interest would set up an arbitrage opportunity, whereby taxpayers can increase housing borrowing and invest the funds. The changes in tax burden would be small in the bottom four-fifths of the income distribution.

The elimination of capital income taxation would also increase the size of the expected budget deficit. Although it would include a revenue pickup from the elimination of the mortgage interest deduction, exempting capital income from taxation would reduce annual federal revenue by about $75 billion, at 2005 levels.

Private saving may not increase under a consumption tax. In theory, a consumption tax could raise private saving by increasing the after-tax rate of return, but statistical studies find little evidence of a positive relationship between saving and the after-tax return. Some research does suggest, however, that employer-funded tax-deferred accounts raise saving, especially for low- and middle-income households. Because a consumption tax would eliminate the tax advantages for such accounts, many employers would probably stop offering retirement plans, many of which currently subsidize low-income employee contributions. Saving could fall for these households.

Rethinking the current tax treatment of savings' returns could be an alternative to eliminating capital income taxes. Various approaches to reform would simplify the current complex set of rules for retirement saving plans, add new provisions to tax capital income of high-income individuals and corporations more uniformly, or introduce a value-added tax to replace a portion of the revenues from individual and corporate income taxes.

NOTES

1. Provisions in Treasury I that were dropped included indexing of the basis for capital gains and depreciation, a partial exclusion of interest income and deductions (as an ad hoc indexing measure), reduction of the double taxation of corporate dividends, elimination of accelerated depreciation (relative to economic depreciation) on machinery and equipment investments, and capitalization of intangible drilling and development costs for oil and gas and mining properties. Congress also retained an alternative minimum tax and enacted limitations on deductions of passive losses to curb tax shelters; both of these provisions were not in the original Treasury proposals because they were not needed under a comprehensive income base.

2. Shakow (1986) describes how such a tax might work. Alternatively, the normal return to capital might be taxed, as in the Dutch imputation scheme (Cnossen and Bovenberg 2002). Under certain circumstances, this is economically equivalent to a tax on accruals and possibly more practical. It does raise enormous political challenges, however (Burman and White 2003).

3. With graduated tax rates, a consumption tax could impose a positive tax rate on income from capital, if the return to saving raises an individual's tax base enough in the future to make his marginal tax rate on future consumption higher than the marginal tax rate at which he deducts current saving.

4. Investment need not just be purchases of physical assets, such as machines or buildings. An individual who defers consuming the bottle of wine in his cellar for five years instead of consuming it today, in anticipation that the wine's quality will improve, is investing in capital just as much as the producer who buys better casks to hold the wine before bottling. The key to whether an item of expenditure represents current consumption or investment is in the timing of the benefits from the outlay; if the benefits are immediate, the outlay is consumption; if the benefits are received over time, the outlay is investment.

5. This is only a problem for a wage tax, since under a system that taxed consumption directly the entrepreneur would pay taxes when he or she consumes out of accrued income from any source.

6. In a situation with no flat-rate tax, the rate of return will stay the same as long as the person doesn't change tax brackets.

7. Similarly, Weisbach (2000) notes that the fundamental difference between a consumption and income tax is in the treatment of capital outlays; if capital outlays are deductible under a consumption tax, returns should be taxed the same as under an income tax.

8. Where there are no limits on the scale of the profitable investment, government participation limits the return but also bears part of the risk. Alternatively, the investor can restore his return in the "no-tax" world simply by increasing the scale of the investment. In what we view as a more typical case of super normal returns, the entrepreneur or investor is subject to diminishing returns on his investment with increases in scale, and does not want to share his above-normal profit with the government.

9. These data are consistent with personal observations that the people who become very rich are those who succeeded in a start-up business, not those who invested an unusually large percentage of their earnings in a diversified portfolio.

10. An R-base tax system is one in which corporate real assets are taxed while financial assets are not. For more discussion of R-base tax systems, see Gordon, Kalambokidis, and colleagues (2004). We add back net interest payments and subtract net capital gains and dividends received from their measure of the size of the 2004 corporate tax base to derive a rough estimate of taxable profits from both equity-financed and debt-financed real assets in the corporate sector.

11. Earlier studies include those by Modigliani (1988) and Kotlikoff (1988). More recently, Gale and Scholz (1994) estimated that over half of wealth and Wolff (1999) estimated that about two-thirds of wealth comes from gifts and bequests.

12. Levy and Murnane (1992) and Piketty and Saez (2003) provide evidence on widening income inequality.

13. Goods are often categorized as complements or substitutes. Complements are goods that are more often consumed together, or if one good is consumed more the other is likely to increase as well—for example, hamburgers and french fries. In contrast, substitutes are goods that are more often consumed instead of each other—hamburgers or hot dogs.

14. Judd (1985) finds that the optimal tax rate on saving is zero and, in follow-on work (1997) that relaxes the assumption of perfect competition, finds that the optimal tax rate is negative because higher saving will lift nonsavers' earnings.

15. *Blueprints for Basic Tax Reform.* This report was released at the end of the Ford administration (Bradford and U.S. Tax Policy staff 1984; U.S. Treasury Department 1977).

16. The *Blueprints* proposal attempted to avoid this complexity by allowing tax-payers to "prepay" tax on saving and exempt returns on assets held outside of qualified accounts, but as discussed above, exemption of returns is equivalent to consumption tax treatment only under certain restrictive assumptions. In addition, allowing alternative treatment of assets could give rise to substantial tax avoidance opportunities by enabling individuals to exploit the difference in timing rules between the two treatments of saving. For a discussion of implementation issues in a *Blueprints*-type consumption tax, see Graetz (1979).

17. Ginsburg (1995) discusses how transition rules and preferences for mortgage interest and municipal bonds in the USA tax could have led to tax avoidance and reduced saving, contrary to the intention of its sponsors.

18. If businesses deduct economic depreciation, the resulting system is an income-type value-added tax.

19. The HR framework of combining an R-base tax for businesses with a wage tax for individuals could also be the basis for an alternative way of implementing an income tax, if business investments are capitalized instead of being expensed. Such an approach was suggested in the Comprehensive Business Income Tax plan for integrating the corporate and personal income taxes (U.S. Department of the Treasury 1992).

20. See also Bankman and Schler, chapter 6, this volume.

21. Our methods resemble those of Gordon, Kalambokidis, and Slemrod (2004).

22. Even if the mortgage interest deduction is retained, about 9 percent of tax units still receive tax increases. This is due to the elimination of the deduction for student loan interest (this largely affects those earning less than $100,000), disallowing Schedule-D losses and investment interest, and taxing some business income at higher effective rates. The R tax broadens the base through adjustments to Schedule-C, -E, and -F income or loss amounts, similar to those done in Gordon, Kalambokidis, and Slemrod (2004). The main reason the tax base increases for some types of business income is that the elimination of interest deductions outweighs any reduction in the tax base through changes in capital recovery and inventory rules.

23. We assume that house values for itemizers are 100 times the value of itemized deductions for real estate taxes. We derived this assumption from data on the ratio of property taxes to housing value of owner-occupied housing calculated from the 2000 census. Simulation results are available from authors upon request.

24. Proportionate increases would lead to the individual income tax rates, the alternative minimum tax rates, and the corporate income rate being increased by 6.8 percent. Increasing the corporate tax rate from 35 to 37.4 percent results in corporate tax revenue that is 81 percent of its current-law value. This is assuming that the mortgage interest deduction is repealed; if it were retained, tax rates would need to increase by 14 to 18 percent (depending whether the amount of mortgage interest deductions changed). Simulations assuming the mortgage interest deduction is retained are available from the authors. The lowest-income groups include some taxpayers with substantial amounts of interest, dividends, and capital gains, offset by business losses that reduce their net income.

25. The entire set of individual income tax rates would change from 10, 15, 25, 28, 33, and 35 percent to 9.5, 14.2, 23.5, 32.3, 37.4, and 43.9 percent.

26. Information on the stock of household wealth comes from the Federal Reserve Flow of Fund Accounts. We estimated the basis of private assets by excluding housing assets, pension funds, and the net value of life insurance, and by assuming the value of unrealized capital gains in publicly traded stock and mutual funds is 26.8 percent of asset value, based on Poterba and Weisbenner (2001).

27. Compared with current law, their taxes would fall only to the extent that they are saving more than the amounts they are currently allowed to deposit in IRAs, 401(k) plans, and other tax-deferred saving plans. Most people, however, currently deposit less than the allowable limits, so they would not benefit from consumption tax treatment of all their saving.

28. For reviews of these studies, see Gravelle (1994) and Congressional Budget Office (1997).

29. For example, a widely cited study of the economic effects of tax reform by Altig and colleagues (2001) assumes a "modest" substitution elasticity of 0.25 between present and future consumption, suggesting a mainstream view that saving behavior is somewhat but not very responsive to rates of return. The relationship between the assumed elasticity of substitution between present and future consumption and the interest-elasticity of savings depends on other parameters of the model.

30. Auerbach and Hassett (2005) summarize the theoretical literature of adopting an ideal consumption tax, reporting estimates of increased economic output that range from 5 to 10 percent. However, these gains in output are not fully realized when actual proposed reforms are evaluated. For example, Auerbach (1996), using a life-cycle model, examines the likely efficiency gains of adopting specific reforms under discussion in the 1990s. He finds that depending on the reform adopted, efficiency gains vary between 0.1 and 6.4 percent, assuming no adjustment costs. (The highest gains require moving to a national sales tax or VAT system with a single rate.) If adjustment costs are assumed or transition relief is included, these gains fall dramatically.

31. This increase will hurt older transitional generations because of the implicit levy on their existing capital, and the transition rules combined with the flat rate structure will leave lower-income households worse off.

32. See U.S. Census, Survey of Income and Program Participation (1996).

33. For college and graduate students, the portion of education expenses deductible as forgone earnings is also likely to be subject to a positive effective tax rate on the capital income it produces, because the marginal tax rate on the forgone earnings will usually be much lower than the marginal tax rate on the earnings that their education produces.

REFERENCES

Altig, David, Alan J. Auerbach, Laurence J. Kotlikoff, Kent A. Smetters, and Jan Walliser. 2001. "Simulating Fundamental Tax Reform in the United States." *American Economic Review* 91:574–95.

Atkinson, Anthony B., and Joseph E. Stiglitz. 1976. "The Design of Tax Structure: Direct Versus Indirect Taxation." *Journal of Public Economics* 6:55–75.

Auerbach, Alan. 1996. "Tax Reform, Capital Allocation, Efficiency, and Growth." In *Economic Effects of Fundamental Tax Reform,* edited by Henry J. Aaron and William G. Gale (29–73). Washington, DC: Brookings Institution Press.

Auerbach, Alan J., and Kevin A. Hassett, eds. 2005. *Toward Fundamental Tax Reform*. Washington, DC: American Enterprise Institute.

Blinder, Alan S., and Angus Deaton. 1985. "The Time Series Consumption Function Revisited." *Brookings Papers on Economic Activity* 2:465–511.

Boskin, Michael. 1978. "Taxation, Savings, and the Rate of Interest." *Journal of Political Economy* 86(January): s3–s27.

Bosworth, Barry. 1984. *Tax Incentives and Economic Growth*. Washington, DC: Brookings Institution Press.

Bradford, David F. 1986. *Untangling the Income Tax*. Cambridge MA: Harvard University Press.

———. 2005. "A Tax System for the Twenty-First Century." In *Toward Fundamental Tax Reform*, edited by Alan J. Auerbach and Kevin A. Hassett (81–94). Washington DC: AEI Press.

Bradford, David F., and U.S. Treasury Tax Policy Staff. 1984. *Blueprints for Basic Tax Reform, 2nd Edition*. Arlington, VA: Tax Analysts.

Burman, Leonard E., and David White. 2003. "Taxing Capital Gains in New Zealand." *New Zealand Journal of Taxation Law and Policy:* 355–86.

Carlino, Gerald A. 1982. "Interest Rate Effects and Temporary Consumption." *Journal of Monetary Economics* (March): 223–34.

Carroll, Christopher A. 2000. "Why Do the Rich Save So Much?" In *Does Atlas Shrug? The Economic Consequences of Taxing the Rich*, edited by Joel Slemrod (465–484). Cambridge, MA: Harvard University Press.

Choi, James J., David Laibson, Brigette C. Madrian, and Andrew Metrick. 2006. "Saving for Retirement on the Path of Least Resistance." In *Behavioral Public Finance: Toward a New Agenda*, edited by Edward McCaffrey and Joel Slemrod (304–351). New York: Russell Sage Foundation.

Christian, Ernest, and Gary Robbins. 2002. "Stealth Approach to Tax Reform." *Washington Times*, November 1.

Cnossen, Sijbren, and Lans Bovenberg. 2002. "Fundamental Tax Reform in the Netherlands." *International Tax and Public Finance* 7:471–84.

Congressional Budget Office. 1997. *The Economic Effects of Comprehensive Tax Reform*. CBO Study, July. Washington, DC: Congressional Budget Office.

Cremer, Helmuth, Pierre Pestieau, and Jean-Charles Rochet. 2001. "Direct Versus Indirect Taxation: The Design of the Tax Structure Revisited." *International Economic Review* 42(3): 781–800.

Engen, Eric, and William G. Gale. 2000. "The Effects of 401(k) Plans on Household Wealth: Differences across Earnings Groups." NBER Working Paper No. 8032. Cambridge, MA: National Bureau of Economic Research.

Engen, Eric, William G. Gale, and John Karl Scholz. 1996. "The Illusory Effects of Saving Incentives on Saving." *Journal of Economic Perspectives* 10(4): 113–38.

Engen, Eric, William G. Gale, and Cori E. Uccello. 1999. "The Adequacy of Household Saving." *Brookings Papers on Economic Activity* 2:65–165.

Friend, Irwin, and Joel Hasbrouck. 1983. "Saving and After-Tax Rates of Return." *Review of Economics and Statistics* 65(November): 537–43.

Gale, William G., and John Karl Scholz. 1994. "IRAs and Household Saving." *American Economic Review* 84(December): 1233–60.

Gale, William, Mark Iwry, and Peter R. Orszag. 2005. "The Saver's Credit: Expanding Retirement Savings for Middle- and Lower-Income Americans." Washington, DC: Retirement Security Project, March. http://www.brook.edu/views/papers/20050310orszag.pdf.

Ginsburg, Martin D. 1995. "Life under a Personal Consumption Tax: Some Thoughts on Working, Saving, and Consuming in Nunn-Domenici's Tax World." *National Tax Journal* 68:585–602.

Gordon, Roger, Laura Kalambokidis, and Joel Slemrod. 2004. "Do We Now Collect Any Revenue from Taxing Capital Income?" *Journal of Public Economics* 88(5): 981–1009.

Gordon, Roger, Laura Kalambokidis, Jeffrey Rohaly, and Joel Slemrod. 2004. "Toward a Consumption Tax and Beyond." *American Economic Review. Papers and Proceedings* 94(2): 161–65.

Graetz, Michael. 1979. "Implementing a Progressive Consumption Tax." *Harvard Law Review* 92(8): 1575–1661.

———. 1997. *The Decline (and Fall?) of the Income Tax.* New York: W. W. Norton & Company.

Gravelle, Jane. 1994. *The Economic Effects of Taxing Capital Income.* Cambridge, MA: MIT Press.

Grubert, Harry, and T. Scott Newlon. 1995. "The International Implications of Consumption Tax Proposals." *National Tax Journal* 48(4): 619–47.

Hall, Robert E., and Alvin Rabushka. 1995. *The Flat Tax.* Stanford, CA: Hoover Institution Press.

Howrey, E. Philip, and Saul H. Hymans. 1980. "The Measurement and Determination of Loanable Funds Saving." *Brookings Papers on Economic Activity* 3:655–705.

Hubbard, R. Glenn, and William M. Gentry. 2000. "Entrepreneurship and Household Saving." NBER Working Paper no. 7894. Cambridge, MA: National Bureau of Economic Research.

Judd, Kenneth L. 1985. "Redistributive Income in a Simple Perfect Foresight Model." *Journal of Public Economics* 28:59–83.

———. 1997. "The Optimal Tax Rate for Capital Income is Negative." NBER Working Paper No. 6004. Cambridge, MA: National Bureau of Economic Research.

Kotlikoff, Laurence J. 1988. "Intergenerational Transfers and Saving." *Journal of Economic Perspectives* 2(2): 41–58.

Levy, Frank, and Richard Murnane. 1992. "U.S. Earnings Levels and Earnings Inequality: A Review of Recent Trends and Proposed Explanations." *Journal of Economic Literature* 30:1331–81.

Modigliani, Franco. 1988. "The Role of Intergenerational Transfers and Life-Cycle Saving in the Accumulation of Wealth." *Journal of Economic Perspectives* 2(2): 15–40.

Neuberger, Zoe, Robert Greenstein, and Eileen Sweeney. 2005. "Protecting Low-Income Families? Retirement Savings: How Retirement Accounts Are Treated in Means-Tested Programs and Steps to Remove Barriers to Retirement Saving." Washington, DC: Retirement Security Project, June. http://www.cbpp.org/6-21-05socsec.pdf.

Office of Management and Budget. 2005. *Budget of the United States Government, Analytical Perspectives.* Washington, DC: Office of Management and Budget.

Piketty, Thomas, and Emmanuel Saez. 2003. "Income Inequality in the United States, 1913–1998." *Quarterly Journal of Economics* 118:1–39.

Poterba, James M., and Scott Weisbenner. 2001. "The Distributional Burden of Taxing Estates and Unrealized Capital Gains at Death." In *Rethinking Estate and Gift Taxation*, edited by William G. Gale, James R. Hines Jr., and Joel Slemrod (422–49). Washington, DC: Brookings Institution Press.

Poterba, James M., Steven F. Venti, and David A. Wise. 1996. "How Retirement Programs Increase Savings." *Journal of Economic Perspectives* 10(4): 91–112.

Saez, Emmanuel. 2002. "The Desirability of Commodity Taxation under Non-Linear Income Taxation and Heterogeneous Tastes." *Journal of Public Economics* 83:217–30.

Shakow, David J. 1986. "Taxation Without Realization: A Proposal for Accrual Taxation." *University of Pennsylvania Law Review* 134:1111–1205.

Skinner, Jonathan, and Daniel Feenberg. 1991. "The Impact of the 1986 Tax Reform Act on Personal Saving." In *Do Taxes Matter? The Impact of the Tax Reform Act of 1986,* edited by Joel Slemrod (50–79). Cambridge, MA: MIT Press.

Steuerle, C. Eugene. 2005. "Taxing the Capital Income of Only the Poor and the Middle Class." *Tax Notes,* April 11, 239.

Toder, Eric. 1997. "Consumption Tax Proposals in the United States." In *Tax Conversations: A Guide to the Key Issues in the Tax Reform Debate,* edited by Richard Krevor. Alphen aan den Rijn, The Netherlands: Kluwer Law International.

U.S. Department of the Treasury. 1977. *Blueprints for Basic Tax Reform.* Washington DC: U.S. Government Printing Office.

———. 1984. *Tax Reform for Fairness, Simplicity, and Economic Growth.* Treasury Department Report to the President, November. Washington, DC: U.S. Department of the Treasury.

———. 1992. *Integration of the Individual and Corporate Tax Systems: Taxing Business Income Once.* Washington DC: U.S. Government Printing Office.

Weisbach, David A. 2000. "Ironing Out the Flat Tax." *Stanford Law Review* 52:599–664.

Wolff, Edward N. 1999. "Wealth Accumulation by Age Cohort in the U.S., 1962–1992: The Role of Savings, Capital Gains, and Intergenerational Transfers." *Geneva Papers on Risk and Insurance* 24(1): 27–49.

David A. Weisbach

George Zodrow in chapter 2 and Eric Toder and Kim Rueben in chapter 3 have ably reviewed the literature comparing income and consumption taxes. Zodrow has cautiously concluded that a consumption tax is desirable, while Toder and Rueben argue that the consumption tax is problematic. I believe that the case is clear: consumption taxes are strongly preferable to income taxes. In these comments, I give a brief illustration why, building arguments made in Kaplow (2006) and Atkinson and Stiglitz (1976). Along the way, I offer comments on some of the points Zodrow and Toder and Rueben make.

One of the most common arguments about the choice between an income tax and a consumption tax relies on what might be called the trade-off theory. To illustrate, consider a single individual subject to an ideal income tax and suppose that we are considering replacing the income tax with a revenue-neutral consumption tax. To keep things simple, assume that the individual does not have existing assets, so taxing him on the transition is not an issue. The income tax imposes a nominal tax on labor income and a nominal tax (at the same rate) on the return to capital. A consumption tax does not tax the normal return to capital. Because of this narrower base, the tax rate on labor income would seemingly have to be higher under a consumption tax than under an income tax. One might think, therefore, that the choice between an income tax and a consumption tax reflects a trade-off between taxing labor income more and capital income less, and that this trade-off depends on the relative elasticities of labor and savings. Toder and Rueben seem to endorse this view when they worry that the distributionally neutral consumption tax rate on the top bracket would have to be inefficiently high. They have company in making this argument.[1] Jane Gravelle, for example, states,

> the efficiency effects [of the choice between an income tax and a consumption tax] depend on assumptions about behavioral effects. If individuals are relatively unwilling to substitute consumption over time and relatively willing to substitute leisure for consumption of goods, then a significant tax on capital income would constitute part of an optimal tax system. These behavior effects are difficult to estimate empirically. (1994, 31)

This argument is incorrect—it misses a fundamental effect of taxing capital income. A tax on capital income reduces future consumption; by reducing future consumption, it reduces the reward for working. If an individual is working hard today to save for some future event, taxing the return to savings reduces the return from that work—the individual can consume less in the future for a given hour of labor. The effective tax on labor income under an income tax is a composite of the nominal labor tax rate and the effect on labor of taxing the return to savings. Once this effect is taken into account, a distributionally neutral and revenue-neutral consumption tax does not impose a higher tax on labor than an income tax does. Instead, the two impose the same tax on labor income, which means there is no trade-off. The only difference is that an income tax imposes offsetting subsidies and taxes on spending and saving. These offsetting subsidies and taxes, which have no distributional or revenue consequences, are undesirable.

We can see this point more clearly by restating the income tax so that the explicit tax rate on labor income is equal to the implicit rate, the composite of the nominal rate and the effect of reducing consumption through the tax on the return to savings. This normalized rate on labor will be higher than the nominal rate on labor income under an income tax but, by construction, equal to the actual, implicit rate on labor income under an income tax. The normalized rate will vary by savings rates. If our sample individual saves more, the effect of the tax on the return to savings will be greater and the normalized rate on labor income will be higher.

An income tax, by taxing savings, not only reduces the return to labor. It also skews the choice between current consumption and future consumption. To capture this effect once we have restated the tax rate on labor, we have to restate the tax on savings as both a tax on savings and an offsetting subsidy for spending. The tax and the subsidy must perfectly offset (in amount), or the normalized labor tax rate will be wrong. If the tax and subsidy do not offset, there is a net tax (or subsidy) on future consumption, which is effectively an additional tax on labor, contrary to how the normalized tax on labor was set. Thus, we can restate an income tax as a tax on labor income (at the composite rate) plus a zero-revenue residual, made up of offsetting taxes on savings and subsidies for spending.

To illustrate, suppose that there is a 20 percent income tax. Suppose also that an individual earns $250 before taxes, pays a $50 tax on his labor income, and is left with $200 to spend. Finally, suppose that the individual spends $100 today and saves $100 for his retirement in 25 years. The annual interest rate on savings is 5 percent.

Under the income tax, as normally conceived, the tax on capital income reduces the return on the savings by the tax rate, here from 5 to 4 percent. Thus, with no taxes on savings, the individual in retirement would have the future value of $100 at 5 percent, or roughly $340 to spend. With taxes, the individual earns only 4 percent and his future consumption is reduced to about $270. The reduction in future consumption from $340 to $270 is like a 20 percent excise tax on that future consumption.[2]

Suppose that instead of the conventional income tax, we impose a tax on labor income at 29 percent, a subsidy of 12 percent for current consumption, and a 12 percent tax on future consumption. Under this tax, the individual has after-tax wages of approximately $180. If he spends half this amount, $90, and receives the 12 percent subsidy, he can spend $100 today as before. He saves the other half of his after-wage-tax earnings and must pay the additional 12 percent tax on savings. This leaves him with about $80, which grows at the pretax interest rate to the same $270. The consumption opportunities, present and future, are the same under this normalized tax and the conventional income tax. If the individual would choose this pattern under the usual income tax, he could also choose this pattern under the normalized income tax.

With this normalization, we can now compare the 20 percent income tax with a revenue-neutral 29 percent consumption (or wage) tax. By construction, they both impose the same tax on labor income. Therefore, labor effort and the labor/leisure distortion will be the same under the two taxes. This also means that both taxes raise the same revenue from wages. The income tax, however, has the offsetting tax and subsidy. This combination produces no additional revenue but distorts savings decisions. The consumption tax eliminates this distortion. Leaving aside the possible second-best issues (discussed below), the consumption tax is, therefore, superior for this individual. The individual has the same distortion in work effort and government revenues are the same, but the individual is able to make less distorted savings decisions.

The analysis above concerned only a single individual and, therefore, did not take into account distributional effects. We can, however, perform the same normalization within each wage class. Those with higher wage income are likely to save more. The implicit tax on labor income, therefore, will be relatively higher for wage classes, which means that the normalized rate on labor income will be correspondingly higher for these classes. Thus, the normalized income tax rate in the example was 29 percent because of the enormously high 50 percent savings rate. If the individual earned less and saved less, say he saved 5 percent of after-tax earnings, the normalized tax on labor income would be 21 percent. We can find the normalized tax rate on labor within each wage or income class. If the rich tend to save more than the poor, the normalization will produce a higher wage tax rate on the rich than the poor.

We can then compare an income tax with a consumption tax that uses the normalized rates. For the same reasons that applied to the single-individual example, for each income class, individuals in that class would be better off facing a consumption tax at the normalized rate than facing the income tax. If we replace the income tax with a consumption tax using these rates, therefore, individuals in each class—poor, middle, rich, and filthy rich—would be better off. Distributional concerns would be entirely resolved, and efficiency improved. That is, we can view choice between an income tax and a consumption tax as merely the choice of whether to impose the residual, a revenue- and *distributionally neutral* subsidy for spending and tax on savings. Imposing this residual tax might sometimes be desirable (as discussed below), but penalizing savings purely to subsidize spending is not. For this reason, a consumption tax is likely preferable to an income tax.

Seen this way, saving or spending are just consumption choices, like chocolate or vanilla. The income tax distorts this choice without producing an offsetting benefit, such as better redistribution or less distortion in labor effort. We normally think it best to let individuals make consumption decisions based on market prices, with exceptions where we think the market is imperfect or where individuals make systematic mistakes. We do not think these exceptions apply in the case of chocolate or vanilla, and few would propose a tax that distorts such a choice. Many seem to believe that savings are different, however. Perhaps the problem is that high-wage individuals save relatively more than low-wage individuals, but the argument above is adjusted for this effect. In fact, this argument for taxing savings is identical to the argument for a luxury tax. Just as the rich save more, making a tax on savings look attractive for distributional purposes, the rich consume more luxuries, making a tax on luxuries look attractive for distributional purposes. We know, however, that we are better off with higher but broad-based tax rates and no luxury tax; we can achieve the appropriate redistribution without the additional distortions created by taxing luxuries. The same holds true for savings. Perhaps the argument is that individuals make systematic mistakes about the amount to save, but in the United States today, they seem unlikely to save too much. Penalizing savings, as under an income tax, is a move in the wrong direction.

This argument illustrates why the trade-off theory is incorrect. Thus, under the Toder and Rueben simulation, the highest marginal consumption tax rate under a distributionally neutral consumption tax would have to be 44 percent. They worry that this rate would be too high, causing undue economic distortions. But high-income individuals already face that rate implicitly under the income tax. The distributionally neutral tax rate is just the normalized rate calculated above. Worries that the rate is too high are unrelated to the choice of the tax base. For the same reasons, measurements of the relative elasticities of labor and savings are not needed (Gravelle 1994; Gruber 2005). We do not have to know this information to know that a consumption tax is superior to an income tax.

Like any simplified economic model, there are exceptions and qualifications to the reasoning given above. One mentioned by both Zodrow and Toder and Rueben is that savings might be a relative complement to leisure. If so, taxing savings may reduce the labor/leisure distortion. If, however, saving is a relative substitute for leisure, we might want to subsidize savings. We do not have good data on this, but my initial guess is that savings should be subsidized because it is a relative substitute. As Roger Gordon (2000) notes, "hours of work and retirement ages tend to be higher for the more able, suggesting a subsidy rather than a tax on capital income" (29–30). Another possibility is that saving within wage classes is heterogeneous, and that for two people with the same wage income, the one with higher savings is the more able (Saez 2002). Neither Zodrow nor Toder and Reuben seem to think this reason is likely to lead to an income tax, and I agree.

The argument described above is compelling. So what arguments, in the face of this reasoning, might lead to support of an income tax? There are many, although most of them, upon close examination, fall apart.

The most serious concern is that consumption taxes, when actually enacted, would not be sufficiently progressive. The issue is more subtle than it first appears. Zodrow asks whether capital income should be taxed under a consumption method, while Toder and Rueben ask whether we should eliminate the taxation of capital income. These are not the same thing. In particular, a well-designed consumption tax would tax economic rents and, therefore, would not eliminate taxes on capital income. The difference between an income tax and a consumption tax is solely the taxation of the risk-free, time value return, not the entire return to capital. Therefore, we could answer no to Toder and Rueben's question and still support a consumption tax. Progressivity may depend on the taxation of rents because rents may be even more heavily distributed toward the wealthy than other types of capital income. If so, the distributional implications of switching to a consumption tax might be quite different from what they otherwise would be, and the rates necessary to make a consumption tax distributionally equivalent to a given income tax would be lower.

No one yet knows for certain whether implementing a sufficiently progressive consumption tax is possible. Some studies suggest that taxing the very highest earners at the correct rates would be difficult. Bankman and Schler (chapter 6) suggest that implementation would be problematic. However, agreement that a consumption tax is desirable in theory and that the only real questions are ones of design would be a large step forward. Moreover, if this is the case, the attitude we should take is optimistic— we should try to design a workable system. Although designing such a system will unquestionably be difficult, we should expect consumption taxes to be easier to implement than income taxes. Both taxes have the same implicit wage tax, but the income tax also has the tax on savings and the subsidy for spending. It is hard to believe that progressive consumption taxes would be more difficult to collect than income taxes. This view, however, is just a hypothesis, and may be proven wrong. Jumping to the conclusion that an income tax is superior because we do not yet have a final design for a consumption tax seems unjustified. Moreover, if anyone were to suggest current law as a design for an income tax, they would be laughed at, so a perfect design for a consumption tax should not be the standard. Even if we fully accept the concerns raised by Bankman and Schler's skepticism, the resulting tax is unlikely to be harder to implement than a realization-based income tax.

Another concern Toder and Rueben raise is that the data on savings elasticity are unclear, and we cannot know that switching to a consumption tax will increase savings. I don't know whether increasing savings is a good idea, and I don't know how anyone else knows. The argument made above did not rely on an increase in savings to show that a consumption tax is superior to an income tax. Perhaps those who look for an increase in savings are making the trade-off mistake illustrated above. Large-scale simulations tend to look at savings as a way of increasing growth and growth as a measure of welfare. However, this is an indirect method of measuring welfare gains. The argument made above shows that we should expect welfare gains without regard to whether savings increases or decreases.

Yet another concern is that savings produces more than just future consumption; savings creates power, prestige, and security. An income tax, so the argument goes, is needed to reduce these additional benefits to savings. If we have a distributionally neutral consumption tax, however, we have already adjusted the system for high and low earners' different savings propensities. Therefore, to the extent that differences in power and prestige are due to differences in savings rates, we are discussing savings choices within an income class, not across income classes. We are comparing who is better off: a lawyer making $400,000 a year who spends, or a lawyer making $400,000 a year who saves. Savings within an income class, however, is a choice, like any other choice. Some may choose to save because they value the benefits—future consumption, power, prestige— and some may choose to spend because they value the benefits. The entire set of benefits from each choice will be relevant to individuals making these decisions; that more than one source of benefits to savings exists is not particularly relevant. Moreover, if we are seriously concerned about power, we should address it directly, such as through reform of the campaign finance system. And if we are going to tax sources of power and prestige, we would have to go far beyond savings, taxing such items as admittance to universities and social clubs, awards, and promotion to management positions. Supporting an income tax as a method of limiting or redistributing power and prestige is not a good argument.

Another critical aspect of this tax-base choice is the transition from an income to a consumption tax. Many have argued that the problem of transition either makes switching to a consumption tax prohibitive or, in the other direction, desirable. Transition might make the change impossible, if transition relief must be provided and such relief is both expensive and complex. Yet, a consumption tax might be all the more desirable if transition creates a lump-sum tax on existing capital. (Note, however, that the argument for a consumption tax made above did not rely at all on a lump-sum tax. Any potential lump-sum tax would just make the argument stronger.)

Some have argued that a consumption tax must, by definition, include a tax on old capital on transition, and because such a tax is infeasible, so is a consumption tax (e.g., Gravelle 1995). Arguing by definition, however, forecloses debate rather than advances understanding. And two can play that game. An income tax is defined as a tax on consumption plus the return to savings. A consumption tax is defined as a tax on wages plus old capital. Therefore, following the syllogism, an income tax imposes a tax on wages, old capital, and the return to savings. If we are to retain an income tax, we must, by definition, tax existing capital in exactly the same way (although possibly at a different rate) as under a consumption tax. Fortunately for tax policy, however, definitions should not be given any weight. Instead, whether to tax old capital is a question of policy, to be evaluated by the consequences for welfare.

Significant unresolved issues are associated with transition, such as whether transition relief is desirable and how transition relief (or lack of relief) would affect asset prices. These issues are likely to be sensitive to the design of the consumption tax. For example, whether transition to a consumption tax creates a lump-sum tax on old capital seems to depend on whether individuals, having had their basis wiped out once on transition to the consumption tax, believe it can happen again. They might think the transition was a one-time event because under a cash flow system, which is a possible consumption tax system, there is no basis and therefore nothing to wipe out in the future. Taxpayers will recover their costs from the government up front and will no longer have to rely on (bad) promises of recovery in the future. But under a basis system, which is an alternative consumption tax regime (with basis increased in each period by inflation and the risk-free rate of return and recovered as assets depreciate), basis is around to be wiped out again. Thus, whether the tax is lump sum may depend on details of implementation and the psychology of individual investors rather than on deep questions of economic theory.

The final issue is the claim that the United States should not switch to a consumption tax because of unspecified fear about the consequences. Major tax reform might produce substantial effects and we cannot confidently predict them all. Caution is justified. At the same time, if we believe that a consumption tax *should* produce gains, whether in welfare, collection costs, gross domestic product, or any other preferred measure, we should study concerns to see if they are real and if so, solvable. Generalized fear, if taken too far, becomes a trump card used by those in favor of the status quo against any change. Analysts cannot respond because generalized fear of the unknown, by definition, raises no specific concerns. Even if all specific concerns were addressed, there is always the possibility that something has been missed. We owe it to ourselves and to posterity to make better arguments.

NOTES

1. Gravelle (1994) and Gruber (2005), for example, both make this argument.

2. Throughout this comment, I employ extremely crude rounding to make the examples readable. The actual implicit rate is 21.28 percent. Apologies to those who wish for precision. The basic points remain, notwithstanding.

REFERENCES

Atkinson, Anthony B., and Joseph E. Stiglitz. 1976. "The Design of Tax Structure: Direct versus Indirect Taxation." *Journal of Public Economics* 6:55–75.

Gordon, Roger H. 2000. "Taxation of Capital Income vs. Labour Income: An Overview." In *Taxing Capital in the European Union,* edited by Sijbren Cnossen (15–45). Oxford, UK: Oxford University Press.

Gravelle, Jane G. 1994. *The Economic Effects of Taxing Capital Income.* Boston: MIT Press.

———. 1995. *The Flat Tax and Other Proposals: Who Will Bear the Tax Burden?* Report for Congress 95-1141E. Washington, DC: Congressional Research Service.

Gruber, Jonathan. 2005. *Public Finance and Public Policy.* New York: Worth Publishers.

Kaplow, Louis. 2006. "On the Undesirability of Commodity Taxation Even When Income Taxation Is Not Optimal." *Journal of Public Economics* 90(6–7): 1235–50.

Saez, Emmanuel. 2002. "The Desirability of Commodity Taxation under Non-Linear Income Taxation and Heterogeneous Tastes." *Journal of Public Economics* 83(2): 217–30.

Joseph J. Thorndike

Should we tax capital income? It's an old question, older even than the income tax itself. Indeed, the modern American income tax emerged as an *answer*—although hardly a definitive one—to this question. The tax treatment of capital income has long been at the center of our fiscal policy, and it seems likely to remain there.

"Should we," of course, is a question of political economy, crossing disciplinary boundaries to engage economists, political scientists, and legal scholars. These tax experts have developed an impressive body of literature on the question. Many—perhaps even most—have concluded that we should not tax capital income. They have argued for a shift to consumption taxation, offering arguments for efficiency and equity to bolster the case for sweeping reform.

But if the expert consensus seems clear, popular opinion remains unsettled. Discontent with the income tax pervades contemporary politics. Academic plans for consumption tax reform have entered the rough-and-tumble world of national politics. A few plans have even developed a political constituency: the flat tax became an issue in the 1996 presidential campaign. A national retail sales tax enjoys vocal support in Congress. Such proposals promise a dramatic break with our fiscal history. Their sheer audacity seems to generate an initial flush of enthusiasm. To date, however, such ambitious plans have consistently foundered in the political arena.

What, then, are the prospects for consumption tax reform? As they say on Wall Street, past performance is no indication of future results. Such caveats aside, any effort to relieve the tax burden on capital income will be a tough sell. For almost a century, the comprehensive income tax has been a resilient feature of American society, fending off a series of powerful challenges. American leaders have consistently embraced the notion that *all* income should be subject to tax—in theory, if not always in practice. Just as surely, lawmakers have rejected efforts to impose broad-based consumption taxes, either as a replacement for the income tax, or as a supplement to it.[1]

To some degree, inertia can explain the failure of consumption tax proposals. Sweeping change is always difficult, especially once lawmakers move from the general to the specific. But inertia tells just part of the story. To fully understand the longevity—and tenacity—of the modern income tax, we must consider American political culture. Specifically, one must appreciate the ambiguous moral status that American society has long attached to money, wealth, and income.

Two elements of American tax history shed some light on the gap between expert theory and political reality, at least when it comes to taxing capital income. The first element is the conflicted American attitude toward wealth and saving, including moral distinctions between different types of income. Such distinctions will almost certainly bedevil efforts to reduce or eliminate the tax burden on capital income.

The second consideration is the nation's brief mid-century flirtation with a cash-flow tax on personal consumption: the "spendings tax" of 1942. As Toder and Rueben observe, the tax is attractive in theory but daunting in prospect. "No country has a tax system of this type," they point out, although, for a few brief moments it looked like the United States might. The ultimate failure of this novel idea—a failure both rapid and predictable—might well serve as an object lesson in the perils of fundamental tax reform.

The Moral Status of Capital Income

Since its inception, the modern American income tax has been levied on many types of capital income, including interest, dividends, and capital gains.[2] Committed, at least ostensibly, to a comprehensive definition of income, 20th-century policymakers generally rejected claims that capital income should remain outside the scope of the federal income tax. These same policymakers, however, have willingly differentiated among various kinds of income. Over the past century, they have allowed deferral of taxation on capital gains and excluded a varying portion of capital gains from taxation or applied lower rates than those on labor income. And this differentiation has been consistently inconsistent: lawmakers have been willing, for instance, to grant preferential treatment to labor income (the earned income credit is an example), even as they offered other preferences to certain types of capital income, especially capital gains.[3]

This contradiction reflects a broader tension within American political culture. As legal historian Marjorie Kornhauser has pointed out in her outstanding article on money and morality, Americans aren't sure how they feel about wealth. They show a reverence for it, and an admiration for those who earn it. But they also harbor a deep-seated suspicion that wealth is also a source of contagion, the root of moral, political, and economic corruption (Kornhauser 1994).

The pro-wealth strand of American political culture draws on an ingrained form of individualism, according to Kornhauser, loosely rooted in classical liberal theory. The anti-wealth strand, drawing on the tradition of small-r republicanism, tends toward a more communal, egalitarian view of society. Programmatically, liberalism has been used to buttress property rights and economic freedom, while republicanism has been called to the service of equality and social justice. Such distinctions are easily overdrawn, but the division is real enough, at least in the abstract world of political theory. In the messy world of political reality, however, the dichotomy breaks down. An effort to reconcile the discordant strains of their ideological heritage led Americans to craft a hybrid ideology: "moral economic individualism." This amalgamation ties the liberal rights of the individual to a republican notion of the common good (Kornhauser 1994, 124–28).[4]

Moral economic individualism—and the ambiguous moral status it grants to wealth—has shaped American political development for more than two centuries. It has had a particularly strong influence on the nation's fiscal history. And nowhere is this influence more obvious than on the subject of capital income.

While policymakers have long paid homage to the ideal of a comprehensive tax base, the income tax has, in practice, frequently distinguished among types of income. In particular, it has reflected a preference for "earned" income from labor, imbuing it with a higher moral status than "unearned" income from capital (Kornhauser 1994, 119).[5] Today's call to eliminate income taxation of capital income starkly contrasts with this tradition.

The American preference for earned income, actively debated from the 1890s onward, was not enshrined in legislation until 1924. The timing seems ironic. The 1920s are often remembered as the age of Andrew Mellon and his wealth-friendly tax cuts. But it was Mellon who actually championed the preference for earned income. Amid his sweeping tax cuts, this patron saint of modern supply-siders urged lawmakers to grant a tax credit (in the form of a deduction) for a certain amount of labor income.[6] Mellon, like many of his contemporaries, saw a moral distinction between different types of income.

> The fairness of taxing more lightly income from wages, salaries or from investments is beyond question. In the first case, the income is uncertain and limited in duration; sickness or death destroys it and old age diminishes it; in the other, the source of income continues; the income may be disposed of during a man's life and it descends to his heirs (1924, 56–57).[7]

Such arguments enjoyed broad support across the political spectrum, and around the world as well. British lawmakers had created an earned income credit (EIC) in 1907. Some supporters traced its origin to John Stuart Mill. Others insisted that agitation had begun shortly after William Pitt the Younger introduced the first income tax in 1798.[8] Some supporters of the earned income credit also insisted that the provision was a backdoor means of taxing wealth. This was not an argument embraced by Mellon or most of his fellow Republicans. But it did reflect an element of the republican tradition, including its suspicion of accumulated fortunes, and helps explain why the Mellon EIC enjoyed overwhelming support among lawmakers.[9]

In operation, the EIC proved troublesome. In 1928, William R. Green, chair of the House Ways and Means Committee, suggested that it might be responsible for 10 percent of all individual income tax return errors. But lawmakers refused to back down, insisting on the moral necessity of such a preference. Legislators would never abandon the credit, insisted William R. Green, chairman of the House Ways and Means Committee. They were firmly convinced by "every argument in the way of reason and justice supporting it" (1928, 95).

The EIC disappeared in the early years of the Great Depression, a casualty of soaring deficits. But the fairness of this preference remained unchallenged, and the EIC reappeared in 1934. It remained a fixture of federal taxation through the end of World War II. Finally, Congress repealed it once again in 1947. Still dogged by complaints that it was unnecessarily complex, it ultimately succumbed to charges that it impeded capital formation.[10]

The odyssey of Andrew Mellon's earned income credit demonstrates the ambiguity and malleability of American attitudes toward wealth and income. The rise of the credit reflected a popular conviction, prevalent throughout the first half of the 20th century, that while all types of income are ostensibly equal, some forms are more equal than others. The credit's fall, by contrast, reveals the resurgent power of liberalism in the postwar version of moral economic individualism. Indeed, the latter half of the 20th century has witnessed a steady increase in the influence of this ideological tradition, especially around tax policy.[11]

The "Spendings Tax" of 1942

Given modern interest in cash-flow taxes on personal expenditure, it seems reasonable to recount one of the most serious efforts in our history to establish such a levy.[12]

Treasury Secretary Henry Morgenthau offered his plan for a progressive spendings tax on September 3, 1942. At the time, Congress was well into its work on the mammoth Revenue Act of 1942 (later described by its chief architect as "the Greatest Tax Bill in American History"). Morgenthau (1942) offered his plan with two aims in mind. First, he needed money. Expenditures for fiscal year 1942 were expected to top $80 billion, while revenue projections for the 1942 act were running at only $24 billion. Second, Treasury officials were still seeking ways to control inflation. By draining Americans of additional income, the spendings tax would help slow the powerful war-borne price rise.

The spendings tax was designed to supplement, not replace, the individual income tax. The Treasury suggested that the two taxes could be administered jointly. Taxpayers would file a combined return and send in a single payment. Individuals would calculate their total spending indirectly, subtracting savings from the total amount of available funds (including current income, borrowing, and reductions in capital). Savings were broadly defined to include debt repayment, life insurance premiums, purchases of capital assets, gifts and contributions, tax payments, and increases in bank balances. The spendings tax would then be imposed in two parts: a flat-rate tax of 10 percent to be refunded after the war, and a progressive surtax. The refundable portion was to be a flat tax on all spending. It would have applied to all individuals already paying the income tax. The proposal made no provision for any deductions or exempt spending level. This portion of the tax amounted to a compulsory, interest-free loan from the taxpayer to the government. The surtax, by contrast, was to be imposed at progressive rates ranging from 10 to 75 percent on all expenditures in excess of certain exempt amounts. The Treasury left open the possibility that various "extraordinary expenditures" might be made deductible (Morgenthau 1942).

The Treasury proposal drew on earlier studies of spendings taxation, including proposals by economists Thomas S. Adams (1921) and Irving Fisher (1939), not to mention a 1921 plan by Rep. Ogden Mills, (R-NY) who later served as secretary of the Treasury under Herbert Hoover. Unlike some of these earlier proposals, however, the Treasury version was never conceived as a replacement for the income tax.[13]

The spendings tax enjoyed several advantages over alternatives, principally a further increase in income tax rates or the enactment of a general sales tax. In comparison with the former, it would more effectively curtail consumer spending, making it a better weapon for fighting inflation. Second, a steep progressive rate structure might permit fairly close regulation of individual spending levels. Third, the spendings tax was thought to be more politically palatable than further extension of the income tax. Because most taxpayers had some discretion over how much to spend, they could become their "own tax assessor" (Paul 1954, 294).

Treasury officials also believed the spendings tax enjoyed several important advantages over a general sales tax. First, it allowed for a simple way of granting personal exemptions and would be less inflationary than a sales tax. In addition, it would not upset wartime price controls, then in their early stages and already under considerable strain. Finally, sales taxes were considered more administratively burdensome, demanding an entirely new collection structure, while the spendings tax would piggyback on the income tax (Blough 1942).

Perhaps the most attractive quality of the spendings tax, however, was its supposed political palatability. Franklin Roosevelt, long opposed to a national retail sales tax, briefly flirted with it because of wartime revenue needs. But organized labor helped kill that idea, and Roosevelt agreed to advance the spendings tax as an alternative.

Lawmakers, however, regarded the spendings tax as too complicated. They rejected Treasury claims that it would present no great difficulty for anyone already filing an income tax return. Treasury even offered sample returns, but to no avail. Randolph Paul (1954) later observed that such complaints are almost inevitable whenever a tax plan is offered in substantive detail.

The Senate Finance Committee dispensed with the spendings tax summarily. As *Time* magazine (1942) observed: "Henry Morgenthau and his tax experts marched up Capitol Hill and marched right down again. They came up to propose a new tax program; for all political purposes, they were almost kicked downhill" ("Congress" 1942). Robert C. Albright of the *Washington Post* provided a memorable epitaph. The spendings tax, he quipped, was "Morgenthau's morning glory. It opened Tuesday morning and it folded before noon" (1942).[14]

NOTES

1. Three examples come to mind. In 1921, conservative Republicans tried to replace the young income tax—still less than a decade old—with a national retail sales tax. They abandoned the effort only after Treasury Secretary Andrew Mellon signaled his opposition. In 1932, Democratic congressional leaders endorsed a manufacturers' sales tax, eager to cloak themselves in the mantle of fiscal probity as the Great Depression wreaked havoc with the federal budget. Open rebellion among the party's rank and file quickly derailed the plan. And in 1942, lawmakers across the political spectrum nearly approved a retail sales tax to help pay for World War II. They opted for broad-based income taxes only after President Franklin Roosevelt signaled his implacable opposition to any sort of broad-based consumption levy.

2. When I refer to the modern federal income tax, I mean the fiscal innovation enacted in 1913. While both the Union and the Confederacy levied income taxes during the Civil War, such taxes are best viewed as collateral, not lineal, ancestors of the 20th-century tax. For the best modern treatment of the Civil War income tax, including its effort to tax certain types of capital income, see Stanley (1993).

3. On the history of capital gains preferences, see Kornhauser (1985) and Lee (2005).

4. Recent historiography rejects any dichotomy between liberalism and republicanism. The literature on this debate is vast, but for a reasonable starting point, see Pocock (1975), Rodgers (1992), and Wood (1969, 1991).

5. For Americans of the early 20th century, "earned income" included any income derived from "personal exertion," according to the era's leading economist, Edwin R. A. Seligman. "Unearned income," by contrast, was any money flowing from investments (Seligman 1921, 23).

6. Lawmakers granted earned income, defined to include any income under $5,000, a 25 percent credit. The Treasury estimated this provision would cost the government $60 million in calendar year 1925, but in an era of buoyant revenue, such a loss seemed trifling (Blakey 1924).

7. Mellon continued,

> Surely we can afford to make a distinction between the people whose only capital is their mental and physical energy and the people whose income is derived from investments. Such a distinction would mean much to millions of American workers and would be an added inspiration to the man who must provide a competence during his few productive years to care for himself and his family when his earnings capacity is at an end. (1924, 56–57)

8. British tax officials later noted that that differentiation between earned and unearned income was "desirable and just," as well as politically popular. Critics objected that any effort to distinguish between different types of income was prone to error. Even more damning, the preference for earned income worked to the disadvantage of certain worthy taxpayers, such as widows living off returns to their husband's accumulated savings (Daunton 2002, 115–16).

On the British rationale for the earned income preference, see Pigou (1920, 614–15) and Stamp (1915). For William Pitt observation, see Comstock (1920, 495).

9. For a critical assessment of the wealth-tax argument for an earned income preference, see Goode (1964, 255). See also Kornhauser (1994, 143).

10. On the changing fortunes of the earned income credit throughout the 1920s and 1930s, see U.S. Department of the Treasury (1937).

11. On the rise of pro-growth ideology among American tax experts and congressional taxwriters, see Ventry (2003).

12. See, for instance, Seidman (1997). See also, more recently, MacGuineas (2004).

13. Many of the earlier plans for a spendings tax were designed to correct a perceived flaw in the income tax: the so-called "double taxation" of savings. The 1942 proposal recognized no such flaw, merely suggesting the spendings tax as a source of additional income during the war emergency.

14. Over the next year or so, Treasury did continue to study the levy, convinced of its virtues. But it never again received serious consideration.

REFERENCES

Adams, Thomas S. 1921. "Fundamental Problems of Federal Income Taxation." *Quarterly Journal of Economics* 35(4): 527–56.

Albright, Robert C. 1942. "Gallery Glimpses." *Washington Post,* September 6.

Blakey, Roy G. 1924. "The Revenue Act of 1924." *American Economic Review* 14(3): 475–504.

Blough, Roy. 1942. "The Spendings Tax." In *Box 6, Papers of Roy Blough.* Independence, MO: Harry S. Truman Presidential Library.

Comstock, Alzada. 1920. "British Income Tax Reform." *American Economic Review* 10(3): 488–506.

"Congress Gives Orders." 1942. *Time,* September 14.

Daunton, Martin. 2002. *Just Taxes: The Politics of Taxation in Britain, 1914–1979.* Cambridge, UK: Cambridge University Press.

Fisher, Irving. 1939. "The Double Taxation of Savings." *American Economic Review* 29(1): 16–33.

Goode, Richard B. 1964. *The Individual Income Tax.* Washington, DC: Brookings Institution Press.

Green, William R. 1928. "Simplification and the Federal Tax on Earned Incomes." *American Economic Review* 18(1): 95–101.

Kornhauser, Marjorie E. 1985. "The Origins of Capital Gains Taxation: What's Law Got to Do with It?" *Southwestern Law Journal* 39(4): 900.

———. 1994. "The Morality of Money: American Attitudes toward Wealth and the Income Tax." *Indiana Law Journal* 70(Winter): 119–20.

Lee, John W., III. 2005. "The Capital Gains 'Sieve' and the 'Farce' of Progressivity, 1921–1986." *Hastings Business Law Journal* 1(1): 1–86.

MacGuineas, Maya. 2004. "Radical Tax Reform." *Atlantic Monthly* 291(1).

Mellon, Andrew W. 1924. *Taxation: The People's Business.* New York: The Macmillan Company.

Morgenthau, Henry. 1942. "Statement before the Senate Finance Committee." In *Box 6, Papers of Roy Blough.* Independence, MO: Harry S. Truman Presidential Library.

Paul, Randolph E. 1954. *Taxation in the United States.* Boston: Little, Brown and Co.

Pigou, A. C. 1920. "The Report of the Royal Commission on the British Income Tax." *Quarterly Journal of Economics* 34(4): 607–25.

Pocock, J. G. A. 1975. *The Machiavellian Moment: Florentine Political Thought and the Atlantic Republican Tradition* Princeton, NJ: Princeton University Press.

Rodgers, Daniel T. 1992. "Republicanism: The Career of a Concept." *Journal of American History* 79(1): 11–38.

Seidman, Laurence S. 1997. *The USA Tax: A Progressive Consumption Tax.* Cambridge, MA: MIT Press.

Seligman, Edwin Robert Anderson. 1921. *The Income Tax; a Study of the History, Theory, and Practice of Income Taxation at Home and Abroad,* 2nd ed. New York: The Macmillan Company.

Stamp, J. C. 1915. "The Meaning of 'Unearned Income.' " *Economic Journal* 25(98): 165–74.

Stanley, Robert. 1993. *Dimensions of Law in the Service of Order: Origins of the Federal Income Tax, 1861–1913.* New York: Oxford University Press.

U.S. Department of the Treasury. 1937. "Tax Revision Studies: Income, Capital Stock, and Excess-Profits Taxes." In *Tax Revision Studies, 1937; Tax Reform Programs and Studies;* Records of the Office of Tax Analysis/Division of Tax Research; General Records of the Department of the Treasury, Record Group 56. College Park, MD: National Archives of the Treasury.

Ventry, Dennis J., Jr. 2003. "Equity Versus Efficiency and the U.S. Tax System in His-torical Perspective." In *Tax Justice: The Ongoing Debate*, edited by Joseph J. Thorndike and Dennis J. Ventry Jr. (25–70). Washington, DC: Urban Institute Press.

Wood, Gordon S. 1969. *The Creation of the American Republic, 1776–1787*. Chapel Hill: University of North Carolina Press. Published for the Institute of Early American History and Culture at Williamsburg, VA.

———. 1991. *The Radicalism of the American Revolution*, 1st ed. New York: A. A. Knopf.

PART III
Can We Tax
Capital Income?

4

Designing an Income Tax on Capital

Edward D. Kleinbard

The current system for taxing business income and business capital is in complete disarray. The underlying problems are so deeply embedded in the current structure as to require fundamental reforms. The periodic appearance of new and exotic financial capital instruments, and the complex technical tax rules subsequently announced to address these instruments, reflect the corrosive effects of the current system's incoherence. Those instruments' names—"MIPs," "Feline PRIDES," "contingent convertible debt," "income deposit securities," "E-CAPS"[1]—mean nothing outside a small circle of capital markets professionals, their advisors, and their regulators. Yet, for all their exoticism, every one of these instruments reflects a different strategy for making a tax pastry, in which some traditional "equity" feature is stuffed inside a "debt" wrapper (or vice versa).

The reason for these unnatural concoctions stems from two logical discontinuities. First, there is a fundamental division in tax treatment between debt instruments, on the one hand, and equity and most other forms of financial capital, on the other. Second, the government taxes inconsistently instruments with different labels but which offer an investor similar, but uncertain, cash flows (for example, common stock, options, or contingent interest debt).

Thus, today two parallel and incompatible income tax systems exist. In the debt model, the tax code affords issuers current ordinary deductions and requires current ordinary income inclusions of holders. In the "most everything else" model, the tax code affords issuers no deductions for the capital deployed in their businesses but taxes holders on a realization basis: sometimes at capital gains rates, sometimes at ordinary income rates, and sometimes (as is currently true of corporate dividends) at the same rate as capital gains, but with different secondary characteristics. Moreover, the same contingent cash flows—that is, flows identical in amount and triggered by precisely the same contingency—may be taxed at different rates, depending on the formal characteristics of the instrument (e.g., corporate stock or contingent interest bonds).

This lack of consensus in the tax system was thought for years to be untidy but tolerable, because issuers and investors had diametrically opposed tax interests, with tax anomalies from one party's perspective balanced by equal and offsetting tax costs to the other. But corporate stock *never* has enjoyed this bilateral treatment, because issuers obtain no deduction for the cost of equity capital. Moreover, today's capital markets are supremely efficient at matching taxable issuers and nontaxable investors (such as charities and pension plans), or vice versa, to maximize their collective after-tax returns.[2] In reality, then, tax anomalies that subsidize the cost of issuing one form of security are not balanced by a commensurate incremental cost to holding that security as an investor.[3]

It has been suggested that the current tax system might be salvageable if each complex financial capital instrument were divided into its basic constituent units, in order then to tax that instrument as the sum of the tax liabilities attaching to those units. That premise assumes that tax building blocks exist that cannot be further divided, but that belief is no more accurate than the thought that a proton or neutron is indivisible. The economic equivalent of stock can be expressed as a bond plus two options, and 15 years ago, Randall Kau (1990) demonstrated 13 ways of creating a bond-like return without the inconvenience of using a debt instrument (see also Kleinbard 1989). Because bifurcation—dividing any particular instrument into some exact mix of familiar components—raises such difficult categorization and valuation issues, the tax system has understandably rejected this approach. Accordingly, the system generally still taxes complex or compound financial capital instruments as a unitary whole.

What, then, does the tax system do today when confronted by an exotic new financial capital instrument? Tax practitioners and the IRS analyze that instrument and use arguments based on analogy and correspondence to determine which one idealized type most closely resembles the new instrument under inspection—like placing instruments into metaphysical cubbyholes (Kleinbard 1991).

Economics plays only a peripheral role in defining these metaphysical cubbyholes. The tax jurisprudence does not, for example, define "debt" by reference to the actual probability of repayment, but rather to certain formal characteristics of the instrument (e.g., stated maturity date, legal remedies on default, seniority in the capital structure). The distinction between deductible interest payments and nondeductible dividends, or the distinction between contingent returns taxed only when paid (and then at capital gains rates) and contingencies that give rise to current ordinary income inclusions, thus turns almost entirely on legal niceties, not on the probabilities of outcomes.

In sum, the primal flaw—our "tax original sin" with respect to financial capital—has been to develop in practice two parallel and incompatible income tax systems (the "debt" and "most everything else" models, with all their subvariants), in which the timing and amount of tax to issuers and holders depend on the purely formal characteristics of an instrument. The result is a system in which the returns on financial instruments are taxed at effective rates that vary widely for no discernable reason.

Why Tax Returns to Capital?

One understandable reaction to the current tax morass is to give up on the idea of taxing current returns to capital and to design our tax base around consumption rather than income. There is a large and sometimes heated literature analyzing which tax system is more appropriate.

A well-designed income tax should be like a wealth tax, which operates by taxing all lifetime accretions to wealth once (and only once) more or less concurrently with the creation of that wealth. A well-designed consumption tax, by contrast, also seeks to tax wealth once, and only once, but defers the timing of that taxation until that wealth is withdrawn from investment activities and consumed. The consumption tax does not directly tax the economic returns to capital but instead taxes those returns as and when they are used to finance consumption. By definition, a consumption tax has a smaller base than a comparable income tax has, and so must impose a higher nominal tax rate to raise the same current revenues (Shaviro 2004).

The arguments supporting income taxes are strongest when policy issues that go beyond economics in its narrowest sense are considered.

For example, income tax proponents point to the corrosive effects on a democracy of great concentrations of wealth and associated power, which suggest the benefits of a system that taxes such wealth as it is accumulated, not simply as it is spent. Moreover, any consumption tax likely will increase the absolute disparity in incomes (and wealth) between the richest and poorest citizens. Income tax supporters also point to the vulnerability of a consumption tax both to evasion (because of its higher nominal rates) and to "one-time" tax holidays couched as incentives to kick-start the economy.[4]

Conversely, consumption tax advocates point out that the current income tax raises little revenue from taxing returns to capital and distorts investment and financing decisions. These criticisms plainly are valid; indeed, the defects of our current system for taxing financial capital instruments are so pervasive, some observers embrace consumption taxes for that reason alone.

This chapter does not purport to resolve the debate between advocates of income and consumption taxes. Instead, it focuses on how we might go about reforming our income tax system to tax more rationally the returns to capital. The hope is that, if we can engineer a more successful income tax, we can then rationally compare the relative costs and benefits of that overhauled income tax to consumption tax alternatives.

Economic Returns to Capital—Capturing the Time Value of Money and Other Returns

The academic literature divides the economic returns to capital into three buckets: a pure *time value of money return* (what economists call the "normal" return), *risky returns* (returns from transactions that on a portfolio basis have an expected risk-adjusted return, but whose individual payoffs may vary substantially from that expected return), and *extraordinary returns* (what the literature describes as "economic rents," or "inframarginal" returns).[5] That literature also demonstrates that a well-designed income tax taxes time value of money returns, but a consumption tax does not. Thus, success in accurately taxing time value of money returns is the primary determinant of whether a tax system is a successful income tax.

By contrast, the literature argues that neither system taxes risky returns—at least in a world where losses are fully deductible—because taxpayers can "scale up" the size of their bets to put themselves in the same position after tax as with no tax. (For the same reason, the literature reminds us of the distortions that can result from artificial limitations on the deductibility of losses.) Finally, that literature demonstrates that both an ideal consumption tax and an ideal income tax reach extraordinary returns.

We can employ financial theory's division of all investment results into normal returns, risky returns, and extraordinary returns to measure the efficacy of any income tax. First, the primary determinant of whether a tax system is a successful *income* tax will be whether the system taxes the time value of money returns accurately and consistently. Second, it must minimize the distortions that result from artificial limitations on the deductibility of losses (or the double inclusion of income). Finally, it must ensure that extraordinary returns bear the same effective tax rate, whatever legal form those extraordinary returns might take.

Time Value of Money Returns

The current tax system fails to honor the primary income tax imperative of accurately and fairly taxing the time value of money. It simply ignores time-value concepts for many financial capital instruments (e.g., stocks, options). By contrast, rules for taxing most debt instruments (or debt-like derivatives such as interest rate swaps) honor time-value principles, but those rules then excuse enormous portions of collective financial wealth (e.g., pension funds and tax-deferred accounts) from the income tax system.

In a simplified, "Edenic" world of entirely equity-funded sole proprietorships, taxing the time value of money would come down simply to aligning tax depreciation with economic depreciation. That is, if tax depreciation precisely followed economic depreciation, investment in a marginal asset that earns normal (time value of money) returns would result in taxable income each year exactly equal to the cash returns from the asset, less the economic depreciation on that asset (i.e., taxable income = normal return * unrecovered investment). In such a world, the term "financial instrument" would have no meaning, and the recovery of direct investment in real assets (through accurate depreciation schedules) would be the sole mechanism for taxing time value of money returns.

Now imagine that one adds the possibility of borrowing to that ideal world. If the resulting tax system permitted the asset owner to deduct the interest paid on that borrowing and required the lender to include the interest in income, the tax system would continue to capture time value of money returns to all parties: to the owner through economic depreciation and interest expense, and to the lender through interest income.[6] This is the conceptual origin of the tax deductibility of interest expense.

This primitive model also was the first bite of the apple that led to the "original sin" of treating the cost of some forms of financial capital instrument as deductible and others as not. The fall from income tax grace was complete when this model was employed to explain the capital structure of corporations. As a result, "stockholders" were treated as the indirect owners of *all* of the enterprise, and "bondholders" as temporary renters of money.[7]

This simplistic model collapses under the weight of overwhelming contrary factors in the modern world. Most relevant to this discussion is the simple fact that, in modern capital markets, it is not usually possible to label one financial capital instrument as evidencing "ownership" of a business's underlying real assets, and all other instruments as evidencing the "rental of money" for temporary periods.[8]

Instead, the United States today has debt-like equity (e.g., deeply subordinated debentures and limited-term preferred stock) and equity-like debt (from convertible bonds through all the exotica referred to earlier). The returns paid to investors other than common shareholders do not simply constitute time value of money returns. From the other direction, it is impossible to identify which class of investors should be treated as the functional "owners" of an enterprise (who should recognize normal returns through depreciation of real assets). The only solution is to abandon the premise that holders of claims against a business enterprise can easily be divided into "owners" and "lenders," and instead seek a basis to capture and tax the true time value returns inherent in all such instruments.

Risky and Extraordinary Returns

As described above, modern financial theory implies that attempts to tax "risky" returns in a well-designed tax system are chimerical because taxpayers can scale up their pretax bets to cover the cost of any tax. This last observation is subject, however, to conditions, including that losses be treated symmetrically with gains (so that losses give rise to tax refunds).

The current income tax system completely fails this condition. Because it relies so heavily on the realization principle to tax gains, there is no choice but to adopt mirror antirecognition rules for losses (the capital loss limitation).[9] If policymakers can design a system that permits the deductibility of economic losses without allowing taxpayers to cherry-pick the Treasury to death on their gains, they could substantially advance the cause of designing a good income tax on financial capital instruments and business enterprises.

Modern financial theory also suggests that a well-engineered income tax will reach taxpayers' extraordinary returns (economic rents) by applying internally consistent rules for taxing business income, on the theory that these "super-sized" returns generally arise in the direct conduct of business enterprises. (To this, policymakers should add royalty income from the licensing of intangibles.[10])

Because the United States functions in an open and global economy, many of the best-known recent examples of extraordinary returns to capital achieve their success on a global scale. This observation implies that the most important practical impediment to the proper income taxation of super-sized profits is the perennial problem of intragroup cross-border transfer pricing, particularly with respect to high-value intangibles.[11] The tax problems associated with measuring and taxing extraordinary returns are not, however, problems embedded in the taxation of financial instruments, other than ensuring some coordination between direct and indirect claimants (e.g., a corporation and its security holders) to the same extraordinary income.

Design Criteria for a Good Income Tax

The following sections explain how policymakers could design a good income tax.

Consistently Tax the Different Economic Components of Returns to Capital

First and foremost, a good income tax must consistently identify and tax the different economic components of returns to capital: time value of money (normal) returns, risky returns, and extraordinary returns. In particular, such a system would focus on taxing normal (time value) returns currently and comprehensively. Different designers might reach different conclusions on whether extraordinary and risky concerns should be taxed at ordinary income or capital gain rates, but all presumably would agree that normal returns should lead to ordinary income on as close to a current basis as possible.

Fundamental tax distinctions should not be drawn between financial capital instruments with similar *economic* but different *formal* characteristics. Accordingly, a comprehensive approach to the income taxation of returns to capital must extend to all instruments that put capital to work in a business enterprise, regardless of their labels, including both traditional "debt" and "equity" securities, financial derivatives (such as forward contracts, options, and swaps), and novel hybrid variations yet to be developed.

Stated more generally, a good income tax system will adopt a *featureless topography*. Every distinguishing feature of a tax landscape—financial versus nonfinancial returns in a consumption tax, or the difference between tradable and nontradable assets in most mark-to-market (or "accrual") income tax proposals—is a fissure that invites abuse and leads to economic inefficiency. The only solutions are to embrace the necessity of such distinguishing features, and with them the concomitant necessity of an endless circle of antiabuse rules and new stratagems, or to design a system that introduces as few distinctive features as possible into the tax landscape.

Minimize the Effects of Realization

Given the fundamental distinctive characteristic of an income tax in taxing accretions to wealth concurrently with their creation, it follows that a well-designed income tax should minimize the distortions that follow from a slavish adherence to realization precepts. The Constitution does not demand the current implementation of the realization principle, and an income tax cannot achieve its objectives without restricting realization's scope in some fashion.[12]

A practical income tax cannot wholly abandon realization precepts. Still, reducing the scope of realization principles could eliminate many concerns about taxpayers' opportunistic "cherry-picking" and loosen current laws' artificial limitations on the deductibility of economic losses. It also would reduce the economic inefficiencies of "locked-in" investments, in which investors hold onto investments that they would sell in a tax-free world solely to avoid the tax cost of that sale.

Embrace Economic Neutrality

A well-designed tax should be neutral—affecting neither "the allocation of investment spending between different assets, nor the method by which this investment is financed" (Devereux and Freeman 1991). In addition to the features described above, a neutral system must tax the returns to capital invested in a business enterprise once and only once, regardless of the legal form of the business enterprise earning that income.

A well-engineered income tax system thus achieves *integration* between issuer and investor tax bases. Integration, properly understood, simply implies coordination between the taxation of business enterprises and holders of financial capital instruments, to capture time value of money returns once (the income principle) and only once (the neutrality principle).

Finally, a neutral system should logically connect the depreciation of a business's real assets and the taxation of the financial capital instruments that represent the indirect claims on those real assets. For both policy and political reasons, however, the tax depreciation (or expensing) deductions actually allowed for a business's real assets (which include not only plant and machinery, but self-developed intangible assets) often deviate significantly from the economic depreciation of those assets. This reality introduces substantial problems for designers of real-world income tax systems.

Comport with International Tax Norms

All income tax systems struggle with the issues posed by international capital flows.[13] These difficulties reflect in part the incompatibilities of different sovereign tax systems, not all of which are equally internally consistent or effective, and which in some cases have completely different design goals.

Given the liquidity of modern global capital markets, a system that does not produce results consistent across different investment scenarios, and consistent with purely domestic investments, will lead to profoundly nonneutral results. Against this backdrop, the best that can be expected of an income tax system for a large open economy is that the system honor its internal principles to the extent consistent with international norms and rely on the tax treaty process to achieve more theoretically satisfactory (and neutral) results.[14]

Address Inflation

Many observers rightly note that most income tax systems do a bad job of addressing inflation; in particular, most systems tax as "gains" amounts that economists would all agree are simply due to inflation. Some analysts have proposed to address this problem through basis indexation systems for investors. In my view, however, inflation should be dealt with squarely as a political and monetary policy issue, not as one of tax policy.[15]

Reduce Administrative Complexity

Most tax reform proposals urge simplifying tax return preparation as a design goal. This criterion makes a sense when applied to the personal income tax, but is not so important in the business tax setting, where some bookkeeping skills can be assumed. Business taxpayers are fully capable of making sophisticated cost-benefit analyses—indeed, positively embracing tax complexity—when they can realize significant tax savings, net of the cost of absorbing that complexity. In the business setting, *certainty* of a tax's application should take precedence over simplification as a design goal.

Income Tax Redemptive Strategies

An income tax engineer can respond in different ways to the observation that holders of many modern financial capital instruments cannot be characterized either as indirect owners of real assets or as simple renters of money. Each response begins, in effect, by acknowledging that *all* investors in a business enterprise collectively own the enterprise in some indeterminate fashion, and then creates rules to identify and tax their collective capital income. This section reviews briefly how these proposals address the problems and design criteria summarized to this point.

Investor-Level Solutions

One possible approach to designing a tax system to reach the time value of money returns on capital would be to return directly to the "Edenic" conditions imagined earlier in this chapter. This approach argues that designing a tax system that focuses on financial capital instruments as if they were real is a waste of time: why not instead simply apportion business income in some fashion to all stakeholders, in accordance with their relative claims? In this model, enterprise-level real asset depreciation reasserts itself as the means by which time-value returns are taxed because it determines in part the aggregate taxable income to be divided.

Pass-Through Models

Publicly traded partnerships provide experience with this approach. That experience teaches us that full pass-through models are extraordinarily complex to implement, largely because of the difficulties of relating income realization at the entity level (where income from the business first is determined) to realization events at the investor level, through secondary market trading in those partnership interests.[16]

Pass-through taxation also has significant conceptual limitations. Most important, the pass-through model will tax normal returns accurately only if that model properly implements business enterprise income taxation generally—including, in particular, by adopting economically perfect capitalization/depreciation rules. Decades of experience with the political and administrative process have demonstrated the fragility of that assumption.

The pass-through model's taxation of business income also retains all the problems of current law's income mismeasurement attributable to the realization principle; the pass-through model simply distributes that mismeasured income to investors. Finally, the pass-through model does nothing to align the taxation of financial derivatives—which for this purpose can be viewed as side bets on a business enterprise's income—with the allocation of firm income to the holders of direct claims against the business enterprise.

For these reasons, an investor pass-through model cannot serve as a practical platform from which to tax returns to capital. As described below, some of these shortcomings apply with equal force to other, more realistic, proposals as well.

Mark-to-Market

Another approach to a comprehensive solution to tax returns to capital solely at the investor level is to require individuals to value all their financial assets at the end of the year and tax those gains not already realized.[17]

Under this "mark-to-market" approach, business enterprises would not be taxed because the economic income attributable to them would be recognized currently by their owners.

Even the most dewy-eyed academics, however, recognize the practical problems with such a proposal. Fundamentally, nearly every such proposal limits its reach to publicly traded instruments. This would introduce new instabilities into the tax code—new mountains and valleys in the tax topography—at least as troublesome as current law's debt-equity distinction. Taxpayers would opt out of mark-to-market accounting through factual argumentation about valuation and by holding derivatives that track the returns on publicly traded assets. The proposals also leave unanswered what tax system would apply to financial capital instruments that are *not* viewed as publicly traded.

Further, implementing a mark-to-market accounting system requires resolving important (and largely unexamined) conceptual issues.[18] Even the mark-to-market accounting that should be easiest to implement—the application of that accounting method to the country's largest securities dealers—has proven difficult.[19] The alternative—mark-to-market accounting at the *entity* level, and not separately taxing financial capital instrument holders—is even more problematic in that it would require annual valuations of real assets.[20]

Entity-Level Solutions

If policymakers cannot design practical stakeholder-level solutions, then perhaps the right approach is to forgo the direct taxation of stakeholders and instead capture both time value of money returns and economic rents at the business enterprise level. A comprehensive entity-level income tax could do this. Such a tax would treat the business enterprise as a surrogate for its collective financial instrument stakeholders. Implementation of this idea necessarily presupposes that the enterprise's tax capitalization and depreciation schedules would follow *economic* depreciation precepts and that distributions to holders would be exempt from tax.

This effectively was the core theory behind the U.S. Treasury Department's 1992 proposal for the comprehensive business income tax (CBIT). CBIT would have treated all business enterprises as taxable entities, disallowed all interest expense deductions to business enterprises, and collected all tax on time value returns (and most taxes on extraordinary returns) at the entity level.[21] CBIT thus directly addressed the tax original sin of debt-equity distinctions by treating all debt instruments in a manner similar to current law's treatment of equity, albeit with a zero tax rate on investors.

Certainly, there is much to recommend in CBIT. For example, it would have applied consistent tax rules to all business enterprises, no matter what their legal form. With the recent surge in the popularity of limited liability companies, entities whose attributes carry no commercial liability to individuals but only an income tax liability, this insight has even more power today than it had in 1992. CBIT also aimed to integrate investor and entity-level tax, ensuring that all business income was taxed once, rather than not at all.

Nonetheless, CBIT's designers were forced into a difficult compromise through their fundamental design decision to capture time value of money returns by taxing all business income solely at the business entity level. In particular, this design decision ran afoul of two important problems already discussed in the context of pure pass-through models. First, this approach depended entirely on correctly implementing entity-level income taxation, particularly with respect to capitalization and depreciation rules. Second, the approach almost ensured that income will be mismeasured because of the practical impossibility of finding a substitute for reliance on the realization principle to measure economic appreciation or depreciation of real assets, and the relatively low turnover in noninventory real assets.

The Treasury Department recognized but never fully resolved these problems. It attempted to correct for the inevitable mismeasurement of the returns to capital at the business enterprise level through a compensating tax on entity-level preference income, which would take the form either of an entity-level supplemental tax on distributions or a compensatory tax on holders, in either case to the extent that holders received distributions that had not yet been taxed at the entity level.

The Treasury Department did not develop either compensatory tax in detail. This failing is odd, in light of the compensatory tax's central importance to correcting the systematic undertaxation of income that otherwise would result.[22] The alternative—passing through to holders a mix of taxable and tax-exempt income in respect of each cash distribution, depending on whether the income had previously been taxed to the distributing company—would introduce extraordinary volatility to securities prices as investors react to a changing mix of preference and nonpreference items. Such a system also is surprisingly difficult to draft and implement, as the George W. Bush administration discovered in 2003, when it proposed a narrower version of the idea.[23]

CBIT also never came to grips with investor-level capital gains. The Treasury Department accordingly did not closely integrate the taxation of capital gain and loss with its new distribution rules, likely leading to substantial tax planning or complex (and as yet unexplored) coordination rules. Finally, CBIT proposed no rules for the taxation of financial derivatives. Today, there are trillions of dollars in notional principal amount of outstanding derivative instruments; even if CBIT's designers could choose in 1992 to ignore derivatives, the income tax engineer today no longer has that luxury.

A Hybrid Alternative: The Business Enterprise Income Tax

This section describes briefly the key features of a new plan to reform the income taxation of business enterprises.[24] That proposal, termed the Business Enterprise Income Tax (BEIT), comprises three sets of reforms designed to redefine the income tax base applicable to business operations, and a fourth set of rules—the Cost of Capital Allowance (COCA) system—intended to replace completely current law's treatment of different financial capital instruments (including derivatives) with a single comprehensive regime.[25]

The overall agenda of the BEIT is to reduce as far as possible the role of tax considerations in business thinking. The BEIT does so by replacing current law's multiple elective tax regimes with a single set of tax rules for each stage of a business enterprise's life cycle: choosing the form of a business enterprise, capitalizing that enterprise, and selling or acquiring business assets or entire business enterprises.

The BEIT builds on current tax principles and on earlier reform proposals, like CBIT, by adopting two novel strategies. First, unlike other comprehensive income tax proposals, the BEIT splits the taxation of returns to capital by taxing time value of money (normal) returns only at the *investor* level, while taxing extraordinary returns primarily at the *business enterprise* level. By doing so, the BEIT sidesteps the problems that plague CBIT and similar comprehensive entity-only income tax proposals, all of which accurately tax normal returns only if they get economic depreciation precisely right.

Second, the BEIT seeks to reduce the realization principle to its smallest possible component. By taxing normal returns to investors rather than business enterprises, the BEIT takes advantage of the intuition that investment assets turn over more rapidly than do noninventory real assets, so that the *base* for determining normal returns is closer to the economic ideal. For the same reasons, the BEIT repeals numerous exceptions to the recognition of income and requires mandatory income accruals with respect to normal returns. The result is a system where reported taxable income tracks economic income much more closely than under current law.

The BEIT would apply only to *business enterprises,* which for this purpose means only private-sector, for-profit activities, other than traditional investment vehicles.[26] The BEIT thus would treat any taxpayer (including an individual) engaged in a trade or business as a "business enterprise."

The Non-COCA Components of the BEIT

The components of the BEIT other than its Cost of Capital Allowance operate as follows. First, the BEIT imposes income tax on all business enterprises at the entity level. Partnerships and even sole proprietorships are taxed as separate entities. In this respect, then, the BEIT is similar to a CBIT.

Second, the BEIT adopts true consolidation principles for affiliated business enterprises: that is, affiliated enterprises (regardless of their legal form) are treated as part of one single business enterprise, and the separate tax attributes of consolidated subsidiaries no longer are tracked. Current law's treatment of consolidated groups is more complex than is commonly understood, which leads to both tremendous compliance costs and tax avoidance strategies designed to game those complex rules.[27] By treating all noninvestment, for-profit endeavors as "business enterprises," and adopting true consolidation rules for related enterprises, the BEIT establishes a comprehensive and consistent base from which to measure returns to capital.

Third, the BEIT repeals all "tax-free" organization and reorganization rules. Instead, the BEIT treats all transfers of business assets (or the entry of an entity into a consolidated group) as taxable asset sales. This rule is necessary to coordinate with the true consolidation principles described briefly above (by eliminating entity-level tax attributes following acquisitions), and further advances the income tax objectives of the BEIT by increasing the number of realization events.

If the above business asset/business entity transfer rules were simply grafted onto the current corporate income tax, the consequence would be to exacerbate tax-induced "lock-in" problems for business transfers: a business enterprise's current tax liability from an actual or deemed asset sale at a gain would exceed the present value of the buyer's enhanced depreciation deductions. This asset-level "lock-in" problem does not exist for the BEIT. The reason is that, while the BEIT *as a whole* is an income tax, viewed solely at the business enterprise level, it is a consumption tax—that is, it exempts normal returns from enterprise-level tax.[28] (Normal returns are taxed under the BEIT, but only at the investor level.) In turn, all consumption taxes are neutral with respect to the tax burden imposed on inter-business sales of assets. As a result, there is no tax disincentive (or incentive) to sales of business assets.

The Cost of Capital Allowance and Time Value of Money Returns

The Cost of Capital Allowance system replaces current tax law's different treatment of debt capital, equity capital, and various derivatives with a uniform allowance for issuers and a mandatory income inclusion to investors.[29] The COCA regime should largely eliminate tax considerations in the capitalization of business enterprises by providing issuers and investors with uniform tax rules for all capital-raising activities, measured only by the amount of capital raised. Finally, COCA tightly coordinates the two levels of tax through adopting a quasi-integration regime.[30]

The COCA regime places the taxation of normal returns on investors for two reasons. First, financial capital instruments turn over more rapidly than do noninventory real assets. As a result, investors' tax bases in their financial capital instruments should reflect more closely economic measures of income than do business enterprises' bases in their real assets. Second, investors do not have tax preferences, like accelerated depreciation, that are reflected in investors' bases in their investment assets.

Issuers

Under COCA, a business enterprise deducts each year an annual allowance for the financial capital invested in it, measured at a rate (equal to a fixed percentage over one-year Treasuries) multiplied by the issuer's total capital.[31] This deduction is available regardless of whether any amount is distributed to investors. No further deductions are available to the issuer even if its actual cash payments to investors exceed the annual COCA rate.[32] As a result, any extraordinary returns (returns above the COCA rate) are taxed at the business enterprise level.

Since balance sheets in fact balance, the total tax-cognizable capital of a business enterprise (the right-hand side of a tax balance sheet) must equal the total tax basis of the issuer's assets (the left-hand side). As a result, the annual COCA deduction is calculated in practice as the statutory COCA rate multiplied by the issuer's total adjusted tax basis in its assets.[33]

Real (that is, nonfinancial) assets that today are depreciable (or amortizable) would remain so under the COCA system. Since the effect of depreciation is to reduce asset basis, a business enterprise's COCA deductions would decrease as it depreciates its nonfinancial assets. Thus, the COCA deduction is in addition to, not in place of, asset depreciation. The relationship among depreciation, the BEIT's treatment of asset sales, and the COCA regime is explored below.

A holder of a financial capital instrument that itself is a business enterprise (other than financial institutions, which are subject to special rules summarized below) would be treated like any other investor in respect of that asset, and therefore would be required to follow the income inclusion rules described below, including recognizing in income each year what the BEIT terms the "*minimum inclusion*" on that financial capital instrument (that is, the business enterprise's tax basis in that instrument multiplied by the COCA rate). At the same time, financial capital instruments that a business enterprise owns constitute part of that enterprise's asset base and therefore also enter into the enterprise's COCA expense calculations. Accordingly, a business enterprise would obtain a COCA *deduction* measured by the COCA rate applied to its tax basis in a portfolio investment and would include in income from that investment at least its minimum inclusion equal to the same amount.[34] The net result is that there would be no tax at the business enterprise level on interfirm investments unless the returns on those investments exceeded the COCA/minimum inclusion rate.

In sum, under the COCA system, issuers no longer will face a tax imperative to employ as much debt financing as possible or to issue complex financial instruments designed to give issuers tax-deductible interest expense in respect of contingent returns. Instead, issuers will minimize the *economic* cost of their financial capital, secure in the knowledge that there is no tax component to that calculus.

Investors

The COCA system (in its idealized form) requires all holders—including tax-exempt institutions other than pension plans—to include each year in ordinary income a minimum inclusion, which equals each investor's tax basis in its investments in business enterprises multiplied by the COCA rate for that year. Minimum inclusions are taxed currently at ordinary income rates, regardless of the amount received in cash. If those minimum inclusions are not actually received in cash, the accrued but unpaid amount is added to a taxpayer's basis in its investment and compounded at the COCA/minimum inclusion rate.

Holders of financial capital instruments calculate their minimum inclusions by looking only to their tax basis in the instruments they own. As a result, the aggregate of investors' minimum inclusions will *not* equal the sum of issuers' COCA deductions, and generally will exceed those deductions for two reasons. First, market trading in securities is likely to lead to more realization events at the investor level than will corresponding sales by business enterprises of noninventory real assets. Second, current law effectively permits business enterprises to deduct the cost of developing many intangibles; these immediate deductions reduce an enterprise's aggregate tax basis in its assets but not the actual economic capital invested in the enterprise (which presumptively would be reflected in market prices for the enterprise's securities).

In addition to minimum inclusions, under the BEIT, an investor must include in taxable income gains on the sale of a financial capital instrument or cash distributions, in either case only to the extent of any excess over prior accrued minimum inclusions. These "*excess distributions*" are taxed at a low rate (e.g., 10 to 15 percent) and are not taxable in the hands of tax-exempt institutions.[35] Gains from dealings in other than business property are taxed at ordinary income rates.

An investor's losses are currently deductible without regard to capital loss limitation principles.[36] The COCA regime treats those losses essentially as reversing prior income inclusions; as a result, the rates at which those losses are deductible vary.

Cash distributions are treated first as tax-free returns of prior accruals of minimum inclusions and then as excess distributions. Just as minimum inclusions increase a holder's tax basis in a financial capital instrument, cash distributions treated as tax-free returns of prior minimum inclusions decrease an investor's tax basis in that tax instrument.[37]

The COCA system applicable to holders requires no special record-keeping by the issuer or information from prior holders. In particular, calculations of minimum inclusions and excess distributions are personal to each investor; no minimum inclusion or excess distribution accounts carry over from a prior third-party investor from which the current investor purchased that security. The COCA system applicable to holders admittedly requires significant recordkeeping by each holder, but that recordkeeping would be mathematically straightforward and, if reflected on each year's tax return, can be kept up to date even by individual investors.

The examples in the appendix and in the notes illustrate these principles in more detail, but a simple example is desirable here. Imagine that Investor pays $1,000 on January 1 to acquire an Issuer security (which might be denominated as debt, or stock, or an exotic hybrid—it does not matter which). Assume for simplicity that the COCA rate is 6 percent in every year. Issuer immediately purchases an asset that is depreciated on a five-year straight line basis.

Issuer's COCA deductions each year will equal the sum of the tax bases of all its assets. Assuming for this example a rule that simply looks to asset basis at the start of each year, Issuer's COCA deduction for this asset will equal $60 in year 1, $48 in year 2, and so on. (Issuer also will obtain a COCA deduction for any asset basis attributable to any net cash the asset generates and Issuer retains.) At the end of five years, Issuer's tax basis in the asset will be zero, and Issuer will no longer obtain any COCA deductions.

Investor, meanwhile, continues to own his Issuer security. Each year, Investor takes into ordinary income a 6 percent yield on his tax basis in his financial capital instrument. If Issuer happens to distribute exactly $60 a year to Investor in respect of that security, Investor will include that $60 a year in income. If Issuer distributes nothing, Investor will include $60 in year 1, $64 in year 2 (6 percent of $1,060 tax basis), and so on. If Issuer makes no current cash distribution and Investor sells the security at the end of year 1 for $1,200, the first $60 of sales proceeds are tax-free returns of prior minimum inclusions, and the remaining $140 of gain is taxed at excess distribution rates.[38] New Investor will now recognize $72 of minimum inclusion income in her first year of ownership. Issuer's COCA deductions continue unaffected.

Derivatives

The COCA system taxes derivatives (which in practice can encompass significant capital-raising components) in a manner similar to how physical securities (e.g., stocks and bonds) are taxed. For complex reasons, however, the applicable rules must be modified slightly in the case of losses arising from derivatives.[39] Readers who review the examples in the appendix will see that COCA seeks to tax financial derivatives by dividing the returns from such instruments into returns on invested capital (which is not necessarily a trivial asset, even when speaking of derivatives) and pure returns to risk (i.e., bets). Each component is then separately taxed.

Special Rules

A modified form of the COCA system applies to financial institutions; their financial assets and liabilities are subject to mandatory mark-to-market accounting, and they obtain a COCA deduction for their net investment in financial assets, plus their basis in nonfinancial assets.[40] Other investors can elect mark-to-market accounting for all traded financial capital instruments that they hold, thereby mitigating the effect of any potential minimum inclusions in excess of cash receipts. A special small-business rule mitigates the risk of current minimum inclusion income to, say, a sole proprietor, while her sole proprietorship incurs COCA deductions that yield no current benefits because of start-up losses. Finally, business-enterprise net operating losses are grossed up each year by a time value of money factor.

Results

The COCA system is a time value of money income inclusion system that uses the best possible information—market prices for securities that change hands—to identify the total capital invested in businesses, without introducing the overwhelming administrative and valuation complexities of a pure mark-to-market system. In the absence of current market sales, financial assets are presumed to increase in value annually at the COCA rate, less any cash distributions.

COCA should largely eliminate the role of tax engineering in shaping a business enterprise's capital structure, because the labels attached to the financial capital instruments that the enterprise issues do not affect its COCA deduction. Capital in turn should be fairly priced, because the system integrates treatment of the providers and users of capital. The COCA system distinguishes, in a logical and consistent manner, ordinary (time value of money) returns (minimum inclusions) and risky or extraordinary returns (excess distributions). Including a current time value return on all financial instruments reduces the opportunities for indefinite deferral, and its concomitant distortive effects of understating income and locking in investments. Finally, replacing today's capital loss limitations with (tax-effected) full utilization of losses eliminates a substantial economic distortion that limits the attractiveness of risky investments.[41]

Coordination between COCA and Asset Depreciation Rules

The COCA system operates alongside, not in place of, standard asset depreciation rules. An issuer's COCA deductions interact in interesting ways with the issuer's deductions for asset depreciation. These interactions reflect the COCA system's simultaneous roles as a depreciation corrective, an integration device, and a mark-to-market surrogate. This section explores some of these interactions.

COCA and Asset Depreciation

If tax depreciation perfectly tracked economic depreciation, a business enterprise could simply use that depreciation to recognize time value of money income inclusions at the entity level(for the reasons summarized earlier). In that world, the COCA system in practice operates simply to tax investors rather than issuers on time value of money returns. Under these assumptions, CBIT is a more logically compelling alternative, because it is simpler: the issuer obtains *only* a depreciation deduction (in turn corresponding with economic depreciation) in respect of the capital deployed in its business, and investors would receive returns out of tax-paid earnings free of additional tax.

In practice, of course, tax depreciation systems depart in two important respects from economic norms. First, the tax system no longer makes even a half-hearted attempt to tailor tax depreciation schedules to reflect estimates of economic useful lives. Second, the tax code permits the tax expensing of many costs that arguably should be capitalized, with the result that the intangible assets that those costs create are not reflected in the tax system as assets in the first place.

Because a business enterprise's aggregate asset basis is used to calculate its COCA deduction, the COCA system effectively mitigates distortions attributable to too-fast or too-slow depreciation. Thus (to take the two extremes), an issuer that deducts rather than capitalizes an expenditure forfeits any COCA deduction with respect to the capital invested, while an issuer that treats that same cost as a nondepreciable capital expenditure receives a COCA deduction in perpetuity. The net result of this self-correcting mechanism is that the present value of the sum of a business enterprise's COCA and depreciation deductions will remain a constant percentage of the enterprise's capital (measured as historic cost), *regardless* of the depreciation and capitalization rules the business employs. By contrast, the tax base for investors' income inclusions reflects the capital they have invested (through market transactions), not the after-depreciation carrying value of the business entity.

In other words, at the business enterprise level, the present value of the sum of the enterprise's COCA deduction and *any* asset depreciation schedule will always equal the present value of *excluding* from income tax a time value (normal) rate of return on the enterprise's economic capital (albeit measured at historic cost, and assuming that the COCA rate is set at precisely the normal rate of return).[42] This is precisely the appropriate integrated result desired: exemption of a normal rate of return from tax at the business enterprise level (as in a consumption tax), and inclusion of a normal return on investment at the investor level.[43]

This observation in turn leads to a powerful question: why not retain the COCA concept for investors but dispense with it at the business enterprise level? If the result is equivalent, why not disallow all deductions on financial capital instruments and permit issuers to deduct all investments as they are made?

There are several good reasons not to do so. First, as David Bradford pointed out, a COCA/depreciation system has the advantage over a simple asset expensing rule of mitigating the effects of changes in tax rates (Bradford 2004).[44] Second, the COCA system is designed to encourage a "featureless topography" by employing one universal set of tax rules that apply to financial derivatives as well as physical securities (e.g., stocks and bonds). Unlike the latter instruments, where one can draw neat distinctions between issuers and investors, derivatives are employed by both. Moreover, a derivative can change its character from asset to liability and back. At the same time, a derivative can move substantial cash from one party to the other. The COCA system therefore seems to be a necessary (or at least a convenient) part of taxing derivative instruments. The importance of preserving a "featureless topography" in turn requires that no important distinctions be introduced between how a derivative's cash flows are taxed, on the one hand, and how those of a physical security are taxed, on the other.[45]

Finally, there are important ancillary reasons for retaining COCA/depreciation for issuers rather than adopting a simpler asset expensing solution.[46]

COCA and the BEIT's Asset Sales Rules

Imagine a business enterprise ("Seller") that holds a depreciable asset with a tax basis of zero and a value of $100, and which sells that asset to Buyer for $100, incurring $20 of tax on the sale.[47] Under the BEIT's asset sales tax rates regime, this $20 in tax liability also represents the present value of the buyer's future tax savings from depreciating its $100 tax basis for the asset. This follows from the fact that the BEIT, when viewed solely at the business enterprise level, functions as a consumption tax. In a cash flow tax, for example, which is a species of consumption tax, every purchase of a business asset is immediately deductible; the buyer's tax benefit in the above example thus would be $20. The BEIT achieves the same result in present value terms through the combination of its COCA allowance and asset depreciation.

One can alternatively phrase this result by saying that Seller and Buyer will be in the same aggregate after-tax position as if the asset were transferred tax-free (and with a carryover basis) to Buyer.[48] Unlike tax-free incorporations and reorganizations under current law, however, the BEIT system does not duplicate gain (or loss). Buyer has invested $100 for an asset with a tax basis of $100 (as would be true of any other investment), and Seller does not take a carryover basis in any asset or security Buyer issues.

Seller appears to be in a better COCA position after the sale, however, than it was before, because it now has $80 of after-tax sales proceeds (cash), and therefore tax basis, it did not have before. What should be done about this problem?

The answer is that this phenomenon is an optical illusion. The "extra" basis that seller obtains simply represents the final cash flow in respect of seller's returns from its investment in the asset that it sold: the present value at the time of investment of the tax-relevant flows (COCA allowance, depreciation, and after-tax sales proceeds) remains constant, even as the quantum of each component varies.

In a similar vein, the fact that investors' aggregate minimum inclusions (normal returns) are expected to outstrip a business enterprise's COCA deduction in respect of its assets is *not* a sign of the system's failure to achieve integration. A business enterprise's value in excess of the tax basis of its assets represents, by definition, the present value of the future rents (super-sized profits) that it will recognize for tax purposes in future years. The BEIT intends to tax those rents at the enterprise level; as a result, the system does not shield them from tax through an artificial COCA deduction that exceeds the actual capital investment that developed the rents. By the same token, once those rents have been identified and valued by the marketplace, a new investor in an enterprise's securities that pays the market price for an interest in that enterprise effectively has capitalized the after-tax value of the enterprise's predicted future rents, just as is true for any other investment. The original investor was the beneficial owner of the enterprise's future rents; to the new investor, the same revenue stream yields simply a normal return.

COCA and Risky Returns

The cost of capital allowance system abolishes the difference between "capital" and "ordinary" returns and instead taxes *all* distributions and gains in excess of an investor's minimum inclusions at a specified low rate. COCA, as currently envisioned, then goes one step further. Relying on the fact that the mandatory minimum inclusion rules mean that investors report substantial ordinary income from their investments every year, COCA permits taxpayers to deduct truly economic losses on a current basis, although those losses are deductible only at tax-effected rates.

As proposed, COCA thus permits taxpayers to cherry-pick their losses while deferring unrealized gains that exceed their minimum inclusion income. The idea, however, is that the minimum inclusion system (which compounds to the extent not paid out currently), together with the abolition of all tax-free organization and reorganization rules, will result in the recognition of a large enough fraction of total economic income from financial capital instruments that the Treasury Department can absorb the costs associated with residual cherry-picking opportunities.[49]

On a related front, the BEIT also contemplates that a business enterprise's net operating losses compound each year at a time value of money rate (presumably, the COCA rate). This rule preserves economic neutrality in the timing of income and loss recognition where a loss produces only a nonrefundable net operating loss carryover.[50]

COCA and Extraordinary Returns

By definition, COCA is largely irrelevant to the taxation of extraordinary returns (economic rents); instead, the main responsibility for taxing those outsized returns falls on the current tax system as modified by the non-COCA elements of the BEIT.

The basic approach of the BEIT to taxing economic rents is to collect that tax at the business enterprise level. The BEIT's treatment of businesses as separate taxable enterprises, subject to a single set of income tax rules, parallels CBIT in this respect. This approach, along with the other BEIT provisions not found in CBIT (true consolidation, elimination of tax-free organization and reorganization rules), creates a uniform tax environment for all business endeavors, increases the number of realization events, and significantly reduces the prospects for tax mischief.

International Application of the BEIT

Foreign Direct Investment

The special issue of cross-border transfer pricing is a matter of great importance to the proper taxation of extraordinary returns. The current system for taxing foreign direct investment by U.S. business enterprises unfortunately is both schizophrenic and in disarray. The BEIT's response to the current system comprises (1) the full inclusion in the U.S. tax base of foreign subsidiaries' income and loss (via the BEIT's super-consolidation rules) and (2) the repeal of the rules allocating U.S. interest expense (now, COCA deductions) in calculating the foreign tax credit.

The result would be a vastly simpler system. Transfer pricing issues would be less important because artificially low intragroup transfer prices from the United States to a foreign affiliate would not reduce current

U.S. tax liability.[51] This last point should lead to a more accurate inclusion of extraordinary returns (economic rents) in the tax base. The resulting system also would be consistent with international norms that grant priority to the source country in taxing income from foreign direct investments (through the U.S. foreign tax credit mechanism).

Foreign Portfolio Investors

The COCA system is premised on the idea that tax on time value of money returns should be collected only from holders of financial capital instruments. This section considers how the BEIT should define the scope of investors subject to tax on their time value of money returns.

Current U.S. law imposes worldwide taxation on the incomes of U.S. persons (defined differently for individuals and entities). The BEIT preserves this basic jurisdictional scope. At the same time, by segregating the taxation of normal returns (taxed to investors) from the taxation of rents and risky returns (taxed primarily to business enterprises), the BEIT permits fine-tuning the application of the tax to each.

Time value of money returns that U.S. citizens and permanent residents earn are subject to the COCA regime, regardless of whether an investment is made in a U.S. or foreign firm. This result preserves neutrality in investment decisions by U.S. investors, and reflects the basic theme that the normal returns on all capital invested by U.S. nonbusinesses in business ventures should be subject to U.S. tax. At the same time, the BEIT's true consolidation principles mean that U.S. resident entities are taxed on their risky returns and rents, regardless of the source of the capital invested in those entities.

Following this logic, one would adopt the view that foreign investors should be wholly exempt from tax under the BEIT. By carving out foreign investors, the ultimate reach of U.S. tax on time value of money returns would be measured by the aggregate capital invested by U.S. residents in business endeavors. This approach also reflects the reality that, in a world of open economies, investors will be able to earn normal returns from many sources; in this environment, imposing U.S. tax on foreign portfolio investors simply raises the cost of capital to U.S. firms. A U.S. person who invests indirectly in a U.S. business enterprise through a foreign intermediary would still be subject to U.S. tax, because the COCA rules would apply to the indirect investment made by the U.S. investor. For all of these reasons, I find this approach to be persuasive.

Conversely, if one defined the time value of money returns that should fall within the BEIT as those derived from investing in U.S. businesses (rather than investments made by U.S. investors), then foreign portfolio investors in U.S. business enterprises should be taxed currently on their minimum inclusion income. I do not favor this conclusion as a matter of logic because it confuses residence-based taxation of normal returns (determined by the investor's residence) with residence-based taxation of risky returns and rents (determined by the entity's residence). It also creates an unavoidable practical conflict between the COCA system, which taxes income before distributions, and withholding tax collection mechanisms, which impose U.S. income tax on foreign portfolio investors, because those mechanisms require cash distributions to operate. (This is one place where CBIT has a practical advantage over COCA.)

The withholding tax administrative problem can be solved through a combination of "catch-up" withholding tax (with interest charges) on subsequent distributions and more extensive broker reporting, and withholding on sales proceeds. While this solution imposes nontrivial administrative costs on the broker community, such a system technically is feasible.[52]

The BEIT is not relevant for nonbusiness enterprise issuers. As a result, regardless of how one decides to treat foreign portfolio investors in U.S. businesses, the U.S. Treasury Department, in particular, will continue to pay interest on its debt obligations held by foreign investors free of withholding tax, in reliance on current law's portfolio interest rules.

Measuring the Effectiveness of the BEIT

Neutrality of Results

The BEIT largely satisfies the condition of neutrality, except as to the absolute scale of economic activity. First, the BEIT taxes all business operations identically (by taxing enterprises, regardless of legal form, consistently). Second, the BEIT renders tax objectives irrelevant to the choice of an issuer's capital structure, because the issuer's cost of capital allowance is determined only by reference to the capital it employs, not the securities it issues. Similarly, the tax liabilities of investors are driven by the capital they invest and the cash returns they earn, not the label of the instruments they hold.

Third, the BEIT (unlike CBIT) is neutral in that it takes a broad view of what constitutes an issuer's capital structure by including all financial derivatives in its system and conforming the rules for derivatives to those applicable to more traditional financial capital instruments. Fourth, the BEIT is "self-righting" for too fast or too slow tax depreciation (or expensing) of specific assets, through the interaction between a business enterprise's COCA deduction and its unrecovered adjusted tax basis in its assets. CBIT's success in this respect, by contrast, would depend entirely on developing perfect coordination among the tax code's depreciation and capitalization rules for real assets, CBIT's proposed but inchoate compensatory tax, and CBIT's equally ambiguous rules for taxing investor-level capital gains and losses.

The COCA system might prove inferior to CBIT in one important respect: COCA would retain some of current law's "lock-in" effect on investments at the investor level.[53] In the COCA regime, an investor who has achieved extraordinary returns on an investment but who now faces a period of normal returns might prefer to retain that investment rather than face a "step up" in tax basis—and with it, higher minimum inclusions in the future when those sale proceeds are reinvested. If CBIT were implemented without any investor-level capital gains taxes, then an investor subject to the CBIT regime would not face a lock-in effect.

Of course, the original proponents of CBIT were ambiguous as to whether investor-level capital gains taxes had a role in their system. Moreover, COCA ought materially to reduce lock-in effects compared with current law (through the minimum inclusion mechanism). The BEIT proposal therefore accepts some residual lock-in effect as a fair trade for materially improved measurement and taxation of normal returns, compared with current law or a practical implementation of CBIT.

It might also be argued that COCA fails neutrality principles in one other respect, which is that investors' aggregate time value of money inclusions each year (their minimum inclusions) are likely to exceed issuers' aggregate COCA deductions. In fact, the COCA system restores balance to the income tax by effectively measuring time value of money *income* inclusions by reference to enterprise *value*, as reflected in the aggregate bases for investors' interests in that enterprise. That is, the combination of requiring investors to include normal returns in taxable income, regardless of cash receipts, and the faster turnover of financial assets than noninventory real assets can be viewed as producing a rough and ready mark-to-market system. That is, the BEIT looks to market information to determine the total capital invested in a business as and when investments change hands and, in the absence of market transactions, presumes that investments accrue at normal rates of return.

In contrast to the investor side, the realization principle and the practical bias in favor of over-expensing investments in real assets (whether tangible or intangible) cause the aggregate tax balance sheets of business enterprises to understate the total capital deployed in their businesses. By the same token, however, enterprises have enjoyed the current deduction of expenses that arguably should be capitalized and the deferral of economic gains that economically are reflected in secondary market trading prices for that enterprise's financial capital instruments.

The COCA system admittedly veers from strict neutrality on one other point: the tax it proposes on excess distributions. Logic does not require the tax; instead, the excess distribution tax is conceived as a compensatory tax for any residual tax preferences at the business enterprise level, and a nod to the view that those who are extraordinarily lucky should contribute some of their good fortune back to the community.

Susceptibility to Abuses

COCA will be difficult to game, because the legal form of a business enterprise or an investment in that enterprise has no effect on anyone's tax liability. In addition, COCA (like CBIT) essentially forecloses many traditional tax shelters, because "business" losses from classic tax shelter activities (whether real estate, lithographic plates, almond groves, or high-tech windmills) cannot be passed through to individual investors.

COCA does offer taxpayers the opportunity to "cherry-pick" losses by removing current law's capital loss limitations. This proposal is not, however, strictly necessary: if experience warranted, one could limit the absolute amount of losses deductible in a year. More to the point, COCA will put additional pressure on policing "wash sales"—transactions in which a taxpayer purports to sell an investment to claim a loss, but retains or reacquires an economic interest in the investment that purportedly was sold (for example, through selling an investment at a loss and immediately repurchasing it at its fair market value). Taxpayers under COCA will have two reasons to seek out wash sales: first, to obtain deductible losses, and second, to reduce future minimum inclusion income (by reducing the tax basis of the investment to its lower fair market value). Although anti–wash sale rules are in place today,[54] in light of the importance they would assume under COCA, they would require significant refurbishing.

Administrative Burdens

COCA unquestionably will add significantly to the administrative burdens the tax system imposes on investors because investors will be required to track their accrued minimum inclusions and to apply distributions correctly against prior accruals. As a practical matter, however, brokers, mutual fund managers, and other market professionals can perform most of these recordkeeping obligations for investors. That does not mean these services will be free: incremental costs presumably will be reflected in increased custodial or management fees. Nonetheless, the cost *per investor* should be reasonably low, because brokers and other professionals will build systems to capture and record the relevant data for their many thousands of customers.[55]

The brokerage industry also would be expected to carry an important responsibility in withholding proceeds (e.g., from sales of securities paid to foreign investors) as the means of collecting tax on such investors' minimum inclusion income. This again will translate into higher custodial and management fees with some resulting loss of liquidity.[56]

Transition Issues

Transition issues are extremely important in any fundamental tax reform proposal. A new tax system will not only create future winners and losers but will also affect current stores of wealth. Income tax reform obviously poses fewer transition issues than a switch to a consumption tax, but that does not mean the issues are trivial. An overnight switch to COCA, for example, could literally bankrupt highly leveraged companies. The BEIT proposal therefore contemplates different transition rules for its non-COCA components (uniform entity-level tax, true consolidation principles, and a revised business asset and acquisition regime), on the one hand, and COCA, on the other.

The BEIT'S non-COCA rules just do not seem to work under a phase-in model and therefore must apply in toto as of a specified date. Since, in many respects, the rules are simplifications of current law, applying them immediately to operations should not cause irreparable harm to taxpayers.

COCA, in contrast, can be phased in by specifying a multiyear period over which the interest expense deduction scales down and the COCA deduction ramps up. The investor side is more debatable but probably should simply be adopted in toto as of a specified date near the end of the business enterprise phase-in period. To avoid excessive dislocations to entities that today are fiscally transparent, taxpayers should be permitted to elect to move entirely into the COCA regime as early as they wish.

If the BEIT and COCA regime is thought to be attractive, further work on transition issues will be required. Fortunately, because the BEIT and COCA system remains fundamentally an *income* tax system, the difficult transition issues that consumption taxes pose (the taxation of existing wealth) are removed from the table.[57]

Conclusions

A well-designed income tax will reach all time value of money returns once, and only once. That tax also will be neutral, influencing neither the form of business organization nor the mix of financial capital instruments issued to finance that business. To date, most practical comprehensive reform proposals, of which CBIT is the most fully articulated, have placed the taxation of time value of money returns and economic rents at the business enterprise level. The BEIT/COCA system, in contrast, splits the measurement and collection of tax on normal returns, which it places on investors, from the collection of tax on economic rents, which it places on business enterprises.

This chapter has demonstrated why the BEIT/COCA system is the superior practical approach. The non-COCA elements of the BEIT substantially simplify and improve the operation of an income tax imposed on business operations. By treating all business enterprises as taxable entities subject to identical rules and implementing true consolidation principles for affiliated enterprises, the BEIT adopts a uniform and straightforward base on which to impose tax. By repealing all "tax-free" organization and reorganization rules, and instead taxing all transfers of business assets or business enterprises at "tax-neutral" rates, the BEIT attenuates the relevance of the realization principle, more accurately conforms enterprise taxable income to economic income, greatly simplifies the tax system, and eliminates a wide array of potential abuses.

COCA moves the taxation of capital substantially closer to theoretical income tax norms in five critical respects. First, it treats returns on all financial instruments—including derivative contracts—in the same manner. Second, by requiring an investor to include "minimum inclusions" in income every year, regardless of cash distributions, COCA reduces the importance of the realization requirement in the taxation of financial instruments. Third, by measuring capital at the investor level, COCA is more likely than is any method that taxes normal returns at the business enterprise level to approximate an economic measure of the total capital deployed in U.S. businesses (through the faster turnover of financial assets than non-inventory real assets). These last two points can be rephrased by saying that the COCA system operates as an imperfect, but simple, mark-to-market surrogate by using actual market information— the prices at which securities change hands—to identify the total capital invested in a business, and by presuming in the absence of market sales that financial instruments increase in value annually at no less than the COCA rate.

Fourth, COCA advances good income tax design principles by operating as a corrective to noneconomic tax depreciation schedules and capitalization rules, through adjusting the present values of combined depreciation and COCA deductions always to equal a normal return on a business enterprise's economic capital (albeit measured by historical cost). Finally, relying on its minimum inclusions system to reduce cherry-picking, COCA removes current law's capital loss limitation and replaces it with full deductibility of economic losses (at appropriately tax-effected rates). By introducing this symmetry in the taxation of losses and gains, COCA contributes to the fair pricing of (and willingness to assume) risk.

Summary

This chapter identifies the characteristics of a good system for taxing income from business enterprises and financial instruments, and then proposes a solution that embodies those characteristics: the business enterprise income tax (BEIT). It argues that such a hybrid income tax is the most robust approach to implementing a comprehensive and coherent income tax on capital. Conclusions include the following:

The current system for taxing income on capital is broken and requires fundamental reform. The United States arbitrarily defines some forms of financial capital as giving rise to deductible expenses, and others as not. The government taxes economically identical contingent cash flows in wildly varying patterns. Recent congressional fixes have only made matters worse. Meanwhile, modern financial engineering leads to ever more complex financial instruments.

Consistent rules must apply for taxing the different components of economic returns. All financial instruments that put capital to work in a business enterprise should be taxed consistently. To do so requires identifying the constituent components of economic returns: time value of money returns, risky returns, and extraordinary returns.

A good income tax system will adopt a featureless topography. Every distinguishing feature of a tax landscape, such as the debt-equity divide, invites abuse and economic inefficiency. A system must be designed that introduces as few distinctive features as possible into the tax landscape.

The U.S. Treasury's 1992 proposal for a comprehensive business income tax (CBIT) remains an important landmark in developing a rational income tax system. It would have applied consistent tax rules to all business enterprises. Still, its fundamental design decision to tax all returns to capital at the business enterprise level, rather than at the investor level, required difficult compromises that were never fully resolved.

The BEIT offers a hybrid alternative plan to reform the income taxation of business enterprises. The BEIT would reduce the role of tax considerations in business thinking by replacing current law's multiple elective tax regimes with a single set of tax rules for each stage of a business enterprise's life cycle.

The BEIT includes a comprehensive cost of capital allowance (COCA) system as a core component. The COCA system replaces current tax law's different treatment of debt capital, equity capital, and various derivatives with a uniform allowance for issuers and a mandatory income inclusion to investors. Moving the taxation of time value of money returns from issuers (as in CBIT) to investors has important theoretical and practical advantages.

If the BEIT/COCA regime is pursued, further work on transition issues will be required. Although it poses fewer transition issues than does a switch to a consumption tax, it would create winners and losers and have direct effects on existing wealth.

NOTES

This chapter continues the exploration of themes first broached in "The Business Enterprise Income Tax: A Prospectus," 106 *Tax Notes* 97 (January 3, 2005). In preparing this chapter for publication, I have benefited tremendously from comments from readers of that earlier article and of previous drafts. I wish to thank, in particular, Jon Ackerman, Rosanne Altshuler, Alan Auerbach, Peter Canellos, Daniel Halperin, Diane Ring, Daniel Shaviro, and C. Eugene Steuerle for their many helpful comments, and for their patience in helping to explain and resolve prior conceptual errors. All remaining errors should, of course, be laid at the feet of the author, and readers should not assume that any of the individuals listed agrees with the proposals made herein.

1. *Investment Dealer's Digest,* August 22, 2005, page 7.

2. Tax-indifferent participants include not only the usual list of tax-exempt entities and foreign institutions but mark-to-market taxpayers, for which the mark-to-market accounting system essentially overrides the tax rules for different financial instruments.

3. It often is observed that the consequence of the prevalence of tax-indifferent investors and issuers is that corporate income may be taxed once, twice, or not at all (as is the case when interest is paid to a tax-exempt investor). More accurately, if one includes households that incur tax-deductible mortgage debt and use the proceeds to sustain higher investments in tax-favored retirement plans, we should add to that list the possibility of negative tax rates.

4. Before dismissing the last point, readers should reflect carefully on the "Homeland Investment Act" provisions of the Internal Revenue Code (section 965), as enacted in 2004, that offer U.S. corporations a one-year nearly free pass on repatriating their untaxed foreign income, in direct contravention of the "capital export neutrality" principles said to have shaped our international tax rules for the past 45 years.

5. Noneconomists may find it more helpful to think of these as "supersized" returns.

6. Again, if both the loan and the asset yield the same marginal returns, the result will be that the owner and the lender together include in income the time value of money on the capital they collectively invested.

7. One can see this outmoded view of corporate capital structures at work as recently as the studies supporting the Institute of Fiscal Studies's 1991 "Allowance for Corporate Equity," which was premised on the view that "A company is owned by shareholders, who have a right to its assets and the income stream arising from them after paying all costs. These costs legitimately include the payment of interest to investors who have lent to the company" (Devereux and Freeman 1991, 6).

8. The other, more widely understood, problems are (1) the "classical" (or double-tax) corporate tax model, (2) the pervasive market presence of tax-indifferent and tax-exempt entities, and (3) the realization principle.

9. The straddle loss deferral rules are somewhat different or at least more precise; they take aim directly at explicit strategies designed to arbitrage the realization principle without taking substantial market risk.

10. See Simpson, "Irish Subsidiary Lets Microsoft Slash Taxes in U.S. and Europe," *Wall Street Journal,* Nov. 7, 2005, page A-1, column 5.

11. Simpson, "Irish Subsidiary Lets Microsoft Slash Taxes in U.S. and Europe."

12. Some observers turn this point on its head by concluding that realization is the *only* problem with the current income tax and that a direct attack on realization, therefore, can solve all other problems. This chapter, by contrast, begins with the debt-equity distinction as the fundamental source of current tax problems affecting financial capital and argues for minimizing the importance of realization wherever practicable.

13. In particular, the designer of an income tax must bear in mind four forms of international capital flows: foreign direct investment, foreign portfolio investment, inbound direct investment, and inbound portfolio investment.

14. One of the most unfortunate aspects of the global economy today is the success of multilateral tariff agreements (e.g., GATT) and the lack of interest on the part of sovereigns in improving the neutrality and efficiency of capital flows through similar coordination of direct taxes.

15. The reason is not simply dimwittedness, but rather a strongly held (if idiosyncratic) belief that inflation is a great social evil and that indexation is a polite word for partial immunization of the one social class (capital owners) that can resist its spread.

16. In the pass-through model, the entity is not taxable but its income is the measure of what must be allocated among stakeholders. How, though, should one treat an owner's capital gain on selling her stake in the entity when the business enterprise's commensurate gain remains *unrealized*? And how should one treat the subsequent purchaser of that interest (who has paid after-tax dollars for that unrealized gain) when the business enterprise realizes the gain at the entity level?

Not surprisingly, the Internal Revenue Code's partnership rules have an extraordinarily complex set of provisions (sections 734, 743, and 754, among others) to coordinate the two levels of realization events. Partnership tax experts tell me that those rules can work, sometimes, in the simplest cases (although I have never been able to understand them); to my knowledge, no one believes that they can be implemented for a publicly traded partnership.

17. Economists refer to this method of accounting as "accruals" taxation. This terminology is hopelessly confusing to people who practice tax law or who administer the Internal Revenue Code because the term "accruals," in its accounting sense, means the recognition of an income or expense item when the future receipt of payment or the obligation to make a future payment is reasonably certain. To tax professionals, the opposite of "accrual" accounting is the "cash" method of accounting, not the realization principle.

18. For background on the topic, see Kleinbard and Evans (1997); Kleinbard (2001, 2002); and Securities Industry Association, "Submission in Response to Advance Notice Regarding Safe Harbor Under Section 475," July 30, 2003, available through *Tax Notes Today* online at 2003 TNT 177-39.

19. As an aside, mark-to-market accounting works at the investor level to tax the time value of money once and only once only if that accounting system is comprehensive (that is, applies to *all* holders of financial capital instruments in an enterprise) and exclusive (that is, the enterprise itself is not also subject to tax).

20. Mark-to-market accounting works well for securities dealers precisely because their income is not significantly derived from real as well as financial assets. That accounting method today is flawed in that it applies only to dealers' assets, and not dealers' liabilities. However, because dealers fund themselves overwhelmingly with overnight financing, there is little practical distortion (Kleinbard and Evans 1997, 811–12).

Another approach would be to tax entities on a constructive mark-to-market methodology that treats the sum of the net fair market values of an entity's assets as equal to the market capitalization of the entity's stock. This approach raises substantial practical issues, including the problems described earlier of identifying genuine owners of a modern business enterprise with a complex capital structure. In addition, many business people can be expected to object that public equity prices are too volatile to serve as a fair tax base for an entity, which, unlike a stockholder, cannot simply capture fluctuations in value through a sale of the asset being measured.

21. The CBIT was reprised in a presentation in May 2005 for the President's Advisory Panel on Tax Reform and in 2003, when President George W. Bush's Treasury Department offered its first proposal to lower the tax rate on corporate dividend income, the centerpiece of which was an "Excludable Distributions Account" concept borrowed directly from the original CBIT study.

22. A direct compensatory tax also would radically affect an issuer's cash distribution policies and would exacerbate the coordination issues between stakeholder-level capital gains and the entity-level tax.

A direct entity-level compensatory tax on certain distributions is reminiscent of the United Kingdom's advance corporation tax. That tax clearly distorted U.K. companies' dividend distribution policies and was eventually abandoned.

23. Among the difficult questions is how to allocate items of preference and non-preference income among the different stakeholders, such as charities, individuals, and other corporations.

The President's Advisory Panel on Federal Tax Reform adverted to that experience in its final report, when it explained that it had rejected "more complicated regimes that would more precisely track the amount and timing of dividends and capital gains that should be exempt from shareholder-level tax based on the amount of income on which U.S. tax was paid at the business level" (125).

24. Kleinbard (2005) describes the plan in more detail (the "BEIT Prospectus"); several explanatory paragraphs from that paper have been carried over to this one. The material contained in the paper also was presented to the President's Advisory Panel on Federal Tax Reform in an expanded form in May 2005; that presentation is available online at http://www.taxreformpanel.gov/meetings/meeting-05_11-12_2005.shtml. As a historical footnote, Kleinbard originally proposed a rudimentary COCA in 1989 in an obscure article titled "Beyond Good and Evil Debt and Debt Hedges: A Cost of Capital Allowance."

25. "BEIT" is pronounced as "bite," which seems an appropriate term for a tax.

26. Most individuals who today are "traders" in securities would fall on the investment side of the definition. In addition, collective investment vehicles would be treated as investors rather than business enterprises. Leasing and real estate development activities would be treated as business activities; a collective investment fund, however, could engage in net leasing of real estate. Finally, hedge funds and other professional traders would be taxed as business enterprises rather than collective investment vehicles.

27. In fact, of 31 types of transactions that the Internal Revenue Service has listed as "abusive" in recent years, 13 are the direct result of the manipulation of the carryover basis or consolidated return rules, or inconsistencies in the rules applicable to different types of entities—all of which are directly resolved by the non-COCA components of the BEIT.

28. In this sense, the BEIT can be conceptualized as an enterprise-level progressive consumption tax of the income type, like the late David Bradford's X tax, combined with an investor-level tax on expected normal returns.

Compared with current law's elective tax-free reorganization rules, the mandatory BEIT regime also eliminates "loss duplication" tax avoidance trades and removes many administrative problems of tracking asset or securities basis through former owners. The BEIT also does not provide a seller of assets with any net depreciation benefit from selling and replacing its asset with an equivalent one.

29. Some simple examples of the mechanisms described in the text appear in the appendix.

Technically, the cost of capital allowance system applies only to *financial capital instruments*—financial claims against (or measured by) the earnings, assets, or liabilities of a business enterprise. The COCA system thus would *not* apply to U.S. Treasury securities (those instruments are not financial claims against a business enterprise) and would exclude ordinary trade receivables and payables of a business enterprise. While I appreciate that, in some ultimate sense, claims against the government can be described as indirect claims against other households and businesses, that argument is too diffuse, and the connection too attenuated, to have any practical significance.

30. COCA retains some modest residual double taxation at the investor level, both as a disguised minimum tax on business-level tax preferences and as an acknowledgement of traditional populist "ability to pay" sentiments.

31. The BEIT Prospectus discusses briefly some preliminary thinking behind how that rate might be determined. Special rules (not discussed in this brief overview) would apply to financial institutions.

32. Similarly, an issuer has no income inclusion if its cash payments are lower than the COCA rate, and will recognize neither income nor loss on the retirement of a financial capital instrument.

33. As a consequence, *every* distribution by an issuer in respect of its financial capital would reduce the issuer's tax basis in an asset (here, cash and cash equivalents), and therefore automatically would reduce the issuer's COCA deductions in future periods.

34. This rule would not apply within a consolidated group because the consolidated group is treated as a single business enterprise.

35. The reasons for imposing any tax on excess distributions are summarized in note 30.

36. The straddle rules would, however, continue to apply.

37. One source of a great deal of the complexity in the current law's taxation of financial instruments is the desire to distinguish returns *on* investment from returns *of* investment. Both the "earnings and profits" concept applicable to corporate stock and some tax rules for complex debt instruments address that concern. The COCA system dispenses with the "earnings and profits" concept and instead taxes all returns during the life of an instrument as returns *on* investment (either as nonincludable payments of prior minimum inclusions or as excess distributions). Liquidations and similar transactions are treated as sales so that basis is recovered through the normal mechanism of reducing sales proceeds by adjusted basis. Under a special amortizing debt rule, however, distributions made on any fixed-term instrument that reduce of the holder's claim against the business enterprise during the life of the instrument are respected to that extent as returns

of principal, so long as the ongoing contractual return on the instrument is reasonably related to that contractual reduction of the holder's claim against the issuer.

38. As noted above, losses are treated essentially as reversing prior income inclusions. Thus, imagine that ordinary income rates are set at 45 percent, excess distribution rates at 15 percent, and the relevant COCA rate for the year is 6 percent. A taxpayer invests $1,000 in a business enterprise and receives no distributions. At the end of year 1, the taxpayer includes $60 in income. The taxpayer then sells the investment for $940. The first $60 of loss (in effect, from the adjusted tax basis of $1,060 to $1,000) offsets prior minimum inclusions of $60 and is deductible at a 45 percent rate. The next $60 of loss is treated as the mirror of excess distribution income, and therefore one-third of the loss (15/45) is deductible against ordinary income. The taxpayer thus reduces her tax liability by (45% × $60) + (45% × $20), or $36.

39. See the BEIT Prospectus at 105-06. This introduces an unfortunate tax distinction, under which it is necessary to deviate from a perfectly featureless tax topography by maintaining a limited metaphysical infrastructure to define the difference between a derivative instrument and a physical security. The practical consequences of drawing the line incorrectly, however, are much reduced when compared with current law's debt and equity distinctions. In addition, many taxpayers that make extensive use of derivatives, including all financial institutions, are taxed under COCA on a mark-to-market basis. Finally, if one believes that a derivative ordinarily is a fair bet (once the time value component of its returns has been extracted and dealt with separately), how this perturbation in the tax landscape could spawn a tax shelter industry is difficult to see.

40. The practical problems associated with universal mark-to-market accounting for all taxpayers do not apply to financial institutions because they already employ mark-to-market accounting for purposes of risk measurement, risk hedging, trader compensation, and internal capital allocation decisions, as well as for many of their regulatory and financial accounting requirements. Moreover, Section 475 of the Internal Revenue Code *requires* "dealers" in "securities" (both terms have very broad definitions) to mark to market their assets for tax purposes. As a result, every major financial institution has invested hundreds of millions of dollars in developing mark-to-market valuation models and accounting systems.

Section 475(f) of the Internal Revenue Code permits " traders" in securities to elect into Section 475's mark-to-market regime. Taxpayers with the requisite systems and desire make the election, while others to not. I envision that the same range of outcomes will apply to nonfinancial institution business enterprises in respect of the BEIT's analogous election.

41. COCA has some superficial similarities to the "Allowance for Corporate Equity" ("ACE") that the Institute for Fiscal Studies proposed in 1991 and Devereux and Freeman (1991) summarized, but the two systems have different agendas. ACE was conceived as an alternative mechanism for implementing a *consumption* tax: corporations would receive a tax deduction equal to a notional cost of equity, calculated in a manner similar to the COCA deduction (applied, however, to "shareholders' funds," not all assets), and continue to deduct actual interest expense. Distributions to shareholders would in some fashion be exempt from tax; like the drafters of CBIT, however, the proponents of ACE became a bit vague when discussing how preference items would be handled, and capital gains taxed.

Like CBIT, ACE did not advance the taxation of financial derivatives at all. Like COCA, however, ACE deductions for notional capital charges corrected for errors in company-level depreciation practices. Devereux and Freeman (1991, 5).

Unlike both CBIT and COCA, ACE applied only to corporations and retained a distinction between debt and equity: actual interest expense on the former would be deductible, while notional capital charges could be deducted in respect of the latter. The limitation of ACE to one class of business entities and the preservation of the debt-equity distinction seem to be fundamental weaknesses of the proposal. Also unlike CBIT and COCA, there is at least some real-world experience with ACE. See, for example, Keen and King (2002).

42. In the special case where all capital investments are currently expensed, the result essentially equates to an illustration of the famous "Cary Brown theorem," in which deducting an investment's cost equals exempting a normal rate of return on that investment from tax (Brown 1948).

This combination of depreciation and a COCA-like system was explicitly adopted in the Allowance for Corporate Equity system to design a consumption tax. As noted, the designers of that system did so by exempting the normal return on an amount termed "shareholders' funds" from tax in the hands of stockholders.

43. Recall that CBIT achieved integration only through its poorly articulated excludable distributions account concept.

44. By contrast, a simple expensing solution opens up the prospect of large windfalls (or detriments), depending on the timing of a taxpayer's investments relative to the effective date of new tax rates.

45. As noted earlier, there is one small point of difference between the COCA rules for derivatives and the rules applicable to "physical" securities, but that difference is not germane to this point.

46. First, if the COCA rate diverges from the normal rate of return, the COCA/depreciation system resembles more closely the status quo of relative tax burdens across different industries than does an expensing solution. Second, BEIT/COCA's combination of deductions for depreciation and financial capital can roughly be analogized to the current law's deductions for depreciation and interest expense. I believe that presenting the BEIT as building on well understood tax concepts may enhance its political prospects.

Finally, the administrative difficulties associated with depreciation rules seem overstated, at least when applied to larger companies. The reason that capitalization and depreciation rules are contentious today is that the substantive *consequences* of those rules are momentous. In a world where the capitalization/depreciation decision has no great consequences, much of today's tax dramatics should dissipate.

Conversely, there might be merit in exploring a simple expensing rule within BEIT/COCA for small businesses because administrative and systems considerations are more important for small companies than for large firms.

47. In writing this subsection in particular, I benefited from the helpful insights of Daniel Halperin.

48. If asset sales were entirely tax-free, but buyers obtained a carryover tax basis in purchased assets, then Buyer in our example would pay only $80 for the asset (because, by hypothesis, if an asset with $20 in present value tax benefits is worth $100, then an asset with no associated tax benefits is worth $80). Seller would keep the $80 free of any tax and buy a new replacement asset for $80.

In the BEIT/COCA case, Buyer will pay $100 for the same asset to reflect the $20 in tax benefits of ownership. Buyer's total *after-tax* cost for the asset thus remains $80. On the other side, Seller will recognize $80 in after-tax proceeds. Seller will be required to pay $100 for a replacement asset; as a result, Seller will need to invest an additional $20 out of its own pocket to acquire that replacement asset. The replacement asset in turn will bring with it $20 in present value tax benefits to Seller, so that Seller's after-tax cost for purchasing the replacement asset also will remain $80.

49. If this hypothesis proves too optimistic, then one would reimpose an annual cap on such losses, but presumably that cap could be set at levels that are orders of magnitude higher (e.g., 100 times as high) than the $3,000 per year of capital loss that current law permits an individual to use against ordinary income.

50. The same rule was advocated as part of the Allowance for Corporate Equity proposal. See Devereux and Freeman (1991, 7).

51. Transfer pricing would still be relevant in respect of the allocation of a multi-national group's tax liabilities between its country of residence and the tax-source countries in which it operated, but from the multinational enterprise's perspective, this issue is less exciting than the prospect of indefinite reductions in the group's effective tax liabilities to the levels prevalent in some source countries.

52. Publicly traded equities, in particular, trade overwhelmingly on exchanges or in organized over-the-counter markets through recognized (and regulated) broker-dealers. (The same is true for corporate debt, except that the debt market is almost entirely an over-the-counter market.) In every such case, there are financial institutions through which sales proceeds flow, and one or more financial institutions on whose books the beneficial owner of a security is recorded. And of course the power and sophistication of technology systems available to financial intermediaries is vastly superior to that available just a few years ago. Both the information and the technology thus exist to impose broker with-holding on sales proceeds, if there is political will to do so. If, as a consequence, the United States and other jurisdictions are encouraged to eliminate bearer (i.e., anonymous) bonds—a market with little commercial importance—and to improve exchanges of taxpayer financial information between tax authorities, that result would not be regrettable.

53. I thank Alan Auerbach for pointing out this issue to me.

54. The wash sale rules of section 1091 and the wash sale principles of the tax straddle regulations, Treas. Reg. Sec 1.1092(b)-1T.

55. The securities industry today has widely divergent practices in assisting investors to track the tax bases of their investments. Some of the practical problems that the industry faces include having no way to validate a customer's starting basis when an account is established, difficulty in sharing information between brokers using different technology platforms when an account is transferred, and difficulty in ascertaining how to treat various financial instruments and transactions when the attendant tax disclosure indicates that the tax analysis under current law is ambiguous. All of these issues are nettlesome; none are insoluble. Mandatory basis reporting rules (as we have today for dividends and interest) and BEIT/COCA's simplified substantive rules for taxing financial capital instruments and business combinations should allow financial institutions to provide investors with the information they need to prepare accurate income tax returns.

56. One other administrative disadvantage to the COCA approach, when compared to CBIT, is that COCA forces one to address directly the role of tax-exempt institutions in the capital markets, while CBIT hides the issue in the tax imposed on business enter-

prises. The practical effect of this observation depends on whether tax-exempt institutions would have understood that CBIT effectively would have taxed their investment returns.

57. In comparing transition issues under BEIT/COCA and CBIT, COCA would preserve investor-level income and therefore should create more modest price dislocations for current holders of corporate stock or bonds than would CBIT (which would turn all existing corporate securities into tax-exempt securities). COCA also does *not* crowd out municipal bond issuers; by contrast, in a CBIT regime, state and local governments would be required to pay materially higher interest rates because of the huge increase in tax-exempt securities competing for investor dollars.

REFERENCES

Bradford, David F. 2004. *The X Tax in the World Economy.* Washington, DC: AEI Press.

Brown, E. Cary. 1948. "Business-Income Taxation and Investment Incentives." In *Income, Employment and Public Policy: Essays in Honor of A. H. Hansen* (300–16). New York: W. W. Norton & Co.

Devereux, Michael, and Harold Freeman. 1991. "A General Neutral Profits Tax." *Fiscal Studies* 12(3): 1–15.

Kau, Randall K. C. 1990. "Carving Up Assets and Liabilities—Integration of Bifurcation of Financial Products." *Taxes* 68(12): 1003–14.

Keen, Michael, and John King. 2002. "The Croatian Profit Tax: An ACE in Practice." *Fiscal Studies* 23(3): 401–18.

Kleinbard, Edward D. 1989. "Beyond Good and Evil Debt (and Debt Hedges): A Cost of Capital Allowance System." *Taxes* 67(12): 943–61.

———. 1991. "Equity Derivative Products: Financial Innovation's Newest Challenge to the Tax System." *Texas Law Review* 69(6): 1319–68.

———. 2001. "Some Thoughts on Market Valuation of Derivatives." *Tax Notes* 91(7): 1173–75.

———. 2002. "A Short Course in Valuing Derivatives." *Tax Notes* 94(3): 380–83.

———. 2005. "The Business Enterprise Income Tax: A Prospectus." *Tax Notes* 106: 97–107.

Kleinbard, Edward D., and Thomas L. Evans. 1997. "The Role of a Mark-to-Market Accounting System in a Realization-Based Tax System." *Taxes* 75(12): 788–823.

President's Advisory Panel on Federal Tax Reform. 2005. *Report of the President's Advisory Panel on Federal Tax Reform—Simple, Fair, and Pro-Growth: Proposals to Fix America's Tax System.* Washington, DC: U.S. Government Printing Office.

Shaviro, Daniel. 2004. "Replacing the Income Tax with a Progressive Consumption Tax." *Tax Notes* 103: 91–113.

U.S. Department of the Treasury. 1992. *Integration of the Individual and Corporate Tax Systems: Taxing Business Income Once.* Washington, DC: U.S. Government Printing Office.

Examples

Table A.1. Opening of Year 1 Tax Balance Sheet

Assets ($)		Liabilities and equity ($)	
Cash	100	Short-term liabilities	100
Portfolio investment	200	Long-term debt	200
Greasy machinery	500	Funky contingent payment securities	200
Land	200	Preferred stock	100
Total assets	1,000	Common stock	400
		Total assets	1,000

Note: COCA = cost of capital allowance.
Assumptions:

- COCA Rate = 5%
- No cash return on portfolio investment
- Operating business earns $130 EBITDA
- Cash payments to holders of all liabilities and equity = $46
- Tax depreciation on machinery = $50
- For simplicity, COCA calculations are done once annually, using the opening balance sheet

Table A.2. Year 1 Results ($)

Income	
Net income from operations	130
Deemed returns on portfolio investment	10
Total gross income	140
Deductions	
COCA deduction	50
Depreciation	50
Total deductions	100
Taxable income	40
Tax at 35%	14
Cash flow	
Net income from operations	130
Less cash coupons on liabilities and equity	(46)
Less taxes	(14)
Net cash flow	70

Table A.3. Opening of Year 2 Tax Balance Sheet

Assets ($)		Liabilities and equity ($)	
Cash	170	Short-term liabilities	100
Portfolio investment	210	Long-term debt	200
Greasy machinery	450	Funky contingent payment securities	200
Land	200	Preferred stock	100
Total assets	1,030	Common stock	430
		Total liabilities	1,030

Notes: Year 2 COCA = $51.50; issuer does not need to accrete any amount to liabilities for prior year's COCA expense because there is no gain or loss on retirement of any liability or equity.

Figure A.1. Holder Example

Assume a constant 5% COCA rate.
Holder invests $1,000 in a security.
For the first three years, there are no cash coupons, but minimum inclusion = $158.
  The basis is therefore = $1,158.
At end of year 3, cash distribution of $500.
  $158 = tax-free return of accrued but unpaid minimum inclusions (basis => $1,000)
  $342 = excess distribution (taxable at reduced rates)
Hold another two years, no cash coupons, but minimum inclusion = $103
  The basis is therefore = $1,103
a) Sell for $1,303: $200 excess distribution.
b) Sell for $1,000: ($103) loss, deductible at excess distribution rates.
c) Sell for $403: ($700) total loss.
    $342 at excess distribution rates
    $261 at minimum inclusion rate
    Remaining $97 at excess distribution rates

Figure A.2. Derivatives

First priority: tax hedge accounting principles.
* Based on current law (e.g., Reg §1.1275-6).
* The presumption is that financial derivatives of a business enterprise that is a nondealer or nonprofessional trader are balance sheet hedges, and as a result a gain or loss is ignored (i.e., subsumed into general COCA regime, where cash coupons on financial capital instruments are ignored).
* Taxpayer may affirmatively elect out.

Second priority: mark-to-market.
* Generally, the regime is mandatory for dealers/professional traders.
* Dealers/traders may elect tax hedge accounting treatment for their liability hedges.

Third priority: asset/liability model.
* Treat all upfront, periodic, and interim payments as (nondeductible) investments in the contract.
* Apply COCA minimum inclusion/deduction rules to resulting net "derivative asset" or to increase in asset basis corresponding to "derivative liability."
* Amount and direction of derivative asset/liability fluctuates from year to year, with no consequence other than minimum inclusions on any net investment (and COCA deductions on assets).
* At maturity or termination, "settle up" by recognizing gain or loss.
* Maturity or termination gain taxed at excess distribution rates.
* Maturity or termination loss taxed identically to general COCA regime for holders (i.e., first deductible at minimum inclusion rates to extent of prior minimum inclusions, then excess distribution rates).
* Result is identical to general COCA rules for gain, or for loss on derivative assets, but different for derivative liabilities (because gain or loss is recognized).
* The consequence is that a bright line test is still required to distinguish derivatives from financial capital investments.

Figure A.3. Derivatives Example

Assume COCA rate = 5%
X pays $50 to Y for a three-year option on S&P 500.
X has minimum inclusions over three-year life = $8 (rounded).
* So X's basis at maturity = $58.
* Y receives COCA deductions on cash proceeds—that is, on assets, not directly on derivative liability.

At maturity, contract pays either:
* $88—X recognizes $30 in excess distribution gain; Y recognizes $38 (not $30) in loss deductible at excess distribution rates.
* $0—X recognizes $8 loss deductible at minimum inclusion rates, $50 loss deductible at excess distribution rates; Y recognizes $50 gain (not $58), taxable at excess distribution rates.

5

Can Income from Capital Be Taxed?

An International Perspective

Julie A. Roin

This chapter grapples with the prosaic question of whether it is possible to collect an income tax that looks much like our current income tax, in a world with significant international capital mobility. It identifies some of the current obstacles to taxation posed by globalization of the capital markets and then suggests some legislative and regulatory changes that might ameliorate these obstacles. That some or all of these suggestions may be politically unpalatable proves a larger point: the effectiveness (or ineffectiveness) of the income tax depends on public and political support for the tax. In the absence of such support, it will quickly mutate into a wage tax, as wages are the only income subject to mandatory reporting and withholding obligations. Further, some of the required changes can only be effected in concert with other nations, many without the same interest as the United States in stemming tax avoidance. The most substantial barriers to effective income taxation, then, may be political rather than technical.

Understanding how globalization has undermined this country's ability to tax capital income requires understanding at least the basic outlines of the U.S. regime for taxing foreign taxpayers and foreign income. The portion of the Internal Revenue Code dealing with international issues is intricately detailed and amazingly complex. Some problems stem from these intricacies, but the majority result from basic design decisions common to virtually all developed nations.

There are two generally accepted bases of income tax jurisdiction: source (accruing to the country where the income is generated) and residence (accruing to the country where the taxpayer lives). All countries assert a right to tax the income generated within their borders, regardless of the nationality of the taxpayer earning such income. The United States follows the general pattern by levying (as a statutory matter) its income taxes on two categories of income earned by foreign corporations and "nonresident aliens." Foreigners not engaged in a U.S. trade or business are subject to a tax equal to 30 percent of the gross amount of certain types of passive income from U.S. sources; foreigners engaged in a U.S. trade or business must pay tax on the income generated by that business from U.S. sources under the normal income tax rules, just as if the taxpayer were a U.S. resident.

Some countries, including the United States, also claim the right to levy an income tax on their residents' worldwide income. The United States and a few other countries also assert this right with respect to citizens living abroad. With the source and residence tax claims of different nations overlapping, some income is subject to tax by two or more national tax systems. Given the high rates of tax imposed by many jurisdictions, such duplicative or "double" taxation threatens the financial viability of international transactions. Since the 1920s, the international consensus has been that the country of source has "primary" taxing jurisdiction, while the country of residence has "secondary," or residual, taxing jurisdiction. This means that, in the absence of explicit agreement to the contrary, countries have the right to impose their full tax levy on all income derived within their borders, but must take taxes levied by a source country into account when calculating the tax due on the foreign-sourced income of their residents.

Residence countries can take source country taxation into account in a variety of ways. They can allow those taxes as a deduction when calculating the taxpayer's taxable income. They can treat source taxes as a credit against their own taxes imposed on the foreign income. Or they can simply exclude the foreign-sourced income from their tax base altogether. The United States, like most countries, employs a combination of these techniques, although it relies more than do many other developed countries on the foreign tax credit and less on outright exemption of foreign source income. The foreign tax credit allows U.S. residents (and companies) to deduct the foreign income taxes they pay from the U.S. income tax due on their foreign income.

Although much has been written about problems with the foreign tax credit, its defects are a secondary problem. To a large extent, the problems evident in the residence-based tax credit regime stem from defects in the operation of the underlying source tax regimes. These source tax defects undermine the operation of all residence-based taxing regimes, not just tax credit regimes. The underlying problem is that source tax countries, sometimes as a matter of statutory law and sometimes pursuant to treaty agreements, fail to tax income generated within their borders and make no effort to ensure that residence countries take up the slack. The result is complete nontaxation of certain categories of international income, with predictable effects on the growth of such income and accompanying revenue losses to national treasuries. Nontaxation of transnational income rather than double taxation of such income is the more serious problem today. Such nontaxation, as explained below, affects both transnational investment income and transnational business income.

Causes of Double Nontaxation

Although economists often argue whether source taxation or residence taxation is "better" from an economic standpoint, as a practical matter, many circumstances trigger neither form of taxation. Most striking is that countries with primary taxing authority often fail to exercise that authority.

Passive Investment Income

Some untaxed income is explicitly excluded. Other income is protected by tax treaties negotiated, typically on a bilateral basis, between nations.

Explicitly Excluded Income

Although countries have the right to levy an income tax on all income generated within their borders, they lack personal jurisdiction over many of the foreign individuals and entities that earn such income. In particular, a country of source is unlikely to be able to collect unpaid taxes or run an effective audit on foreign investors who are "passive" investors— those not engaged in active business activities in the source country but receiving payments such as interest or dividends from source country entities. Many such taxpayers never enter the source country, conducting all of their income-producing activities through agents, or even through the mail. Because countries can exercise only very limited powers of tax enforcement outside their borders, source countries typically do not even try to impose their normal income tax regimes on such taxpayers. Instead, they impose withholding taxes at flat rates on the gross amount of certain types of investment income paid to such foreigners.

Meanwhile, other types of investment income are excluded from the tax base on grounds of being unsuited to taxation in an international context. The United States, for example, by statute levies a 30 percent withholding tax on the gross amount of U.S. source "fixed, determinable, annual, and periodic income" earned by nonresident aliens and foreign corporations outside the context of a U.S. trade or business (I.R.C. §§871(a), 881(a)). The term "fixed, determinable, annual and periodic income" includes interest income and dividend income but excludes most types of capital gains and even many gains considered ordinary income. Gains have largely been excluded from tax in many countries because a withholding tax on gross sales proceeds threatens to confiscate all, if not more, of sellers' profits from such sales, while an alternate rule imposing a withholding tax equal to a percentage of gains is difficult to administer given buyers' ignorance of sellers' tax bases.[1]

Over time, the category of exempt income has grown. For example, most interest income earned by foreign investors is now legally exempt from U.S. income tax (I.R.C. §§871(h)-(i), 881(c)). These exemptions from source taxation are not conditional on the foreign taxpayer paying taxes on such income in their country of residence. They are not even conditional on the taxpayer reporting such income items to their country of residence. And few taxpayers are believed to report and pay tax on such income in their home countries.[2]

U.S. residents also take advantage of these rules to avoid paying U.S. taxes due on both their foreign income and, increasingly, their U.S. income and specifically the income derived from passive investment in widely traded securities. It is relatively easy for a U.S. resident to masquerade as a foreigner by holding assets, including stocks and bonds issued by U.S. entities, indirectly through an artificial entity such as a corporation created in a foreign jurisdiction. As long as the U.S. issuer can attest that its payment is made to a foreign taxpayer's foreign bank account, the issuer is exempted from any withholding requirement. The identity of the ultimate owner is simply irrelevant to the issuer making the payment. Although in most cases, the U.S. owner of the foreign recipient corporation should be reporting and paying U.S. tax on the foreign corporation's income on a current basis, the chances of the relationship to the foreign corporation being discovered, and the U.S. owner's subsequent liability for the tax, are remote.[3] Indeed, to increase the difficulty of detection, some U.S. taxpayers use tiered entity structures. That is, they interpose several artificial entities between themselves and the U.S. issuer (Sheppard 2005). It helps if the intermediary entities are established in tax haven countries—by definition, those countries that levy low or no income taxes and that have bank secrecy laws—but it is by no means essential. The interest income derived by an American individual investing in U.S. bonds through a French corporation is not much more likely to be discovered by the French or U.S. tax authorities than when such interest income is derived by a French individual.[4]

Treaty-Protected Income

In addition to the U.S. source investment income implicitly or explicitly exempted from tax by statute, additional categories of investment income are exempted from U.S. tax under bilateral tax treaty arrangements with countries no one would consider to be tax havens.[5] Tax treaties go beyond statutory law to provide additional source tax reductions. Although dividends generally remain subject to a reduced rate of withholding tax, the typical tax treaty eliminates the withholding tax on royalties and those categories of interest income that remain subject to source tax by statute.[6] Such reductions are meant to reduce or eliminate inadvertent overtaxation created by withholding taxes levied on gross income, and to substitute in their place the residence country's normal taxation rules.

Treaty exemptions are reciprocal. That is, when the United States gives up its source tax claim with respect to treaty partner residents investing in the United States, the treaty partner gives up its source tax claims against U.S. residents earning similar income within its borders. A treaty partner's waiver of its source tax claim should increase U.S. residence-based tax revenues by reducing the amount of foreign tax credits claimed as an offset against this U.S. tax liability. The treaty partner should also see its source tax revenues decline and its residence tax revenues increase as a result of the treaty.[7] If the treaty rule works correctly, both taxpayers and national treasuries would come out in approximately the same place financially as they would have in a no-treaty world, although each country would collect its tax revenues from its residents rather than from its investors.

These treaty exemptions suffer from the same defect as statutory exemptions do. The source tax concessions are granted by source countries without any proof that the taxpayer has reported or paid tax to the residence country on the associated income.[8] Although tax treaties contain exchange-of-information provisions that require the treaty partners to provide each other with information on the other's residents upon request, resident country taxing authorities often do not know whom or what to ask. Certainly neither source country governments nor foreign payors provide home country tax authorities with anything close to the information returns U.S. payors of investment income are required to send U.S. payees—returns that make machine auditing and substantial tax compliance likely.

Again, though in the first instance this makes avoidance of home country taxes by foreigners more likely, it also provides more locales in which U.S. residents can masquerade as residents. How often they currently take advantage of these locales to evade U.S. taxes is unclear.

The Undertaxation of Business Income

All countries tax the income generated from active business activities undertaken within their borders by nonresidents, usually under the same rules applied to residents.[9] The reasoning behind such equivalent treatment is both practical and political. Few countries could long sustain a taxing regime that systematically favored foreign over domestic businesses.

Business income generated from foreign sources, though, is treated differently because of both jurisdictional and overtaxation concerns. No country has the jurisdiction to tax the foreign income of foreign taxpayers.[10] In addition, many countries exempt the foreign business income of their resident taxpayers from their domestic tax base. The United States takes a different tack. It claims to eventually impose a tax on the foreign income of its businesses equal to the difference between the foreign source taxes paid and what the U.S. tax on such income would have been, had such income been earned domestically. But it allows taxpayers to defer paying this step-up, or residual, tax and sometimes forgives portions of it.[11] The net result of the two approaches is surprisingly close. In both, taxpayers benefit by allocating income to low-tax jurisdictions.

Taxpayers generally succeed in overallocating income to jurisdictions with low income tax rates. The latest U.S. statistics show that 58 percent of the profits earned by U.S. multinationals were allocated to 18 "tax haven" countries, "a figure that far exceeds the share of economic activity that multinationals conduct in these low-tax countries" (Sullivan 2004a, 1190). Taxpayers succeed largely because of defects in the statutory rules for "sourcing" income enacted by high-tax countries.

Tax Havens

Income sourcing schemes would not be worth pursuing if all countries taxed income at similar rates. Rates differ widely, however. Countries maintain low income tax rates for a variety of reasons. Some lack capacity to collect high rates or to spend their proceeds effectively. Others want to attract additional foreign investment or spur domestic investment. Still others seek to raise revenues by facilitating foreign tax avoidance.[12] Mixed motives are common. Ireland, for example, has attracted real business operations because of its low corporate tax rate, but many are suspicious that it also encourages taxpayers to improperly siphon considerable amounts of income away from other jurisdictions (Sullivan 2005).[13]

Taxation of transnational income would be easier without tax havens, but they probably cannot be eliminated. Tax haven behavior is profitable. Tax havens gain both tax revenues and at least a modicum of economic activity when foreign investors run their money through their financial institutions (Littlewood 2004). If the benefits enjoyed by such countries are outweighed by the tax and economic losses suffered by other counties, in theory the other countries ought to be able to bribe tax havens into adopting different tax regimes. However, such side payments are unworkable, given the coordination issues between the nonhaven countries (which would have to agree on their respective contribution levels) and more importantly, the power of each tax haven country to forestall the agreement. Nonhaven countries could not expect to see any benefits, and thus should be unwilling to pay anything unless and until all havens have discontinued their haven regimes. However, every country would have the opportunity to be the last operating haven (generating extraordinary revenues) and could hold out for a payment equal to such an amount. The total demand by all haven countries would thus exceed any conceivable benefit to other countries, while any less compensatory scheme would be inherently unstable. Individual countries would still have an economic incentive to defect and become tax havens.

The only way to neutralize havens, then, is to remove the profit from haven activity. Havens' profitability depends largely on the failure of high-tax countries to find reasonable methods for determining the amount of taxable business income. Tax havens pose a threat only because tax-payers can easily allocate income to them, and away from the high-tax jurisdictions where such income has been earned. Fixing the source rules, in short, may be a more practicable solution than eliminating tax havens.

We must understand the flaws in the current methods of determining the source of income for tax purposes, to see how corrections to these rules can be made. Taxpayers have two primary techniques for misallocating income to tax havens: transfer pricing manipulation and income characterization.

Transfer Pricing Manipulation

Customers tend to view multinational corporations as single, indivisible entities. In fact, however, even the most vertically integrated enterprises are usually operated through strings of separately incorporated, related corporations. For a variety of legal and business (as well as tax) reasons, manufacturing operations are usually undertaken by a corporation established in the country in which such manufacturing operations take place. Customer location generally dictates the residence of corporations undertaking sales operations. Neither of these countries may be the one in which the parent corporation, which handles strategic planning, administration, research and development, and a slew of other corporate functions, is incorporated or located. Although ultimately each of these corporations is owned by the parent company's shareholders, as a formal matter, each is a distinct entity that interacts with the other corporate entities through contractual arrangements. That is, these related corporations buy things from, and sell things to, each other, as well as to the general public. To the extent the source of income for tax purposes depends on which of the related entities happens to earn the income, the tax characterization hangs on the specifics of these intercompany contracts and, in particular, on the prices they charge each other for the goods and services they transfer to each other. The prices at which related companies trade goods or services are called in the tax literature "transfer prices."

As good agents of a common owner, of course, related corporations have an incentive to ensure that the maximum amount of income is earned where it will be subjected to the lowest possible tax rate, an objective that may be advanced by carefully setting transfer prices. Start with the simplest example. Suppose a company, X, manufactures mousetraps in low-tax Ireland (tax rate of 12.5 percent). It sells some of its mousetraps to its wholly owned distributor, Y, in the United States (tax rate of 35 percent) for sale to U.S. customers. Now suppose that these mousetraps cost $6 to make, $6 to market, and are eventually sold for $20. The combined enterprise will make $8 for each mousetrap sold in the United States. But how much of this $8 will be attributed to the Irish manufacturing operations and subject to tax at 12.5 percent, and how much will be attributed to the U.S. sales operations and subject to a 35 percent income tax? In the first instance, it depends on the price X charges Y for the mousetraps. If X charges Y $12 per mousetrap, X will make $6 of profit (taxed at 12.5 percent) and Y, only $2 (taxed at 35 percent). If X charges Y $8 per mousetrap, X's profit will be $2 (taxed at 12.5 percent) and Y's will be $6 (taxed at 35 percent). If left to their own devices, what price do you think X will charge Y?

Other, more elaborate schemes can be used to extend the circumstances in which such transfer pricing manipulations provide tax benefits. Suppose X's manufacturing activities in the above example took place in a high-tax country, the same country in which X was incorporated. X, or X's parent company, could establish an intermediary corporation, Z, in a low-tax country. X could sell the mousetraps to Z, which would then resell the mousetraps to Y. If X sold the mousetraps to Z for $7, and Z resold the mousetraps to Y for $13, X would have $1 profit to declare to the high-tax country of manufacture, Y would have $1 of profit to declare in the country of ultimate sale, and Z would have $6 to declare to the low-tax country.

Of course, tax authorities—and the legislatures that control them— have some idea of what is going on. As in the United States, most countries give tax authorities the power to rewrite, for tax purposes at least, contracts between related parties so that the prices paid conform to the "arm's length" standard—that is, to recompute each related parties' taxable income as if the contractual prices were the same as would have been paid by unrelated companies bargaining at arm's length.[14]

In the real world, however, it is not easy to determine what that arm's length price is. Indeed, most economists are convinced that, at best, there is a range of arm's length prices. Accordingly, the Internal Revenue Service allows taxpayers to choose a price anywhere along that sometimes wide range. But the larger problem is that few intercompany transfers involve fungible items with clearly defined market prices. Intellectual property that is difficult to value, ranging from trademarks to patents to goodwill, infects almost every transaction. So, too, do location factors arising from unique market and supply factors. Nor is it always clear which entity should be allowed to profit from location and supply factors. Finally, transfer-pricing decisions inevitably necessitate allocating the efficiency gains generated by vertical integration of the business enterprise. As a result, it is very hard to specify third-party prices established in comparable transactions to serve as the arm's length standard. At best, taxpayers and tax authorities find themselves relying on loosely similar transactions for comparison, leading to disputes about the type and extent of corrections necessary to make the price terms reasonably comparable.

Transfer pricing disputes tend to degenerate into very expensive contests of dueling experts. The costs of such disputes weigh on tax authorities as well as on taxpayers. Tax authorities lack the resources to challenge more than a tiny fraction of the questionable transactions that exist. As a result, many taxpayers overreach and rely on the audit lottery to escape detection.

Income Recharacterization

Manipulating transfer prices is not the only way to shift income from a high-tax country to a low- or no-tax country. Equally important is taxpayers' ability to structure their transactions to generate particular types of income: different statutory source and tax rules apply to different types of income. Thus, changing income from one type into another may change the applicable statutory source rule. That, in turn, may change the country in which the income is sourced. Alternatively, the change in the type of income may alter the taxing regime under which it will be taxed.

Tax-motivated structuring can be as simple as financing operations with debt rather than with equity, since interest income is often treated as (passive) income earned by the creditor and subject to less tax at source than dividend income. Further, not only may such income be subject to a lower rate of tax in the hands of the creditor—or no tax at all—but the interest payment will reduce the income of the debtor, thus reducing its income tax liability.

A more complicated scheme may involve "slicing and dicing" income into smaller or larger numbers of component parts to generate the best tax results. For example, most lending transactions include a service element (loan processing), an interest element (the time value of money), and a risk (credit risk) charge. In the absence of tax considerations, a bank might charge a single sum for all of these functions, which would be characterized as interest income. However, if a bank split the transaction and its fees into the three parts, one fee would be treated as personal services income and sourced where the services were performed, one would be treated as interest income and sourced accordingly, and the last would be treated as insurance income and sourced under the insurance rules.

The slicing and dicing strategy works for nonfinancial business transactions as well. The owner of intellectual property could simply license the property and set a royalty charge. Alternatively, it could manufacture goods, incorporating the intellectual property for resale, and then sell the goods, generating income from manufacturing and sales with nary an intellectual property return in sight. In yet another variation, the taxpayer could hire someone else to perform manufacturing services and to sell the resulting products on behalf of the taxpayer. Even after paying these independent contractors, the taxpayer could be left with substantial income because of its initial ownership of the intellectual property and its acceptance of business risks, not to mention the recompense it deserves for its exercise of managerial or entrepreneurial skill in locating and overseeing the work of such subcontractors. But its profits would be characterized as general business income, or income generated from the manufacture and sale of inventory property and sourced accordingly, rather than being treated as royalty and insurance income that would be sourced under a different source rule, and perhaps taxed under a different taxing regime altogether—that is, as nonbusiness income.

Tax considerations influence these choices. If they distort real business behaviors, they create what economists call inefficiency. Even when actual business operations remain unchanged, however, governmental revenues decrease because taxpayers rarely choose to pay more tax than required. And as more transactions have a global component, these techniques can be used to avoid an ever-increasing share of corporate tax liability.

Globalization, then, threatens the United States' ability to enforce the taxation of capital income earned by both individuals and corporations. This problem is probably getting worse as more people and businesses gain the knowledge to engage in these tax schemes and the confidence that they will not be caught or seriously punished if they are. The question discussed next is whether anything can be done to change this.

Can the Omitted Income Be Taxed?

Capital income taxation cannot long survive if income generated in international transactions is untaxed. If international income is untaxed, wholly domestic transactions will disappear. Taxpayers will increasingly choose to invest and earn, or appear to invest and earn, abroad. Thus, the answer to the question "can we tax capital income?" is contained in the answer to the question "can we tax transnational capital income?" Few problems have perfect solutions; this one is not an exception. Instead, we have imperfect alternatives.

Taxing Passive Income

Virtually all interest income and much other passive investment income currently goes untaxed by both source and residence countries. In most cases, source countries have unilaterally withdrawn their tax claim while residence countries have found themselves unable to enforce their claim. In other situations, the nontaxation results from treaty relationships. This favorable treatment of cross-border investment income has led many taxpayers earning domestic income to transform it into effectively exempt transnational income by interposing a foreign entity as an intermediate recipient. The question is how to ensure that this income gets taxed somewhere.

Residence Taxation Possibilities

In a perfect world, the solution would come in the form of full residence-country taxation, at least in those situations in which the source country's nontaxation stems from a treaty agreement. It may be the better solution in other cases as well, because it would make taxation of net, rather than gross, income more probable. It would also leave open the possibility of applying progressive rate schedules, though those gains may be offset by some unfavorable revenue allocations.[15] But is it technologically feasible?

To be completely effective, source countries would have to provide residence countries with information returns capable of being seamlessly integrated into their internal audit processes. Ideally, returns could be matched by computer to the taxpayer's account, enabling computer matching and billing as in the United States, with the Form 1099s issued by banks and other financial and brokerage institutions. Such computer matching has improved compliance rates with respect to income in the wholly domestic context. Unmatched or unverified income—such as the income derived from the operation of small businesses (e.g., sole proprietorships and, of course, foreign income)—remains the primary source of the infamous U.S. "tax gap."

This scheme would have to surmount several obvious challenges. Form 1099 issuers would have to have the foreign taxpayer's foreign tax identification number (or its equivalent). Perhaps that number can be obtained by requiring investors to provide it as part of their certification of foreign status ("statements of beneficial ownership"), which they must file to be exempted from backup withholding under current law. And in fact, the United States has managed to do exactly that with one government, Canada. It has shared bank account and other interest information with the Canadian government since 1997 (Kudrle and Eden 2003). As is done with domestic (and suspicious foreign) investors, backup withholding may be imposed if the U.S. government informs the payor that the foreign taxpayer account number is invalid.[16]

A more serious technical issue is that the computer systems of the IRS and the foreign governments would have to be compatible, or payors would be left with the technically challenging, if not impossible, task of creating and maintaining different programming formats for each country's investors. Given the problems the IRS has had modernizing its current computer system, other countries may not want to change their own systems to become more compatible with the U.S. system.[17]

A less-perfect but perhaps more attainable goal would be to require taxpayers to routinely construct and send U.S.-based information returns containing both the taxpayer's source and residence country tax identification numbers to their countries of residence. Although matching in the residence country would have to be done by hand, and costs may prohibit complete matching, there could certainly be more matching than at present. Combined with an increase in penalties for failing to report foreign income, residence country tax compliance should increase.

Whether these measures would be enough remains uncertain, however. Taxpayers may try to avoid residence country taxation by investing through intermediary companies resident in tax haven jurisdictions. The short-term effect may be to increase returns to tax haven treasuries rather than the treasuries of "true" residence countries.[18] Ultimately, the only solution may be for source countries to withhold taxes from payments to all taxpayers "resident" in tax haven countries while providing information returns for others. Whether such an information regime is susceptible to undercutting, if taxpayers substitute derivative contracts for plain-vanilla securities transactions, is also unknown. Such contracts may be even harder to trace than ordinary securities transactions. Further, even when traced, their tax characterization may be more problematic. For example, although the amount payable under a derivative may be linked to the amount of dividends paid with respect to publicly traded stock, the payments under the derivative are not, technically speaking, dividends and may not fall under any tax reporting or withholding scheme.

More information should soon be available on the practicability of such a residence country taxation scheme. The European Union (EU) began implementing its long awaited "savings tax directive" in 2005. After more than a decade of negotiations, the 25 member states of the EU and 15 other countries or territories began implementing mechanisms designed to ensure that cross-border interest income does not escape income taxation. Each of the participating countries agreed either to engage in an automatic information exchange system (which reports a foreigner's interest income to his or her country of residence) or to impose a withholding tax on foreigners' interest income and divide the proceeds between the source and residence countries.

The EU scheme is hardly foolproof. Among other things, it applies only to interest income earned by individual residents of the participating countries. Residents of nonparticipating jurisdictions fall outside the reporting/withholding net. Thus, a resident may continue to avoid both disclosure and taxation by forming a corporation to hold his or her interest-bearing assets or by pretending to be a resident of a nonparticipating country.[19] Nor does the agreement cover every potential source jurisdiction. Neither American nor Asian financial centers agreed to be bound by the regime. And, by its terms, the EU agreement is limited to interest income.

The United States' refusal to participate is particularly interesting and discouraging. Substantial diplomatic pressure was exerted to bring the U.S. into the arrangement, especially by the British, because the European parliament conditioned the savings plan on the EU's "third country trading partners. . . . [having] equivalent measures" in place (Walsh 2005, 260–61).[20] Near the end of the Clinton administration, the Treasury department proposed a regulation that would have required banks to identify and report the income derived by foreign account holders to the Internal Revenue Service, potentially making that information available to other countries' tax authorities. The Bush administration withdrew this proposal in favor of one that would limit the reporting requirement to residents of the EU countries providing similar information. That more limited regulation has neither been finalized nor otherwise made effective. Whether the current administration supports its enactment is unclear.

Meanwhile, the United States has made known that it will not enter into a treaty arrangement with the EU, nor commit itself to more extensive information exchanges than it is obligated to provide under the terms of its bilateral treaties. Although the EU eventually agreed that these bilateral treaty mechanisms were "comparable" to the EU savings directive's mechanisms, this is not true. Not only may most treaty-based information exchange occur only after a specific request by the treaty partner, rather than automatically, but the treaties do not oblige U.S. banks to report interest paid to nonresidents—and so far, the United States does not report such interest.

The United States' failure to sign on to the EU initiative is particularly discouraging because of its reasoning. Although, perhaps, the U.S.'s refusal to participate could be justified by pointing to the weakness of the EU scheme (that is, its very limited reach, which all but encourages taxpayer avoidance), the U.S.'s objections clearly come from the opposite direction. Put in its bluntest terms, many in the current administration seem to believe that the U.S.'s national interest would be better served by aiding foreign tax avoidance to attract investment than by trying to make such avoidance untenable (Kudrle and Eden 2003; Walsh 2005). Others object to the inherent loss of privacy when earnings are disclosed to governmental authorities (Kudrle and Eden 2003).

Neither objection is compelling. The privacy issue is overblown, particularly as applied to the EU. U.S. citizens investing domestically must share this information with U.S. tax authorities. Why should foreigners be entitled to a higher standard of privacy protection?[21] And concern about the economic consequences of reporting is hypocritical at best and misinformed at worst. The whole point of the tax credit mechanism adopted for use by U.S. citizens, and more particularly the elaborate "passive foreign investment company" and subpart F tax regimes, is to ensure that U.S. citizens immediately pay tax at U.S. rates on their passive income, including their interest income. The United States is trying to prevent other countries from using their tax systems to attract U.S. citizens to their banks and financial institutions. Yet, by not reporting foreigners' interest income, the U.S. is attempting to attract them and their assets. Why should tax-motivated investing be fine for foreigners and not for U.S. citizens? Or perhaps more accurately, why is it wrong for other countries but right for the United States to use its tax system to attract investment?

Advocates of continuing the U.S.'s position as a tax haven for foreigners do not seem to realize that, while facilitating widespread underreporting of taxable income may lead to more *foreign* investment in the United States, it is likely to lead to less *domestic* investment in the United States. U.S. residents will avoid taxation by making similarly tax-favored investments abroad. Whether such a trade of foreign for domestic investment is a net benefit to the U.S. economy is uncertain at best, though perhaps the low domestic savings rate means that relatively little domestic investment will be at stake in the future.

The absence of effective and automatic multilateral reporting to residence countries makes taxing residents' foreign investment income difficult and expensive for all countries. Knowing that the tax authorities will not be able to track down more than a small percentage of taxpayers, many residents will decide to play the audit lottery, engaging in dubious or even clearly illegal actions because the expected value of punishment—probability of detection and conviction multiplied by the resulting penalty—is less than the expected gain. And, of course, the more taxpayers play the game, the better the odds become.

Residence country taxation is not the only alternative. Another possibility would be to revert to source taxation. Some increases in source taxation, as explained above, are probably necessary even if a widespread multilateral reporting system exists, as not every country would participate. As explained below, in some respects, source taxation works better than residence country taxation. However, it also has problems that residence taxation does not.

Source Taxation

Gaps would exist even if effective multilateral reporting existed. Tax havens and entities formed in low-tax countries would pose particular problems, since reporting of income to those jurisdictions would be fruitless. Further, moving from source- to residence-based taxation of passive income could shift net revenues from one country's treasury to another, because not all jurisdictions have as much outgoing as incoming foreign investment. Given that much "passive" investment income consists of distributions of business income that are untaxed at the business level, it is far from certain that that shift is defensible. Effective taxation of passive income at its source would solve those problems. Other problems, however, would be created. These other problems probably outweigh the benefits of source taxation in most situations.

It would be relatively simple for source countries to impose flat-rate withholding taxes on many types of passive income, due to their control over the payors of that income. Failure to withhold could be punished either by imposing joint and several liability on the payor (the current rule) or in some other circumstances, the loss of a deduction for the payment being made. But source taxation would be difficult in some situations. If attempts were made to impose taxes on transfers of local securities, for example, taxpayers might try to escape such taxes by trading securities indirectly, holding such shares in companies established in tax haven jurisdictions and trading only the shares of the holding company parent. Of course, a special regime might be applied to shares held by tax haven entities. Every dividend or other cash distribution could be treated (and taxes withheld) as if it were both a dividend distribution and the concurrent sale of the stock. Appreciation in the value of the stock since the prior distribution could be treated as capital gain, and the relevant taxes deducted from the amount of the dividend distributed to the owner. But such a regime might be too complicated for the average taxpayer to understand and operate.

An equally serious problem is that the withholding tax necessarily applies to gross income. Particularly if made to an entity that is part of a complex ownership structure, "cascading" taxation becomes an issue. In the simplest case, assume a Corporation X is established and operating in Country E. Assume further that Country E levies a 30 percent withholding tax on income earned within its borders by foreign passive investors. Corporation Z is established and operating in Country D, which has a 25 percent withholding tax on the income of foreigners, and Corporation Y is established and operated in Country F. Now suppose Corporation X pays a royalty of $10 to Corporation Z, on account of which Corporation Z pays a royalty of $6 to Corporation Y. What taxes should be levied in such a situation? Surely X should withhold and pay $3 (30 percent of 10) to E, leaving Z with $7. But should Z withhold another $2 from its payment to Y, and remit this money either to E or D? If so, what started as a royalty of $10 would be subject to taxes of $5, for an effective tax rate of 50 percent. And the rate would go up if Y pays royalties to yet another party.

That result seems wrong; the total tax exceeds the highest rate applicable in any country. Perhaps Y should be entitled to claim a tax credit against its liability for tax arising out of the second stage of the transaction, as corporations currently can for income taxes paid by their subsidiaries when those subsidiaries pay taxable dividend distributions. But how would this tax credit arrangement work if, for example, the payment to Y took the form of an interest rather than royalty distribution?

We may not have much sympathy when X, Y, and Z are related corporations; after all, they can avoid most, if not all, of their problems by avoiding the complicated ownership or transactional structure. Indeed, some complex structures exist largely to game the income tax system. However, not all X, Y, and Z combinations are related, nor can all complex corporate structures be simplified without generating untoward consequences not due to taxation.

There may be no solution to this problem. That is one reason why so many tax treaties eliminate source taxation on most categories of investment income. Those who have worked with indirect foreign tax credits, the one form of pass-through credit currently used by the U.S. tax system, can attest to its complexities and inevitable failures. These problems would doubtless be magnified if source taxation were expanded to cover more payments. Source taxation on gross amounts of passive income should probably be restricted to potentially abusive situations. But, in the absence of effective residence taxation, that covers almost all transactions involving foreign payees.

Transforming business income into deductible distributions of untaxed passive income is one way to avoid taxation. If such passive income were subject to a substantial tax in a source or residence country, such maneuvers would be less valuable and, accordingly, less troublesome.[22] But it will take more than rationalizing the tax treatment of passive investment income to solve the problem of undertaxation of business income.

Taxing Business Income

The seemingly eternal tax policy debate—"capital import neutrality" versus "capital export neutrality"—has become so important largely because so much foreign-sourced income goes untaxed at its source.[23] If foreign income were subject to a full source tax where earned, the gap between capital import neutrality and capital export neutrality would be reduced in most cases, perhaps to insignificance. But whether such source taxation is possible and politically plausible is unclear. If it is technically possible but politically implausible, of course, that raises questions about political support for the concept of an income tax. One way of getting to a consumption tax is to pretend to have an income tax but not enforce it as it applies to capital income. That is more or less the current situation. Whether the resulting tax regime is the best form of consumption tax is another question entirely.

The problem, as explained earlier, is that the source rules have been constructed in such a way as to allow taxpayers considerable freedom to allocate their income to low-tax jurisdictions, whether or not the income was earned there. Such freedom exists both because of adherence to a pricing standard that does not work in real-world circumstances and because sourcing decisions often depend on formal criteria that have little or no underlying economic significance, leaving taxpayers free to rearrange their facts to minimize their tax obligations. The question is whether anything can be done about this.

The answer is surely yes. The source rules do not have to be constructed so that their outcome depends on how a transaction is structured, as opposed to its economic realities. Neither do they have to depend on the uncertain science of determining arm's length transfer prices. Indeed, there is a model for an alternative approach: formulary taxation as used by U.S. states to allocate the income of multistate enterprises.

Formulary Taxation

Most U.S. states determine their share of a unified business tax base—the entirety of a taxpayer's U.S. income—by a formula based on some weighted average of the ratio of the taxpayer's property, payroll, and sales located within the state to the taxpayer's total property, payroll, and sales. The United States has been inching toward the formulary approach in allocating deductions. Interest deductions, in particular, are allocated as expenses of foreign or domestic income in proportion to the capital employed in the taxpayer's foreign and domestic operations, rather than on the basis of where underlying loans are "booked." Mathematical formulas are also used to allocate other deductible expenses. The formulary method could be expanded to cover the allocation of income as well as the allocation of deductions.

Moving to a formulary system for the taxation of transnational business income would not be simple. Substantial improvements in the design of the formulary mechanism would be required. In addition, international institutions would probably have to be developed to administer the tax system. At the very least, the United States would have to get permission from its treaty partners to use such a mechanism, as most of the tax treaties that bind the United States mandate the arm's length method of allocating transnational income.

Design Flaws

As used in this country, the operation of the formulary method at the state level has revealed design flaws that should be corrected before it becomes the centerpiece of a system for taxing transnational income. Some elements of the allocation formula are as subject to manipulation as the current source rules. These elements would either have to be eliminated or changed if formulary apportionment is to be an improvement over the status quo.

Traditional state income allocation formulas use the weighted average of a taxpayer's in-jurisdiction versus out-of-jurisdiction (or total) payroll costs, property values, and sales. Use of the property factor has become increasingly problematic as intangible property has grown.

Intangible property has neither a fixed location nor, in many cases, a reasonably determinable value. Allocating intangible property to the taxpayer's state of residence has served only to encourage taxpayers to establish residency in a low-tax state. In the international context, it would encourage residency in tax haven jurisdictions.[24] And to determine the valuation of intellectual property such as patents or related items (e.g., "goodwill" or "marketing intangibles") requires exactly the sort of intensive, costly, and ultimately unsatisfactory proceedings currently seen in transfer pricing disputes. Although one solution may be to include only real and tangible property in the allocation formula, a better approach may be to ignore property entirely, and rely on a two-factor formula based on payroll and sales factors.[25]

But even payroll and sales factors can be manipulated. When income is attributable to the use of high-value intangible property, employers may find it beneficial to hire workers in a low-tax jurisdiction simply to divert income away from higher-tax jurisdictions. Moreover, defining a workable definition of "payroll" will not necessarily be easy. For example, the costs of leased employees surely must be included along with the cost of regular employees, to prevent taxpayers from avoiding taxation by leasing rather than directly hiring workers in high-tax jurisdictions. But difficult line drawing problems will arise. Should the costs of hiring outside legal counsel be treated as "payroll costs"? What about the cost of other outside technical experts?

The sales factor has similar problems. The common, everyday understanding of the sales factor would correspond with the ultimate location of the consumers. But a business may not know where that ultimate consumer resides; the business may sell only to middlemen, with its sales taking place where the middlemen reside. In fact, the current legal rule is somewhat worse than that. Under the U.S. source rules, sales of inventory take place where "the rights, title, and interest of the seller in the property are transferred to the buyer" (Treasury Regulation 1.861-7). Although this regulation contains an anti-abuse rule, for the most part, taxpayers have been allowed considerable freedom to determine the source of sales income by expediently drafting their sales agreements to pass title at low tax points in the transshipment process.[26]

If taxpayers are allowed the same freedom in the implementation of a formulary system of taxation, we could readily envision the speedy disappearance of the tax base to tax haven jurisdictions. Such jurisdictions might be forced to build wharves and shipping docks instead of financial institutions, but as long as off- and on-loading cargo is not actually required, these physical requirements need not be overwhelming. The biggest impediment to the success of such schemes, indeed, may be finding independent distributors to serve as intermediaries to the final customers, distributors willing to pay a price for goods that includes the manufacturers' return on the various intangibles incorporated in the product.[27]

It is uncertain how large an obstacle this will prove to be. As for goods and services supplied over the Internet, of course, there is no obstacle to initiating sales "in" tax haven jurisdictions. Although U.S. states have complained about the influence of similar schemes on the operation of their formulary tax systems, such schemes are likely to pose a greater threat to the international operation of a formulary system, simply because national tax rates tend to be so much higher than state or regional income tax rates. The higher stakes will make the costs of engaging in tax avoidance measures more enticing.

Taxpayers are not the only parties to engage in strategic behavior. Even before the economic literature began suggesting that "to the extent tax rates vary across jurisdictions, formula-apportioned corporate income taxes are similar in their incidence to a set of implicit excise taxes on the apportionment factors," U.S. states had begun moving from an allocation formula that equally weighted property, payroll, and taxes toward a single-factor sales allocation formula (Edmiston 2002, 239). This trend has accelerated as the economic literature convinced state legislatures that sales were the least moveable of these factors, so that changing their formula to one heavily or exclusively weighting sales location would reduce the costs of production and stimulate economic development. Should competition force the use of such a single-factor formula, the economic incidence of the tax would closely resemble that of a value added tax. We then must wonder whether the easier road to that result would be to replace the corporate income tax with an explicit value added tax.

Administrating the System

Even if a reasonably effective formula can be designed, the system as a whole must be administrable in an international environment to provide a meaningful alternative to today's arm's length system. Few believe that the formulary method can be successfully applied without greater harmonization of national taxes. For such harmonization to be possible, international cooperation is certainly necessary, and international administrative structures may well be required.

Theoretically, every country could enact and administer its own formulary system. However, the costs of doing so would be enormous for both taxpayers and tax authorities. Each jurisdiction would need taxpayers to compute its worldwide income under its own rules. Further, because tax authorities generally cannot operate outside the borders of their home jurisdictions, they would either find themselves unable to effectively audit large portions of relevant information or would have to force taxpayers to provide enormous amounts of information. In addition to the massive and largely duplicative costs imposed by overlapping audits, taxpayers may have justifiable concerns about how some countries would use this information, ranging from industrial espionage to coordination with criminal gangs to simple extortion through the threat of unfounded tax-based litigation. As one participant in this conference put the matter: "Can you imagine if Zimbabwe [or insert the name of your favorite dictator] had the right to examine and challenge the world-wide income statements of your client?"

Once we start envisioning some sort of centralized auditing function, however, the need for harmonization of the definitions of taxable income becomes acute. Tax-base harmonization has its advocates in many contexts. It would forestall the use of some avoidance techniques and reduce compliance and enforcement costs. However, it has disadvantages as well. At the very least, it would represent a major change in the political landscape. For harmonization to be effective, new institutional structures probably would also have to be established to oversee the interpretation and amendment of tax base rules.

We only have to examine the history of the state-level corporate income tax to see the forces that push toward legal divergence in the absence of strong centralizing institutions. Over time, many states have drifted away from what seems to be a natural focal point, the definition of income used to calculate federal income tax. Sometimes, states refused to accede to tax-base curtailments enacted at the federal level, fearful of their revenue effects. At other times, states reduced their own tax bases as part of efforts to attract desirable businesses or to aid local residents. And still other states simply had somewhat different political priorities than did the federal government. Because economic and political differences among countries are far larger than those among the U.S. states, we could expect even greater pressures on national legislatures and administrators to vary from whatever degree of harmonization was originally established. And of course, the greater the variation, the more difficult the joint auditing function, and the more expensive the operation of a formulary system.

But centralization has costs as well. For better or worse, the advent of international tax authorities will shift considerable power from the national to the international level. "Special interests" may have a harder time prevailing in their attempts to seek special treatment before such an international authority. But national interests would become "special interests" in such a system. Changes, regardless of their merits, would be harder to enact at the international level than at the national level.[28] In the taxation field, where such developments as tax avoidance schemes can change very quickly, relegating the task of coping with those changes to what may be a relatively unresponsive international body carries genuine risks. Given the importance of tax rules in an economy, countries may also find it risky to cede control over those rules to an international organization in which they play only a minor role.

Even if tax bases were completely harmonized, countries would retain the right to set their own tax rates. No discussion of globalization's influence on the taxation of capital income would be complete without a discussion of tax rates or, in short, tax competition.

Tax Competition

The tax haven problem described above is just an extreme version of a more general problem: tax competition. Despite its size, the United States lacks the market power to impose significantly higher income taxes on businesses operating within its borders than those imposed by similar countries. This does not mean that the United States must compete, tax-wise, with Saudi Arabia or Tanzania or a host of other countries. But at the very least, we have to compete with Canada, Europe, and China.[29] Businesses' costs of production, which include taxes as well as labor costs, energy costs, and regulatory costs, must be in the same range as other countries' to attract investment to the United States. Not every individual cost on this list must be the same, but if overall costs are significantly higher in one country than in others, that country's currency will depreciate or its economic base will disappear, leaving it poorer. Certainly, imposing a disproportionately high tax on capital income is a calculated risk.

It is unclear whether, in a globalized economy, the economic burden of taxes that appear to fall on capital income actually stay on capital income, or whether their economic burden shifts elsewhere (such as to labor or consumers, as lower wage rates or higher prices). But it is indisputable that the ability of the United States to tax capital income effectively decreases if other, similar nations do not tax capital income. No matter which way we look at the problem, taxation of capital income in a global economy requires international cooperation.

Summary

Would today's global economy permit income taxes to be levied across international boundaries and among trading partners? This chapter emphasizes that we cannot tax capital income efficiently until we figure out how to tax transnational capital income. Such taxation faces both political and technical barriers.

Increased globalization makes it easier for Americans to adopt the identity of foreigners for tax purposes. Foreigners are largely exempt from U.S. income taxation on their capital income. To combat such tax evasion, the United States will have to increase its taxation of foreigners' U.S.-sourced capital income, invest more in expensive enforcement techniques for U.S. residents (such as net worth audits or close scrutiny of third-party payers' records), work with other countries to establish a credible transnational information return system, or (most likely) engage in some combination of the three.[30]

Globalization makes it easier for all taxpayers to attribute their capital income to foreign rather than U.S. sources. Dealing with these avoidance techniques requires rethinking and revising both the structure and content of the current source rules. This will probably require moving to a variant of formulary taxation, where a taxpayer's worldwide income is allocated among nations in accordance with a mathematical formula based on economically relevant criteria.

Effective capital income taxation requires the taxation of income generated in international transactions. Most domestic transactions can be replaced with economically equivalent international transactions. If the income generated from international transactions is not taxed, the income tax base will soon disappear in various tax evasion schemes. Taxpayers will appear to invest and earn only abroad.

There are no easy answers. In the absence of a perfect solution to this quandary, governments will need to utilize imperfect mechanisms and hope that the combination overcomes rather than magnifies the flaws inherent in each such mechanism.

NOTES

1. Whether this perception is correct is another matter. Congress has mandated withholding from the gross proceeds derived from the sale of U.S. real estate. This withholding obligation is imposed at a rate lower than the standard 30 percent tax, and the amounts withheld are refundable to the extent they exceed the tax due. Whether such a tax regime can be transferred to contexts involving many more transactions, perhaps less formal transfer mechanisms, and (at least in the stock market context) greater susceptibility to replacement by derivative contracts is unclear.

2. Congress knew full well when it added the exclusion for portfolio interest to the tax code that doing so would help foreigners avoid residence country taxes; it only expressed concern, however, about the possibility that the exclusion would "provide

some U.S. persons with a new avenue of tax evasion" (Staff of the Joint Committee on Taxation 1985, 393). See also McIntyre (1992, 48): "Whether by design or otherwise, the Eurobond market provides an ideal investment environment for tax evaders."

3. The Internal Revenue Code requires U.S. shareholders of foreign corporations to currently declare and pay tax on their implicit share of the corporations' passive investment income under one of two specialized tax regimes: the "subpart F" regime found at I.R.C. §§951-965 or the "PFIC" regime found at I.R.C. §§1291-1298.

4. Of course, if it is discovered, it may be preferable to be violating the tax laws of only one country rather than two.

5. The United States cancelled most of its tax treaties with tax haven countries in the 1980s.

6. The statutory exemption covers interest received from unrelated U.S. debtors; treaty-based exemptions usually also cover interest received from related debtors, such as wholly owned subsidiaries.

7. Although many countries, unlike the United States, exempt active foreign-sourced business income from residence country taxation, virtually all countries tax their residents' foreign-sourced nonbusiness income, such as interest income.

8. There are other problems peculiar to the U.S. context that go beyond mis-reporting. For example, even when treaties eliminate the possibility of its being subject to source country taxation, income retains its character as "foreign-sourced income" for U.S. tax purposes. Under the rules pertaining to the operation of the tax credit mechanism used by the United States, this often has the effect of allowing the taxpayer to claim additional tax credits for source taxes paid with respect to other items of foreign income, instead of increasing the U.S. residence tax due on the treaty-protected income. For this reason alone, most tax treaties turn out to be revenue-losing propositions. Given that the taxation of this treaty-protected foreign income is supposed to substitute for the taxation of U.S.-source income earned by foreigners, there is no reason to treat it as other than U.S.-sourced income for U.S. tax purposes.

9. Bilateral tax treaties provide some source taxation relief for marginally active taxpayers.

10. Some U.S. statutes appear to tax the foreign income of foreign residents, but closer examination reveals that in most cases, the income involved should be described, as an economic matter, as U.S.-source income.

11. Technically, U.S. taxpayers are immediately taxable on their worldwide income. However, if a U.S. taxpayer carries out its foreign business operations through a foreign incorporated subsidiary, the subsidiary does not count as a "U.S. taxpayer" and (unless a special tax regime such as subpart F or PFIC applies) its U.S. parent does not become taxable on its share of the subsidiary's foreign earnings and profits, unless and until the subsidiary distributes its earnings and profits to the parent in the form of a dividend or the parent sells the stock of the foreign subsidiary. In both cases, the parent is entitled to claim foreign tax credit for foreign taxes paid by the subsidiary as an offset against the U.S. tax that becomes due on the parent's share of the foreign profits.

In the American Jobs Creation Act of 2004, Congress enacted a provision granting taxpayers, for one year beginning with the date of enactment, an 85 percent deduction for cash dividends received from controlled foreign subsidiaries. This provision guarantees that taxpayers repatriating foreign profits during this taxable year will pay a maximum of 5.25 percent of those profits in U.S. taxes, and less if they can claim offsetting foreign tax credits (I.R.C. §965).

12. Even if a country collects little in the way of revenue from each foreign investor, as long as the expenses incurred in serving that investor are lower than those revenues, a country can reap considerable financial benefits from participating in such transactions. To get a sense of the volumes involved, estimates of the amounts invested in "offshore companies and accounts" range from $5 to $8 *trillion* (Kudrle and Eden 2003).

13. This siphoning is distinct from the question of whether it is acceptable to use low tax rates to attract real investment. The issue of tax competition is discussed in greater detail in the last section.

14. In the United States, this power is granted by I.R.C. §482.

15. Particularly outside of the treaty situation, we must worry that some source countries will give up more in the way of potential source tax revenues than they will gain in the way of residence tax revenues. The effective switch in "primary taxing jurisdiction" from country of source to country of residence may create winners and losers, justifying revenue sharing.

16. The U.S. government would have to be notified of this fact by the affected foreign government first.

17. Of course, the Treasury could use this as an excuse to investigate the computer systems used by other countries and to identify a properly functioning system that could be used as a model. But the United States may not be alone in having a dysfunctional system.

18. That is, the country in which the individuals owning the tax haven entity's shares actually reside.

19. Indeed, Swiss banks routinely offer to form corporations for their individual depositors.

20. EU members worried that in the absence of widespread participation in the scheme, money would simply be moved to nonparticipating countries and the EU would be left worse off.

21. Although there would be reason for concern if the foreigners resided in countries governed by tyrannical or dictatorial regimes, that does not describe the situation of any residents of EU countries. Inasmuch as the information-sharing obligation would have been imposed by treaty, the United States should not have had to worry about its indiscriminate extension to other regimes.

22. These techniques would continue to be valuable to the extent they generated "homemade integration," that is, reduced the two-level tax on corporate earnings to a one-level tax. But that is a separate problem, as pervasive in the wholly domestic sphere as it is in the foreign context.

23. This roughly translates into "which is more desirable, to tax foreign-sourced income at the rate prevailing in the country of source or the rate prevailing in the taxpayer's country of residence?"

24. The concept of "residency" for an artificial entity such as a corporation is quite manipulable, which is one reason this chapter advocates formulary taxation rather than

immediate residence country taxation of profits earned by the foreign subsidiaries of domestic entities. Over time—perhaps not a very long time—entities will all be residents of tax haven countries, undercutting the aim of such reform proposals.

25. To prevent taxpayer manipulation, both leased and self-owned property would have to be taken into account were property to remain a factor. Otherwise, taxpayers would be able to shift their tax liability away from high-tax jurisdictions by renting facilities there while purchasing facilities used in low-tax jurisdictions.

26. "[I]n any case in which the sales transaction is arranged in a particular manner for the primary purpose of tax avoidance, the foregoing rules will not be applied. In such cases, all factors of the transaction, such as negotiations, the execution of the agreement, the location of the property, and the place of payment, will be considered, and the sale will be treated as having been consummated at the place where the substance of the sale occurred" (Treasury Regulation 1.861-7).

27. For the formulary method to have an impact, the income of all related companies engaged in a "unitary business" must be combined and allocated among the jurisdictions in which any of the companies is engaged in business. Otherwise, taxpayers would be able to replicate the tax effects of the arm's length method by strategically incorporating the various parts of its business operations. Thus, the distributors would have to be unrelated corporations, which means that the parties would have to engage in the sort of bargaining over relative profit contributions that the tax authorities try to replicate when applying the arm's length method. If such bargaining is unsuccessful—if the manufacturer and distributor cannot agree on a transfer price—the tax avoidance scheme will fall apart because the taxpayer will be forced to use a related distributor, giving the consumer's country the jurisdiction to tax its allocable portion of the unitary income.

28. Another way of looking at the dilemma in designing such institutions is to see it as a trade-off between giving international bureaucrats flexibility and power—while creating a "democratic deficit"—and having national governments retain considerable control over those bureaucrats, which means operating by consensus and ensuring that changes are made very slowly if at all.

29. Measuring our competitive stance is not as simple as merely comparing tax rates; benefits also have to be taken into account. Businesses in many European countries are subject to higher corporate taxes, but their workers are covered by national health insurance systems. At least some businesses in the United States absorb some of their employees' health insurance costs.

30. For example, some U.S. taxpayers obtained credit cards from foreign banks, and paid the resulting charges out of undeclared foreign income held in undeclared foreign accounts. In 2001, the Treasury began issuing John Doe summonses to these foreign credit card issuers (Hamilton 2003). This initiative identified far more taxpayers than the Internal Revenue Service was capable of auditing or prosecuting. The Service tried to reduce the number by establishing a "voluntary compliance initiative" under which violators could escape civil fraud and information return penalties in return for payment of back taxes, interest, some other penalties, and the provision of information regarding promoters and marketers of such schemes (Internal Revenue Service 2003). Although some taxpayers stepped forward under this initiative, generating a substantial revenue flow, they represented only a small fraction of the identified individuals (Bennett 2004; Sullivan 2004b). The remainder presumably are continuing to play the audit lottery, banking on the IRS's limited enforcement budget.

REFERENCES

Bennett, Heather. 2004. "IRS Offshore Compliance Initiative Collects U.S. $170 Million So Far." *Tax Notes International* 33: 517–18.

Edmiston, Kelly D. 2002. "Strategic Apportionment of the State Corporate Income Tax." *National Tax Journal* 55: 239–40.

Hamilton, Amy. 2003. "Justice Advances Offshore Crackdown by Going After Individuals." *Tax Notes Today* 50: 3.

Internal Revenue Service. 2003. "IRS Announces Amnesty Program for Offshore Credit Card Abusers." IR-2003-5, reprinted in *Tax Notes Today* 10: 11.

Kudrle, Robert T., and Lorraine Eden. 2003. "The Campaign against Tax Havens: Will It Last? Will It Work?" *Stanford Journal of Law, Business & Finance* 9: 37–68.

Littlewood, Michael. 2004. "Tax Competition: Harmful to Whom?" *Michigan Journal of International Law* 26(1): 411–87.

McIntyre, Michael J. 1992. *The International Income Tax Rules of the United States,* 2nd ed. Dayton, OH: LexisNexis Matthew Bender.

Sheppard, Lee A. 2005. "Offshore Investments: Don't Ask, Don't Tell." *Tax Notes* 108: 171–76.

Staff of the Joint Committee on Taxation. 1985. *General Explanation of the Revenue Provisions of the Tax Reform Act of 1984.* Washington, DC: U.S. Government Printing Office.

Sullivan, Martin A. 2004a. "Data Show Dramatic Shift of Profits to Tax Havens." *Tax Notes* 104: 1190.

———. 2004b. "U.S. Citizens Hide Hundreds of Billions in Cayman Accounts." *Tax Notes International* 34: 898–906.

———. 2005. "The IRS Multibillion-Dollar Subsidy for Ireland." *Tax Notes* 108:287.

Walsh, Suzanne. 2005. "Taxation of Cross-Border Interest Flows: The Promises and Failures of the European Union Approach." *George Washington International Law Review* 37: 251–61.

Paul W. Oosterhuis

O ne thing unclear about Ed Kleinbard's chapter (chapter 4) is the impact of taxing capital income on cross-border investments. Kleinbard proposes a notional inclusion for U.S. portfolio investors in foreign companies, even though the foreign companies, obviously, do not get any kind of cost of capital allowance (COCA) deduction. The result is a double tax on corporate income in a system that is not intended to do so. Basically, the United States' and other country's tax systems do not match.

In the opposite circumstance, with foreign portfolio investors in U.S. corporations, Kleinbard proposes withholding on notional income through a deferred catch-up mechanism because, he concludes, you can't withhold out of nothing.

Kleinbard proposes to accrue the withholding amount. Then, when there is a dividend or sale out of which to withhold, the company or a broker would withhold the accrued amount. Thus, there has to be some system to withhold all the gains and losses on the sale of shares.

My reaction is that such a withholding requirement probably will not work. In the end, foreign investors in the United States are going to be exempt from the COCA tax. Unless every major country adopts a COCA, U.S. investors will be double-taxed on their foreign corporate investments and foreign investors will pay no tax on their U.S. corporate investments. Such a result seems to be unstable.

The whole income tax integration system in Europe, the U.K. ACT system, and the German imputation credit floundered largely over the problems of cross-border portfolio investments. And so this is a thread that can unravel some big ideas, including the Business Enterprise Income Tax, which Kleinbard proposes as a hybrid alternative plan to reform the income taxation of business enterprises.

Julie Roin (chapter 5) raises issues with respect to formulary apportionment. As Roin writes, if only one country adopts formulary apportionment, companies can put much of their economic and financial risk in the formulary apportionment country, while putting the formula factors in countries without formula apportionment.

So formulary apportionment, if adopted unilaterally, would permit U.S. multinationals to lower their worldwide tax rate a fair amount, I suspect. But let's assume that the major countries reached a broad consensus to switch to formulary apportionment. Those countries would still have to be careful as to what the formula would be, because most of its elements are easy to manipulate.

If property is a factor, for example, the factor would not be the fair market value of property, since fair market value is just a discount of those cash flows—but that is how arm's length pricing determines value, so its complications are avoided only if the factor is based on book values. If book values are the basis for apportioning, then, for example, companies that produce software and other intangibles can shift most of their income to low-tax countries like Ireland. All of the companies' assets with book value are, for example, receivables, computers, and servers, which are extremely mobile. So book value clearly doesn't work as a basis for apportioning.

Similarly, difficulties emerge when using payroll as a factor. When Section 936 of the tax code was authored in 1976, it provided a U.S. tax credit based on taxable income in Puerto Rico. A few years later, it became apparent that incentives had been provided to increase taxable income in Puerto Rico, but not to increase jobs or investments. Taxable income increased because that is what was incentivized.

When the Treasury was thinking about reform in the early 1980s, it considered tying the incentive more directly to jobs and payrolls. When Treasury analysts looked at the numbers, however, they saw tax savings for companies of up to $300,000 per employee, at a time when the cost of an employee in Puerto Rico was $20,000 to $30,000. Companies could have made a profit by hiring people to do nothing.

President George W. Bush's advisory panel examined formulary apportionment in 2005, and some members concluded that only formulary apportionment based on sales would be workable, because sales are more difficult to move.

Yet even apportionment based on sales creates opportunities for tax planning. If a company wants to sell to customers in a different country, it can either sell by itself or sell through a third party—making country of sale somewhat elective. For example, if a company in a foreign country sells its goods to the United States and elects to sell through a third party, its income is measured by arm's length pricing and it does not pay any U.S. tax. But, if it chooses to sell in the U.S. directly, it will have to pay U.S. tax based on its sales ratio, as applied to global income. This optional element is more difficult to manipulate than some of the other factors that might be used, but is nonetheless capable of manipulation.

An income tax with income apportioned globally by sales, however, may not be attractive to the United States, since many U.S. companies have a high portion of their sales outside the United States but have the bulk of their intellectual property and other intangibles inside the United States.

I conclude that there is no shortcut to dealing more effectively with transfer pricing. We can deal with it better than we do today, not so much by changing the rules, but by enforcing the rules we have. In the United States, the Internal Revenue Service should improve the quality of its transfer-pricing experts. If we could apply more brainpower to transfer-pricing cases, the system could work reasonably well. Our government simply doesn't have the resources to handle today's sophisticated transfer-pricing issues.

6

Tax Planning under the Flat Tax

Joseph Bankman and Michael L. Schler

The basic flat-tax/X-tax proposal under consideration has the following terms:

- Businesses are taxed on gross receipts, less cost of inputs from sellers subject to the tax, less wages. All costs of inputs, including land and inputs purchased with borrowed funds, are immediately deductible. As a result, there is no concept of tax basis—that is, an asset's acquisition price and the key element today in computing capital gain or loss.
- No deduction is allowed for the cost of inputs purchased from exempt persons. Yet a taxable business is fully taxed on resales of goods purchased from exempt persons. Similarly, a taxable business is fully taxable on a sale to an exempt person, even though the exempt purchaser obtains no deduction for the purchase.
- Individuals are taxed on wages at progressive rates. The top individual rate would be the same as the business rate. If an individual is self-employed, the business is taxed under the rules for businesses.
- Financial transactions and financial instruments are not subject to tax, for either businesses or individuals. Interest is not deductible, and dividends and interest are not included in income. An individual does not have income, gain, or loss on personal or investment (i.e., nonbusiness) assets.
- Imports are not deductible (as the foreign seller is exempt); exports are not taxable.

This regime can be thought of as a standard European-style credit-invoice VAT, except that wages are deducted by businesses and taxed at progressive rates to workers. (In general, in a credit-invoice VAT, businesses are subject to VAT on the difference between their sales and their purchases from other VAT taxpayers.) Alternatively, the flat tax/X tax can be viewed as a tax on cash flow at the business level, with individuals taxed on wages but not on investment income or gains.

Tax Avoidance under the Flat Tax/X Tax

European VAT systems, like the current U.S. income tax, are plagued by fraud.[1] A business may buy inputs from an exempt seller, yet provide the tax authorities with a fraudulent credit invoice allegedly from a taxable seller. A business may claim that goods were exported and the proceeds thus exempt from the VAT, with the costs of inputs deductible, while in fact the goods may have been sold domestically for cash. "Carousel" and "missing trader" arrangements may be created in which an intermediate entity subject to the VAT provides a "valid" credit invoice to the buyer (which may or may not be part of the scheme and may even be related to the original seller), but then goes out of existence before the authorities can collect tax from it. These frauds have become so pervasive that they are distorting official trade statistics.[2]

As suggested above, fraud exists in the income tax as well; witness, for example, evasion in the cash economy. It would no doubt continue to exist in a VAT-like system.[3] We do not compare here the vulnerability of the two systems to outright fraud. Rather, we focus on the susceptibility of the flat tax/X tax to tax planning that is either legal or close enough to legal to be carried out under the color of law. This is the category that would encompass most recent tax shelters, for example.

Likelihood of Tax Shelters under the Flat Tax/X Tax

As a theoretical matter, the flat tax/X tax would seem to offer little opportunity for shelter. It adopts a consistent cash flow regime, and imposes a zero tax rate on most investment income.

Nevertheless, this nation has long been a center for financial innovation. Some significant part of that innovation has centered on reducing or avoiding the income tax. Not only tax shelter promoters have devoted time and effort to this enterprise. Tax lawyers, accountants, and tax-savvy executives have done the same (e.g., Bankman 1999; S. Rep. No. 109-54).

One wonders what effect a flat tax/X tax modeled on a European-style VAT would have on the U.S. army of tax advisers, and vice versa. Faced with the prospect of learning a new set of rules that are more coherent and thus less rewarding to tax planning, most tax professionals may simply leave the field.

Alternatively, many professionals might turn their attention to tax minimization under the new system. If they do, there is no way to know what they might come up with. So far, no more than a handful of U.S. tax professionals have considered how to design around a flat tax/X tax. Unfortunately, as we have seen in the tax shelter context, all it takes is a few inspired and well-placed individuals to find and exploit a weakness in a tax regime.

Further, even after a tax regime is fully in place, the best tax professionals find it impossible to guess the provisions that will provide ground for the next shelter. Anticipating future problems is particularly difficult here, since no one has ever attempted to draft the flat tax/X tax.

Generally it is the specific statutory language that creates loopholes. The real test comes only after the drafting is complete, Congress has gone home, and the regulations have been written. At that point, armies of tax professionals devote enormous effort to interpreting the specific language of the regulations in the most taxpayer-favorable ways, and in exploiting any perceived loopholes to the fullest. The biggest dangers of a flat tax/X tax are the flaws not yet identified, or even existing until the specific language is in place.

Relative Incentives for Tax Avoidance under Flat Tax/X Tax and European VAT

By most accounts, less effort has been devoted in Europe to tax avoidance under the VAT than has arisen here under the income tax. Yet even in Europe, constant legislative changes are necessary to counter the latest VAT schemes.[4] Further, several recent European court decisions have considered VAT avoidance schemes using language remarkably similar to the economic substance and form versus substance discussions that appear in the U.S. tax shelter cases.[5]

The incentive for tax avoidance schemes might be greater here under the flat tax/X tax than in Europe under the VAT. In Europe and all other developed nations, the VAT is supplemented by an income tax; the income tax reduces the payoff to some of the ways taxpayers might otherwise reduce VAT liability. For example, some transactions described below, designed to artificially avoid VAT through its exemption for financial transactions, would continue to be subject to the income tax. (Of course, a taxpayer who hides transactions to avoid one tax would probably do the same to avoid the other.)

More significantly, because here the flat tax/X tax would replace the income tax, a higher flat-tax/X-tax rate than the rates in Europe would be required. As a result, U.S. taxpayers would have more incentive to exploit inconsistent or discontinuous treatment for parties and transactions, and to take advantage of the special rules for small business, financial services, and financial instruments.

To be sure, because of the wage deduction here, while the nominal flat-tax/X-tax rate would be higher than the rates in Europe, for profitable labor-intensive industries the actual tax paid would be low. Yet the incentive for tax avoidance is based on marginal rates, and the marginal benefit of avoiding $1 of income (or of creating $1 of deduction) would be greater here than in Europe.

General Structural Issues and Tax Planning Opportunities

Several distinct issues relating to tax planning would arise under a flat tax/X tax.

Deducting All Costs in a Flat Tax/X Tax

Under the flat tax/X tax, the business-level tax is measured by gross receipts, less cost of inputs, less wages. All inputs are immediately deductible (unless purchased from an exempt seller). No attempt is made to determine the relationship of the expenses to the true nature of the business carried on by the entity. Thus, any business may spend money on any nonfinancial asset and deduct its cost. For example, any business can use its entire free cash flow to buy land and possibly eliminate its tax liability. If it wished to distribute its available funds to its shareholders, it could borrow money to buy the land.

Theoretically, nothing is wrong with this, since the buyer of the land obtains the tax deduction only if the seller has taxable flat-tax/X-tax receipts. However, this fundamental aspect of the system creates enormous pressure to ensure that there is no "leakage." When any particular taxpayer can legally wipe out its tax liability at will, the slightest leakage will have enormous revenue consequences to the Treasury. Based on the recent tax shelter era, Schler believes that this aspect of the flat tax/X tax by itself raises serious questions about its practicality.

Purchases from Exempt Sellers

Under the flat tax/X tax, a deduction for business assets can only be allowable to the business purchaser if the seller is a business subject to the flat tax/X tax.[6] The purchaser obtains no deduction for a purchase from an exempt person or entity (such as an exempt small business or a foreigner) or an individual selling an asset held for nonbusiness use. In these cases, if the purchaser resells the asset, the total sale proceeds are treated as taxable proceeds with no offset for the cost of the asset.

Disallowing a deduction for a purchase from an exempt seller is necessary for the tax system's integrity. If a taxable business could freely obtain a deduction for buying an asset from an exempt seller (individual, small business, foreigner, etc.), enormous revenue losses would result.

This rule has unfair results and creates traps for the unwary in some cases. For example, suppose an individual buys land from a taxpayer for personal use for $100, and shortly thereafter either sells it to his wholly owned corporation for $100 or simply contributes it to the corporation. In either case, the corporation will obtain no deduction but will have no basis in the land. If the corporation then sells the land for $100, the corporation will have $100 of taxable cash flow. If the corporation then liquidates, everything is as before, except that tax has been paid on $100 of cash flow.

In addition, this rule creates considerable anomalies. Consider a taxable corporation that wishes to buy a house or a car for use by its executives. If it buys a used house or car from an individual, it will get no deduction. If it buys a new house or car from the builder or manufacturer, the entire cost of the house or car will be deductible. As a result, there will be incentives for new assets to be sold to business users, and used assets (already held by individuals) to be sold to other individuals.

Notwithstanding these results, this rule seems essential. If deductions were freely allowed for purchases from exempt persons (e.g., foreigners), enormous distortions and tax avoidance could arise. For example, all taxpayers could defer their tax liability indefinitely, and create unlimited tax losses in the entire domestic tax system, by buying foreign real estate from foreign sellers.

Small Business Exemption

Most of the world's VATs have a small business exemption (Weisbach 2003).[7] The tax loss from such an exemption may be manageable, since small business is barely in the tax base today, due in large part to the (illegal) nonreporting of cash receipts.

However, the exemption would eliminate whatever tax is now collected from small businesses. It would also eliminate the psychic cost now incurred from illegal evasion. Because of that, the exemption would no doubt cause some individuals now in the large business sector (who would be unwilling to engage in this sort of illegal self-help in the small business sector) to shift to the small business sector. The net result is that the effective subsidy given to the small business sector increases, and the small business sector grows even larger. The European experience may not be representative here because, as noted above, in Europe the VAT is supplemented by an income tax, which does not exempt small business.

But here, as in Europe, some small businesses that supply goods and services to nonexempt business will elect into the flat-tax/X-tax system. In that way, their sales can be deducted by their customers and they can deduct the cost of their supplies. This may be more desirable than selling nondeductible goods to their customers, with neither party receiving a deduction for the cost of supplies.

With respect to more passive investments, such as real property, or businesses whose primary asset consists of real property, the small business exception can be problematic. It exempts not only ongoing profits but also past appreciation. Consider, for example, the individual who purchased rental real property for $100 and now finds the property worth $400. The small business exemption would forgive the $300 of gain realized under an income tax. There is no efficiency-based or equitable reason for this forgiveness. This result is exacerbated if the small business had both gain and loss property: it would sell the loss property before the effective date of the new rules and claim the tax loss, then claim the small business exemption and sell the gain property tax free thereafter. Perhaps the gain property could be sold under the small business exemption even if the business intended shortly thereafter to elect out of the small business exemption for the reasons stated above.

Unfortunately, there is no practical way to tax the existing appreciation in assets under a small business regime. Absent a requirement that all property be valued as of the date of enactment, post-enactment appreciation cannot be separated from pre-enactment appreciation.

If a small business exemption is adopted, aggregation rules will be needed. Otherwise, businesses too large for the exemption will be broken into pieces, each eligible for the exemption. These aggregation rules may have to be quite complex, similar to the rules now in the tax code to prevent the use of multiple related corporations to obtain multiple benefits from the lower tax brackets on corporate income (see Code §§1561, 1563).

Similarly, complex rules will be needed to deal with small businesses that grow out of eligibility for the small business exemption. For example, will such a business begin its life as a taxable entity with a zero basis in all its assets, even though it could have sold all its assets the day before without being subject to any tax? If that is the rule, obviously the business will indeed sell all its assets the day before, then reinvest (with a deduction) the day after. Likewise, rules will be needed to deal with the larger business that "shrinks" into small business status to sell its remaining assets without any tax.

One effect of the small business exemption is to create a two-track economy. The taxable sector is discouraged from purchasing goods or services from the exempt sector because the purchase is not deductible. Consequently, an exempt business may have a good that a nonexempt business wants, but the extra cost arising from the lack of deduction may preclude a sale. Yet an exempt purchaser incurs no such penalty for purchasing from another exempt business. For example, since no deduction is allowed to a taxable business for imported goods, imports are relatively more attractive to an exempt business purchaser than to a nonexempt business purchaser.

Transition Relief

Implementation of a flat tax/X tax without transition relief wipes out all existing basis. Taxpayers lose deductions for amortization and pay tax on gross sale proceeds. Such a tax is equivalent to a lump-sum tax on existing capital.

If a flat tax/X tax is announced without transition relief but with a future effective date, or if its enactment is anticipated, taxpayers will be able to create the equivalent of transition relief on their own. Taxpayers will sell loss assets before the effective date to obtain the tax deduction. Of course, the present system already encourages sale of loss property—a dollar of tax savings today is worth more than the same dollar of tax savings in the future—but here the incentives will be stronger because the effective date of the new system will present a now-or-never opportunity to cash out losses.

Even more significantly, absent transition relief, taxpayers might also sell nonloss business assets before the effective date (even at a gain) to obtain the advantage of the tax basis. If the assets are needed for a business, they could be leased back temporarily. After the effective date, the sale proceeds can be reinvested in the purchase of similar assets, with a full deduction for the purchase. In effect, the existing tax basis of the asset is converted into a net deduction in the same amount. To be sure, the deduction for the purchase under the new system would only be available if the seller at that time had full taxable income on the sale. Nevertheless, the result could be a considerable shifting of assets, as well as taxable income and losses, among business entities both before and after the new system's effective date.

Transition relief would reduce (but not eliminate) these incentives. Yet transition relief would reduce the tax on capital, requiring higher rates on wages and thus increasing the incentive to avoid the wage tax.[8]

Refundability of Losses

Losses under present law may be used (with considerable restrictions) to offset present, past, or future tax liability but do not otherwise generate tax refunds. Losses are not "refundable." For a company that cannot use tax losses as a result of these rules, the government shares in gains but not losses. The restriction on losses presumably discourages some investment and raises the cost of other investment, as the situs of investment shifts to companies that have other sources of income and so can "use" the loss. Loss restrictions also impose transactional costs, as taxpayers attempt end runs around the loss restriction rules, and the law responds with yet more complex rules and doctrines.

The flat tax as originally proposed generally followed present law in this regard, except that any loss carryover would increase by a below-market interest rate.[9] However, enforcing loss restrictions under a flat tax/X tax might be difficult. Because of this, and because of the way in which loss restrictions discourage or raise the cost of risky investment, it can be argued that losses under a flat tax/X tax should be refundable. The argument is supported by the fact that the European-style VAT is refundable.

However, if wages are taxed at a lower rate than business income, refundability of losses creates the potential for tax-related planning and mischief. A family-owned business could overstate wages, generate a loss, and claim a tax refund at the business rate. The refund would exceed the extra tax liability owed by the family employee on the wages at the lower wage rate. This is a pure loss to the Treasury.

This same temptation exists for profitable companies under current law. However, refundability of losses extends this temptation, since the technique would then benefit unprofitable businesses, or profitable businesses that could overpay wages in order to become unprofitable.[10]

Refundability also means that, even aside from wages, almost any business can achieve not only a zero tax (as explained above), but a cash refund from the government. Any business can obtain any size refund if it can find enough cash (including borrowed cash) to buy sufficient business assets. The asset can, for example, be land subject to a long-term net lease, which would provide good security for a lending bank. The business could deduct the cost of the asset, and, if this creates a loss, obtain a cash refund from the government. For example, a start-up company might have a small amount of equity, borrow money and buy land, obtain a tax refund, then dividend the tax refund to its shareholders. If the business makes money, the government will eventually get its refund back with the equivalent of interest. If the business breaks even or loses money, it will have no assets after paying off the debt, and the government will be out of luck.

Refundability also makes the system more vulnerable to unrelated loopholes. Suppose, for example, that a company for some reason finds itself with an ability to manufacture losses—perhaps the company has been set up for just this purpose—and that Congress or the tax authorities will take months to close that loophole. Under current law, exploiting that flaw would require (1) a separate scheme to transfer losses and (2) finding a profitable company willing to take part in that scheme and pay for the losses. Under a refundable loss regime, those subsequent steps would be unnecessary, and the cash would be collected directly from the government.

Likewise, refundability makes the system much more vulnerable to fraudulent deductions. Such fraud will permit a business not only to wipe out the tax liability on its real income, but to obtain "real cash" from the government. This is analogous to fraudulent returns today that claim tax refunds based on refundable credits, such as the earned income tax credit.

On balance, one of us (Bankman) would opt for refundability. The other (Schler) would not. Schler believes that, given the likelihood of abuse, such a system would be like giving taxpayers access to an ATM machine that permitted unlimited daily withdrawals from the Treasury.

Ultimately, refundability is a political decision. It is at least possible that a flat tax/X tax will not have refundability.[11] Thus, we later include a description of techniques that could be used in a nonrefundable system to obtain results similar to refundability, by shifting losses from unprofitable businesses to profitable businesses.

Tax Planning under the Flat Tax/X Tax

A flat tax/X tax offers a variety of opportunities for avoiding taxes by careful planning. Some are similar to and some differ from tax avoidance opportunities under the hybrid income tax that currently exists in the United States.

Financial Transactions

Under the flat tax/X tax as originally proposed, financial transactions are excluded from the system. This creates a number of problems and anomalies.[12]

Mergers and Acquisitions

The exclusion of financial transactions would greatly influence the market for mergers and acquisitions. A stock purchase would be a financial transaction, exempt to the seller and nondeductible to the buyer, who would in effect take the underlying assets with a zero basis. An asset purchase would be fully deductible to the buyer and fully taxable to the seller. These results would exacerbate the illogical differences existing today between various forms of equivalent transactions. As to transactions that are tax-free reorganizations under current law, under the new system, stock transfers would always be tax-free, but rules would be needed to determine the taxable or tax-free status of, say, an asset transfer pursuant to a forward merger that qualifies as a tax-free reorganization today. Thus, a flat tax/X tax will not eliminate the complexities of the reorganization rules.

To be sure, to the extent that the flat tax/X tax is adopted in pristine form and is invulnerable to shelter-like schemes, regardless of how the merger is structured, the present value of all deductions in the tax system would be unchanged. The differences in form will, however, greatly affect the timing of tax receipts, which may be an independent problem as discussed below.

Converting Nonfinancial Sales Income into Financial Income

The exclusion from tax of receipts attributable to financial transactions creates an enormous incentive for businesses to characterize receipts from consumers or other tax-exempt persons as financial income rather than sales income.

For example, major British department store chains recently told customers who used credit cards that a portion of their cost was a "card-handling fee" (the cost, however, was the same for customers who paid with cash). The retailers then contended that the card-handling fee was exempt from the VAT. The U.K. Court of Appeal recently rejected this position.[13] Similar issues are certain to arise under the flat tax/X tax.

The same issue would arise on installment sales to nontaxable purchasers, such as consumers (Weisbach 2000). The days of automobile manufacturers providing low-interest financing of sales to consumers would be over. The new paradigm would be low sales prices accompanied by high-interest financing. A $20,000 car might be sold for $16,000 under an installment contract that requires excessive interest of $4,000. The business would benefit by the understatement of nonfinancial receipts by $4,000 (and would not be taxed on the interest). The individual purchaser would be indifferent. The same tax benefit from low prices and high interest rates would apply to sales to other nontaxable purchasers, such as small businesses.

Forward Contracts for Goods

A forward contract for the purchase or sale of property is a financial asset excluded from the system, creating distortions between economically equivalent transactions. For example, an airline desiring to lock in its future cost of fuel can either enter into forward purchase contracts at the fixed price, or else enter into separate swaps or puts and calls on the price of fuel that would have the same net effect. In the former case, the deductible input is the airline's cost of fuel purchased under the contract at the predetermined price. In the latter case, the deductible input is the actual subsequent market price at which the fuel is purchased, with the hedging gain or loss outside the tax system.

Even more anomalously, suppose the airline enters into the forward contract to buy the fuel at, say, $2 per gallon. If fuel later costs $2.50, the airline could close out or sell the contract for $.50 in cash, spend $2.50 to buy fuel on the market, and deduct $2.50. If fuel costs $1.50 at the time, the airline would take delivery under the contract and deduct $2.00. From the airline's point of view, this is the best of both worlds, since it deducts the greater of the forward contract price or the later market price of the fuel. However, if the other party to the contract is taxable, there is in principle no loss to the tax system. Here, if the other party paid $.50 to close out the contract, the $.50 would not be deductible, and the other party would then have taxable receipts of $2.50 on the sale of the fuel at market price.

Consider the example in which a taxpayer and taxable third parties enter into offsetting long and short forward contracts for delivery of goods (Weisbach 2003). The taxpayer settles the favorable side of the straddle for cash, resulting in nontaxable gain from a financial transaction, and takes delivery on the loss transaction, resulting in a deductible loss. Thus, the taxpayer is guaranteed a tax loss on a transaction with no real economic substance. Of course, the financial gain and deductible loss to the taxpayer is offset by financial loss and taxable gains to the counterparty. Consequently, there is no loss to the tax system as a whole, although shifting of income and loss would still arise.

This example further illustrates the need for the rule described below, that no deduction be allowed for a purchase from a nontaxable party. In the example, if the other party to the contract were exempt from tax, and the treatment of the taxpayer were unchanged, the result would be a transaction with no economic substance that resulted in a guaranteed deductible loss to the taxpayer and no offsetting income in the system.

Suppose, though, that a profitable corporation enters into a forward contract with an individual to purchase goods for $100, the value of goods falls to $60, and the individual sells the now-favorable contract to another business for $40. The corporation elects to take delivery under the contract, pays $100 for the goods, immediately sells them for $60, and claims a loss of $40. The other business bought the contract for $40, bought the goods for $60, and sold the goods for $100. To avoid $40 of leakage out of the tax system, it would be necessary to disallow the other business a deduction for its $40 purchase of the contract, because the payment was to a party outside the tax system. The general rule would have to be that whenever a taxpayer purchased or entered into a forward contract, or a similar contract relating to the delivery of goods, with a nontaxpayer, the taxpayer's payment to the nontaxpayer for the purchase of or entry into the contract would be nondeductible (just as would the price of the goods themselves if paid to a nontaxpayer).

However, when a nontaxpayer pays a taxpayer to enter into or assume a contract, the payment must count in the taxable receipts of the taxpayer. Otherwise, a nontaxpaying individual with a built-in loss of $100 on a supply contract could pay a taxpayer $100 to assume liability on the contract, and the taxpayer would have a loss of $100 on fulfillment of the contract. The individual would have shifted his own nondeductible loss into a deductible loss for the taxpayer. To avoid this result, the taxpayer must have taxable receipts of $100 from the individual. This is an anomalous result, considering that the taxpayer cannot deduct a payment to an individual to assume the taxpayer's obligation under a contract.

Expenses of Financial Transactions

Since receipts from financial transactions are not taxable, salaries and other inputs allocable to such transactions would not be deductible. For example, a business could not deduct the portion of the salaries of its employees allocable to its financial transactions. This raises obvious allocation issues. For example, salaries of employees who work on corporate transactions would have to be allocated between asset purchases and sales (deductible salary) and stock purchases and sales (nondeductible salary). An additional problem would arise for forward contracts that may be settled in cash or by delivery of goods, since it is not known at the time the contract is entered into whether the contract will be closed out in the form of a financial or a real transaction.

Of course, even though salaries paid with respect to financial transactions would not be deductible, the employee would be taxable on his wages. This would provide a strong incentive for the business to pay such salary in a nontaxable manner, since there is no offsetting loss of a tax deduction.[14]

Conclusions

These problems with financial transactions have no easy solutions. The flat tax/X tax would need doctrines like economic substance, business purpose, sham transaction. and so on, and rules similar to the current rules that require all pricing of transactions between related parties to be at arm's length. It would also need record-keeping requirements for financial transactions, since those transactions would not otherwise appear in any tax records. In theory, at least, the taxpayer would have to report every financial transaction, or at least keep records for review on audit.

Of course, these doctrines and statutes already exist under present law, and contracts are already subject to discovery under present law. Whether income shifting as a result of excluding financial products from the tax base would be greater than under present law is unknowable; if not, there would be no net cost in this area. However, this issue alone could eliminate some portion of the simplification otherwise offered by the flat tax/X tax.

In the past, European VAT systems had few antiabuse provisions that prevented the shifting of income from real transactions into income from financial transactions, and vice versa. This is less true today. As noted above, U.S. antishelter doctrines have been incorporated in at least some European VAT regimes.

Income Shifting to Loss Entities (Transferability of Losses)

Under the flat tax/X tax, absent special restrictive rules, it will be very easy for businesses with tax losses to "sell" the losses to businesses with profits. This can be accomplished through shifting income from the profitable business to the loss business, or alternatively, shifting deductions from the loss business to the profitable business. This section discusses a number of such techniques.

Leasing

The simplest technique would be leasing transactions, under which the profitable taxpayer buys an asset and leases it to the taxpayer with losses. The profitable taxpayer obtains an immediate deduction for the full cost of the asset, offset in later years by rental income. The taxpayer with losses obtains no immediate deduction, but obtains rental deductions over the life of the lease. Although the present value of all tax deductions in the system would not change, the actual payment of tax liability would be deferred.[15]

Asset and Stock Transactions

Under the flat tax/X tax, transfers of tax losses could be made even more "efficiently" than by leasing transactions. The result is not merely a timing benefit to the profitable business, but a permanent tax reduction.

Suppose that a profitable corporation has $10 in taxable cash flow and another corporation with losses wishes to buy an asset for $10. The profitable corporation can use the $10 to buy the asset and then contribute that asset to a newly formed subsidiary. It can then sell the stock of the subsidiary to the loss corporation. The profitable corporation would presumably get a deduction for the purchase but not be taxed on the stock sale, since stock is a financial asset. The profitable corporation now has the same $10 in cash it started with, except it now has no tax liability and no further entanglement with the loss corporation. The asset presumably has a zero basis in the subsidiary and will generate $10 of income to the subsidiary or (if the subsidiary is liquidated) to the loss corporation. If, as is supposed, the loss corporation has otherwise unusable losses and the tax system includes a consolidated return concept or a tax-free liquidation concept,[16] the additional income is of no consequence. The result is an upfront and permanent shift of the tax deduction from the loss corporation to the profitable corporation, in contrast to a lease transaction in which the tax shift reverses over time as rent is paid.

This technique would work equally well if the profitable corporation owned an existing asset, for which it had deducted the purchase price, that it wished to sell to a loss corporation. The profitable corporation can do so tax-free, by contributing the asset to a subsidiary and selling the stock of the subsidiary. The subsidiary, again, will have a zero basis in the asset and will recognize gain on the sale of the asset or on income produced by the asset. But so long as a corporation with losses purchases the subsidiary, that gain or income can be recognized tax-free, again assuming a tax-free liquidation concept or consolidated return concept.

In either case, the profitable corporation can either distribute the cash sale proceeds to its shareholders, or reinvest the cash in an asset identical to the asset that it had just sold, or even reinvest the cash in an asset that it will immediately resell using the same technique. In fact, the profitable corporation could do the same transaction repeatedly, generating a tax deduction and no offsetting income each time, by rolling over the sale proceeds indefinitely.

Intermediary Transactions

A loss corporation could effectively "sell" its losses to a profitable corpora-tion by acting as an intermediary. Suppose a profitable corporation (seller) has a subsidiary holding business assets that it desires to sell to another prof-itable corporation (buyer). Normally, either the seller would sell the under-lying assets to the buyer, resulting in offsetting income to the seller and deduction to the buyer equal to the sale price, or the seller would sell the stock of the subsidiary to the buyer, resulting in neither income nor deduc-tion. Both of these alternatives are revenue neutral to the government.

However, suppose the loss corporation buys the stock from the seller, and then has the purchased subsidiary sell its assets to the buyer. The seller has no income on the stock sale, the buyer has a deduction for its purchase price of the assets, and the loss corporation group has a gain on the asset sale that (again assuming a consolidated return concept or tax-free liquidation concept) is sheltered by its losses.

Similarly, suppose a taxable business desires to purchase an asset from a nontaxable entity. The taxable business would obtain no deduction for such a purchase. However, a loss corporation could first buy the asset from the nontaxable entity (not obtaining a deduction for such purchase), then sell the asset to the taxable business. The taxable business would obtain a deduction, since it is buying from a taxable business that just happens to have losses.

In all of these cases, a new deduction for the purchase price has been created in the tax system, offset by a reduction in the losses of the inter-mediary loss corporation. This technique is very similar to a transaction involving intermediary loss corporations that developed under existing law, under which a buyer would obtain a stepped-up tax basis in assets to increase its depreciation deductions.[17] These transactions usually had little substance, and the IRS designated them as a "listed transaction."[18] The flat tax/X tax would increase the incentive for this type of transaction, because the buyer would obtain not merely a stepped-up tax basis in the purchased assets, but an immediate deduction of the entire purchase price of the assets.

High or Low Interest Rates

Since sale proceeds are taxable but interest is not, a profitable corporation could sell goods on the installment basis to a corporation with losses for a low price and a high interest rate. Likewise, since purchase price is deductible but interest is not, a loss corporation could sell goods to a profitable corporation for a high price and a low interest rate.

Possible Solutions

If losses are refundable, a loss corporation would have no reason to engage in a transaction to shift its losses to a profitable corporation. Assuming refundability of losses is rejected, unlimited "self-help refundability" through loss shifting would be difficult to justify.

How much non-tax "substance" should be required to shift losses from one taxpayer to another? Historically, leasing has required some (small) amount of substance, except in the days of "safe harbor leasing."[19] While the existing rules for leasing could be retained, this would do nothing to prevent the types of loss shifting that result from transferring assets to corporate subsidiaries and selling the subsidiaries' stock.

A number of approaches can prevent this type of loss shifting. However, none of them seems both practicable and likely to be effective. First, the flat tax/X tax could adopt the complicated set of anti-loss-shifting rules found in our present tax system.[20] These rules have had only limited success in stopping loss shifting under current law, and there is no reason to think they would work better under the flat tax/X tax.

Second, the above transactions and similar transactions could be made subject to the kinds of doctrines now used to attack tax shelters, such as economic substance, business purpose, and step transaction. Reporting requirements could also be imposed on these transactions. However, just as today, these doctrines would be relatively easy to avoid. In particular, property could be contributed to a subsidiary without any advance plan to sell the stock of that subsidiary to a loss corporation. Since the subsidiary's stock would carry with it an embedded tax liability (underlying property with zero basis and no deduction upon purchase of the stock), only businesses with unusable losses might be expected to purchase it.

Third, a contribution of assets to a subsidiary might be treated as a sale of the assets. The contributing party, with a zero basis in business assets, would recognize income equal to the fair market value of the property and the subsidiary would receive a deduction in like amount for its issuance, actual or deemed, of stock to purchase the property. This rule would prevent the tax-free sales described above, since the profitable corporation would now recognize income upon contributing the property to the subsidiary.[21] However, the rule also would discourage the transfer of property to subsidiaries in normal business transactions. For this reason, present law does not treat these transactions in this manner. The rule would also require taxpayers to value, and authorities to monitor the value of, all such transferred property.[22]

Fourth, the tax-free sale of subsidiary stock might be allowed, but neither the tax-free liquidation of a subsidiary nor the filing of consolidated returns would be allowed. These bans would prevent a loss corporation that purchased a target corporation with appreciated assets from using its losses to shelter the gain on the assets. However, those restrictions would be major changes from present law—changes that would enormously reduce flexibility in nonabusive transactions.

Finally, all sales of subsidiaries' stock could be treated as sales of the underlying assets, with income to the seller and a deduction to the buyer. This would also be a vast change from existing law, and would either prevent an enormous number of ordinary business transactions now accomplished as tax-free reorganizations, or require retention of the complex existing rules for tax-free reorganizations. The first alternative is not realistic. The second would add excessive complexity to the flat tax/X tax.

Consequences of Transferability of Losses

If losses are transferable, a profitable corporation can in effect buy losses from a loss corporation and use the losses to obtain a current reduction in its own tax liability. The result is very similar to the loss corporation receiving a direct refund from the government for its tax losses. Thus, transferability of losses can be seen as a way of granting refundability.

As noted above, Schler and Bankman differ on the merits of such refundability. Schler believes that transferability, like refundability, will lead to permanent revenue losses as well as timing benefits that greatly reduce tax revenues. He therefore finds transferability undesirable even if it does not lead to unproductive tax-engineered transactions. Bankman believes that transferability is a second-best way to achieve the efficiency advantages of refundability. He finds transferability undesirable to the extent it leads to unproductive and expensive tax-engineered transactions (for example, refundability of losses realized by foreign persons).

Income Shifting through Partnerships

In recent years, partnerships have played a critical role in many tax shelters because of their pass-through nature. Whether partnerships would continue to exist under a flat tax/X tax is not clear.[23] A number of arguments can be made in favor of retaining the partnership concept, or alternatively in favor of eliminating the concept and treating all partnerships as separate taxable entities. These arguments are summarized in appendix A. The question discussed here is whether, if partnerships continue to exist, they could be used in tax shelter transactions under the flat tax/X tax.

A partnership might give rise to considerable opportunity to shelter income under the flat tax/X tax. A partnership will have income (gross receipts) and deductions (costs of inputs and wages). If today's partnership rules are continued, a partnership could allocate deductions to a partner that can utilize deductions, and income to a tax-exempt partner or a partner with losses.[24] Similarly, taxable cash flow as determined under the flat tax/X tax might be allocated to a tax-exempt or loss partner, even though the economic benefit of the cash flow might remain with the taxable partner. Today, such allocations are subject to the rules concerning "substantial economic effect." Such rules would have to be continued. Yet if a loophole could be found in those rules, which is certainly not without historical precedent,[25] completely artificial tax deductions can be created for taxable partners, or taxable partners' economic profits can be allocated for tax purposes to tax-exempt or loss partners.

In addition, whether or not a partnership interest is a financial asset, a pass-through partnership regime allows prepaid income to be allocated to a tax-exempt or loss partner, then a taxable partner to buy the partnership interest, then the corresponding deduction to be allowed to the partnership and passed through to the taxable partner. The lease-strip shelters of the early 1990s illustrate this problem (Bankman 1999).[26]

More generally, taxpayers have exploited ambiguities and inconsistencies in the existing partnership regulations to create tax shelters, and the regulations (and statute) have had to be constantly updated to shut down various perceived abuses. If an entirely new set of partnership regulations were required to reflect the flat tax/X tax, this cycle would start again from the beginning, and taxpayers would no doubt have many opportunities to take advantage of unintended results in the new regulations for many years to come.

To be sure, the particular problem of lease strips described above has apparently been resolved under present law.[27] While the issues differ under the flat tax/X tax, the prepayment problem could be solved by importing the result, if not the reasoning, into that latter tax.[28] Alternatively, a prepayment could be recharacterized in the theoretically correct manner as a loan.[29]

However, even solving lease strip and prepayment problems would do nothing to prevent the next tax shelter involving partnership allocations. If partnerships are retained, the partnership antiabuse doctrines now in the tax code would have to be retained (if not expanded). Among other things, this might require a rule that a partnership having a tax-exempt partner must meet stringent rules concerning allocations of income and deductions, similar to rules that are applied today in some situations to prevent abusive allocations to tax-exempt entities [Code §§168(h)(6), 514(c)(9)(E)].

One additional possibility for reducing abuse potential is to limit who may be a partner in a partnership. For example, flow-through treatment could be precluded for any venture with a nontaxable partner, such as a small business. A domestic loss corporation might be permitted as a partner because there would be less concern about income shifting between domestic entities. An individual could also be permitted as a partner, with that interest in the partnership being treated in the same manner as a taxable sole proprietorship.[30] Likewise, a foreign partner might be allowed if the partner's interest in the partnership was treated as if the partner carried on the underlying business directly. However, these rules would increase the complexity of current law and raise significant new issues.[31]

In conclusion, if the concept of partnerships is retained under the flat tax/X tax, all existing complexities of the partnership rules will have to be retained, including the many antiabuse rules contained in the tax code and in the partnership tax regulations. In addition, excluding tax-exempt persons as partners altogether may be necessary. Even so, preventing partnership tax shelters under the flat tax/X tax may be impossible.

Income Shifting between Financial Institutions and Nonfinancial Affiliates

Because financial institutions would not be subject to the flat tax/X tax, they would have considerable incentive to shift their deductions to their affiliates. For example, instead of the institution buying or leasing a building from a third party, the institution might cause an affiliate to buy the building (fully deductible) from the third party and lease it to the financial institution. Aside from the timing benefit of having the purchase deduction in (rather than outside) the tax system, the rent might be below market, resulting in a permanent shift of income from the taxable to the nontaxable sector.[32] Endless variations are possible. For example, a bank might sell the rights to its name to a trademark affiliate for a high price (deductible to the affiliate, exempt to the bank), then license it back from the affiliate for a relatively low annual payment stream. The IRS's inability to police intercompany pricing makes such attempts likely to succeed.

Income Shifting and Other Transactions between Individuals and Businesses

Shifting income among taxpayers presents avenues of tax avoidance that would be important to minimize. The problem presents itself in several forms.

Transfers of Property from Individuals to Businesses

Under the flat tax/X tax, a business would not receive a deduction for the purchase of personal property from an individual. In addition, the business would have a zero basis for the property. This rule means that the value of the property at the time of the contribution has no tax significance.

From this rule, it necessarily follows that a business cannot be allowed to deduct a contribution of personal property from an individual shareholder. Such a deduction would provide a way around the "no deduction for purchase" rule. An individual could transfer property to a wholly owned subsidiary and immediately have the subsidiary sell the property to another business. The deduction generated by the contribution would offset the sale proceeds. The subsidiary could then distribute the sale proceeds tax-free. Meanwhile, the transaction would generate a deduction for the purchasing business. The net result would be a business deduction with no tax on the individual.

The rule disallowing the business a deduction for contributed property may seem anomalous. After all, the shareholder could sell the property to a taxable third party (e.g., a corporation) without having any taxable gain, contribute the sale proceeds to the business, and have the business buy the property from the third party for the same price. The business would be entitled to a deduction in that case. However, this deduction is offset by the third party having no deduction for the purchase from the individual shareholder, but having income on the resale to the business.

Of course, if the taxable third party has losses, this is yet another way of shifting those losses to the individual's wholly owned business. The individual sells the property to the unrelated third party (with no income to the individual or deduction to the third party) and the third party resells it to the business (with income to the third party and deduction to the business). The net effect is that the business gets a deduction at the expense of a reduced-loss carryover to the third party.

In addition, note that a direct sale from the individual to the wholly owned business would not raise valuation issues. Regardless of the sale price, the individual would have no income and the business would have a zero basis for the property. By contrast, when the sale runs through the intermediate third party with losses, the parties have a considerable incentive to overvalue the property. This increases the deduction to the business with no additional tax cost to anyone else. No matter how high the price, the individual is untaxed on the sale to the third party, and the third party is assumed to have losses to shelter its proceeds on the sale to the business.

Finally, to shift deductions to a business, an individual could sell the property tax-free (perhaps to another individual) and contribute the proceeds to the business. The business would use the cash to buy property from a taxable person, thus starting off life with deductions equal to the amount of such contributions. This would occur even if there were no transition relief for businesses, so that all assets previously held by businesses received a zero basis. No tax would be due from the business sector until distributions (i.e., taxable cash flow) exceeded the fair market value of contributed cash proceeds. Adding full transition relief to this rule would give businesses a tax shield (comprised of basis and deductions) larger than they now have.[33]

Transfers of Property from Businesses to Individual Shareholders

Suppose a business sells or rents property to an individual shareholder that will not use it in a business. The business will have a taxable sales or rental receipt. Likewise, suppose the business distributes such property to an individual shareholder. The distribution must be treated as a deemed sale, generating income to the business, or else all tax would be avoided if property were distributed to a nontaxable shareholder.

In both of these situations, the incentive will be to minimize the sale price, rental price, or deemed sale price, to reduce the taxable income to the business. The shareholder will be indifferent from a tax point of view, since (in the case of a property acquisition) a later sale of the property will not be taxed and (in the case of property rental) any rent paid to the business is not deductible. The IRS will have extreme difficulty in enforcing proper valuation in these situations, making this area ripe for abuse. The incentive to minimize the sale and rental prices also exists today. However, in the case of a sale, the incentive under the flat tax/X tax will be greater than it is today, because today a reduced sale price will result in additional taxable gain to the shareholder on a later sale of the property, which will not be the case under the flat tax/X tax.

"Untaxed" Fringe Benefits

The flat tax/X tax will not reduce (and under some circumstances may increase) the incentive under current law to channel benefits to employees as nontaxable fringe benefits. If any such benefits are tax-free, and if the employer is entitled to a deduction for such benefits, a gap in the tax base will arise comparable to that which exists today. Even if the employer cannot deduct the benefits, the employer could defer its tax liability using other techniques. In either case, both the wage base and the corporate tax base would be eroded. Note that the integrity of the wage base is even more critical to the overall tax base under the flat tax/X tax than under the current tax system. As a result, even if the incentives to pay nontaxable fringe benefits are unchanged under the flat tax/X tax as compared to the present system, the risk to the Treasury from untaxed fringe benefits under the flat tax/X tax may be greater than it is today.

In fact, under the flat tax/X tax, in some situations, a business will have a greater incentive than today to improperly allow its shareholder or employee to use business assets without reporting wage income to the individual. For example, suppose that the individual shareholder needs a car for personal use, and the business has cash to buy the car. Assume the only practical choices are (1) the business pays the car payment to the individual as salary, (2) the business pays the car payment to the individual as a dividend, or (3) the business buys the car and allows the individual to use it without consideration. The first two alternatives result in no tax savings, while the third results in a tax saving from the deduction of the cost of the car. The same incentive exists under present law to choose the third alternative. However, the immediate deduction of the car results in a greater tax savings under the flat tax/X tax, so the expected tax savings as a result of the technique has increased. As a result, the incentive for improper tax reporting has increased.

But in other factual situations, the incentive to provide improper non-taxable fringe benefits to an employee may be no greater under the flat tax/X tax than it is today. Suppose the choice is between (1) the business buying a car that will be used by the shareholder, or (2) the business buying another business asset for its own business use. In that situation, under both the flat tax/X tax and the current system, the business obtains the same tax benefit under both alternatives, and the shareholder obtains the same relative benefit (tax-free use of a car) under alternative (1) as compared to alternative (2).

Recharacterization of Wages as Business Income, and Vice Versa

Many owner-employees will have some ability to recharacterize wage income as business income, or to recharacterize business income as wage income, by setting their salaries either too low or too high. Even employees who do not have an ownership interest in their employers could form independent contracting companies, in the hope of recharacterizing current wage income into business income.

If employees and businesses are subject to tax at the same rate, there generally will be no advantage on a present value basis to changing the label given a distribution from a business. Neither the characterization of distributions as wages or dividends, nor the timing of the distributions, will affect the present value of net tax liability.[34]

Recharacterizing wages as business profits, which can be invested tax-deferred, might be desirable, however, if the business wishes to defer taxes, even without reducing the present value of its tax liability. Such recharacterization will be even more desirable, and reduce the present value of tax liability, if the business is tax exempt, if the business tax can be partially evaded, if the business has the opportunities to earn a very high return and is otherwise capital constrained, if tax rates are thought likely to fall, or if (perhaps due to the continued existence of payroll taxes) the marginal rates on wages exceed the marginal rates on dividends. Yet recharacterizing business profits as wages would be desirable for those individuals who are in a lower marginal tax bracket than the business, or if tax rates were thought likely to rise.

The IRS has great difficulty under present law policing the proper amount of compensation to be paid to a shareholder of a closely held business (Bittker and Lokken 1999, ¶¶22.2.1, 22.2.2). It is not clear whether the flat tax/X tax makes this problem worse as a theoretical matter, though the problem may be worse as a practical matter because the significance of the wage tax would increase. In any event, it is doubtful that the flat tax/X tax will ameliorate today's problem of determining the proper amount of compensation.

Sole Proprietorships

Today, it is sometimes necessary to distinguish an individual's personal, investment, and business assets (and activities). The nature of an asset or activity can affect whether a loss is deductible at all, and the capital or ordinary nature of any taxable income, gain, or loss.

Under a flat tax/X tax, the distinction will be solely between business and nonbusiness activities. Nonbusiness activities will be completely exempt from tax, while business activities will be subject to the flat tax/ X tax unless the small business exemption applies. Thus the distinction will be even more important than under existing law, and there will be considerable incentive on the part of an individual to categorize activities as investment activities. Given the elusive nature of the distinction in many cases, this area will be very hard for the tax authorities to police. This issue has a large potential for revenue loss.

In addition, if an individual is in a business, and the small business exemption does not apply, the business activities will have to be viewed as operated through a sole proprietorship subject to the flat tax/X tax. Further, transactions between the proprietorship and the individual will need to be treated the same as transactions between the individual and any other business. For example, if an individual converts an asset from business use to investment (or personal) use, the proprietorship should be subject to the flat tax/X tax as if it had sold the asset to the individual for its fair market value. Otherwise, the value of the asset will permanently leave the tax base. Individuals are not likely to volunteer this tax and may, in some cases, rely on the small business exemption. At a minimum, the incentive will be to place an extremely low value on the asset. The different treatment of business and individual assets also creates incentives for mischief with respect to assets not currently held in business form. An individual might buy an asset, claim it is a business asset, deduct it under the flat tax/X tax, quietly begin using it for personal use, then sell it and claim it is an exempt personal asset.

Alternatively, an individual might buy a home for $100, live in it, then move out and convert it into rental property. As noted above, this should be treated as a sale to the sole proprietorship. The individual is exempt, but the proprietorship gets no deduction for the purchase of the house. If the small business exemption does not apply, the proprietorship obtains a zero basis for the house, the rental income is fully taxable, and any proceeds of the sale of the house are fully taxable to the proprietorship. Even if the sale is for the individual's original purchase price of $100, the full $100 is taxable to the proprietorship. In fact, the individual cannot even avoid this disastrous result by moving back into the house. As discussed in the preceding paragraph, this would be a taxable sale to the individual for the value of the house and would subject the proprietorship to flat tax/X tax.

Income Shifting among Individuals

Under current law, the progressive rate structure creates an incentive to shift income to low-bracket family members or friends. The flat tax/X tax should eliminate the incentive to shift income from capital, since such income is not subject to tax.

However, the flat tax/X tax assumes progressive tax rates on wages and so would produce incentives for shifting of wage income to those in lower tax brackets. In one respect, income shifting of wages under the flat tax/X tax might be worse than under present law. The reason is that under present law, a high-bracket taxpayer who wishes to shift taxable income must give up the cash, and thus will generally shift income only to a family member, or to another lower-bracket person to whom the individual wishes to make a gift. Under the flat tax/X tax, a high-bracket individual might shift income to an unrelated lower-bracket individual, with income later recouped through a nontaxable financial transaction. This would turn income shifting into a transaction without real consequences and greatly expand the incentive do so.

Consider, for example, a business about to distribute funds as either wages or dividends to a high-bracket employee or owner. The recipient convinces the business to put a low-bracket friend on the payroll and to distribute the funds to the friend. The high-bracket employee recoups the funds through a financial transaction with the friend. For example, the high-bracket employee loans the friend money at a usurious interest rate.

Will a Flat Tax/X Tax Lead to Undesirable Deferral of Tax?

Under the flat tax/X tax, all business taxpayers will be able to legally defer all of their tax liability for the indefinite future. Shareholders of a business that uses these techniques can then in effect cash out, tax-free, by simply selling their equity interests to a third party.

Strategies for Deferring Tax Liability

A business can defer its tax liability indefinitely by merely reinvesting all its profits in a deductible manner each year. There is no limit on the ability of a business to do so. For example, a business can use its profits to buy vacant land, to buy assets already subject to a net lease, or to buy property that it will lease to another taxpayer, with tax losses. If the business desires to distribute its cash profits to its shareholders, it can borrow the equivalent amount of money so that it has enough funds for both the reinvestment and the distribution.

A shareholder or employee of a closely held business can also minimize the current combined tax liability of the business and its shareholder by minimizing the salary the business pays to the shareholder, and using the resulting increased pretax profit of the business to buy deductible assets.

In addition, the closely held business could use strategies to reinvest its earnings in a deductible manner—strategies that go beyond the strategies available to a large public corporation. For example, the business might buy a house from a taxable seller and lease it to the shareholder. The business would obtain a tax deduction for the full purchase price. This strategy converts a personal expense of the shareholder into a deductible expense of the business (offset in future years by rental income and gain on a later sale of the house). If the shareholder wished to move, the business would sell the house at a taxable gain and buy a new house with deductible purchase price. This would allow a tax-free "rollover" as long as the new house cost as much as the sale price of the old house.

Results of Deferral of Tax Liability

On a current basis, these strategies will have the effect of allowing free shifting of current losses among taxpayers. Further, current deductions may tend to migrate to taxpayers that have the greatest current use for the deductions.

Yet under these strategies for deferring tax liability, the amount of income subject to tax will increase with the period of deferral and the accumulation of capital. In present value, then, assuming monies are ever withdrawn, the total tax liability should remain unchanged. The timing of tax payments, however, would be deferred. In addition, deferred tax on the buildup of capital inside the business sector may be lost due to changes in the political climate (for example, an administration may issue a tax holiday on withdrawals) or loopholes in the system.[35]

Implications of Ability to Defer Tax Liability

Bankman is willing to live with the possibility of deferring tax liability under the flat tax/X tax. He doubts that taxpayers will prefer to leave money in the business sector, subject to future tax, as opposed to paying tax today and then investing the money tax-free in financial assets. The choice is essentially one between a Roth individual retirement account (IRA) and a traditional IRA. He believes that the possibility that the government will reduce tax on the eventual distribution of funds from the business sector is offset by the possibility that the government will increase the tax on that distribution. The net incentives for a risk-adverse taxpayer might well be to pull funds out of the sector sooner than would otherwise be the case in a no-tax world.[36] He is willing to accept the risk of increased borrowing by the government to reflect deferral of tax liability by taxpayers.

Schler believes that the ability to freely defer tax liability is a fundamental flaw in the flat tax/X tax and is sufficient reason in itself to reject the tax. He believes that taxpayers will invariably prefer to postpone tax, even at the "theoretical" expense of paying more tax later.

He also believes that this incentive to defer tax will be further increased by the possibility of future tax holidays, newly discovered loopholes in the system, or (in the case of closely held businesses) non–arm's length transactions with their shareholders.[37] In fact, the future discovery of a single tax shelter that technically "works" might permit the elimination of a substantial part of the system's deferred tax liability before the government could shut down the shelter. In any of those situations, deferral of tax liability will also reduce the present value of tax liability.

As a result, Schler believes that the flat tax/X tax will dramatically reduce government revenues for years to come. The net result will be a forced reduction on government spending, an increase in an already-large deficit, or, most likely, some combination of both. Further, Schler believes that even if it is not clear that taxpayers will act in this manner, the risk that they will do so, and the risk that they could begin doing so at any time, makes adopting the flat tax/X tax an enormous gamble on future tax revenues.

Conclusions

The flat tax/X tax will present considerable opportunities for tax planning. Some of these opportunities will lead to schemes that resemble today's tax shelters. The flat tax/X tax will clearly require rules similar to the antiabuse provisions of current law. Further, while some of the general avenues for tax planning under a flat tax/X tax can be seen today, other forms of tax planning are certain to arise after specific legislation is enacted, and after the practitioner community has the opportunity and incentive to minimize taxes under the new law. Some of the areas for tax planning will result in a permanent reduction in the present value of tax liability, while other areas will merely defer tax liability without a reduction in present values.

The authors agree that the flat tax/X tax presents opportunities for socially unproductive tax planning. However, they disagree on the relative vulnerability of the flat tax/X tax and income tax to this form of behavior. Bankman believes that, notwithstanding the areas of vulnerability outlined in this article, the flat tax/X tax offers fewer opportunities for tax planning than present law. Schler believes that the full deductibility of costs makes the flat tax/X tax particularly vulnerable to tax minimizing schemes and that, even aside from policy objections to the flat tax, this vulnerability is reason enough not to adopt it.

Summary

This chapter considers the possibilities for tax planning (or tax avoidance) that arise under a consumption tax, in particular in the context of the (somewhat misnamed) flat tax, or X tax. Would such a tax produce the same sort of undesirable tax planning that bedevils the current income tax (e.g., Bankman 1999; Schler 2002)? If so, this would reduce or eliminate a principal reason for switching to a consumption tax.

The flat tax/X tax, just like the present income tax, will be subject to various tax avoidance transactions:

Fraud. A flat tax/X tax will attract a certain amount of fraudulent behavior. This is true today of the European value-added tax, or VAT, and will no doubt be true of any similar tax adopted in the United States.

Legal shifting of income to tax-exempt taxpayers. Under the flat tax/ X tax, some entities will be tax-exempt (e.g., small business and financial institutions). As a result, the tax can potentially give rise to "legal" tax avoidance transactions in which income is shifted from taxable to nontaxable entities. Such transactions might involve, for example, financial instruments or partnership transactions. Enormous effort will be required to draft the statute and regulations to minimize such shifting of income—and this effort may not be successful.

Related-party pricing issues. Under the flat tax/X tax, in many situations, unduly high or low pricing between related parties can greatly affect their combined tax liability. It is very difficult, if not impossible, for the Internal Revenue Service (IRS) to police transactions that depend on the valuation of assets or services.

Transactions between profitable businesses and loss businesses. Under the flat tax/X tax, shifting income between taxable entities will be relatively easy. In particular, income can be shifted from profitable businesses to businesses with losses, with the outcome that neither entity pays tax.

Unknown loopholes. Under any tax system, creative taxpayers will make every effort to discover unintended loopholes, and there will be a constant race to take advantage of those loopholes before the government can close them. It is as yet impossible to predict what those loopholes might be in the flat tax/X tax, but based on experience, they are sure to exist. This problem may be exacerbated under the flat tax/X tax as compared to current law, because in any new system, government and taxpayers will be starting "fresh." In other words, while the current tax code and regulations have been revised innumerable times to stop tax avoidance transactions, this cycle will be starting anew with an entirely new system.

These possibilities for tax avoidance under the flat tax/X tax will require that the new tax system contain numerous antiabuse rules. The need for such rules is further demonstrated by European countries, in recent years, being forced to adopt antiabuse rules for their VAT systems. The complexity and uncertain effectiveness of such rules may reduce the benefits of the conversion to a flat tax/X tax.

In addition, the flat tax/X tax is unique in that it permits any business taxpayer to defer its tax liability indefinitely in a variety of completely legal ways. These techniques will require the taxpayer to pay additional tax (i.e., with an interest factor) in the future. In theory, the techniques will not reduce a business's true tax liability, but as a practical matter, the longer tax payments may be deferred, the greater the chance that they will escape the tax net altogether.

The two authors disagree on the implications of these conclusions. As to tax avoidance transactions, Bankman believes that, despite the vulnerabilities we describe, the possibilities for tax avoidance under the flat tax/X tax are fewer than under current law and should not preclude the adoption of the flat tax/X tax. Schler believes that the possibilities for and the unknowable risk of tax avoidance under such a new system, are major problems and sufficient reason not to adopt the tax.

As to tax deferral transactions, Schler believes that the possibility of deferring tax liability (even without reduction in the present value of such liability) has the potential to greatly reduce government revenues for years to come. Further, any number of events (e.g., the discovery of new tax shelters) might prevent the deferred tax from ever being paid. As a result, Schler believes that the possibility of deferral is itself an independent reason not to adopt the flat tax/X tax. Bankman does not think the flat tax/X tax encourages deferral and so does not see deferral as grounds for rejecting the tax.

Appendix
Should Partnerships Continue to Exist under the Flat Tax/X Tax?

Partnerships and other flow-through entities are an important part of the present economic landscape. A number of arguments can be made for and against retaining partnerships under the flat tax/X tax.[38]

Arguments for Eliminating Partnerships as Pass-Through Entities

Current partnership provisions are enormously complex, requiring hundreds of pages of very technical regulations in the tax code. All of those regulations are based on the existing income tax, and would have to be rewritten to reflect an entirely new tax system. The retention of such complexity, and the need to rewrite these regulations, would considerably reduce any simplification benefits of a flat tax/X tax.

Much of the existing rules' complexity arises from the differences between so-called "book capital accounts" and "tax capital accounts." Those accounts reflect, respectively, the fair market value and tax basis of property contributed to a partnership. Thus, under a set of very complicated rules, gain or loss on the sale of property with a tax basis that differs from its fair market value is generally allocated to the partner that contributed the property [Code 704(c)]. A similar provision applies when a new partner buys into a partnership that already holds appreciated or depreciated property. The magnitude of the resulting adjustments would be greatly increased by the flat tax/X tax, because the tax basis of all partnership assets would be zero.

Some features of current law simply would not fit within a flat-tax/X-tax framework. For example, operating income from appreciated property contributed by a partner (in contrast to gain on a sale of the property) is not specially allocated to the contributing partner, probably because tracing the source of operating income is difficult. Instead, the noncontributing partner is given a disproportionate share of the depreciation deductions thrown off by the property. Under a flat tax/X tax, however, the contributed property will have no basis and thus generate no tax depreciation. To prevent misallocation of income, elective (and very complicated) provisions under current law that provide for fictitious depreciation deductions would have to be made mandatory.

Finally, the tax code now treats a partnership in some respects as an entity and in other respects as an aggregate of assets held by the individual partners. This approach does not fit the structure of the flat tax/X tax. Consider, for example, the sale of partnership interests. Under the flat tax/X tax, either a partnership interest would have to be treated as a financial asset, with no gain or loss on the sale of the interest, or a sale and purchase of a partnership interest would be treated as a sale and purchase of the underlying assets, taxable to the seller and deductible to the buyer.

The first approach would make the partnership particularly susceptible to income shifting. Any time a partnership was about to sell an appreciated asset, with taxable proceeds to be passed through to the partners, a partner could avoid this tax by first selling the partnership interest tax-free. More generally, under current law, nontaxation of appreciated property and other forms of built-in gain, along with misallocation of income for tax purposes, is offset at the time of sale of the partnership interest. A partner whose interest has gone up in value but who has avoided recognition of income will recognize that income upon sale. The advantages of nonrecognition are offset (though not on a present value basis) upon sale. If a partnership interest is treated as a financial asset, this offset would not occur.[39]

The second approach also raises the possibility of income shifting. The partner would start off with a zero basis for his interest. Suppose the partnership delayed reinvesting current taxable cash flow, and the partner then sold his interest. The partner would recognize gain on the cash flow that was not reinvested and (because of the no-basis rule) gain again when he sold his interest. This result could be avoided only by either allocating a part of the sale price to the current value of the cash deposits, and treating this part of the sale price as tax-exempt investment income, or by specially importing the concept of basis into the flat tax/X tax. Either of these approaches would be quite complex. In addition, some variation of the first alternative would be necessary for the buyer in any event, since the buyer should not obtain a greater deduction for buying a partnership interest than if it had bought the underlying assets directly.

Arguments for Retaining Partnerships as Pass-Through Entities

Fairness may require the retention of partnerships. Suppose that two loss corporations create a profitable 50/50 joint venture. Absent the partnership concept, the joint venture would be subject to tax even though the partners had plenty of losses to shelter the income of the venture. The same problem would arise if the joint venture were generating losses and corporate partners were profitable. These results could be viewed as quite unfair.

The flow-through nature of current partnership taxation can, at least in theory, be replicated by contractual provisions outside of partnership. To be sure, the government could rely on existing doctrines (such as substance over form) to recharacterize the relationship as a partnership. The difficulty with this approach is that the boundaries of partnership are unclear as a conceptual matter and hard (and expensive) to police as a practical matter. As a result, the statutory elimination of partnerships may do little except shift the partnership results into a different area.

An additional issue concerns transition to a new system. Suppose that immediately before enactment of a flat tax/X-tax, a profitable corporation had contributed property with a basis of $100 and a value of $400 to a 50/50 partnership with a loss corporation, and that property is sold for $400 after enactment. The first $300 of gain on the sale of the property (here, all the gain) would be taxed to the profitable corporation [§704(c)]. If tax is now collected on entities, that tax is now borne by the coventurers. If the venture pays tax at the maximum rate, there is no loss of tax revenue to the government. However, the liability for the tax shifts from the profitable corporation to the venture, which is 50 percent owned by the loss corporation. This would greatly upset the settled expectations of the parties. Alternatively, if the property had been contributed by the loss corporation, the expectation would have been that there would be no tax to either party on the sale of the property. If partnerships were eliminated under the flat tax/X tax, the entity would bear a new tax liability that would be shared by the coventurers. This would be even more upsetting to the parties.

If the flat tax/X tax is adopted with transition relief, and contributed property were to receive a carryover basis, elimination of partnerships could also reduce government revenues. Consider, for example, the reverse of the situation described immediately above: the loss corporation contributes property with a basis of $400 and value of $100 immediately prior to enactment, and the property is sold after enactment for $100. Assume the entity itself has $300 of income aside from this loss. Under current law, the $300 income of the entity is split 50/50, but the $300 loss on the property sticks with the loss corporation. Assuming the loss corporation has sufficient existing losses, none of the loss on the asset produces a tax benefit, and the government collects tax from the profitable corporation on income of $150. If partnerships were eliminated, the entire $300 loss on the property reduces entity-level income of $300, and so the government does not collect any tax on the income of the entity.

NOTES

1. See Commission of the European Communities (2004); OECD (2004), describing various estimates of VAT revenue leakage ranging from 4–6 percent to 17.5 percent; and President's Advisory Panel (2005), quoting a U.K. Inland Revenue estimate that as of April 2004, the VAT tax evasion rate was 12.9 percent.

2. See "Distorted Trade Data Point to Massive Tax Fraud" and "Fraud Makes Presence Felt in Trade Figures," *Financial Times*, August 10, 2005; "A Bit of This, a Bit of

VAT: The Scam That's Costing Britain Billions," http://telegraph.co.uk, August 15, 2005 (describing carousel schemes and stating that these and similar schemes are so large that the U.K. government admitted they are distorting Britain's trade balance); "Taxpayers Losing Billions in Systematic VAT Fraud," *Belfast Telegraph Digital*, August 10, 2005 (quoting a U.K. government official referring to "a systematic criminal attack on the VAT system"); "Court Report Finds VAT Fraud, Possible Terrorist Link," *Tax Notes International*, August 8, 2005, at 489 (generally discussing VAT fraud and describing a confidential German report on VAT fraud said to estimate German revenue loss in 2003 at €17.6 billion, representing 11 percent of annual VAT revenues, and said to conclude that some of the lost revenue ends up in the hands of terrorists and is used by them to finance their activities). Most recently, see "U.K. Pre-Budget Report, Press Notices," PN03, December 6, 2006, available at http://www.hmrc.gov.uk/pbr2006/pn-all.pdf (which refers to the "rapid increase in attempted [VAT missing trader] fraud" in recent periods and estimates the attempted fraud in the 2005–2006 fiscal year to be between £3.5 billion and £4.75 billion, and the actual loss of VAT receipts from such fraud between £2 billion and £3 billion).

3. See President's Advisory Panel (2005), at 202, stating that the Treasury Department revenue estimates for the effect of a VAT system (not the flat tax/X tax) assumed a noncompliance rate of 15 percent.

4. See proposed Dutch legislation discussed below. The United Kingdom has adopted legislation, very similar to the U.S. rules for "listed transactions" and "reportable transactions," that requires disclosure of schemes whose main purpose is obtaining a tax advantage. This legislation applies to VAT schemes. The scope of the disclosure obligation, as it applies to VAT, was recently expanded in Schedule 1 to the Finance (No 2) Act 2005, effective August 1, 2005, because the existing legislation was not broad enough to pick up all the schemes that were being used by taxpayers. See HM Revenue and Customs (2005).

Most recently, to combat missing trader frauds, the U.K. Budget 2006, released March 22, 2006, proposed that the U.K. revenue service be given additional authority to require individual business to keep specified records for goods they have traded. See the related "BN 43-VAT: Power for HMRC to Direct Additional Record-Keeping Requirements," available at http://www.hmrc.gov.uk/budget2006/bn43.htm; and "Regulatory Impact Assessment for VAT: Power for HMRC to Direct Individual Businesses" (describing missing trader fraud and referring to it as a "systematic criminal attack on the VAT system, which is prevalent throughout the EU"), available at http://www.hmrc.gov.uk/budget2006/index.htm#news.

5. See the Debenhams case discussed below. See also decisions of the European Court of Justice (ECJ) in Halifax plc (case C-255/02) and University of Huddersfield (case C-223/03), both issued Feb. 21, 2006. The Halifax case involved a financial institution that bought supplies through a nonfinancial subsidiary in order to be able to reclaim its VAT costs. The decision reviews the United Kingdom's rejection of the VAT recovery. It states that a taxpayer has no right to deduct input VAT "where the transactions from which that right derives constitute an abusive practice," and discusses the meaning of "abusive practice." The importance of the VAT abuse issue is demonstrated by the U.K. tax authorities placing 175 contested VAT cases on hold pending the outcome of these cases, and the tax authorities anticipate that in the "vast majority" of these cases the ECJ decisions will support disallowing the contested VAT benefits. See HMRC Business Brief 02/06 (February 27, 2006), available at http://www.hmrc.gov.uk. See also the decision of the ECJ in *Emsland-Stärke GmbH and Hauptzollamt Hamburg-Jonas*, December 14, 2000, Case C-110/99, also characterizing a VAT refund scheme as abusive.

Under the scheme, goods were exported, the exporter received a VAT refund on the export, and the goods were immediately reimported under an existing arrangement and became subject to a lower VAT rate than the refund rate. The ECJ opinions can be found at http://curia.eu.int/en/content/juris/index_form.htm by going to "Case Law/ Search Form" and entering the case numbers stated above.

6. See President's Advisory Panel (2005) also proposing this rule.

7. Compare this with President's Advisory Panel (2005) at 162, which does not provide an exemption for small business and provides that the income of a sole proprietorship would be taxed to the owner at the graduated individual rates. To the extent that a small business's income is taxed at less than the regular business rate, the issues discussed herein would still arise. In fact, some of the issues would be exacerbated, because a business taxed at regular rates would be entitled to a full deduction for goods purchased from a sole proprietorship whose income might be taxed at a very low marginal rate.

8. See President's Advisory Panel (2005, 172–73), generally proposing that depreciation deductions for existing assets, and interest deductions on existing debt, be phased out over five years. See also Bankman (2003); Engler and Knoll (2003); and Shaviro (2000).

9. More recently, see President's Advisory Panel (2005, 167), proposing that unused losses increase by a market interest rate.

10. Of course, if the flat tax/X tax retains a small business exception, taxpayers eligible for that exemption would have no incentive to increase taxable wages with no tax benefit to the small business.

11. See President's Advisory Panel (2005, 167), proposing that losses not be refundable.

12. We do not discuss the tax treatment of the financial services sector itself. If that sector is exempt from the flat tax/X tax, then taxable businesses would have a disincentive to deal with that sector because they would get no deduction for goods or services purchased from that sector. By contrast, consumers would have an incentive to deal with that sector because that sector could set its prices without regard to any flat tax/X tax.

13. *HMRC v. Debenhams Retail PLC,* [2005] EWCA Civ 892 (July 18, 2005) (the charge slip stated that 2.5 percent of the retail price would go to Debenhams Card Handling Services Ltd., a wholly owned subsidiary). This case can be found at http:// www.bailii.org/ew/cases/EWCA/Civ/ under Debenhams in the alphabetical listing of cases. The arrangement is reported to be worth about £300 million per year in U.K. revenues and to have been adopted by more than 70 retailers (*International Tax Review,* Weekly News, August 1, 2005).

14. For example, consider a hedge fund or other investment partnership that compensates its investment manager with a profits interest in the fund. Under the flat tax/ X tax, no one is taxed on the fund's profits. As a result, unless the manager is taxable (unlike today) on the receipt of the profits interest, the compensation will permanently escape taxation under the flat tax/X tax.

15. See below for a discussion of this deferral issue.

16. The consolidated return concept would allow the subsidiary to have $10 of income sheltered by losses of its parent. The tax-free liquidation concept would allow the subsidiary to liquidate into its parent tax free, and for the parent to then have $10 of income sheltered by its own losses.

17. The situation arose when the owner of a target corporation had a higher tax basis in the stock of the target than the underlying asset basis in the target. Normally in that case, the owner would sell the stock rather than the underlying assets to reduce its taxable gain, but this would provide the buyer with a carryover tax basis in the underlying assets rather than a stepped up basis. To avoid this result, a loss corporation would buy the target's stock (reducing the gain to the seller), then have the target corporation sell the underlying assets to a buyer (providing a stepped up basis in the underlying assets to the buyer).

18. "Listed transactions" are those the IRS considers most abusive (Notice 2001-16, 2001-1 Cum. Bull. 730).

19. Those rules, since repealed, allowed the use of leases that had no economic substance. The so-called lessee had all the economic benefits and burdens of ownership of the property, and the so-called lessor received all the tax benefits of owning the property but none of the economic benefits or burdens of ownership.

20. See President's Advisory Panel (2005, 167), proposing the adoption of rules limiting transferability of losses similar to those that exist today.

21. Of course, if the subsidiary already held the asset, the profitable parent corporation could still sell the stock of the subsidiary, rather than the assets of the subsidiary, to a loss corporation.

22. This rule would make it easier, rather than more difficult, to transfer losses where a business with unusable losses contributes property to a subsidiary jointly controlled by a profitable corporation. The loss corporation would recognize gain tax free, and the deduction for the property would go automatically to the subsidiary. However, this result may not be troublesome, since a similar result could be obtained in these circumstances simply having the subsidiary purchase property from the loss corporation.

23. See President's Advisory Panel (2005, 162), contemplating that pass-through entities would continue to exist, and that income of such entities would be taxed at the business rate and reported on a separate schedule of the owners' tax returns.

24. To some extent, the problem would be less than today. For example, today a partnership can allocate investment gains to a foreign partner and investment losses to a U.S. partner, resulting in a deduction to the U.S. partner and no taxable income to the foreign partner. Under the flat tax/X tax, all investment gains and losses are exempt from tax, so there is no benefit to such a shift. Moreover, if business income were artificially allocated to a foreign partner, and business losses to a domestic partner, it would be necessary to tax the foreign partner as if it earned the business income directly.

25. See, for example, 342 F. Supp.2d 94 (D. Conn. 2004), rev'd, 459 F3d 220 (2d Cir. 2006), in which taxable income was artificially allocated to a foreign bank. See Burke (2005).

26. As a variation of those transactions, assume a profitable corporation enters into a partnership with a loss corporation. The partnership is funded with a $1 billion contribution from the profitable corporation. On December 30, the partnership contractually agrees to lease aircraft for substantially their entire useful lives. In return, the lessees prepay $1 billion. The partnership agreement allocates the entire sum to the loss corporation and its capital account is increased by that amount. The loss corporation, however, is required under the agreement to bear the cost of purchasing $1 billion worth of aircraft for use in the lease. The $1 billion expense, when incurred, will reduce the loss corporation's capital account back to zero. On December 31, the loss corporation sells its interest to a subsidiary of the profitable corporation. On January 1, the partnership

purchases the planes and deducts the $1 billion expense; the deduction flows through to the profitable corporation subsidiary.

The same result could be obtained if the loss corporation were replaced by a tax-exempt entity, such as a foreign person. Moreover, similar shelters are possible any time a payment is made to a nontaxable person in exchange for future goods and services, and the nontaxable person's responsibilities are assumed by a taxable person.

27. See, for example, Notice 2003-55, 2003-34 I.R.B. 395; *Andantech L.L.C. v. Commissioner,* Nos. 02-1213; 02-1215, (D.C. Cir. June 17, 2003), 2003 U.S. App. LEXIS 11908, affg. in part and remanding for reconsideration of other issues T.C. Memo 2002–97 (2002); *Nicole Rose v. Commissioner,* 320 F.3d 282 (2d Cir. 2002), affg. per curiam, 17 T.C. 328 (2001).

28. The treatment relied upon by the taxpayer—acceleration of rental income—was clearly inconsistent with the income tax base but not inconsistent with the cash flow tax base.

29. The proper treatment is to treat a prepayment as a loan, which is repaid with interest, followed by a payment of the loan amount plus interest to the party providing goods and services. Deemed interest on the loan is outside the system. The interest and principal on the loan are considered to be paid at the time the expense for the goods and services is incurred. This would defer the inclusion of income until after the exempt party exits the scene, leaving the income and expense with the profitable corporation.

30. Individual sole proprietorships raise other issues, discussed below, but the relevant point here is that an individual's interest in a business partnership does not raise any additional issues.

31. For example, if the partnership had domestic business losses and foreign business income (not connected to a U.S. business), rules would be needed to prevent allocation of the losses to U.S. partners and the income to foreign partners. This issue also arises today.

32. The Dutch government recently introduced legislation to stop this abuse. Ruben de Wie, "Dutch Officials Propose Transfer Pricing Tactics to Combat VAT Avoidance," *Tax Notes International,* May 23, 2005, 634. The *Halifax plc* case discussed above is another real-world example of a financial institution attempting to artificially shift expenses to a nonfinancial subsidiary to obtain VAT recovery available only to a non-financial subsidiary.

33. For example, assume that individuals hold assets with $20 of basis and $50 of value. If they sell half of those assets and contribute the proceeds to corporations, and there is no transition relief, corporations start life with deductions of $25. No tax would then be due until corporate distributions exceeded this amount, so the first $25 of consumption would be tax free. Note that the problem here is not the deduction given to corporations but the exemption of the individually held assets from tax, since individuals could alternatively keep all the assets and consume the $25 of sale proceeds tax free. If corporations receive full transition relief, they could distribute an additional amount tax free equal to the existing tax basis of their assets.

34. Suppose, for example, that a corporation earns $100 from the services of its owner-employee, that the prevailing interest rate is 10 percent and that the business and individual tax rate is 30 percent. If the corporation pays out all $100 as wages, it pays no tax and the owner-employee has $70. If the employee invests that sum for one year, she has $77. If the corporation pays no wages (treating the $100 as receipts) and

invests the $100 (wiping out the tax due on the $100), it would have $110 the following year. If it pays the $110 out as dividend, it would pay $33 in tax, leaving $77 for the employee. The same result would arise if the corporation characterized the $110 payment in the second year as wages. In that case, the employee would pay the $33 tax and again have $77 to consume.

35. For example, as discussed above, a permanent loss to the tax system would arise if the closely held corporation leased the house to the shareholder/employee at a below-market rent. For the IRS to enforce a fair rent in this situation would be difficult if not impossible.

36. A more complete analysis would have to take into account the possibility (less likely, in Bankman's view) that the government might raise taxes not by increasing the tax on the business sector but by instituting a tax on financial returns.

37. A good precedent for a tax holiday is Code §965. Under the general rules of the Code, a corporation can indefinitely defer U.S. tax on the earnings of its foreign subsidiaries by keeping the earnings offshore, but repatriation of the earnings results in tax at the regular corporate rate. This regime is somewhat analogous to the ability of a taxpayer under the flat tax/X tax to defer tax indefinitely by reinvesting earnings. However, under Code §965, corporations are able to bring back most of their accumulated earnings during 2004 or 2005 with an 85 percent dividends-received deduction. One theory behind this provision is that corporations were not bringing back the money anyway, so the United States might as well encourage repatriation and collect whatever tax it could. The same theory might arise under the flat tax/X tax, to encourage businesses to at least pay some tax on their accumulated reinvested earnings.

38. Note that under the European VAT, partnerships are treated as separate taxable entities rather than pass-through entities.

39. As discussed above, this same problem as to built-in gain (although not misallocated income) arises in the flat tax/X tax if a corporation can sell a subsidiary's stock tax free.

REFERENCES

Bankman, Joseph. 1999. "The New Market in Corporate Tax Shelters." *Tax Notes* 82 (June 21): 1775–95.

———. 2003. "The Engler-Knoll Consumption Tax Proposal: What Transition Rule Does Fairness (or Politics) Require?" *SMU Law Review* 56: 83–97.

Bankman, Joseph, and David A. Weisbach. 2005. "The Superiority of an Ideal Consumption Tax over an Ideal Income Tax." Olin Working Paper 251. Chicago: University of Chicago. http://ssrn.com/abstract=758645.

Bittker, Boris I., and Lawrence Lokken. 1999. *Federal Taxation of Income, Estates and Gifts,* 3rd ed. Boston: Warren, Gorham & Lamont.

Burke, Karen C., 2005. "*Castle Harbour:* Economic Substance and the Overall-Tax-Effect Test." *Tax Notes* 107(May 30): 1163.

Commission of the European Communities. 2004. "Report from the Commission to the Council and the European Parliament on the Use of Administrative Cooperation Arrangements in the Fight against VAT Fraud." Brussels: Commission of the European Communities. http://europa.eu.int/eur-lex/lex/LexUriServ/site/en/com/2004/com2004_0260en01.pdf

Engler, Mitchell A., and Michael S. Knoll. 2003. "Simplifying the Transition to a (Progressive) Consumption Tax." *SMU Law Review* 56: 53–81.

HM Revenue and Customs. 2005. "TAIA (Tax Avoidance Impact Assessment): Section 6 and Schedule 1 to the Finance (No 2) Act 2005." London: HM Revenue and Customs. Available at http://www.hmrc.gov.uk/library.htm under "Reference Documents," then under "Tax Avoidance Impact Assessments."

OECD (Organisation for Economic Co-operation and Development). 2004. *Consumption Tax Trends: VAT/GST and Excise Rates, Trends and Administration Issues.* Paris: OECD.

President's Advisory Panel on Federal Tax Reform. 2005. "Simple, Fair, and Pro-Growth: Proposals to Fix America's Tax System." Washington, DC: U.S. Government Printing Office.

Schler, Michael L. 2002. "Ten More Truths About Tax Shelters: The Problem, Possible Solutions, and a Reply to Professor Weisbach." *Tax Law Review* 55(3): 325.

Shaviro, Dan. 2000. *When Rules Change: An Economic and Political Analysis of Transition Relief and Retroactivity.* Chicago: University of Chicago Press.

U.S. Senate. 2005. *The Role of Professional Firms in the U.S. Tax Shelter Industry.* Report of the Permanent Subcommittee on Investigations of the Committee on Homeland Security and Governmental Affairs, April 13. Washington, DC: U.S. Senate.

Weisbach, David A. 2000. "Ironing Out the Flat Tax." *Stanford Law Review* 52:599–664.

———. 2003. "Does the X-Tax Mark the Spot?" *SMU Law Review* 56:201–38.

Edmund Outslay

ere I address the practical problems of taxing capital under the current U.S. income tax system and speculate on the potential problems of taxing capital under some form of consumption tax. This volume raises fertile areas of tax planning for those of us in tax accounting, to manage both tax liabilities and financial accounting net income (through reduction of the "income tax provision" subtracted from net income before taxes). These transactions provide the framework for master's-level business administration and tax planning courses built around the impact of taxes on managers' decisionmaking.[1] Little wonder, then, that as a tax accountant, I am most excited by the chapters presented in this session.

Each chapter, but particularly Joseph Bankman and Michael Schler's (chapter 6), eloquently points out that behavioral issues "bedeviling" the current income tax system are likely to remain under a consumption tax system. In addition, the reader quickly finds that the "devil is in the details" when it comes to crafting a new tax system, particularly with respect to transition rules. Faced with the daunting prospect of adopting a system that likely will be every bit as complex as the current system, readers could conclude "better the devil we know than the devil we don't know" when it comes to radical tax reform. A pessimist, or perhaps a pragmatist, might also conclude that, given the boundless ingenuity of tax practitioners, we are "doomed if we do and doomed if we don't" switch from an income tax system to a consumption tax system.

The Devil in the Details

Bankman and Schler point out that switching from an income tax to a modified (X-tax) consumption system presents formidable transition issues involving old capital (existing capital expenditures that are being depreciated over time) versus new capital (future capital expenditures that will be expensed). A plan without transition relief would amount to a tax on consumption from existing capital, which Bankman and Schler view as efficient but others see as promoting inefficient asset sales prior to the enactment date of the new law, to take advantage of the tax basis that otherwise would expire unused. As with the accelerated depreciation rules adopted in 1986 that applied only to new capital expenditures, complex "anti-churning" rules would have to be adopted to keep taxpayers from converting old capital into new capital through sales, exchanges, or leases. Similar issues involve whether to provide exemptions for small businesses, and how to handle the refundability of existing losses (many corporations currently have net operating loss carryovers in the billions of dollars) and future losses. The authors point out that, under an X-tax system, losses could be transferred through purchases of assets by profitable corporations using a subsidiary and then transferred to the ultimate user of the asset through sale of the subsidiary stock. All of these transactions would require retaining the subjective "judicial doctrines"—economic substance, business purpose, step transactions, "substance over form"—that currently plague the administration of the tax shelters that arose under the income tax system, necessitating rules to limit "trafficking in losses" and income shifting through transfer pricing and related party transactions (e.g., closely held corporations and their shareholders).

Better the Devil We Know

Bankman and Schler, as well as Edward Kleinbard (chapter 4) and Julie Roin (chapter 5), point out the "legal" ways in which taxpayers avoid taxes under the current income tax system, often through exploiting ambiguities in the technical language of the tax code. Kleinbard focuses on hybrid financial instruments that take on characteristics of debt and equity. Roin examines the shifting of income and deductions through the transfer pricing of cross-jurisdictional transactions between related parties. Bankman and Schler focus on "tax shelters" that involve the creation of noneconomic losses through basis shifting. In every case, the authors discuss the elaborate and highly complex rules developed under the current system to combat abuse of these tax strategies.

Roin and Bankman and Schler acknowledge that it is difficult to determine how susceptible their proposed changes to the tax system will be to avoidance or evasion activities. Roin points out that a shift to a territorial system would require cooperation with other taxing jurisdictions, which is no sure thing. Schler, the pragmatist, fears that taxpayer ingenuity will ultimately devise "loopholes" that he and Bankman haven't considered, and that the potential revenue loss from these yet undevised strategies may be even greater than the revenue loss from existing income-tax strategies. Bankman, the optimist, acknowledges the potential losses in revenue that could accrue from an X-tax system, but believes the opportunities for tax planning under a consumption tax are fewer than for under the current system. Kleinbard sees his cost of capital allowance proposal as impervious to gaming, but his proposal "fixes" only one feature of the current income tax system (financial instruments).

Reflections on the Broad Issues

In each of the chapters in this section, the authors analyzed each proposed shift from an income-based tax system to a consumption-based tax system, using primarily a tax (one-dimensional) perspective—revenues gained or lost, administrability, fairness. As someone who teaches tax accounting, I live in a two-dimensional world, one that encompasses taxation and financial reporting. Kleinbard touches on this second dimension in his discussion of how corporate tax directors pursue tax strategies to provide financial reporting reductions in the company's effective tax rate.[2] I believe we must consider that publicly traded companies will continue to live in an income world for financial reporting purposes, even if their tax world switches to a consumption tax.

In addition, a corporation's state and local taxes and a substantial portion of its international taxes will continue to be based on income. Although none of the authors touched on state taxes, my guess is that states would decouple their tax regimes from the federal regime and continue to use an income-based system. This would require corporations to compute both a consumption tax base and an income tax base for their activities, which would add to the cost and complexity of meeting their tax obligations.

The irony of ignoring the financial reporting implications of switching to a consumption tax is that the relation between financial reporting of net income and taxable income has never been under more scrutiny.[3] Since the 2003 Enron hearings conducted by the Senate Committee on Finance, Congress and the Treasury have explored ways to make a corporation's tax status more transparent on reported financial profits or losses (one result of which is the new Schedule M-3 to Form 1120, which asks for an extensive reconciliation of a corporation's book and tax differences). Treasury-supplied data from analysis of corporations with assets in excess of $2.5 billion (a surrogate for publicly traded corporations) indicate that such corporations paid approximately 65 percent of corporate income taxes collected from 1999 to 2003. No longer clandestine, corporations now seem proud to announce how much they paid to the U.S. Treasury in income taxes (Berkshire Hathaway announced it paid $3.3 billion in its 2003 annual report, and Wal-Mart announced it paid $4 billion in its 2004 annual report).

A shift to a consumption tax with full deductibility of capital expenditures would create significant financial reporting implications, which in the short run would reduce earnings. Under current accounting rules,[4] a "basis difference" between an asset's tax basis and its financial reporting basis creates deferred tax assets and liabilities on a company's balance sheet. In the case of capital assets, where tax depreciation generally exceeds book depreciation, the tax effects of the difference create a deferred tax liability. An immediate loss of existing tax basis would create a significant increase in such liabilities, with the resulting "debit" to tax expense, which would reduce net income. Going forward, the Financial Accounting Standards Board would have to reconsider how to account for consumption taxes, which likely would become "above the line" expenses (reducing net income before income taxes). Whether such taxes would lose what transparency they have under existing rules is an unresolved issue not addressed in this volume.

The "tone at the top" with respect to corporate tax planning has changed dramatically in the past several years. After the collapse of

Enron and WorldCom and the subsequent advent of the Sarbanes-Oxley Act and the Public Company Accounting Oversight Board, boards of directors of public companies have become much more reluctant to sanction aggressive ("uncertain") tax planning strategies. Where before "enhancing shareholder value" was a key driver behind tax-planning strategies, tax risk management has taken center stage at most publicly traded corporate tax departments and with their tax advisors. The disclosure rules, coupled with the resulting sanctions for failure to meet the requirements, led one of my colleagues to observe that the *practice* of taxation was now more complex than the tax rules themselves. The corporate governance environment in which publicly traded corporations now operate is such that corporations are not likely to indulge in the tax planning strategies described by Bankman and Schler unless motivated by a legitimate business purpose.

Whether or not a consumption tax is implemented at the corporate level, I concur with Kleinbard and Roin that corporations will continue to seek out lower-tax jurisdictions in which to earn their income, regardless of the type of tax regime in place. Any radical change in the U.S. tax system must consider the international tax-reduction opportunities such a switch would create. As much as some members of the European Union have tried to eliminate "harmful competition," I find it difficult to believe that tax base harmonization will ever be achieved.

Ultimately, the success of switching to a consumption tax rests with a commitment from Congress to refrain from using the tax system to affect taxpayer behavior. Congress has shown no inclination to make such a commitment. Absent such a pledge, a consumption tax system is likely to suffer the same fate as the 1986 tax reform changes, a slow deterioration to a special interest group–eroded tax system. Also, as this volume makes abundantly clear, a transition to a consumption tax system will not obviate the need for a tax administrative agency such as the Internal Revenue Service. Nor will it offer much relief from complexity. Despite the strong theoretical arguments in favor of a consumption tax system, the cost in dollars and in taxpayers' comprehension of instituting transition rules seem to outweigh the benefits. The reality is that we do not have a clean slate on which to devise a new system. That is not to say that we should throw up our hands in despair and live with the current system. Our willpower is lacking, not our brainpower.

NOTES

1. The popularity of such courses, particularly in master's-level business administration classes, can be traced to *Taxes and Business Strategy: A Planning Approach* (1992), coauthored by Mark A. Wolfson and Myron S. Scholes. The authors' objective in writing this text was to "equip readers with the ability to adapt quickly to the ever-changing set of tax rules they confront, and to improve their accuracy in predicting how the economic environment will change under alternative tax regimes" (xvii). One review described the text as being about "maximizing private wealth at the expense of the income tax. It is about private optimization without remorse" (Sims and Sunley 1992, 455).

2. For a more detailed discussion of the relationship between tax planning and financial reporting, see McGill and Outslay (2004).

3. See, for example, Boynton, DeFilippes, and Legel (2005); Mills, Newberry, and Trautman (2002); Mills and Plesko (2003); and Plesko (2002).

4. Income tax accounting is governed by Financial Accounting Statement No. 109, *Accounting for Income Taxes.*

REFERENCES

Boynton, Charles, Portia DeFilippes, and Ellen Legel. 2005. "Prelude to Schedule M-2: Schedule M-1 Corporate Book-Tax Difference Data 1990–2003." Working Paper. Washington, DC: U.S. Department of the Treasury.

McGill, Gary A., and Edmund Outslay. 2004. "Lost in Translation: Detecting Tax Shelter Activity in Financial Statements." *National Tax Journal* 57(3): 739–56.

Mills, Lillian, and George Plesko. 2003. "Bridging the Reporting Gap: A Proposal for More Informative Reconciling of Book and Tax Income." *National Tax Journal* 56(4): 865–93.

Mills, Lillian, Kaye Newberry, and William B. Trautman. 2002. "Trends in Book-Tax Income and Balance Sheet Differences." *Tax Notes* 96(8): 1109–24.

Plesko, George. 2002. "Reconciling Corporation Book and Tax Net Income, Tax Years 1996–1998." *SOI Bulletin* 21(4): 111–32.

Sims, Theodore S., and Emil M. Sunley. 1992. "Taxes and Business Strategy: A Planning Approach (Review)." *National Tax Journal* 45(4): 451–55.

Wolfson, Mark A., and Myron S. Scholes. 1992. *Taxes and Business Strategy: A Planning Approach.* New York: Prentice Hall.

George A. Plesko

In Joseph Bankman and Michael Schler's chapter 6, "Tax Planning under the Flat Tax," two scholars look at the same facts but reach different conclusions. Reading it with an open mind allowed me to decide which set of arguments was more persuasive. I came down on the side of Schler, who expressed general concern that the possibilities for both tax avoidance and the increased risk of new avoidance opportunities under a redesigned system are sufficient reasons not to abandon the current tax system.

I share Schler's overall concerns about how we would get from where we are now to a new tax system, and about what the system would eventually look like. While I am not afraid of uncertainty per se, I do worry about this particular uncertainty, especially when I compare the risks of implementing a new system against the alternative of improving the efficiency and administration of the current one. This chapter and the others in this volume further discuss moving to a consumption tax, helping us identify ways we could incrementally reform the current tax system.[1]

The historical evidence shows that people will adapt faster than structures during a transition to a new tax system. When it comes to taxes, the intelligent design of a new system is going to be trumped by the evolution of the participants. Bankman and Schler appear to agree that there would be fewer tax avoidance constraints under a consumption tax than under current law.

Even if the ability to avoid taxes is eventually controlled under an alternative system, its efficacy would rely, as Bankman and Schler describe, on the eventual collection of taxes with the same present value as is collected through a system that generates a specific stream, based on an annual levy with lower nominal values but collected earlier. The timing of receipts matters. Inherent in the consumption tax system outlined by Bankman and Schler is that the federal government would give up some—perhaps a lot of—control over the how receipts would be received. When taxpayers control deferral, the expected present value of those taxes may not be realized. Let me provide two current examples.

First, U.S. corporations have accumulated a large amount of unrepatriated foreign earnings. Under the U.S. tax system, corporations may defer domestic taxation on foreign earnings until those earnings are repatriated. Further, corporations do not report any income tax liability on their financial statements for foreign earnings classified as permanently reinvested. If repatriated, these earnings are subject to the regular corporate tax rates, less any adjustments for the foreign tax credit. Unrepatriated earnings have grown and companies' desire to bring those funds back to the United States has increased. Coupled with the current political climate, this desire has led Congress to enact a tax holiday that puts repatriations "on sale." That is, earnings held abroad, which under prior law would have been taxed at ordinary corporate income tax rates when repatriated, can for a time be brought back at a greatly reduced rate. Such rate changes in rates violate the assumptions that the political process will allow the amount of deferred tax owed to accumulate and that the Treasury will be able to collect large amounts of revenue at some undetermined date in the future. A casual observation: political pressures tend either to coincide with, or be created by, the periods when such large liabilities would be paid, and those political pressures work to eliminate or greatly reduce the liability.

The second example comes from intergenerational transfers. Large transfers of accumulated wealth will soon be taking place in the United States. Normally, such transfers would be subject to the estate tax, but recent political activity has revealed enormous political pressure to repeal or otherwise minimize it. This example also raises a basic question—what will happen in the future when there is pressure to engage in transactions that would cause massive realizations and tax liabilities. The ability to collect those revenues will depend on the political climate at that time, and such uncertainty, coupled with the possibility of influencing future tax rates, will affect companies' decisions in ways no one can yet anticipate.

Financial Reporting Considerations

Eliminating the corporate income tax would not end the need to measure corporate income. Publicly traded corporations are currently subject to two different sets of accounting rules: one to measure income and another to report it. Neither set is designed to assist in the preparation or reporting of the other and neither is designed to provide information to the users of the other. The one based on the tax code provides information to the government. The second, based on generally accepted accounting principles, provides financial information to external financial statement users. Over time, because of the evolution of U.S. capital markets, these two related but distinct measures have come to yield more information to the markets than either one alone.

The starting point for the corporate tax audit is reconciling financial reporting income with income reported on the tax return.[2] These numbers should not be the same, but the differences between the two must be explained. The importance of income reconciliation can be seen in the addition of the Form 1120, Schedule M-3.[3] Beginning in tax year 2004, the Schedule M-3 superseded the Schedule M-1 for large corporations. The new form requires detailed accounting of the various sources of income and expense differences between the two systems, as well as classifying the difference as temporary or permanent. A key feature of the M-3 is the requirement that companies reconcile their worldwide financial reporting income with the financial reporting income attributable to their tax entities. Some of this external validation of the firm's economic activity would be lost under a consumption tax. Other tools would have to be developed to assist in auditing.

The second issue is the general nature of financial reporting and financial information. Companies report tax expenses to their shareholders based on financial reporting income. They segregate current expense (which should approximate what is reported on their tax returns), from deferred expense (what they expect to pay in the future, or in the case of a deferred asset, to have refunded). While research reveals possible problems with using financial statements to infer taxable income or taxes paid, empirical evidence suggests that these data provide incremental information useful to the market for valuation (Hanlon 2003; McGill and Outslay 2004; Plesko 2000, 2003). Therefore, the existence of two reporting systems, and the current connections between them, appear to reinforce the value of data disseminated under each.[4] No one knows for sure whether consumption tax information might effectively replace the information currently available, but it appears that we would lose some information now used to value companies.

The last issue goes to the heart of the tax shelter debate and stems from the observation that we have dual accounting of the same underlying economic activity. Currently, the two accounting methods provide checks on both financial and tax earnings management. If businesses aggressively report financial earnings, for example, by reporting greater sales, they may pay a price through a higher current tax liability. Conversely, managers may assert less aggressive tax positions or use less aggressive tax planning devices because of the effect on reported earnings. Empirical evidence suggests that firms balance these competing reporting effects.[5] Replacement of the current system with a consumption tax base would eliminate this tradeoff because transactions aggressively executed to avoid the consumption tax would have no financial reporting cost. Aggressive financial reporting not only would have no tax consequence, it might not even be observed in the tax system.[6]

Accounting research should devote more thought to the economic foundations of capital income taxation and to the legal and reporting issues that would need to be addressed under a consumption tax. Accounting research, however, has much to contribute when trying to understand how the tax system affects the supply of information and the usefulness of the information provided.

Administrative Issues

I will close with three observations about the shift to a consumption tax and its effects. This list does not cover of all of the transition issues, nor is my discussion intended to be complete. These issues were not raised in any of the chapters and are largely beyond the scope of this volume, but will nevertheless need to be addressed either administratively or through legislation.

First, the notion of corporate income and its measurement predates not only the U.S. income tax and the Haig and Simons income concept, but the United States itself. As a result, an enormous taxation infrastructure is built on some sense of income, however defined.

National Income and Product Accounts

The National Income and Product Accounts (NIPA) measures *income.* One of the components of national income is corporate profits, based on tax return data collected by the Statistics of Income. While the amounts of corporate profits are driven by tax-return data, these data are supplemented with financial information to produce timely estimates of gross domestic product.[7] Current methods use a combination of both sets of data. Financial statement information becomes available three months after the end of a firm's fiscal year, while tax return data may not be available for an additional two years. The NIPA methodology uses financial reporting information to project future taxable income until the tax return data become available. This is another example of how two sets of measures of the same economic activity complement each other. The absence of a tax return–based measure of income under a consumption tax implies that, at a minimum, the methodology of the national accounts' corporate profits component would need to be substantially revised if *income* tax data were not available.

State Tax Systems

Most states impose their own income taxes on corporate income. Administratively, state tax reporting often starts with the first page of the federal tax return or substantially the same information. Without a federal income tax, states clearly would have to substantially change their own tax systems. If states retained their own income taxes and imposed the reporting requirements necessary to maintain them, federal abandonment of income taxation could actually *increase* compliance costs.[8]

Internal Revenue Service Transition

Even if the replacement of income taxation with consumption taxation were otherwise quick and seamless, with legislation passed in one year and regulations issued by the beginning of the next, substantial resources would still have to be left in place to administer the old income tax system. For at least four to five years, and probably more, the Internal Revenue Service would need to devote substantial resources to auditing the last year of income tax returns, and many additional years would be needed to litigate and ultimately resolve any disputes.

NOTES

1. See Kleinbard's proposal (chapter 4) for reforming the taxation of financial instruments.

2. See Manzon and Plesko (2002), and Plesko (2002, 2004), for an introduction to book-tax differences and the magnitude of the adjustments based on both publicly available and proprietary (tax return) data. Boynton, DeFilippes, and Legel (2005) provide a long-time series of differences in the amounts of reported income based on tax return tabulations.

3. The foundations for these differences can be found in Mills and Plesko (2003).

4. See Hanlon and Shevlin (2005) for an overview and discussion of these issues.

5. Mills (1998) shows that differences in reported book and taxable income can affect the tax audit. Mills and Sansing (2000) address strategic issues in reporting. Erickson, Hanlon, and Maydew (2003) show that some firms were willing to pay additional taxes to report fraudulently higher earnings. Plesko (2005) estimates the extent that discretionary reporting under each system is reflected in the other. For a general discussion of the role of tax and financial reporting tradeoffs, see Shackelford and Shevlin (2001).

6. Because consumption taxes are generally treated like any other expense, the firm's incentives actually become aligned—minimizing consumption tax payments would *increase* reported earnings.

7. Financial statement information becomes available three months after the end of a company's fiscal year, while tax return data may not be available for an additional two years.

8. Strauss (1997) provides a thorough introduction and analysis of the state and local implications of a federal consumption tax.

REFERENCES

Boynton, Charles, Portia DeFilippes, and Ellen Legel. 2005. "Prelude to Schedule M-3: Schedule M-1 Corporate Book-Tax Difference Data 1990–2003." Working Paper. Washington, DC: U.S. Department of the Treasury.

Erickson, Merle, Michelle Hanlon, and Edward L. Maydew. 2003. "How Much Will Firms Pay for Earnings that Do Not Exist? Evidence of Taxes Paid on Allegedly Fraudulent Earnings." *Accounting Review* 79(2): 387–408.

Hanlon, Michelle. 2003. "What Can We Infer about a Firm's Taxable Income from Its Financial Statements?" *National Tax Journal* 56(4): 831–63.

Hanlon, Michelle, and Terry J. Shevlin. 2005. "Book-Tax Conformity for Corporate Income: An Introduction to the Issues." *Tax Policy and the Economy* 19:101–34.

Manzon, Gil B., and George A. Plesko. 2002. "The Relation between Financial and Tax Reporting Measures of Income." *Tax Law Review* 55(2): 175–214.

McGill, Gary A., and Edmund Outslay. 2004. "Lost in Translation: Detecting Tax Shelter Activity in Financial Statements." *National Tax Journal* 57(3): 739–56.

Mills, Lillian F. 1998. "Book-Tax Differences and Internal Revenue Service Adjustments." *Journal of Accounting Research* 36(2): 343–56.

Mills, Lillian F., and George A. Plesko. 2003. "Bridging the Reporting Gap: A Proposal for More Informative Reconciling of Book and Tax Income." *National Tax Journal* 56(4): 865–93.

Mills, Lillian F., and Richard C. Sansing. 2000. "Strategic Tax and Financial Reporting Decisions: Theory and Evidence." *Contemporary Accounting Research* 17(1): 85–106.

Plesko, George A. 2000. "Book-Tax Differences and the Measurement of Corporate Income." In *Proceedings of the Ninety-Second Annual Conference on Taxation, 1999* (171–76). Washington, DC: National Tax Association.

———. 2002. "Reconciling Corporation Book and Tax Net Income, Tax Years 1996–1998." *SOI Bulletin* 21(4): 1–16.

———. 2003. "An Evaluation of Alternative Measures of Corporate Tax Rates." *Journal of Accounting and Economics* 35(2): 201–26.

———. 2004. "Corporate Tax Avoidance and the Properties of Corporate Earnings." *National Tax Journal* 57(3): 729–37.

———. 2005. "Estimates of the Magnitude of Financial and Tax Reporting Conflicts." Working Paper. Storrs: University of Connecticut School of Business.

Shackelford, Douglas A., and Terry J. Shevlin. 2001. "Empirical Tax Research in Accounting." *Journal of Accounting and Economics* 31(1-3): 321–87.

Strauss, Robert. 1997. "Administrative and Revenue Implications of Federal Consumption Taxes for the State and Local Sector." *American Journal of Tax Policy* 14(8): 361–452.

PART IV
Concluding Comments

Henry J. Aaron

The chapters and comments in this book have considerably advanced our understanding of the issues surrounding the taxation of capital income. William Gentry and Glenn Hubbard, George Zodrow, Al Warren, Joe Bankman, David Weisbach, and others have helped clarify the differences between a pure income and a pure consumption tax. The basic conclusion of these authors seems to be that the shift from a pure income to a pure consumption tax is less consequential than many of us think it is. By implication, the choice between these two pure forms of taxation relies more on administrative considerations than on philosophy or even distributional preference. In the remarkably clear exposition of David Weisbach,

> The risk-free return has historically been close to zero. All that an income tax taxes that a consumption tax does not is this amount. Therefore, an income tax taxes vanishingly little not taxed under a consumption tax. Notwithstanding the long debate over the two tax bases, they are essentially the same. (2005)

Is this view correct? Weisbach himself wonders why, if his analysis is correct, intense debate on whether to tax income or consumption has gone on for centuries. I shall attempt to answer that very question.

The literature dismissing the significance of the distinction between income and consumption tax uses an abstract model; the first step is to determine if it provides useful guidance about changes in our messy tax system. We all know the clichéd story about the drunk who looked under the lamppost for the object he lost because "that is where the light is." My impression is that this literature makes a similar mistake. It conjures up an imaginary world in which certain relationships hold and then applies those relationships to a real world in which those relationships do not hold.[1]

The current tax system is not close to an ideal tax system of any stripe, income or consumption. What we have, as many have noted, is a hybrid system that violates the canons of both pure forms. Most filers are subject to a system approximating the consumption tax, in the sense that income from most of their directly owned assets is substantially untaxed. Few people have significant assets besides their owned home, social security, qualified retirement accounts, and other tax-sheltered saving. All of those assets receive consumption tax treatment—or better, since taxpayers display remarkable skill at deducting interest and other capital payments while deferring or avoiding tax altogether on capital income.

Current taxes differ in at least the following ways from idealized consumption and income taxes:

- some equity investments are taxed not once, but twice; others are taxed less than once, at concessionary rates, or not at all; still others are subsidized;
- depreciation does not reflect loss of economic value;
- inflation gains are taxed;
- taxes on gains are taxed not as accrued, but are deferred or are permanently forgiven;
- tax arbitrage and shelters result in negative effective rates of tax to some forms of investment; and
- diverse tax regimes in different nations create large and, it would seem, growing opportunities to avoid or evade tax altogether, not just on the risk-free component of capital income, but on the whole package and on labor income to boot.

It is difficult and often unwise, therefore, to draw inferences from distinctions that exist in the imaginary world of idealized income and consumption taxes about how to deal with these and other problems. The practical questions raised by Bankman and Schler (chapter 6) tell me—and should tell Bankman—that moving to a progressive wage tax on individuals and some sort of value-added tax (VAT) on businesses that have a wage deduction is so fraught with risks that the trip is not worth taking. And these risks are magnified by the inevitable complexities of transition rules.

This book also instructs me that the differences between the two regimes, even in the imaginary worlds of idealized taxes, are not as insignificant as some of the literature suggests. Consider the difference between an income VAT and a consumption VAT. The former requires depreciation; the latter permits expensing. The present value of expensing is larger than the present value of the same nominal quantity of depreciation. The difference depends on the discount rate. If the discount rate is 0.5 percent, for example, straight-line depreciation over 20 years is worth a bit more than 95 percent as much as expensing. The difference hardly seems worth much excitement. When the interest rate gets up to 3 percent, then depreciation is worth only 76 percent of expensing. And at the unthinkable rate of 10 percent, which is well below the hurdle rate used by many corporations in planning investments, straight-line depreciation over 20 years is worth only 44 percent as much as expensing.

But what is the right interest rate to use? According to various contributors to the "it doesn't make much difference" literature, the answer to this question is the riskless spot rate. Individuals or the government can alter their portfolios, buy or sell short, or engage in other transactions that would excuse from tax most or all capital income other than the reward for waiting, which doesn't need to be much if time preference is a measly 0.5 percent. Almost all that is involved is timing. The present value of the tax collected on all components of capital income other than the reward to waiting is unaffected by when it is collected (assuming constant tax rates).

But no one, to the best of my knowledge, has shown that people actually base economic decisions, private or public, on such rates. Few businesses would prefer straight-line depreciation on a 20-year asset over expensing 95 percent of the purchase price. Does cash in hand not matter?

To approach matters from a different perspective, the "it doesn't matter much" reasoning is based on infinite horizon models.[2] But over any finite horizon, income tax revenues (discounted) are often substantially in excess of consumption tax revenues, since much consumption is deferred beyond any finite period. Invoking infinity leads to a different conclusion from one that applies over any finite period. And then, since the capital stock usually grows at about the same rate as income, the tax is never collected. The advantage to net savers endures, even if they pass on higher amounts of tax liability to future generations.

For a moment, grant that only the tax on the return to waiting distinguishes income and consumption taxation. U.S. gross domestic product

(GDP) in 2006 was approximately $13 trillion. If we take the U.S. capital/output ratio as approximately three to one, the U.S. capital stock would be $39 trillion. (I ignore whether that capital is owned by people subject to U.S. or foreign taxes, but the figure for capital ownership by U.S. citizens is still approximately correct.) The labor share of GDP is about 0.7; the share of capital is about 0.3. The average tax rate—federal, state, and local—is about 0.33.

The average effective rate of tax on capital income is 0.1 (rounding Slemrod's chapter 1 estimate down), which means that total effective taxes on capital income are $13 trillion × 0.3 × 0.1 = $390 billion.

If the riskless rate of return is 1 percent (a bit higher than Bankman and Schler [chapter 6]), then the riskless yield on the U.S. capital stock is $39 trillion × 0.01 = $390 billion. This crude arithmetic suggests one of the following possibilities: (1) Slemrod's estimate of the tax burden on capital is too high; (2) capital taxes actually fall on a lot more than the riskless return to capital; (3) the riskless return is a lot more than 1 percent. We have a puzzle!

And I haven't even mentioned the possibility that a switch from an income to a consumption tax could impose unacceptable burdens on the poor, necessitating offsetting tax and expenditure programs with their own sets of costs. Redistribution does matter. Whether Gentry and Hubbard (1998) or Toder and Rueben (chapter 3) are right about distribution, this debate is *not* about chump change.

NOTES

1. For example, Weisbach posits unlimited lending, so that investors subject to tax can create the same objective investment situation that would have existed in the no tax world. Unlimited borrowing does not exist.

2. Infinite horizon models include all events, stretching in to the infinite future, discounted to present value.

REFERENCES

Gentry, William M., and R. Glenn Hubbard. 1998. "Fundamental Tax Reform and Corporate Financial Policy." In *Tax Policy and the Economy*, vol. 12, edited by James M. Poterba (191–227). Cambridge, MA: MIT Press.

Weisbach, David. 2005. "The (Non)taxation of Risk." *Tax Law Review* 58(1).

CONCLUDING COMMENT

C. Eugene Steuerle

T his book does a marvelous job in expanding on the continuous debate over the taxation of property and income from property—a debate as old as civilization itself. A few issues stand out in my mind.

Too little attention is given to one anomalous consequence of simply converting the income tax to a consumption tax: the rich would be taxed on the basis of consumption, but the poor and middle class, mainly on their income. That is, even if the income tax is replaced with a consumption tax, all but the wealthiest will continue to face an income tax through the phaseout of various program benefits, ranging from educational aid to wage subsidies. This qualification is not a minor one, as the implicit income tax rates resulting from these benefit phaseouts are often quite high. No one suggests similarly converting these income-tax-like benefit phaseouts to a consumption base. Given the high income tax rates faced by low- and moderate-income taxpayers, removal of capital taxation ought to begin with those with modest incomes or, alternatively, for the first few percentage points of a return on assets. The reason for the opposite, upside-down focus on the richer members of society seems mainly political.

If much of the income tax accounting remains even as the income tax is replaced, much of the alleged simplification (other than substituting expensing for depreciation) stressed by consumption tax advocates simply goes out the window. In fact, our tax system could become more complicated, since it would include major elements of both consumption tax and income tax accounting and reporting systems. Moreover, income accounting for capital income is still required for financial accounting purposes.

Yet another issue often ignored in the consumption tax debate is that big up-front deductions for capital expenses can reduce competition from new businesses. During the debate over President Ronald Reagan's tax reform, the Treasury maintained correctly that large "front-loaded" deductions under the accelerated cost recovery system "are of little value to new and rapidly growing firms or to firms in ailing industries, neither of which can fully utilize their benefits" (Office of the Secretary, U.S. Treasury 1984, 109). This problem would arise under many types of consumption taxes, threatening to increase the concentration of power among fewer companies. In principle, this problem could be mitigated by allowing firms to sell their deductions or carry them forward with interest, but, in practice, we probably would not trust government to be able to deal with the resulting compliance problems.

Compliance is a major issue under a consumption tax because the amount at stake is sometimes bigger than under an income tax, as Bankman and Schler (chapter 6) make clear. Taxpayers do try to reduce taxes today, in the hope that they will not have to pay tomorrow—that the law will change, that they won't be caught, or, if they are bankrupt, that someone else will be left with the tab. When taxpayers play this game, the government gets stuck with the risk that the taxpayer might be right. In effect, taxpayers decide if the government will make the equivalent of loans to them at a market interest rate. Who is left insuring the loan?

Perhaps we should refocus the consumption–income tax debate on how best to tax society's "winners"—those with unusually high earnings or supernormal rates of return on savings—rather than whether to tax capital income. Taxing winners involves more than figuring out whether to tax extraordinary returns or the return to risk. According to the benefit theory of taxation, people should be taxed based on the benefits they are receiving now. That theory justifies taxes on wealth because wealth accumulation depends on public services such as defense and a legal system that allows it. The theory of consumption taxation contradicts this line of argument when it suggests that future generations should pay a delayed tax for some benefits purchased today.

Likewise, how should a nation distribute the variety of costs that society accepts for itself when the motive is more altruistic and the taxpayer receives few benefits? For instance, consider compensating the victims of natural disasters. Does a smaller amount of current consumption, regardless of wealth, provide an appealing case for reducing one's share of the burden of helping Hurricane Katrina's victims?

I once showed that we do collect tax on capital—but mainly through the corporate tax, not the personal tax (Steuerle 1985). This seems consistent with findings by Joel Slemrod (chapter 1). Corporations and businesses also withhold most of the taxes individuals pay. Whatever the tax world of the future, corporations and businesses will likely continue to be the principal tax collectors for the government. The consumption–income tax debate will be settled in part by just how well they can continue to perform that role, whether or not we collect taxes on capital income.

Finally, two factors weigh in favor of moving at least partially toward consumption taxation. From an equity standpoint, it seems fairer to tax those with equal earnings equally, and not penalize those who save their wages. From an efficiency standpoint, educational outlays are (almost always) expensed. Most are provided by government or by business through learning on the job. Why physical investment should be treated less favorably is unclear, unless the choice is dictated by distributional considerations. Distributional issues, however, might be just as easily solved through rules of transfer programs like Social Security or, where necessary, supplementary estate or inheritance taxes.

REFERENCES

Office of the Secretary, U.S. Treasury. 1984. *Tax Reform for Fairness, Simplicity, and Economic Growth*, vol. 1. Washington, DC: U.S. Treasury.

Steuerle, C. Eugene. 1985. *Taxes, Loans, and Inflation: How the Nation's Wealth Becomes Misallocated.* Washington, DC: Brookings Institution Press.

Daniel Halperin

This book addresses two distinct questions: the first concerns the distribution of tax burdens, the second, incentives.

First, if we switched to consumption taxation, would we be able to maintain the current distribution of tax burdens? The present income tax falls on investment income, which is received mostly by high-income households. Second, would a shift from income to consumption taxation significantly change incentives to save and invest? In addition, if we consider differences in tax rates across various sectors, would a real-life consumption tax actually be more uniform than an income tax in dealing with the sectors?

It has been argued that neither an income nor a consumption tax taxes the return to capital, even if a tax is nominally imposed (Weisbach 2005). I am skeptical that this is true for an income tax because the argument rests on a belief that borrowing without limit is possible. Is this assumption realistic in all circumstances?

But a fundamental question is, if we want the tax system to remain as progressive as it is today, how would we count the tax that is nominally paid on the return to risk? Will this amount count as a tax burden on investors that has to be replicated under a new, equally progressive system? Or do we say that since nobody has ever really paid tax on the return to risk, we don't have to duplicate it?

I am not convinced that a change to a consumption tax makes sense. Eric Toder and Kim Rueben (chapter 3) closely summarize why I think adopting a consumption tax would be a bad idea. David Weisbach, in his remarks on Toder and Rueben and George Zodrow (chapter 2), questions skepticism about a consumption tax—anticipating the questions I would raise. It is not enough to believe that a consumption tax may well be simpler or more economically efficient than an income tax. We need to know much more than we do now about these supposed improvements. If we are going to undertake an experiment of this size and this uncertainty, we should have strong evidence that the payoff will be large, not just that there is some potential gain. Because generous transition rules are a virtual certainty, the evidence suggests to me that efficiency gains would be small.

I am also concerned about whether we can keep the same relative distribution of after-tax income under a consumption tax. Toder and Rueben show that to do so, nominal rates would have to be significantly higher than they are now. Imposing higher nominal rates under a consumption tax would be more difficult because many who would face these rates would actually have a significant tax increase. Only those who get almost all of their income from capital and very little from labor would get a tax cut. Therefore, that such a large group of high-income people would accept this tax increase strikes me as unlikely.

One further point: the important goal when transitioning to a consumption tax would be to maintain the distribution of after-tax income, which is not the same as maintaining equality of tax payments. The taxpayers' burden may go up, while their after-tax income increases—particularly if investors now earn lower before-tax income when the income tax burden is reduced. However, the normal practice in the legislative process is to consider nominal tax payments. If this practice were followed, the distribution of after-tax income would more likely be distorted in favor of the wealthy.

The argument that a consumption tax would be both simpler and cause fewer distortions is equally troubling. A zero tax rate on capital income is not the minimum rate. Congress would want to perpetuate tax expenditures and to provide incentives through the tax system. Much, if not most, of the distortion in the income tax results from explicit congressional policy, not from the technical difficulties of measuring income. I would be shocked if favoritism for housing and the mortgage interest deduction disappeared. State and local governments would continue to insist on preferences for their bonds. Other sectors that enjoy preferences today would want to retain them. We have seen the difficulty with efforts to integrate corporate and shareholder taxes or to make relief of taxes on dividends depend upon whether the corporation actually paid taxes. Those corporations with preferences fought that proposal which could have reduced the overall tax burden on corporations to zero. Corporations that were closer to zero didn't want to extend that benefit to other corporations if the tax burden on the shareholders of the former would be unchanged.

I also question whether personal savings will increase under a consumption tax, particularly if we expect generous transition rules. Much depends on whether we believe that the difference in the tax burden on savings between the current income tax and a consumption tax is large or small. If the difference is small, as I believe would be true for most people, the chances of increasing savings significantly must be fairly small. As far as saving is concerned, we should worry whether qualified pension plans will continue to exist in a consumption tax world. If they don't, overall saving might increase as saving by lower- and moderate-income filers falls—at least if other saving incentives were not introduced; these incentives could be complex and, again, require less-than-zero rates on at least some capital income.

On the other side, we do need to worry that the income tax system, with all the pressures on it, may well self-destruct, particularly given current political forces. The nation could then end up with no federal tax on capital and an interest deduction. If that is the case, obviously a consumption tax would be preferable.

Of course, we are not there yet. If we have the will, the current debate indicates that we can improve America's income tax system.

REFERENCE

Weisbach, David. 2005. "The (Non)Taxation of Risk." *Tax Law Review* 58(1).

Glossary

2005 Advisory Panel on Federal Tax Reform: A bipartisan panel established by President George W. Bush to advise on reforming the tax code. The panel proposed two options: a simplified income tax and a variant on the Hall-Rabushka flat tax with an additional tax on some capital income. See Hall-Rabushka flat tax.

Accelerated depreciation: A measure that allows businesses to write off the value of assets faster than some normal schedule that in theory represents the rate at which they actually wear out or become obsolete. See depreciation, straight-line depreciation.

Alternative minimum tax (AMT): A floor on individual or corporate income tax liability. The floor is computed by adding certain so-called "preference items" to regular taxable income and calculating tax under an alternate rate schedule. Technically, the AMT is the difference between regular income tax and the tax computed under the AMT rules.

Average effective tax rate: The ratio of taxes collected to the pretax return. See collections-based measure.

Business Enterprise Income Tax (BEIT): A tax reform proposal that redefines the income tax base applicable to business operations and addresses the different types of taxes on different capital instruments (including derivatives) with a single comprehensive regime. The BEIT includes imputations of returns when income is not recognized immediately.

Capital export neutrality: A theoretical system in which the overall burden of taxation on capital owned by residents of a given country is the same whether that capital is invested abroad or at home. See capital import neutrality.

Capital import neutrality: A theoretical system in which overall burden of taxation on capital income earned within a given country is the same, regardless of the investor's country of residence. See capital export neutrality.

Capital income: Income derived from capital assets such as interest, dividends, capital gains, rents, and royalties.

Collections-based measure: A measure used to estimate income taxes that involves dividing collected taxes by income or pretax returns. For capital income, this requires allocating shares of proprietors' income and partners' income between capital and labor and estimating individual taxes on capital income. See investment-based measure.

Comprehensive business income tax: A tax proposed by the U.S. Treasury in 1992 that would have applied consistent tax rules to all forms of capital income generated by business, regardless of whether financed by debt or equity.

Consumption tax: Taxation based on consumption instead of some other measure of ability to pay (most commonly, income). A tax on consumption can be levied directly through sales, excise taxes, or value-added taxes, or indirectly through a tax on income with a deduction for net saving.

Cost of capital allowance system: A provision of the Business Enterprise Income Tax that replaces the current treatment of debt capital, equity capital, and the various species of derivatives with a uniform allowance for issuers, and a mandatory income inclusion to investors. See Business Enterprise Income Tax.

Deadweight loss: The cost to society of a wasteful allocation of resources arising from taxation or other market imperfections. For example, tax arbitrage can make low-yielding investments profitable, even though their poor yield represents a loss to society. Deadweight loss also includes the transaction costs involved in engaging in tax-motivated activities.

Depreciation: A measure of the decrease in the value of the capital stock, or a method of attributing the cost of an asset across the useful life of the asset. In theory, depreciation is simply the change in the value of a physical asset that is wearing away or becoming obsolete.

Discount rate: The rate of return required to postpone the use of capital for a year, also called the time value of money. The discount rate is used to determine the present value of future cash flows. For example, at a 5 percent discount rate, the present value of $105 in an account next year is equal to $100 this year.

Economic income: A comprehensive measure of income that includes wages and salaries, other returns to labor, returns to capital (whether realized or not), and other income.

Economic rents: See inframarginal returns.

Entrepreneurial household: A household that owns one or more active businesses.

Excise tax: A tax on the manufacture or sale of a particular good or service.

Extraordinary returns: See inframarginal returns.

Flat tax: A more progressive variant of the value-added tax in which labor costs are deductible to the employer and taxable to the employee. Employees are taxed at one rate on their labor incomes above a threshold amount. Business cash flow is taxed at the same flat rate.

Formulary taxation: A taxation approach in which a multinational firm's profits would be allocated among different jurisdictions in proportion to payroll, property, or sales, or some combination, in each jurisdiction. Most U.S. states determine their share of a taxpayer's U.S. income by a formula based on some weighted average of the ratio of the taxpayer's property, payroll, and sales located within the state to the taxpayer's total property, payroll, and sales.

Haig-Simons income: The sum of a person's consumption expenditures and the increase (or decrease) in that person's net worth in a given time period. (This definition of income includes both realized and unrealized capital gains, for example.) See economic income.

Hall-Rabushka flat tax: A flat tax proposal, developed in the 1980s, that assesses a 19 percent tax on all businesses (corporate or otherwise). It is identical to a version of value-added taxation, except that wages, pension contributions, materials costs, and capital investments are deducted from the tax base. Individuals (or households) are assessed a 19 percent flat-rate tax on wages and pension benefits above an exemption of $25,500 for a family of four. See flat tax.

Horizontal equity: The principle that similarly situated people (e.g., with a similar ability to pay taxes) should be treated similarly (e.g., taxed equally). See vertical equity.

Income shifting: Shifting profits or losses from one division of a business to another so that deductions are taken in high-tax jurisdictions and profits in low-tax ones.

Infinite horizon models: Economic models in which agents live forever and plan accordingly. The models approximate a situation in which people care about future generations. Because people's behavior depends in part on future policies, the use of these models requires analysts to make assumptions about budgetary policies beyond the immediate term.

Inflation-protected securities: Securities whose principal is tied to the an inflation index, such as the consumer price index. For United States Treasury Inflation-Protected Securities (TIPS), the principal increases with inflation and decreases with deflation. When a TIPS matures, the holder is paid the original or adjusted principal, whichever is greater.

Inframarginal returns: Returns to assets that are greater than the normal returns necessary to compensate the asset's owner for bearing risk and deferring consumption. Alternately associated with super-normal returns, windfall profits, or rents.

Interest rate swaps: A transaction in which one party exchanges a stream of interest for another party's stream to hedge exposure to interest rate fluctuations.

Investment-based measure: A measure used to estimate capital income taxes based on the stream of returns from investments using an aftertax discount rate and estimates of the pretax return based on statutory provisions (tax rate, depreciation schedules, taxations of pensions) and how they play out over time. See collections-based measure.

Labor income: Income derived from working (including salary, wages, employee benefits).

Marginal effective tax rate: The share of return paid in tax on the last dollar of investment. It is the ratio of the difference between expected pretax rate of return and the expected aftertax rate of return to the pretax rate of return for the marginal investment.

Nominal payments: Payments that are unadjusted for inflation. For example, a payment of $10,000 today and a payment of $10,000 in 30 years are the same nominally but not in real terms. See real payments.

Nominal rate of return: The rate of return (e.g., interest rate) unadjusted for inflation. See real rate of return.

Normal returns: Minimum returns on assets necessary to compensate for the time value of money plus any risk. See inframarginal return, discount rate, risk premium.

Notional income: Income that a person is *treated* as having even though it is not currently received in cash. See economic income, Haig-Simons income.

Partnership: Defined by the Internal Revenue Service as an unincorporated organization whose two or more members carry on a trade, business, financial operation, or venture and divide its profits. A partnership is subject to complex rules of taxation under the current U.S. tax code (designed to allocate income and loss for tax purposes properly among the partners).

Progressivity: See vertical equity.

Progressive consumption tax: A consumption tax with a graduated rate structure. For example, see X tax, flat tax.

R-based tax: A consumption tax that ignores financial transactions. That is, the tax applies to real transactions but not financial transactions.

Real payments: Payments on assets after removing the effects of inflation. See nominal payments.

Real rate of return: Returns to assets over and above the rate of inflation. See nominal rate of return.

Refundability: Feature of certain tax credits in which the excess of the benefit one is entitled to claim over the taxes due is refunded to the taxpayer. For example, if one is entitled to claim a $1,000 refundable tax credit and owed $700 in income tax before the credit, the credit would offset the entire $700 in tax liability and the remaining $300 would be rebated as a tax refund.

Return to risk bearing: Since a certain level of return can be achieved without assuming any risk (the risk-free rate of return), financial instruments of greater risk must pay a higher expected (or average) return. See risk premium.

Risk premium: The higher expected return for a risky investment that is necessary to compensate holders for the risk. See return to risk bearing.

Risk-free return: In theory, the risk-free rate of return is the return paid on safe investments. In practice, inflation-protected United States Treasury bills are sometimes viewed as riskless because of their low probability of default and short maturation period. Also known as the riskless rate of return.

Risky returns: See return to risk bearing and investment-based measure.

Straight-line depreciation: Deduction of the cost of an asset in equal installments over a number of years (the depreciation period). See accelerated depreciation.

Super-normal returns: See inframarginal returns.

Tax arbitrage: Taking advantage of an imbalance in a market or markets (e.g., two different prices for the same thing) to produce a zero- or low-risk investment strategy that yields positive returns. Tax arbitrage takes advantage of different taxation of economically equivalent activities. Thus, for example, if an investor can produce a set of financial transactions that generates fully deductible losses that are eventually repaid in the form of lightly taxed capital gains, he or she can profit after taxes even if the overall investment just breaks even or produces a small loss.

Transfer prices: The prices of goods and services exchanged within a multidivisional organization. Firms have incentives to manipulate transfer prices so that profit is allocated to jurisdictions with low tax rates and deductions are allocated to high-tax jurisdictions.

Transferability of losses: See income shifting.

Uniform commodity taxation: A tax system in which all goods and services are taxed at the same rate, whether consumed today or in the future.

Uniform taxation of present and future consumption goods is equivalent to a zero tax rate on the normal return to capital.

Urban–Brookings Tax Policy Center Microsimulation Model: A large-scale microsimulation model of the U.S. federal tax system—similar to models the Congressional Budget Office, the Joint Committee on Taxation, and the Treasury's Office of Tax Analysis use—that calculates the tax liability for a representative sample of households, both under current rules and under alternative scenarios. Based on these calculations, the model produces estimates of the revenue consequences of different tax policy choices, as well as their effects on the distribution of tax liabilities and marginal effective tax rates.

Value-added tax: A broad-based business tax imposed at each stage of the production and distribution process that, when applied nationally, is typically designed to tax final household consumption. See flat tax.

Vertical equity: A concept of fairness that people with greater means or lesser needs should pay on net more in taxes less benefits. As applied to the tax system, it is commonly taken also to imply that they should pay a higher *share* of income in taxes. Also called progressivity. See horizontal equity.

Windfall profits tax: See inframarginal returns.

X tax: A tax similar to a flat tax except that it allows for multiple rates for labor income above the exemption level. The remainder of the value-added tax base is taxed the highest tax rate applied to labor income. See flat tax.

Yield-exempt income tax: An income tax that applies to earnings only and exempts returns on investments (interest, dividends, and capital gains). The Roth IRA, in which contributions to the account come from after-tax income, but the returns and withdrawals from the account are tax-free, is an example of yield-exempt treatment of income.

About the Editors

Henry J. Aaron is currently a Bruce and Virginia MacLaury Senior Fellow in the Economic Studies Program at the Brookings Institution. From 1990 through 1996, he was the director of the Economic Studies Program. In 1996, he was a Guggenheim Fellow at the Center for Advanced Studies in the Behavioral Sciences at Stanford University. From 1967 to 1989, he taught economics at the University of Maryland. He also served as assistant secretary for planning and evaluation in 1977 and 1978 at the Department of Health, Education, and Welfare, and in 1979, chaired the Advisory Council on Social Security. He has been vice-president and member of the executive committee of the American Economic Association and president of the Association of Public Policy and Management.

Leonard E. Burman is director of the Tax Policy Center, senior fellow at the Urban Institute, and visiting professor at Georgetown University. Dr. Burman served as deputy assistant secretary of the Treasury for Tax Analysis from 1998 to 2000, and as senior analyst at the Congressional Budget Office from 1988 to 1997. He is the author of *The Labyrinth of Capital Gains Tax Policy: A Guide for the Perplexed*, and numerous articles, studies, and reports. He is also a commentator for *Marketplace*. His recent research has examined the individual alternative minimum tax, the changing role of taxation in social policy, and tax incentives for savings, retirement, and health insurance.

C. Eugene Steuerle is a senior fellow at the Urban Institute and codirector of the Urban–Brookings Tax Policy Center. He is also the author, coauthor, editor, or coeditor of eleven books and close to 1,000 articles, columns, testimonies, and reports. His latest book is *Contemporary U.S. Tax Policy*. Among many other positions, he has served as deputy assistant secretary of the Treasury for Tax Analysis (1987–1989), president of the National Tax Association (2001–2002), chair of the 1999 Technical Panel advising Social Security on its methods and assumptions, and president of the National Economists Club Educational Foundation. Between 1984 and 1986, he served as Economic Coordinator and original organizer of the Treasury's tax reform effort, for which one top Treasury wrote that 1986 tax reform "would not have moved forward without your early leadership."

About the Contributors

Alan J. Auerbach is the Robert D. Burch Professor of Economics and Law, director of the Burch Center for Tax Policy and Public Finance, and former chair of the economics department at the University of California, Berkeley. He is also a research associate of the National Bureau of Economic Research and previously taught at Harvard and the University of Pennsylvania, where he also served as economics department chair. Professor Auerbach was deputy chief of staff of the U.S. Joint Committee on Taxation in 1992 and has been a consultant to several government agencies and institutions in the United States and abroad. A former vice president of the American Economic Association, he was editor of that association's *Journal of Economic Perspectives* and is now editor of its new *American Economic Journal: Economic Policy*. Professor Auerbach is a fellow of the Econometric Society and of the American Academy of Arts and Sciences.

Joseph Bankman is a leading scholar in the field of tax law and the author of two widely used casebooks on the subject. His writings on tax policy cover topics such as progressivity, consumption tax, and the role of tax in the structure of Silicon Valley start-ups. He has gained wide attention for his work on how government might control the use of tax shelters and has testified before Congress and other legislative bodies on tax compliance problems posed by the cash economy. He has worked with the state of California, coauthoring a bill that helps simplify tax filing by giving low-income taxpayers the option of receiving a Ready Return—a completed tax return prepared by the state. Before joining the Stanford faculty in 1989, Professor Bankman was a professor at the University of Southern California Law Center and a tax practitioner with the Los Angeles firm of Tuttle & Taylor.

Jane G. Gravelle is currently a senior specialist in economic policy in the government and finance division of CRS. She specializes in the economics of taxation, particularly the effects of tax policies on economic growth and resource allocation. Recent papers have addressed consumption taxes, dynamic revenue estimating, investment subsidies, capital gains taxes, individual retirement accounts, estate and gift taxes, family tax issues, charitable contributions, and corporate taxation. In addition to her work at CRS, she is the author of numerous articles in books and professional journals, including recent papers on the tax burdens across families and tax reform proposals. She is the author of *The Economic Effects of Taxing Capital Income* and coeditor of *The Encyclopedia of Taxation and Tax Policy*. She is the editor of the Tax Expenditure Compendium, published every two years by the Senate Budget Committee. She is past president of the National Tax Association.

Daniel Halperin is the Stanley S. Surrey Professor at Harvard Law School. After beginning his career in private practice in New York, Professor Halperin served in the Treasury Department from 1967 to 1970. After seven years as a professor at the University of Pennsylvania Law School, he returned to the Treasury Department, first as tax legislative counsel and then as deputy assistant secretary for tax legislation. Professor Halperin was a professor of law at Georgetown University Law Center for 15 years before coming to Harvard in 1996. He was also a visiting professor at both Yale and Harvard Law Schools. Professor Halperin has written numerous articles in the area of tax law and policy.

Edward D. Kleinbard is a partner at international law firm Cleary Gottlieb Steen & Hamilton LLP. Widely recognized as a leading tax lawyer in the United States, he is consistently listed in *The International Who's Who of Corporate Tax Lawyers*, *International Tax Review*'s "World Tax" yearbook, *Chambers USA: America's Leading Lawyers for Business*, and Chambers Global *The World's Leading Lawyers*. His practice focuses on federal income tax matters, including taxation of new financial products, financial institutions, and international mergers and acquisitions. Mr. Kleinbard regularly publishes on tax matters and is an adjunct professor at Yale Law School. Mr. Kleinbard has testified before several congressional committees and the President's Advisory Panel on Federal Tax Reform.

Paul W. Oosterhuis is a partner at Skadden, Arps, Slate, Meagher & Flom LLP & Affiliates and coordinator of the international tax practice. He represents clients on a wide range of international and domestic tax matters, including international mergers and acquisitions, post-acquisition integration transactions, spin-off transactions, internal restructurings, and joint venture transactions. Mr. Oosterhuis has regularly been selected for inclusion in *Chambers USA: America's Leading Lawyers for Business* and has been consistently rated one of the top tax lawyers in Washington, D.C., by the Chambers and Partners Global Survey. He is the author of several publications on international and corporate tax law. He was a legislation attorney and legislation counsel for the Joint Committee on Taxation and an adjunct professor of law at Georgetown University Law Center.

Edmund Outslay is a professor of accounting and the Deloitte/Michael Licata Teaching Fellow in the Eli Broad Graduate School of Management at Michigan State University. His primary teaching and research interests are in accounting for income taxes, international taxation, and mergers and acquisitions. He has published numerous articles in journals such as *The Accounting Review, Journal of Accounting Research, Journal of the American Taxation Association*, and the *National Tax Journal* and is a coauthor of the text *U.S. Tax Aspects of Doing Business Abroad.* In February 2003, he testified before the Senate Finance Committee on the Joint Committee on Taxation Report on Enron Corporation.

George A. Plesko is an associate professor of accounting at the University of Connecticut in Storrs, CT, and has also served on the faculties of the MIT Sloan School of Management, the John F. Kennedy School of Government at Harvard University, the International Tax Program at Harvard Law School, and Northeastern University. Plesko's research focuses on corporate tax policy, the interactions of financial and tax reporting, the characteristics and magnitude of book-tax differences, and the behavior of loss firms. His research has appeared in *The Accounting*

Review, the *Journal of Accounting and Economics,* the *Journal of Accounting Research,* and the *National Tax Journal,* and he has testified before the Senate Finance Committee on corporate tax policy issues. His 2003 *National Tax Journal* paper with Lillian Mills, "Bridging the Reporting Gap: A Proposal for More Informative Reconciling of Book and Tax Income," was awarded the 2005 American Accounting Association/ Deloitte Wildman Medal. He is a member of the Internal Revenue Service Advisory Council's Tax Gap Subgroup, the Statistics of Income Consulting Panel, and has been an advisor to tax reform projects for the states of Massachusetts and Maine.

Julie A. Roin is the Seymour Logan Professor of Law at the University of Chicago Law School. She teaches both federal income tax and state and local finance courses. Her primary research interest is federal income taxation, in particular its treatment of transnational transactions. She is the author of a number of law journal articles and the coauthor, with Paul Stephan and Don Wallace, Jr., of a casebook entitled *International Business and Economics—Law and Policy.*

Kim Rueben is a senior research associate at the Urban Institute and the Tax Policy Center, where she currently heads up the state policy effort, and an adjunct professor at the Georgetown Public Policy Institute. She has recently completed studies on California's infrastructure financing system, an evaluation of the impact of changing federal deductibility of state and local taxes, an examination of the economic effects of Colorado's Taxpayer Bill of Rights Law, and an evaluation of states' fiscal capacity. She was a visiting scholar at the San Francisco Federal Reserve Bank, an adjunct professor at the Goldman School of Public Policy at the University of California at Berkeley, and a research fellow at the Public Policy Institute of California, where she is now an adjunct fellow.

Michael L. Schler is a tax partner in the New York City law firm of Cravath, Swaine & Moore LLP. He practices in the areas of mergers and acquisitions, corporate tax, consolidated returns, financial products, and asset-bracket securitization. He was chair of the New York State Bar Association Tax Section from 1994 to 1995, and has been a member of the executive committee since 1985. He is a trustee and the vice president of the American Tax Policy Institute. He is the chair of the New

York Tax Forum and a member of the American College of Tax Counsel. He has been a consultant to the American Law Institute Federal Income Tax Project on Integration of the Individual and Corporate Income Taxes, and to the Institute's Project on Taxation of Private Business Enterprises. He is the author of numerous published articles in the tax field, a speaker at numerous tax conferences, and the cochair of the annual UCLA Mergers and Acquisitions tax conference.

Reed Shuldiner is the Alvin L. Snowiss Professor of Law at the University of Pennsylvania Law School, where he has taught since 1990. He has been a visiting professor at Harvard Law School and Yale Law School. Prior to Penn, he served as an attorney advisor in the Office of Tax Legislative Counsel at the Treasury Department (1986 to 1989). He was an associate with the Washington, D.C., law firm of Wilmer, Cutler, and Pickering (1984 to 1986) and a counsel with Cadwalader, Wickersham, and Taft (1989 to 1990). He has acted as an adviser to foreign governments on behalf of the Treasury Department and the International Monetary Fund. He is the author of numerous articles on the taxation of capital.

Joel Slemrod is the Paul W. McCracken Collegiate Professor of Business Economics and Public Policy at the Stephen M. Ross School of Business, professor of economics in the department of economics, and director of the Office of Tax Policy Research at the University of Michigan. He joined the economics department at the University of Minnesota in 1979. From 1983 to 1984, he was a National Fellow at the Hoover Institution, and from 1984 to 1985, he was the senior staff economist for tax policy at the President's Council of Economic Advisers. He has been at Michigan since 1987. From 1992 to 1998, Professor Slemrod was editor of the *National Tax Journal*, and between 2005 and 2006, he was president of the National Tax Association. He is coauthor with Jon Bakija of *Taxing Ourselves: A Citizen's Guide to the Debate over Taxes*, soon to be in its fourth edition.

Joseph J. Thorndike is director of the Tax History Project at Tax Analysts and a contributing editor for *Tax Notes* magazine. He is the author of numerous articles on tax history and policy, coeditor (with Dennis J. Ventry, Jr.) of *Tax Justice: The Ongoing Debate* (Urban Institute Press, 2002) and coauthor (with Steven Bank and Kirk Stark) of *War and Taxes*

(Urban Institute Press, forthcoming). He is currently writing a history of tax fairness and social justice during the Great Depression and World War II.

Eric Toder is a senior fellow at the Urban Institute and the Urban–Brookings Tax Policy Center, where he specializes in retirement policy and tax policy issues. Between 2001 and 2004, he served as director, National Headquarters Office of Research, at the Internal Revenue Service. Dr. Toder previously held a number of positions in tax policy offices in the U.S. government and overseas, including deputy assistant secretary for Tax Analysis at the U.S. Treasury Department, deputy assistant director for Tax Analysis at the Congressional Budget Office, and consultant to the New Zealand Treasury.

David A. Weisbach is the Walter J. Blum Professor and director of the Olin Program in Law and Economics at the University of Chicago Law School. He previously held positions at Georgetown University Law Center, the Office of Tax Policy in the Treasury Department, and in private law practice. He is the author of numerous articles on taxation and was a consultant to the President's Commission on Tax Reform in 2005. His current research interests include the differences between income and consumption taxation, the structure of the corporate tax, tax expenditures, and the use of taxation for redistribution with respect to factors other than income (such as disability).

George R. Zodrow is professor of economics and Rice Scholar, Baker Institute for Public Policy, at Rice University. He also holds an appointment as International Research Fellow at the Centre on Business Taxation at Oxford University. His research interests are tax reform in the United States and in developing countries and state and local public finance, and his articles have appeared in numerous publications and books on taxation. Professor Zodrow is currently editor of the *National Tax Journal* and recently served as the editor of the "Policy Watch" section of *International Tax and Public Finance*. He is the author of *State Sales and Income Taxes* and the coeditor of *Fundamental Tax Reform: Issues, Choices and Implications* and *United States Tax Reform in the 21st Century*. He was a visiting economist at the U.S. Treasury Office of Tax Analysis from 1984 to 1985 and has participated in tax reform projects in numerous countries.

Index